UNIVERSITY OF NOTTINGHAM

WITHDRAWN

FROM THE L

10 0296140 6

D0548198

OWL

Fourth Among Equals

FOURTH AMONG EQUALS

Bill Rodgers

First published in Great Britain 2000
by Politico's Publishing
8 Artillery Row, London, SW1P 1RZ, England

Tel. 020 7931 0090
Email publishing@politicos.co.uk
Website http://www.politicos.co.uk/publishing

© Bill Rodgers 2000

The right of Bill Rodgers to be identified as author of this work has
been asserted by him in accordance with the Copyright, Designs and
Patents Act, 1988.

A catalogue record for this book is available from the British Library.

ISBN 1 90230 136 6

Printed and bound in Great Britain by St Edmundsbury Press.
Cover design by AdVantage.

100296 1406

All rights reserved. No part of this publication may be reproduced or
transmitted in any form or by any means, electronic or mechanical
including photocopying, recording or any information storage or
retrieval system, without prior permission in writing from the
publishers.

This book is sold subject to the condition that it shall not by way of
trade or otherwise be lent, resold, hired out, or otherwise circulated
without the publisher's prior consent in writing in any form of
binding or cover other than that in which it is published and without
a similar condition including this condition being imposed on the
subsequent purchaser.

Contents

Illustrations

Preface

There is no account in this book of meetings with Mikhail Gorbachev, conversations with Dr Henry Kissinger or visits to Balmoral to see the Queen. Readers who enjoy sharing such occasions must look elsewhere. There are also few extracts from my speeches, although I doubt whether this will cause much disappointment.

I started to write my story as an exercise, or test. I proposed to distil the essence of the occasional diaries I have kept from the age of sixteen, and the papers and other records I have accumulated. I wanted to reflect on my journey from a Liverpool childhood to the drama of Westminster, where, for almost half a century, I have witnessed – and often experienced – the heights and pain of politics. There was the challenge of placing my own career in context, together with the development of my ideas on the purposes of it all. More difficult was how to write freely and openly about colleagues, when, in the bruising world of politics, even close friends infuriate and behave badly from time to time. Now, at the end of my task, what I hope I have done is to contribute at least a footnote to history.

So, after the opening chapter, this is primarily an account of a public life. I would like to have mentioned Reg, Joyce, Cyril, Mary – friends from my earlier years and adolescence – and more of my brother Peter, of school friends and of all those men and women who have given me loyalty, pleasure and affection. I see them like that great host on a heavenly stairway in *A Matter of Life and Death,* that magnificent film of the 1940s. Happily, most of them are still very much alive, and I remember them better than they know. I acknowledge them in their anonymity, because without them this story would not have been there to write.

But I acknowledge particularly those who made a direct contribution to the book's publication. Roger Liddle read all the chapters in draft, except the last one; John Perkin read many of them. Chapters were also read by John Grigg, John Harris, Dick Newby and Pamela Dunbar. I am very grateful to them for the suggestions for improvements they made, and to the Rev. P. R. Owen of Bangor-on-Dee, Philip Waller of Merton College, Oxford, Fred Lloyd of Liverpool, the City of Liverpool Librarian, and the staff of the House of Lords Library for help on certain points. I am in debt to my agent, Laura Morris, to my publisher, Iain Dale, whose tight schedule put other publishers to shame, and to my editor, Duncan Brack, who more than kept up with it. John Roper rapidly read the proofs at short notice and saved me from some howlers; and Roy Jenkins read them in the very final stages and saved me from some others. Tina Knight and Charlie Marks both contributed to the typing of the original copy and subsequent redrafts, although most of the chapters were typed and corrected by Maureen Kruger. They all showed patience and care, and fortitude in dealing with my handwriting.

I owe most to my wife Silvia, whose comments on every chapter were typically uncompromising and led to significant revisions, and whose experience in writing her own, very different and highly acclaimed autobiography, *Red Saint, Pink Daughter,* was always at my disposal in writing mine.

Needless to say, what now appears between these covers is my responsibility alone.

Bill Rodgers
January 2000

For my grandchildren,
Laura, Millie, Alexander, Thomas, Jacob and Isobel

Chapter 1
A Liverpool Childhood

Cross Offa's Dyke, near Llawnt, and the land falls sharply to the border town of Oswestry. Generations of Welshmen have trickled into England this way from hill farms and more distant quarries in search of something better than a meagre living. Two hundred years ago, some moved south to Shrewsbury, still an inland port and a centre of the cloth trade, and some north to the forges and foundries of Wrexham that were feeding the industrial revolution. But others headed across the glacial plain that stretches eastwards towards the upper valley of the River Trent and Arnold Bennett's five towns that comprise the Potteries. On this route for more than 800 years has stood Wem, or 'Weme', as Doomsday Book has it, meaning marshy ground.

Wem was home for much of his youth to William Hazlitt, who was visited here by Coleridge. Earlier, Judge Jeffries, one of the most hated of Lord Chancellors, had earned his reputation as a prosecutor and judge in the neighbouring parishes. In the late eighteenth century Wem was a small market town of no great distinction, serving the isolated farms of the post-Enclosure landscape. Few buildings had survived the Great Fire of 1677 that marked off its medieval past.

It is not clear when the Rodgers family (sometimes spelt without the 'd', as 'Rogers') became Welsh immigrants to Wem, but Andrew Rodgers (1778–1854), a farm labourer, married Ann Tilley and produced eight children in that generation. Many of the family stayed in Wem and are recorded in the parish register. They earned a living on the land and in ancillary trades, one as a blacksmith and some as farriers. Others moved on and socially upwards, and by 1848 there was a John Rodgers established as a tailor fifty miles to the north at Frodsham, near where the Mersey widens to fill with sandbanks at low tide; and shortly afterwards, a Samuel Rodgers, also a tailor, at Bangor-on-Dee. Perhaps it was one of the less successful members of the extended Rodgers family who continued across the river to seek his fortune in the rapidly growing seaport of Liverpool. Be that as it may, my great-grandfather was born in Carter Street, off Park Road, in what is now Liverpool 8, in 1830. He began his working life as a sailmaker on sailing ships to China, and carried to a peaceful grave in his nineties a permanent scar earned in a brush with Chinese pirates. But in the intervals of a long seafaring career he fathered three daughters and three sons, Alfred, Will and John. Alfred, who learnt a trade and became a whitesmith, also fathered six children, of whom the eldest was William Arthur who, in due course, fathered me.

I was born, my parents' second son, on 28 October 1928 at 4 Westgate Road, a short terrace of late Victorian houses behind the tram sheds at the better end of Smithdown Road. The district was known as Wavertree and was inhabited mainly by the respectable working class. It bordered on the newer and distinctly more prosperous suburb of Allerton, from which it was divided by Queen's Drive, Liverpool's earliest ring road. But the sub-district took its name from Penny Lane, an older thoroughfare which, many years later, the Beatles made famous. Penny Lane was a junction and a terminus for the tramcars and, later, for the municipal buses. It was convenient for the city centre and half a mile from where my father's mother lived at 31 Portman Road, a house that in my childhood was lit only by gas mantles which would flare into life when lit with a wax taper and burn with a hard, white light and a steady, gentle hiss.

But after a few years we moved to another rented house at 6 Horringford Road in Aigburth, within a quarter mile of the river. This was much bigger and, although terraced, had black and white mock half-timbering below the eaves. But there was no garden, and an alleyway that smelt of rubbish and dogs separated us from the backs of the houses in the neighbouring road. All the houses in our road had net curtains and heavy velveteen drapes which looked weighed down by accumulated dust. Aspidistras in brass pots were common. But so, too, were exotic pieces of inlaid furniture and pale blue vases with oriental designs. For Liverpool was a great seaport, and almost every other family in that neighbourhood had fathers or sons who made their living as ships' captains, mates and engineers on the long routes to South America and the East.

Liverpool's five miles of docks ended at what was inappropriately called 'The Dingle', halfway between where we lived and the Pier Head. But except for the relic of a never-used dock excavated by a foolish Victorian entrepreneur, the part of Aigburth where we lived was residential. Close to the river there were the big houses of once-prosperous merchants, now occupied by professional people; and farm buildings built of sandstone. Since the 1920s, semi-detached houses had spread across the green fields. But in the middle of the road, outside our house, stood a great oak tree that forced the traffic (such as it was) into a dual carriageway either side. It had survived for more than 200 years, a remnant from a deciduous forest that had once reached along the Mersey, upstream to Delamere and beyond.

Born in 1891 into a respectable working-class family, my father might have been expected to serve his time apprenticed to a carpenter or a plumber. But with a withered ankle and club foot, he was unfit for anything involving manual labour. Like many boys cut off by illness or disability from team games and physical activities, he was left to his thoughts and the books he could buy for a penny or tuppence in the junk shops and street stalls. Leaving Windsor Wesleyan Higher Grade School at thirteen, he took a job as an office boy in one of the small ironmongers and workshops that served the city and the docks. Then, rejected for military service amongst those who volunteered for Kitchener's Army, he found in 1915 a place as a clerk in the Municipal Buildings of the Liverpool Corporation. It was a secure job which nepotism would have filled in days of peace. He remained there for forty years, Clerk to the Health Committee for much of his service.

I would visit him in his gloomy place of work, beside the Victorian oak desks and behind the frosted glass. He would take me to the stamp shops of Moorfields and 'behind-the-market', the narrow street where rabbits and other household pets were sold. We would walk to the Town Hall and then across Exchange Flags, in the shipping and banking heart of the city. We would go to the Pier Head, to watch the great Atlantic liners tie up at the largest floating landing stage in the world. He enjoyed my visits as much as I enjoyed them. They were a relief from the monotony of his day and a change from a lonely sandwich lunch.

I was aware of the extraordinary regularity of his life. In the years of my earliest memories, he would leave home at twenty minutes past eight, walk to Mersey Road station on the Cheshire Lines Railway, take the train to Liverpool Central Station and be in his office on the dot of nine o'clock. Then, in the evenings, exactly at 5.40, we would hear his key in the door. By the time he had taken off his coat and hat and walked into the kitchen, my mother was bringing in his dinner. If he was not home by 5.45 he was late, and would offer an explanation; if he was not home by ten to six, it was a serious cause for concern.

Thoughtful and reflective, my father did not easily make close friends. He was highly intelligent and, born a generation later, would have gone to university. As it was, he taught himself Pitman's shorthand, and went to evening classes at the Toxteth Technical Institute to learn Spanish and to paint watercolours. He joined Boots Circulating Library and bought books by Galsworthy, Conan Doyle and J. B. Priestley, whose views, as reflected in *The Good Companions*, were very much his own. Apart from a desultory interest in the football pools, his main hope of a modest fortune came from 'Bullets', a form of epigram that comprised a competition for readers of *John Bull*, a popular weekly from Odhams Press of a kind that might have been favoured by H. G. Wells and Mr Polly. Brought up a Presbyterian, taught at a Methodist school and married in a Baptist church, he was an agnostic. In politics he was an undefined radical, restless about the state of the world and rather despairing of its getting better. He was prejudiced against 'the Yanks' for their brashness and for the corruption of the English language by American accents and expressions; and made only one trip abroad, to Dublin in 1915. Until he retired, by which time I was on the edge of a political career, he felt it wrong to reveal, even to me, how he had voted. He limited himself to saying that he had been put off socialism by attending a meeting in the early years of the century which had been entirely devoted to attacking the memory of the recently dead Queen Victoria. Later he confessed to always voting Liberal or Labour, except in 1931 when he had voted for the National Government.

His reticence about his political views was part of a deep belief in the obligations and integrity of those in the public service. His opinions of the aldermen and councillors with whom he came into daily contact were entirely determined by how conscientiously they did their job and whether they sought any personal advantage from it. Alderman Mrs Elizabeth ('Bessie') Braddock, Labour, although a fishwife in the council chamber, was tireless in visiting hospitals and old people's homes. My father had respect for her. So, too, for Councillor Gregson, a high Tory but one who eschewed partisanship in committee. My father would have thought it improper for any elected member to enquire as to his own political views or to interfere in the responsibilities of paid officials. He could never had imagined – or survived – life under Derek Hatton.

My father believed that a job well done should be its own reward. As a result, he was himself well respected by councillors and senior officials, and also by the matrons of the hospitals with which he dealt when the city had responsibility for them before the NHS. But he was never pushy and, at a crucial stage in his career, was passed over for promotion. Sir Thomas Baines, Town Clerk of Liverpool 1935–46, was responsible, and he is the only person I can remember of whom my father spoke with real bitterness. On the other hand, although a stickler with young staff, who were not always eager to work for him, he taught them well and took great pride in their success. His particular favourite was Sir Stanley Holmes, who worked for him as an office junior and later became Town Clerk of Liverpool and then Chief Executive of the Metropolitan County of Merseyside.

The weekends were time for the allotment, and then the beloved garden he made at 104 South Sudley Road when we moved there in 1936. Sunday meant tea with cold meat, cakes and tinned fruit in the dining room which was otherwise little used. There was music on the wireless from Albert Sandler and the Palm Court Orchestra, although this was more my mother's taste than his. There was also the 'Week's Good Cause', the Sunday charity appeal on the wireless, to which he often sent a donation. We had no car and, until preparations for civil defence on the eve of war led to uncertain and late evenings at the office, no telephone. My father never thought of himself as a good man and had little time for the pious and the Godly, but neither did he care for vulgarity or ostentation. On retirement, he did two days of voluntary work a week for the Family Service Units, but was content to look after their office without further recognition.

When my early political reading led me to identify the *petite bourgeoisie,* I decided that my family, provincial, suburban and just a cut above the skilled working class, fitted neatly into that category. But there were difficulties. Our neighbour, Mr Hughes, the butcher, drove a car, sent his children to private schools and kept strong drink in the house with which, to my surprise, he regularly entertained police officers. He was clearly better off than my father, but there were no books in his house. Our other neighbour had served in India with British Insulated Callander Cables and was wholly the part as Major Fish, with Sam Browne and smart uniform, in the wartime Home Guard. His voice, unlike that of Mr Hughes, was vaguely patrician. As for my friends at school, there was no social gap except with a handful who came from the slums of Garston, although the son of a doctor would return to a four-bedroomed house in the best part of Allerton, beyond my parents' means.

Given these fine gradations of social status, my mother – Gertrude Helen, known as 'Gert' – came from a slightly better class than my father and was thought to have married beneath her. Her father, Thomas Christmas Owen, had been a manufacturer of cardboard boxes in Caernarfon, North Wales, and she had been brought up in a spacious house built of stone, with a living-in maid. But some time before the First World War the business collapsed and the family moved, either in disgrace or out of necessity, to Crosby on the north side of Liverpool. My mother, now in her twenties, was sent out to work as a secretary, but the family fortunes were never restored. When I knew my mother's father in the 1930s, he was living on his own and selling smoker's requisites from a suitcase, door to door. He was a silent man with a bushy Edwardian moustache who smoked a pipe, wore brown suits and never spoke to his grandson. There was a certain mystery about past events, a hint of a veil better not drawn aside. My mother's brother, Uncle Len, who had been gassed in the war, was a fairly frequent visitor to our house, but Uncle Herbert would arrive unannounced after a long interval to borrow money and then vanish until the next time. Eventually he vanished altogether.

My mother's first child, a girl, was stillborn. Then followed my brother Peter, and I arrived four years later, by which time my mother was thirty-eight and hoping for a girl to replace her previous loss. Appropriately in a Welsh-speaking Welshwoman whose party piece for her children was to pronounce Llanfairpwllgwyngyllgogerychwyrndrobwllllantysiliogogogoch with impeccable fluency, music and choral singing were her pleasures. My brother Peter was taught to play the piano, and it was a disappointment that I never chose to learn. After a long pause while her children were growing up, she returned to a choir and sang regularly until her eighties. In her later years she took to reading romantic novels, but during my childhood I cannot remember her reading anything except the evening paper. She had a mother's pride in the achievements of her sons, keeping press cuttings of my progress right up to her death at the age of eighty-nine. She would have liked me to go into business in the commercial heart of Liverpool, with a regular income and a clear job description she could quietly boast about. When I eventually left for London it would have given her the greatest satisfaction had I worked for the BBC. That would have been the acme of success.

In 1934, shortly before my sixth birthday, I started school. The Liverpool (Sudley Road) Temporary Council School No. 72 had been built in 1904 to meet the new responsibilities of the City Corporation following the Balfour Act of two years earlier and the rapid growth of population. It was a wood and corrugated iron building because, in the verdict of the Association of School Boards, 'it had been ascertained that in large manufacturing towns where the atmosphere is often charged with chemical impurities, such a building will last about ten years'. But the school had already lasted thirty years at the time of my arrival and remained in use for another thirty until burnt down. It was an all-age school which pupils attended from five to the end of compulsory education at fourteen. The exceptions were those who passed the Junior City Scholarship Examination at eleven and left for a grammar school or, in the next tier of assumed ability, were transferred to a technical institute, mainly, it seemed, to become Post Office engineers. For the girls in particular, any serious study appeared to stop for those who remained behind at eleven. Cooking, sewing and hygiene would henceforth occupy their time.

Sudley Road was a good school. The headmaster, Mr Clayton, a slightly built man in his early fifties, had played football for Chelsea as a student and then served in the Great War in the Royal Flying Corps. He had a devoted staff, mainly of unmarried women teachers who achieved remarkable results with their pupils, despite the classes of fifty or more in which we were often taught. There were 300 such oversized classes in elementary schools in the city, but the prejudice against women in work (especially during high male unemployment) meant that the Liverpool Education Committee would employ married women only reluctantly and if they were 'in necessitous circumstances'. I remember with gratitude the names of Miss Caird, Miss Christian and Miss Kirkham, the quality of whose teaching far outweighed the importance of bricks and mortar (or wood and corrugated iron), but especially the name of Miss Budd, who took the scholarship class. In 1993 I discovered that she was still alive and, finding her address, called on her unannounced. She opened the door, looked at me for a moment, and said, 'Come in, Billy'. It was the first time I had seen her for over fifty years. Now in her 101st year, she is one of those who can say that they have lived in three centuries.

My school had been built on the edge of a criss-cross of narrow streets named after the great Imperial proconsuls Cromer, Lugard and Milner. They were lined with turn-of-the-century terraced homes, many of them rented but some of them owned, with well-scrubbed steps and stained glass in the doors. The catchment area of the school also included some modern semi-detached houses, pebble-dashed with bay windows and gardens front and back. This was not the shifting inner city or the rough end of deprived Liverpool, and the background of the children made teaching easier. Sudley Road Council School had an excellent record of scholarships at eleven. Classes of fifty seldom produced comparable results elsewhere.

In my early years at Sudley Road, escorted by my brother Peter, I walked for ten minutes to school and back twice a day, going home for midday dinner. Later, when we moved half a mile to our new house, I caught the tramcar for two stops along Aigburth Boulevard. For the morning break, when we were given the regulation third of a pint of milk, I took four small ginger snaps or biscuits, but always gave one away to the policeman who guided us across the busy main road. The school had a small asphalt playground and a larger paved one which was used for physical training. There was also a cinder-strewn clay patch suitable for scratch games of football. For anything more serious and for the annual sports day – where my main successes were in the egg-and-spoon race – we went to a stretch of land rented by the City Corporation from Miss Emma Holt, whose family owned the Blue Funnel shipping line.

Holt's Field, not more than 200 yards from the school, marked the point where speculative housing development had stopped short of the substantial detached villas of the Victorian nearly-rich. Most of Sudley Road (or North Sudley Road, as it had recently become) was 'unadopted' by the Corporation, and it was barely paved and full of potholes. Along it there were high sandstone walls punctuated by doors that led to courtyards and coach-houses. There were fine, although neglected, glasshouses and an occasional walled garden. There were two meadows in which horses grazed. I took a delight in the texture of the sandstone and marvelled at the size of the oak and chestnut trees. I was fascinated to think of how life had been lived eighty years ago in these great decaying mansions. When similar houses, further from my school, fell vacant and awaited demolition, I explored their corridors and kitchens and pulled the communication cords that had once summoned domestic servants to spacious drawing rooms. This part of the city, stretching along the river from Fulwood to Cressington Park – private parks of comfortable Victorian residences – and inland to Mossley Hill and Allerton, was a pleasant place to live. By the standards of the time and the condition of much of Liverpool, mine seemed a privileged childhood.

A seafaring family background led my father to believe that learning to swim was a necessity and, soon after I was able to walk, I was taken before breakfast on Sundays to Garston Public Baths, a mile or so south of where we lived at the terminus of the trams. Beyond Garston there was the new Speke Airport and beyond the airport what we called 'the country'. These were open fields that mainly grew potatoes; and woods that stretched down to the River Mersey at Hale, where there was a lighthouse, and Dungeon Lane, where prisoners from the Napoleonic Wars had been held. Outings to 'the country' gave me the greatest pleasure. Standing on the shore and looking across the river at the widest point, upstream from the half-hidden entrance to the Manchester Ship Canal, the streets of the city seemed a long way away.

But I was not cut off from an awareness of what life was like in Liverpool for many other children. Garston itself was an industrial village of mean streets dominated by the gasworks from which stale odours would penetrate our house when the wind was in the wrong direction. The railway docks were the reason for its existence, but there was also a small shipyard, a copper works and a tannery. When I first explored Garston on my bicycle I could see nothing that redeemed it, not a tree, not a blade of grass, not a flower.

Garston was a microcosm of much larger areas of Liverpool that stretched behind the docks. Off Park Road and Park Lane (which were far from any park), narrow streets of terraced houses sloped down to the Dock Road. These were the slums of Liverpool, even where council tenements had replaced the stinking alleys and courts in which the labouring classes of Victorian England had lived. If anything, the slums on the north side of the city centre, off Scotland Road, were worse. Seen from the top of a tramcar, there was a pub on every corner, with children, often without shoes and as ragged as anything in Dickens, hanging about outside. When the wartime evacuation took place in 1939, the description 'Plimsoll City' was coined as so many children had cheap and shoddy footwear or none at all. A high proportion were verminous, which was hardly surprising when forty per cent of homes were without baths.

The sight of these children gathered on street corners, both before the war and in wartime (most returned from evacuation long before the serious bombing began), was my first and most formative political experience. The difference between their condition and mine, and between the slums where they lived and suburbia where I lived, was striking. My father did not claim that it was an inescapable fact of human nature or seek to put the blame on those who lived in the slums, except for any neglect of their children that arose from drinking habits. He did not argue, as others did in the columns of the *Liverpool Daily Post,* that rehousing them was pointless because they would only keep coal in the bath.

But the sight and smell of the slums also made me suspicious, at an early age, of romanticising working-class life. Later, I came to believe in the loyalties forged by common experience in the mining villages of Wales and County Durham, given appalling disasters like that at Gresford Colliery in 1934 (photographs of which I could just recall), when 265 men died. But if poverty and the slums occasionally bred saints and heroes, for the most part they meant misery and an ugly fight for survival. Liverpool was to produce successive generations of popular comedians, from Arthur Askey (a corporation clerk in my father's time) to Ken Dodd but, as with all clowns, behind the laughter there were tears. More recently, Liverpool playwrights and film-makers have made a decent living out of Scouse courage and humour in the face of adversity. There is nothing wrong with that, or with depicting the sharp, tough street-wise people, but another thing to attribute values to working-class life in the slums that it rarely possessed.

I never acquired a strong Scouse accent. Identifying emotionally with Liverpool, as I have done all my life, has not required me to wear as a badge of membership the peculiarly nasal dialect with its own vocabulary, grammar and syntax that emerged from a fusion of immigrant Irish, Welsh and Scottish, and native Lancastrian, voices. But my 'a' remains short and my children, born and brought up in London, took delight, when they were young, in what they regarded as my distinctive rendering of 'raspberry jam in the bath'.

The romance I found was in the docks and the Pier Head and every aspect of one of the great seaports of the world. The Overhead Railway that ran from Dingle to Seaforth was designed to take dockers and seafarers to their place of work, and for sixty years it was a unique feature of the city. It ran alongside and above the Dock Road, which was crowded at all times with horse-drawn carts loaded with bales of cotton and steam-driven traction engines in which a coal fire glowed beneath the boiler that occupied the space of an internal combustion engine in a modern vehicle. This was long before the days of featureless container ships, so the nature of the cargoes could be clearly seen as they were lifted out from the holds of the ships. I watched Elder Dempster ships unloading bananas from the Canaries and ships of the Bibby Line bringing cotton from India and rice from Burma; and learnt the distinguishing flags and funnel colours of Lamport and Holt, Moss Hutchison and the Pacific Steam Navigation Company.

Despite its original purpose, and as motor vehicles began to provide alternative transport for dockers, the Overhead Railway became a weekend and holiday attraction and I enjoyed travelling past docks named after statesmen with Liverpool associations, from Canning and Huskisson to Gladstone. Better still was to pass through the dock gates on to the quays, accompanied by my Uncle Harold who, apprenticed as a plumber, was first employed as a rat-catcher, and ended forty years of service doing much the same thing as a senior Port Health Inspector. Uncle Harold – my father's brother – was my favourite uncle. He gave me foreign postage stamps for my collection and a banana spider, pickled in pink spirit in a tightly sealed bottle that I kept for many years.

By the 1930s, Liverpool as the port for the transatlantic passenger trade to New York and Boston was in decline, with much of it already transferred to Southampton. But great ocean-going liners still sailed to the outposts of the Empire; Shaw Savill to

Australia and New Zealand, Union-Castle to South Africa, and Canadian Pacific, with its glamorous fleet of 'Empress' class ships, to Quebec and Montreal. They sometimes tied up at the landing stage, towering like skyscrapers above the ferry boats that criss-crossed the river and the packet steamers to Ireland and the Isle of Man. I would stand at the Pier Head and gaze out to the estuary, wondering whether I would ever sail away across the ocean to North America and, through the Panama Canal, to the most distant parts of the world. Passengers stayed overnight at the Adelphi Hotel which had grand bedrooms on the lower floors and rooms suitable for servants at the top. The ground floor lounge was immense and the elaborate luggage of rich travellers was piled high, awaiting transportation to the great liners. As the hotel was on rising ground, these could be seen as they were guided by tugs to the docks or landing stage prior to embarkation. The Adelphi was an Edwardian railway hotel, popular with Grand National racegoers as well as travellers by sea. It was fashionable and expensive enough for me to speculate on whether I might ever afford to pass through its doors and order coffee.

However, despite my awareness of the slums and the excitement of the city and its docks, family, sunshine and holidays on the North Wales coast and the Isle of Man were much of my childhood through the 1930s. I learnt to kindle the kitchen fire using orange peel dried in the oven, which burned with a vigorous heat to light the wooden 'chips' which, in turn, lit the coal. When we moved in 1936 to our new, heavily mortgaged semi, I got tar on my shoes from the newly-made roads and went to sleep to the sound of lawnmowers being pushed across newly-established lawns. In cold weather I put garlic in my shoes to ward off influenza (wholly unaware of any culinary uses for it), but with little obvious success. I delivered milk in the neighbourhood from the horse-drawn 'float' of the local dairyman, cycled increasing distances from home, crossing the Mersey by the Widnes transporter bridge to Runcorn and beyond, and began to use the black and white half-timbered Carnegie public library. It was an unexceptional peacetime growing-up in a suburb in the provinces.

After the opening few weeks in September 1939, the war did not greatly change this pattern of life. My brother Peter was evacuated immediately to Wrexham, but Sudley Road Council School stayed put while closing its doors for lessons. As a result, for some months I was taught twice weekly at home, and in the home of a neighbour by a chain-smoking schoolmaster of military bearing who squeezed my knee under the dining room table, claiming he did so to reward a right answer or encourage a better one. This mahogany table, used by Peter and me for occasional table tennis in peacetime, was now a safe place beneath which we all sheltered when the air-raid sirens sounded. No modern semi-detached house had a cellar, which was the safest place of all, and ours had no space under the stairs, which was regarded as second best. On the days in the week when I was not being taught, I joined a group of boys pushing around a barrow belonging to the local Scouts, collecting aluminium saucepans from housewives to be melted down for use in aircraft production.

In peacetime I had earned sixpence a time for trimming garden hedges in our neighbourhood. Now I offered my services with a pot of paint, whitening garden steps and kerbstones so they could be identified by pedestrians during the blackout, when no lights could be shown. The expectation was of heavy bombing and many buildings in 'town' – which is what we called the inner city – were being strengthened with concrete and sandbags. My father had become an air-raid warden, and with whistle, gas mask and tin hat was on a regular rota of patrols from the sector post, established in an old carriage house across the road. But this was still the period of 'phoney war', and when it was said on the BBC that a German aircraft had been in the vicinity, the news was greeted with ridicule. In 1939 and early 1940, for Liverpool the real war was at sea, where enemy mines and submarines were starting to sink ships, causing bereavement in many homes.

With the fall of France and evacuation from Dunkirk, things were different. Within days of Churchill's call to the nation to brace itself so that men would say 'This was their finest hour', my father's Aunt Emma sent a message from Ottawa that Peter and I would be welcome in Canada for the duration of the war. We did not go, and shortly afterwards the ship in which we might have sailed was sunk in the Atlantic by a U-boat. But frequent air-raids on Liverpool now began. I was quite old enough to be scared by the bombing but too young to have a role to play, even in fire-watching. I would sit under the table and count each bomb as a stick of five or six screamed closer. I came to judge the distance away of an explosion, rather like counting the seconds between lightning and its thunder. What I liked least were the landmines, a ton of explosive on the end of a fluttering parachute that would drift downwards and explode on impact, thus doing a great deal more damage by surface blast than a bomb, which would partially bury itself, leaving a crater. There was no possible mental preparation for a landmine, and it was a landmine that blew in our windows and blew off our front door on 28 November 1940. Two hundred people were killed in Liverpool that night.

In all, there were sixty-eight night bombing attacks on Liverpool between September 1940 and May 1941, with little before and very little after. Nearly 2,000 tons of high explosives were dropped, more than on Birmingham or Plymouth or Glasgow and twice as much as on Coventry in its famous one-night raid. But the 'May Blitz' of the following year was Liverpool's most dramatic experience of war. It lasted for seven consecutive nights, causing devastation in the centre of the city and the loss of 1,900 lives. As an air-raid warden, my father was on duty from when the sirens went, soon after 10 P.M., until the all-clear, sometimes as late as 4 A.M. Then, with public transport at a standstill, he cycled to work, keeping the same office hours as in times of peace. Amongst buildings badly damaged by high explosives and fire was the William Brown Library, which lost nearly 300,000 books. I was standing in our garden one afternoon when the sky suddenly darkened and large, black flakes began to fall, like snow in winter. The burning pages had been carried upwards in the vortex of the blaze and were now floating down, cinders with the faint imprint of language, four miles from the city centre. When the sky cleared again and the wind blew fresh, it brought the sweet smell of cattlecake that burnt for days on the docks and was so persistent that even now, over fifty years later, I can almost smell it.

But through the bombing and its aftermath, despite continued loss of life at sea and the disappearance of my Canadian cousin, 'missing believed killed' when piloting a Mosquito fighter-bomber over France, I grew up much as I would have done in peacetime. There was rationing, but I was never hungry. My father, whose passion was his garden, diversified into tomatoes and kohlrabi to supplement our diet, but was mainly concerned with planting his daffodils, tulips and dahlias on time and pruning his Paul Scarlet roses promptly at the end of March. He hoped that I, in turn, would acquire a liking for gardening, 'because,' as he wrote in his wartime diary, 'it may teach him patience.'

Early in the war, I organised what I called a garden fête and sale (in a garden of perhaps fifty square yards) and sent a postal order for £1 17s 6d to the Lord Mayor's War Fund. I was flattered to receive a letter personally signed by Alderman Sir Sidney Jones, and then see my name in the newspaper. Greatly encouraged, I went one better and raised £5 6s od towards the cost of a rifle, and received a letter from the office of the Chancellor of the Exchequer, Sir Kingsley Wood. But my organising skills went mainly into the Semper Victor Sports Club which, despite its name, had a chequered history between its origins amongst a group of friends in 1941, when we were all thirteen or fourteen, and its extinction three years later. 'Their club meetings,' my father noted in his diary, 'are vigorously conducted and should be good experience for future MPs or councillors'. But we had no such thoughts, only where to play and who to play at football or cricket on Saturday mornings.

I had listened on the eve of war to BBC broadcasts by Vernon Bartlett, then a *News Chronicle* journalist, and Stephen King-Hall, the publisher of an influential private *Newsletter*. They had awakened my interest in international affairs. Now I followed events closely on the wireless and in the *Liverpool Daily Post* and drew maps of battles won and lost in the Western Desert, at Stalingrad, in Burma or on the Arno.

Having been awarded a Junior City Scholarship (equivalent to passing the eleven-plus examination in the days of selective entry to secondary education) I went in the autumn of 1940 to Quarry Bank High School in Allerton, about two miles from where we lived. My father had chosen the school, first for Peter and then for me, partly because of its congenial location in a leafy area close to Calderstones Park. But more important was the reputation it had acquired under a remarkable headmaster, Richard Fitzroy Bailey, who had been appointed at its foundation in 1922. Other schools in the city, like the Liverpool Institute and the Liverpool Collegiate, had begun life in the nineteenth century and were well known for conventional discipline and good academic results. Quarry Bank was liberal and relaxed, and was said never to have expelled a boy. It was modelled on Shrewsbury School, where R. F. Bailey had been a housemaster, with prefects and monitors largely responsible for discipline (including the use of the slipper on recalcitrant boys), and a wide range of extramural activities that could be pursued at the close of the normal school day. It also supported the Unity Boys' Club, a club for working-class boys from the poorest parts of Liverpool, with a flavour of Toynbee Hall. R. F. Bailey was a bachelor of private means and a scholar of Eton, who could have considered prestigious jobs elsewhere, but he stayed at Quarry Bank for a quarter of a century until retirement. Perhaps many of the grammar schools established at that time had inspired headmasters and dedicated young teachers who encouraged those wanting to learn without neglecting those less gifted. There were few boys at Quarry Bank during R. F. Bailey's headship who did not leave with an affection for the school and a great respect for him.

There was no cramming or specially privileged treatment for those who might bring the school academic distinction, but throughout the 1930s boys left to take up university places, and scholarships were won to Oxford and Cambridge. One name to conjure with when I arrived at Quarry Bank was that of Dan Pettit, a Cambridge Blue who had played football for England as an amateur international. It was thirty years before I met him and longer still before we worked together when he was Chairman of the National Freight Corporation. A contemporary of my brother was David Basnett, later Chairman of the TUC, a decent man who nevertheless disappointed his friends at a critical time for the Labour Party in the 1980s. Another was Peter Shore, with whom I was frequently to cross paths and eventually join in the cabinet. Although I did not know him at Quarry Bank, I also overlapped with James Stirling, who was to become one of the outstanding British architects of the twentieth century. Derek Nimmo, comic actor and theatrical impresario, was a year or two behind me. After playing Jasper Keene in the popular school play *Guinea for the Ghost*, he took my place as Brutus in *Julius Ceasar* when I left school. I remember him best riding a bicycle, heels on the pedals and toes pointing outwards, a rather clerical figure, as if rehearsing the roles he was soon to play. John Lennon was a much later pupil at Quarry Bank, well after R. F. Bailey's retirement. He and the school do not appear to have been made for each other.

I did not enjoy my first year at Quarry Bank. In Form 3A I found the academic competition difficult, and was no good at Latin. But the second year was better and I successfully proposed two motions for debate: 'That communism would be a good thing for England', and: 'That hanging should be abolished.' My speech on communism was largely based on the Red Dean of Canterbury's *The Socialist Sixth of the World*, a eulogy of the Soviet Union under Stalin that I had found on my father's bookshelf. Perhaps because Russia was then Britain's acceptable wartime ally, the motion was carried without dissent.

But I came into my own in the sixth form with the freedom to study chosen subjects and the confidence to pursue special interests as Secretary of the Social Science Society, Chairman of Debating and organiser of the annual exhibition of the Literary, Scientific and Field Club. I decided to do history, economics, English literature and geography for my Higher School Certificate, two at scholarship level. Geography was probably a mistake, leaving little room for argument, which was now what I most enjoyed. English literature I found exciting, reading Shakespeare seriously and discovering T. S. Eliot. I was fortunate in having in my class David Best, the son of a Jewish bookmaker and an active member of the Young Communist League, who had slipped away from school to spend six months in the merchant navy and, as a result, seemed far more mature than the rest of us. He did remarkable lino cuts for the school magazine, derived equally from Picasso and social realism, and wrote advanced poetry which did homage to W. H. Auden. He knew the language of the Modern Movement and took me to soirées and discussion meetings attended by what I took for the intellectual elite of Liverpool. I benefited greatly from the stimulus of his personality. He became a successful architect in Israel and has remained a good friend.

But it was economics, and particularly social history, that absorbed me. These were taught by R. A. Roberts, who had arrived at Quarry Bank a year or two before after a mysterious war career, having been either invalided out of the army or – the more exciting version we preferred – been cashiered for desertion. He was a little over thirty and had taken a fouth class degree in PPE at Magdalen College, Oxford. He had a large head, with the lips and jowls of the Emperor Nero, and seldom seemed to wash. He spoke from his throat with what we took to be the accent of an Oxford aesthete, and was not good at keeping discipline. But Alec Roberts was an inspired sixth-form teacher, thoroughly knowledgeable in his subjects, cynical in his judgement of people and at all times willing to treat us as adults. We teased him and showed little respect, but he made us work and bothered about our progress. Most of all he taught us scepticism – to ask 'why?' and to take nothing for granted. If the mainly middle-class boys of a sixth form grammar school were challenged by socialism, so much the better for their education. In practice, we turned the scepticism he recommended on his own political ideas and there was no indoctrination.

I already felt strongly about social conditions in Liverpool, and Alec Roberts and arguments in the sixth form began to give intellectual substance to my hitherto inchoate thoughts. I visited his untidy flat in a Georgian terrace in unfashionable Toxteth, and marvelled at his books. The mantelshelf was crowded with every book published by Allen Lane since establishing his Penguin imprint ten years earlier. There were also the red covers of the Left Book Club and other, yellow-jacketed, publications from Victor Gollancz like *Why You Should be a Socialist* by Wing-Commander John Strachey and *Guilty Men* by Frank Owen, Michael Foot and Peter Howard. I borrowed these and found others to interest me in the public library.

I identified with John Wilkes in his fight for freedom of speech; and with the Chartists, about whom I wrote an essay which won the Ashlar Prize presented by old boys of the school. I was fascinated by how industrial and technological development led to social change and, in turn, created new political challenges. I read about Dolfuss and the shelling of workers' flats in the Karl Marx Hof in Vienna and wondered why the Labour Party had not dispatched its own brigade to fight for the republican cause in Spain. (I did *not* read George Orwell's *Homage to Catalonia,* which offered an explanation). But the book that made the greatest political impact on me should have pushed me in quite another direction. Professor A. V. Dicey, a distinguished but conservative academic lawyer, had given a series of lectures at Harvard which were published in 1905 as *Law and Opinion in England*. This traced the way in which the movement of public opinion in the nineteenth century had been reflected in legislation and the growth of collectivism.

The opportunity to test my political ideas came in the summer of 1945 and the general election, the first for ten years. I attended every Tory meeting I could in order to heckle, using *Your MP* – another Gollancz special – as a guide to the awkward questions I should ask. Victor Raikes, a local MP, was an excellent target because of his pre-war neo-Nazi association with the Anglo-German Link movement. So was Patrick Buchan-Hepburn, who was to become Churchill's Chief Whip after 1951. In my own constituency of East Toxteth, I supported the Liberal candidate, Professor Lyon Blease, an immensely tall man with a long black coat, who strode through the streets, head held high in the air, oblivious to the world around him, including his potential voters. Unfortunately he lost. Otherwise I unequivocally associated myself with Labour.

The Conservative manifesto, based on his standing as the successful war leader, was called simply *Mr Churchill's Declaration of Policy to the Electors*; Labour's was *Let us Face the Future*, and had a large red 'V' on the front cover. It made the case for the nationalisation of coal, gas, electricity, the railways and iron and steel, promised to raise the school leaving age to sixteen, and argued for a massive housing programme. But at its heart, and at the heart of much of Labour's campaigning, was the idea of security for the individual and his family, in a job, in old age and in sickness through a

National Health Service. This was the welfare state, highly appealing to those who had experienced pre-war unemployment or, like my father, had found it difficult from time to time to pay doctors' bills. 'Security' was what William Beveridge had recommended in his famous report of 1942, and it had an appeal in the suburbs as well as in the inner city.

On polling day most of Quarry Bank's arts sixth form decided to stay away from school, although whether all went electioneering was later in dispute. The Headmaster was incensed and awarded us a Saturday morning detention. But it was a small price to pay when three weeks later (because of the need to wait for the ballot papers of those in the Forces who had voted overseas) I stood on the steps of St George's Hall in the heart of the city where the results were displayed for all the world to see.

Liverpool politics had long been complicated by the antagonism of Protestants and Irish Catholics, rivalling Glasgow in this respect, and not far behind Belfast. A Protestant party was represented on the city council and Alderman Longbottom, later Grand Master of the Orange Order, was heartily disliked by my father for his rabble-rousing bigotry. Despite a large Catholic minority amongst the voters, no Catholic was nominated as Lord Mayor until 1943.

The Conservative Party had captured most of the Protestant working-class vote at the turn of the century, when the ship-owning and unitarian Liberals had failed to move with the times. A tight Conservative caucus had been established by Sir Archibald Salvidge, controlled since 1938 by Sir Alfred Shennan, an architect who prospered by combining his practice with the chairmanship of key council committees and a close association with Bents Brewery, which was remarkably successful in obtaining lucrative corner sites for its public houses. An early beneficiary of the long Conservative ascendancy, based on religious prejudice and a cheap populism towards Liverpool's 'alien immigration' of Germans, Italians, Chinese and Jews, had been F. E. Smith, who sat in Parliament for Liverpool constituencies from 1906 until becoming Lord Birkenhead in 1919. Since 1935 Liverpool had been represented by eight Conservative and three Labour MPs, but now fortunes had been precisely reversed to give Labour eight seats in Parliament, and the Conservatives only three. It was a marvellous moment and a time for rejoicing. I put out the Union Jack at home – a slightly incongruous act, as the Conservatives had treated it as their own property during the election – and stencilled: 'Well Done Labour' on the fence round the Air-Raid Warden's Sector Post. I was confident that the right side had won and, as a symbol of my political manhood, I gave up the *Aeroplane Spotter*, my weekly reading since 1941, in favour of the *New Statesman and Nation*.

A fortnight later I was off on my bicycle to ride to London, with a friend, via the Wye Valley and the Cotswolds. But the eve of my departure was marked by a remarkable event. Listening idly to the wireless for war news from the Far East, I heard the announcement that an atom bomb been dropped on the Japanese city of Hiroshima. I knew of Lord Rutherford's work in nuclear physics, but understood that an unsolved problem about splitting the atom was how to avoid a chain reaction leading to an uncontrolled explosion that would destroy the planet. Plainly I was wrong, because here we were, unaffected by what had happened. I shouted the news to my mother, but her response took a less than global view of events. 'Yes dear,' she said, humouring me, 'but do you want cheese or ham in your sandwiches?'

The next day I set off by bicycle as planned, to stay my first night in London at a youth hostel in Highgate, very close to where fifty years later I came permanently to live. The uniforms of servicemen and women on the streets seemed slightly anomalous, because London's war was over and bomb damage to the West End seemed slight. On my return journey, I celebrated V-J Day – the end of the war with Japan – in Leicester at a huge public party in the centre of the town. After that, I hurried home to Liverpool, cycling 100 miles in a day, to commence the next stage of my life.

In order to find a channel for my political energy, I decided to join a political party. Alec Roberts advised me against any hasty choice, so I wrote to the Liberals, the Communists, Common Wealth (a short-lived middle-class party that had flourished during wartime but had won few votes in the election) as well as Labour. From the Liberals and Common Wealth I received a packet of leaflets, and from the Communists a long closely argued letter. From the Labour Party there was not even an acknowledgment. But I increasingly felt that Labour policies offered the nearest approximation to my developing ideas.

Existing inequalities of wealth seemed to me particularly unjust. For very many years the 17th Earl of Derby had been known as the 'King of Lancashire' through his apparent ownership of half the county and his influence in the Conservative Party. He had been Secretary of State for War in the Lloyd George coalition when Field Marshal Haig had said of him: 'Like the feather pillow, he bears the mark of the last person who sat on him.' But this did not diminish the huge respect with which he was treated when, now reaching his eighties, he appeared at victory celebrations. I was furious when he was profusely thanked for heading any list of charity donations because in relation to his immense wealth, his contributions to charity meant far less than my father's to the Week's Good Cause. In any case, such contributions were a form of Danegeld, designed to deflect attention from the injustice of his riches. One day I cycled through the Victorian streets and the 1920s council estates of Walton and Knotty Ash, past iron gates on to a quiet road that led to rolling parkland on the northern edge of the city. This was Knowsley, Lord Derby's estate of 20,000 acres. I planned to investigate a country house, said to be larger than Buckingham Palace, where Lord Derby lived on a lavish scale (when he wasn't living at another of his many houses) with at least forty servants. I was stopped by a bailiff and ejected; this, he said, was private land and I was trespassing. 'But,' I protested, knowing my lines, 'the land is the people's.' 'No it ain't my son, not here,' was the half-genial reply, and I was escorted out to re-join the plebs. My feelings about the landed aristocracy had already been provoked when I had tried to fish, using a piece of string and a bent pin, from a municipal park in Bakewell in Derbyshire. I was sharply told that although the public had access to the riverbank, the river and its fish were the property of the Duke of Rutland. So even when they didn't own the people's land, these fabulously rich men owned the people's water.

Despite such experiences, most of my time was given over to the widening pleasures of growing up and school work that I increasingly enjoyed. I joined the Methodist Youth Club, played tennis, went to the cinema and began to like girls. There were occasional visits to the Wallasey Jazz Club, where the Merseysippi Jazz Band gave a fair imitation of genuine Dixieland; and late-night listening to AFN Munich, the American forces radio that brought us Woody Herman, Tommy Dorsey and the late Glenn Miller. With the school I went for the first time to the Philharmonic Hall, to be introduced to classical orchestral music with Sir Malcolm Sargent conducting.

On the basis of my results in the Higher School Certificate examination I was of-fered a place at Liverpool University, but not until the following year because of the need to accommodate returning servicemen. As this left me with some months to spare before my eighteenth birthday and call-up to National Service, Alec Roberts suggested that I should try for a scholarship to Oxford or Cambridge. I was given a table in the book-room at the very top of the school, where textbooks were stored. It had the musty smell of a church vestry and little natural light, but I could work there undisturbed. I wrote two essays a week, taken from previous examination pa-pers, for the group of Oxford colleges that included Balliol, Magdalen and New Col-lege, and decided to follow Alec Roberts to Magdalen if I could.

Early in January 1947 I took a train from Lime Street Station, changed at Bletchley and found myself in Oxford for the first time. I was daunted by the knowl-edge of the other examinees, who talked with learning about reredos, transomed windows and ornamental quatrefoils, and other features of the architecture of the medieval college. More to the point, their mothers had apparently entertained the relevant Fellows of the College to lunch and discussed the abilities of their progeny. It cannot have been quite like that and there may have been a majority of silent and uneasy examinees like me, but the confidence of those who vouchsafed their views as we drank sherry with the President was alarming. I remember little else of my visit except a long essay on: 'Liberty is the absence of restraint; discuss', on which I had enough to say; and an interview when I expressed a wish to visit Greece to show support for ELAS, the communist-backed movement in the civil war which the British Army was helping to suppress. Snow was falling on Oxford as I left to return to Liverpool, and the attractions of spending some time there in the future began to grow on me. When, ten days later, I received a letter saying that I had been awarded an Open Exhibition in Modern History at Magdalen, I was surprised and delighted.

I heard from Magdalen about my Exhibition on 20 January 1947 and, exactly a month later, I joined the King's Regiment, Liverpool's own indigenous force of fighting men. Although my brother Peter was in the Army policing Palestine in the last ugly and dangerous days of the Mandate, I would have preferred the Navy for my National Service, reviving life at sea as a family tradition; or the RAF, the glamorous wartime service, at least for flying crew. But the Army alone was recruiting and I wanted to get my National Service over.

The 20 January had seen the beginning of the most severe cold spell of the century, with freezing weather and much snow. Three weeks later an unprecedented national fuel crisis began, greatly damaging to the Labour Government, with power stations running out of coal, factories closing and no heating in many homes. These conditions persisted until the last week in March. In the wooden huts amongst the sandhills of Formby, where I had begun my initial training, there was no fuel for the primitive stoves that were intended to provide us with minimum warmth. All pipes froze and the only sanitation was in buckets placed on open ground on which we had to break the ice. The ends of every one of my fingers split and the raw wounds were deepened by the sharp-edged metal buttons which were not easily forced through the apertures of a stiff new khaki uniform. It was almost too cold for parade-ground drill or the noisy bayonet charges at distended sacks of horsehair which were designed to make us killers.

But the temporary experience of physical privation, which any fit eighteen year-old should be capable of enduring, was as nothing compared with the culture shock of my new existence. I quickly learnt that hitherto my life had been sheltered. For one thing, I could both read and write, and soon found myself writing letters on behalf of those who found it hard to do either. For another, I found that arguments were usually settled by a quick scuffle and one of us on the floor, rather than discussion. Nor were the sergeants and corporals who ruled our lives inclined to explain the reasons for the orders they gave. 'Because I say so,' was their only answer to the simple question: 'Why?' The rational and liberal standards of Quarry Bank High School had no relevance here. The best I could do was learn to survive.

For almost two years I did so with tolerable success. Sent to a War Office Selection Board for officers, I complained about the rigidity of army discipline, defended the Soviet Union and showed myself an awkward non-conformer in tactical military exercises. I was regarded as wholly unsatisfactory, and quite properly failed.

The spring of 1947 was spent learning to drive heavy lorries through the narrow lanes of Devon and Somerset, and the summer in washing out latrines, until my startled sergeant-major found me teaching him English in the Adult Education Centre when the regular lecturer fell sick. Feeling that one of my roles reflected on his own dignity as my pupil, Sergeant-Major Varley promptly took me off routine duties, and henceforth I was my own man, free to read a novel a day, leave camp to watch cricket or sink into a stupor induced by endless pints of local cider. Then in November I sailed from Harwich to the Hook-of-Holland, en route for Göttingen and the Army College of the Rhine. Three months later, as a sergeant in the Royal Army Education Corps, I was teaching English and history and giving vocational advice to soldiers awaiting demobilisation at the Further Education Centre in Hamburg. It was a fate similar to that of many grammar school boys during National Service who found themselves either teaching soldiers or serving in the Intelligence Corps, often learning Russian.

But 1948 was an absorbing year to be in Hamburg. The war had been over for less than three years, and I was part of the army of occupation. The bombing of Hamburg by the RAF, code-named 'Operation Gomorrah', had as its objective its total destruction. The docks of the fine Hanseatic port had been destroyed and the skeletons of office blocks and once-great bonded warehouses stood gaunt and precarious, awaiting demolition. On the single night of 28 July 1943, 42,000 civilians had been killed in a firestorm that raged through the inner city, more than had been killed in the German blitz on Britain. But as in virtually all cities devastated by bombing, a surprising number of buildings remained standing and some areas were almost untouched. The baroque Hauptkirche St Michaelis had survived, as had the Rathaus with its campanile. Churches seemed as prominent on the skyline as those of Wren and Hawksmoor in the City of London.

I visited Hagenbeck Zoo, went regularly to concerts, where I heard the great Wilhelm Furtwangler conduct, sailed down the Elbe, and attended a rally of the SPD, the first such socialist meeting to be held in Hamburg since 1933. Christmas 1948 was spent snowbound in a Gothic castle hidden in deep woods, seventy kilometres north of Hamburg, near Lübeck.

However, the enjoyment of these pleasures was only one aspect of my complex response to living in Germany so soon after the war. Everything – leather goods, cameras, women – could easily be purchased with cigarettes, and the black market was more generally accepted by the authorities than fraternisation, although this was now permitted. I attended a war crimes trial of a former colonel in the Waffen SS, who was accused of (and later executed for) the murder of men of the Norfolk Regiment. All around me were Germans who had applauded Hitler and acquiesced in the liquidation of the Jews. Jews, waiting to board ship to the United States, had been seized from the Hamburg docks in 1939 and, two years later, a thousand had been rounded up and deported. There was no doubt in my mind about collective guilt, and while I excused those of my own age or a little older, I felt unqualified hostility towards the middle-aged. When, towards the end of my time in Hamburg, I was put in charge of the Education Centre, I insisted that my civilian German staff watch a film of the German invasion of Poland, showing corpses of Polish civilians hanging from roadside trees. The accompanying soundtrack was the second movement of Beethoven's Seventh Symphony, and I have never since been able to listen to it without reliving the film and feeling again my own quite savage anger. Despite the July 1944 plot against Hitler and the terrible retribution suffered by the conspirators, I still believe that, with few exceptions, the only 'good' Germans – amongst those who were adults in 1933 – who survived the war did so in concentration camps or in exile.

Germany's remarkable economic recovery began while I was in Hamburg. At the beginning of 1948 Germany was the defeated enemy; by the end of the year it was moving inexorably towards becoming an ally of the Western powers. In June came currency reform in West Germany, master-minded on the German side by Ludwig Erhard. By July the Berlin airlift was underway and a turning point in East-West relations had been reached. By the autumn a constitutional convention was meeting in Bonn to draft what became the Basic Law of the Federal Republic, confirming the division of Germany which was to last forty years.

My own sense of a new era was marked less by these events than by the death of Jan Masaryk, the charismatic Czech leader who, during his wartime exile in London, had become a symbol of the freedom to which his people were entitled. It was described as suicide, but was widely believed to be murder by the Soviet secret police. A few months earlier I had stood on a hill outside Bad Harzburg and looked east to the ominous watchtowers on the heavily guarded frontier between the British and Soviet zones of a divided Germany. Now the democratically elected multi-party government of the Czechoslovak Republic, hitherto seen to be a bridge between East and West, had been overthrown and the country was suffering a fate as terrible as its betrayal by Britain at Munich only ten years before. The end of democracy in Czechoslovakia was as politically decisive for me as the crushing of the Hungarian rising was to be for many in the communist parties of the West in 1956.

But despite Czechoslovakia and the Berlin Airlift, I did not applaud the sudden rush to soften attitudes towards the Germans and diminish what might offend them. In contravention of army regulations, I submitted an article to the *New Statesman* (it was not published), complaining that the NAAFI 'Victory Club' had been named 'Hamburg House' in deference to German susceptibilities; and that British troops could no longer wear civilian clothes because Germans had complained that this was contrary to their own military tradition. For me, these developments were coming much too soon. The Germans were being embraced for the wrong reasons and long before they had earned redemption for the misdeeds of the Hitler years.

Despite that, I had become fascinated by Germany. Hamburg in 1948 had both the sleazy, dangerous mystery of the Vienna of Harry Lime and *The Third Man* and an underlying, vaguely arrogant, resilience. Before Hitler there had been Weimar. After defeat and devastation there was to be the 'economic miracle'. Thirty years later, the brilliant film *Heimat* was to bring out all the contradictions of Germany through those generations.

But my years of National Service were less a chapter in my life than a short story, complete in itself, with a beginning and an end. Son after Christmas I sailed back to Harwich, and on 23 January 1949 was formally discharged from the Army. Nine days earlier I had carried my belongings in my army kit box into the porter's lodge at Magdalen College.

Chapter 2
Oxford and After

The marvellous pleasure of arriving at Oxford was knowing that my time was now my own. What I should do with it was quite another matter. Alec Roberts, who was most responsible for my being there, advised that I should work for a First but without much hope of getting one unless I was very single-minded. This was not what I intended to be, although I had only the haziest idea about other choices open to me. There was no 'Freshers' Week' in Oxford in the 1940s – we would have disdained such a pedestrian introduction to our new lives – and certainly no attempt to brief those undergraduates foolish enough to arrive a term late. My real loss in arriving in January was to be cut off from the dozen or so first-year Magdalen undergraduates, also reading history, who had arrived in the autumn.

But I did not feel lonely in those first weeks in Magdalen so much as on my own, an experience to which I had become accustomed through my Army years. I was also fortunate to meet J. S. Perkin, who was reading English, and he became my closest friend in college throughout my Oxford time. John had been born and brought up in Macclesfield with a healthy suspicion of southern ways and I learnt from him about F. R. Leavis and *Scrutiny* and caught up again with modern poetry. In the vacations he taught me to tickle trout in the streams of Derbyshire and to ignore angry farmers when we walked across their land. Later he was to become, for twenty-five years, the editor of the *Manchester Guardian Weekly*, transforming it from a regional institution in decline into an international newspaper with a circulation of over 100,000.

My rooms in Magdalen were at the bottom of Staircase IV in the Cloisters, which dated from the fifteenth century (although much restored in Victorian times). The sitting room or study was heated by an electric fire with two bars that glowed faintly but did not lift the temperature much above freezing point in winter. The bedroom had an iron bedstead of the kind found in hospitals, and a jug of cold water and a wash bowl on a painted wooden stand. There was also a chamber pot. This provided me with a difficulty. The nearest lavatories and running water were either across the lawns to the New Buildings or in the Gothics, a discrete construction falsely attributed to Pugin and entirely devoted to bodily functions.

I did not fancy a long walk in urgent circumstances at night, but I was uneasy about the chamber pot being emptied by my scout, a kind of batman whose task it was to make my bed and clean my rooms. I did not like the idea of personal servants and also found their presence an intrusion into my privacy. I certainly had no idea how to tip them when they were called upon to exceed their normal duties. As a result, the New Buildings and the Gothics saw me as often in the middle of the night as by day.

Magdalen had adopted a cafeteria system for breakfast and lunch, the first Oxford college to do so. Magdalen was also the first – perhaps the only – college to serve whale meat to supplement the limited products of food rationing. We boasted of it almost as a test of manhood, for it was fibrous and foul-tasting. But either the Bursar organised Magdalen's food supplies badly or the grey post-war skies were lightening, because by the time John Strachey, who as Minister of Food had been conducting 'palatability tests' on whale meat, was entertained to dinner by the Labour Club at the Cadena Cafe in May 1950, oxtail soup, roast duckling and Astoria trifle were on the menu. There was also a decent three-course lunch regularly to be had at a popular restaurant, Long John's, for two shillings and ninepence.

My memory is of spending most of my first two terms talking with John Perkin, learning slowly to study again, exploring the buildings and gardens of the colleges and dipping into any event that interested me. It was all I had hoped from a residential university where the stimulus of discussion and activity lasted for at least sixteen hours in every day. I sat at the feet of T. S. Eliot, there being no other room when over 200 undergraduates turned up to hear him at Pusey House, and found him disappointingly ordinary; saw De Sica's *Bicycle Thieves* and Rossellini's *Paisa* at the Scala in Walton Street (then an 'art cinema', showing only continental films); drank beer and listened to New Orleans jazz at the Perch Inn; and wrote a sonnet (so my diary reminds me) to a girlfriend on St Valentine's Day.

Magdalen, I discovered, was not a college from which to launch oneself on to the university. It had none of the corporate spirit which helped Balliol men achieve success through the loyalty of their colleagues; nor the cosy supportive warmth of smaller colleges like Jesus or Lincoln. Magdalen's tradition was to disdain collective activity in favour of private life, even within its walls. Together with Peter Lowell, a rather older undergraduate and pre-war refugee from Hitler's Europe, I launched the Waynflete Society, named after Magdalen's fifteenth century founder, as a college debating society. It flourished for a couple of terms but died quickly when we withdrew our attention. It was difficult for organised groups to take root in Magdalen unless they were dining clubs.

Kenneth Tynan – already a legend – had lately rocked the university while reading English, but there seemed to be relief at his departure from Magdalen rather than pride in his notoriety. I was to meet Jock Bruce-Gardyne, Tim Renton and Christopher

Chataway, all of whom overlapped with me, again when they became Conservative MPs, but only Chataway made much impact on the university and that was as President of the Athletic Club and a record-breaking middle-distance runner. Magdalen's most prominent political figure at the time of my arrival was Keith Kyle, Secretary of the Union, an active and well-liked Liberal (he later joined the Labour Party under the influence of Hugh Gaitskell, and later again the SDP). Keith, a tall, gaunt man with a beak of a nose, would swoop, like an eagle, into college for a tutorial. At a casual meeting I drew his attention to a huge accumulation of mail in his pigeonhole in the college lodge. 'Like Lord Melbourne,' he said in a voice more attuned to a public pronouncement than conversation, 'one leaves correspondence long enough for it to answer itself.' I was impressed and wondered whether Oxford life required every remark to be laced with a quotation or historical analogy.

I was already learning that the generic use of 'you' as in: 'when *you* are ill *you* send for a doctor' was regarded as ill-bred in Oxford discourse. What Fowler in his classic *Modern English Usage* called 'the false first-personal one' was all the rage. It was, Fowler said, writing in 1926, a new invention of the self-conscious journalist and he called for its supression. Oxford made it smart – 'one goes to a tutorial when one's tutor asks one' – although even Oxford thought it precious when carried to extremes.

The President of the Junior Common Room – effectively the undergraduate representative in any discussions with the college authorities – in my first term was Julian Bullard, whom I was to meet again when he was H. M. Ambassador in Bonn. His opposite number at that time in a still divided Germany, H. M. Ambassador to the German Democratic Republic, was Tim Everard, our joint contemporary at Magdalen in 1949, who became a friend when his diplomatic and my political career converged in the 1970s.

Julian Bullard had been at Rugby and Tim at Uppingham, and the overall feel of the college was public school. But with twenty-four grammar school boys amongst the eighty-five freshmen of 1948, it had a slightly higher proportion than Balliol (twenty out of seventy-nine) and much higher than Christ Church (ten out of seventy-eight) and Trinity (seven out of ninety-eight). Nevertheless, a disengaged *hauteur* coupled with quiet scholarship was the general tone. This was set by the President of the College, T. S. R. Boase, a bachelor art historian who seemed to bother with few undergraduates except those with significant social standing. I remember him mainly for his reluctant handshake and weak smile. But what mattered most to me about the college was how I would find those who were to teach me.

Magdalen had four history tutors. The two newest had just been appointed and were destined to remain Fellows for almost forty years. One was John Stoye. He had a shy smile and gentle ways, and I liked him without quite knowing where the force of his personality lay. Karl Leyser was a more flamboyant character, but a figure of some fun. He was frequently seen in the uniform of an officer in the Black Watch (he had been mentioned in dispatches), striding across the lawns of the college wearing a kilt and waving his swagger stick. That he should have such a passion for military display in peacetime was a legitimate object of surprise, but in some undergraduate remarks there was an unpleasant undercurrent of ridicule. Karl was a German Jew, still with a distinct accent which could make him almost unintelligible at moments of excitement. But if a few mocked what they saw as his pretensions, he was much admired for his vast and recondite learning.

The senior history tutor, and the man whose letter had told me that I was to go to Magdalen, was K. B. MacFarlane. He was a tallish, square man who carried his head slightly on one side. Although a major figure in the Senior Common Room and an earlier candidate for President, Bruce MacFarlane seemed at first a remote, self-contained scholar. In a tribute many years later, Alan Bennett, in his book *Writing Home,* described him as 'a man of great austerity and singleness of mind … the most impressive teacher, and in some ways the most impressive man, I have ever come across'. MacFarlane had published very little (he would have had a hard time in today's output-driven universities), but the outcome of his long study of John Wycliffe, the late medieval heretic and reformer, was eagerly awaited. I had enormous respect for him and hung around nervously outside his rooms, plucking up courage to knock on the door and go to my tutorials. An essay I did for him on 'Church life in England in the thirteenth century' was one of the few I wrote for my Magdalen tutors of which I was not more than half ashamed, but his shyness and scholarship made me feel clumsy and was a barrier to intimacy. I was surprised when he invited me back to college for a weekend after I had gone down, and was tortured by the decision about when I could start calling him 'Bruce', rather than 'MacFarlane', which in those days was the accepted halfway house between surname-with-prefix (*Mr* MacFarlane) and Christian name. For some years I continued to call on him in Magdalen on all my visits to Oxford until in a foolish and tactless way I broke the spell by declining an invitation to another weekend.

The fourth of my tutors was far more worldly than Bruce. Although he had not yet achieved notoriety as a television performer, A. J. P. Taylor's name was already one to conjure with. Like many other undergraduates, I had enjoyed his *The Course of German History*, which was at the same time polemical (anti-German) and informed. His Oxford lectures, given without notes to an audience of hundreds, were immensely popular. I admired his ability to recapture with a provocative anecdote the attention of his audience when it appeared to wander. His eye would roam over his listeners to detect anything less than rapt attention. Then his voice would rasp and squeak as it changed gear, and we would become his captives again.

But as tutor and pupil we did not get on. This was mainly my fault. He began to teach me at a moment when my essays for him were last in the queue as a call upon my time. For the first twenty minutes of a tutorial we would talk about the political story of the week. Then his eyes would fall ominously to the papers on my lap, and it was inescapably time to read. I would apologise for the shortcomings in what followed, but he continued to judge my essays by the standards they should have reached. In addition, he found irritating – with every reason – my inability (owing to mild dyslexia) to pronounce foreign names. I would refer to the Austrian Foreign Minister with whom Disraeli dealt over the Eastern Question as 'Andrassy', a fair phonetical rendering of the way he was spelt. *'Andracky!'* Alan Taylor would shout, adopting the proper pronunciation of his Hungarian name. I would try again, and then a third time, before ending up thoroughly demoralised, with my tutor wondering what was the point of trying to teach me.

But there were also political and temperamental differences. The iconoclasm and cynical wit that made him such an attractive lecturer were less comfortable to me when it came to discussing contemporary politics one to one. In home affairs I was already a Fabian; abroad, while lacking the vehement anti-Soviet instincts of friends like Oleg Kerensky (whose grandfather had been head of the Provisional Government of Russia in 1917), I had come to accept Soviet responsibility for the Cold War. But as a man of the maverick left, Alan saw things differently, although it was difficult to know what he really cared about and whether his expressed views were serious or contrived.

In my second term with him as my tutor, exhausted by too many activities and too little sleep, I suddenly found myself unable to finish reading an essay or even to speak. I opened my mouth but no sound came. Alan was deeply embarrassed. He eventually told me to catch a bus to Dorchester and go for a long country walk; pastoral care was not his strength. I knew nothing at the time of his own confused and difficult family life or that his first marriage was finally breaking up. His house at Holywell Ford, where he taught his pupils, seemed as full of children as of books. That he was profoundly unhappy and restlessly discontented never occurred to me.

My next encounter with AJP (as Magdalen history undergraduates called him) was eight years later. The explosion of a Soviet hydrogen bomb and American policies under President Eisenhower and his hard-line Secretary of State, John Foster Dulles, led to a widespread feeling that nuclear war was now a crucial issue. I shared this anxiety and saw myself as a nuclear disarmer, although uncertain about how disarmament might be achieved. When I was told about a meeting at Central Hall, Westminster, on 17 February 1958, called by the new Campaign for Nuclear Disarmament, I naturally attended. The distinguished platform included Bertrand Russell, J. B. Priestley and Alan Taylor, and when Alan spoke he was in coruscating rhetorical form. He correctly judged the expectant mood of the audience and played it for all he was worth. As he came to the climax of his speech he told how, when politicians appeared on public platforms at the time of the suffragettes, women would rise in their places and cry: 'votes for women.' He paused and put all his contemptuous authority into the gravel of his voice. 'I say to you,' he declared, 'whenever any politician appears on a platform today you should rise in your place and cry: "murderer".' The audience was ecstatic, but I was profoundly shocked. It was one thing to tease undergraduates about the foibles of Bismarck or the shortcomings of Ramsay MacDonald, but quite another to simpify a great contemporary issue and accuse those who took a different view of not even caring. Not for the last time in politics, I moved from agnosticism to a firm position – in favour of *multi*lateral not *uni*lateral disarmament – because I was unconvinced by the alternative case.

It was a dozen years before I met him again or forgave him for what seemed dangerous self-indulgence throughout the 1950s and 1960s, whether in pursuit of unilateral disarmament or, even less acceptably, as an acolyte of Lord Beaverbrook, the owner of the *Sunday Express,* for which Alan wrote pot-boiling articles. But then I sat next to him at a dinner at Magdalen, enjoyed his gossipy company in the wasteland of my prematurely middle-aged contemporaries and sensed all passion spent. 'Why did you give up CND?' I asked. There was a sparkle in his eye which challenged me to decide for myself whether what followed was cynicism or provocation. 'I had spoken in the Central Hall, Westminster; in the Free Trade Hall, Manchester; in the Usher Hall, Edinburgh … what else was there left for me to do?' It was his party piece, but more than half true. Reconciled, and much easier with him than when he had taught me, in 1974 I arranged a small dinner for him at the House of Commons with some of his former pupils now in public life. At his suggestion, these included Robert Kee (the source of so much of his personal misery thirty years before, because of a triangular relationship involving his wife); Paul Johnson, in the early stages of transition from the *New Statesman* left to the *Spectator* right; David Marquand; and Keith Kyle. I also invited Maurice Oldfield, said to be John le Carré's model for George Smiley, who I was soon to meet as head of MI6 and of whom Alan spoke fondly as a former pupil from his Manchester days. It was a happy occasion and I was pleased that my own antipathy towards him had drained away.

I saw him occasionally in his final years. Once he called at Patshull Road, where I lived, with his young son Daniel (by his second wife, Tony Crosland's sister), who had a present for my eldest daughter, Rachel, with whom he was at school. On another occasion we met at dinner at Keith Kyle's, with Keith, himself unwell, nursing him through a rather subdued evening in a very hot room. But mostly I remember him, hunched up and anonymous, pulling his shopping basket on wheels through the decaying streets of Kentish Town. It seemed a long, sad way from Holywell Ford.

An early attempt to venture out into the university from Magdalen was my submission of two short stories to the editor of *Cherwell*, then the leading undergraduate literary journal. They were both rejected. I also became an occasional reporter for *Isis*, the highly professional student weekly, whose editor was on a par with the President of the Union and the President of OUDS (the Oxford University Dramatic Society) in the superstar esteem accorded them by many undergraduates. My editor was Robert Robinson, who already possessed the light-tenor friendliness that was to make him a highly successful quizmaster and talk-show impresario thirty years later, although in 1950 he described television – whose popular appeal had just caught on – as 'the ulcer on twentieth century civilisation'. 'How's your mum?', addressed to Shirley Catlin (Shirley Williams as she became), were the first words I heard Bob Robinson utter. I thought it a very familiar way of referring to Vera Brittain, whose literary reputation made her a distinctly un-mum-like figure.

The idea of working for *Isis* was attractive, but I knew that in the highly competitive world of undergraduate writing I was not destined to succeed. I had a romantic notion of myself as a poet rather than a politician, reflecting what I hoped was my temperament. But the reality was that I fitted most easily into politics, where the participation of a newcomer was positively welcomed either for his contributions to discussion or his willingness to undertake some of the burden of organisation.

There were two layers of involvement open to undergraduates: the political clubs and the Oxford Union. The main political clubs were large and active and holding office in them was modestly prestigious. In Michaelmas Term 1948 (the beginning of the academic year in October), the Conservative Association had 1,800 members, the Labour Club 1,500 and the Liberals 1,200. As membership involved no political test or commitment, freshmen undergraduates sometimes joined all three. Nevertheless, in the Hilary Term (spring) when I arrived, each still retained a membership of about two-thirds of that number. The Labour Club held at least one weekly meeting, often addressed by a cabinet minister and attended by several hundred members. Unlike the late 1930s, when the democratic socialists, led by Tony Crosland and Roy Jenkins, split off from the communist-dominated Labour Club (a process to be repeated in the 1960s and 1970s), the Labour Club in my time was not fissiparous. The far left, both communist and non-communist, were corralled in the Socialist Club, a bit-player in university politics whose main asset was a stunningly beautiful Chairman, Caroline Carter.

The main division, or so it seemed to me, was between 'BR' and 'White's' socialists. 'BR socialists' ate modest meals at the British Restaurant – a branch of municipal catering dating from wartime – on the Plain, to the east of Magdalen Bridge in the direction of industrial Cowley; they wore raincoats and rode bicycles. 'White's socialists' frequented a fashionable eating house on the High, near Carfax; they carried umbrellas whatever the weather. This division had more to do with pretensions than class or ideology. Amongst the BR socialists was David Donnison, formerly of Marlborough College, son of a distinguished Indian civil servant, who became Professor of Social Administration at LSE and a major influence on social policy for three decades. Amongst those who preferred White's was John Gilbert, the son of a clerk in the Inland Revenue with a background much like my own, who retained his polished arrogance as an MP and middle-rank Labour minister in the 1970s, and again, as an effective spokesman for the Blair Government in the House of Lords after 1997. What I found more surprising than these trivial differences in style was that the Labour Club appeared to be run not by grammar-school products or by those students with a genuine working-class background from Ruskin College, but by the sons and daughters of the professional middle classes from public schools. Dick Taverne, Oleg Kerensky, Michael Summerskill and Shirley Catlin, successively Chairmen of the Club, had been respectively at Charterhouse, Westminster, St Paul's and St Paul's Girls. We were quite unselfconscious in our relationship, respecting each other equally for what we were: all clever enough to be at Oxford. But there were even fewer grammar-school boys active in the Labour Club than the proportion in the university as a whole. It seemed improbable to me that they were less inclined towards the Labour Party than their public-school counterparts. The more likely explanation was that they were keeping their eyes to their books and following the advice of their former teachers that they should seek to excel – as the launchpad for their future careers – in the academic studies that had brought them to Oxford. Later, reflecting on those undergraduates who were prominent in the university as a whole, I concluded that, with notable exceptions, those who came from public schools had the bonus of an articulate self-confidence that made them quicker off the mark in journalism, acting and politics, where every term saw the mushroom rise of reputations.

This was particularly so in the Oxford Union, to whose Presidency most of the leaders of the political clubs aspired. The reputation of the Union in the world outside, and the airs and graces of its senior elected officers, could easily discourage an undergraduate who contemplated taking part. I joined the Union in my first term, but it was a year before I made my maiden speech. Although pleased to receive the standard mark of approbation from the President, Uwe Kitzinger, an invitation to become a teller in the next debate, it was already too late in my Oxford time to consider serious progress in the Union. But even if I had the application to climb the ladder of committees and offices, I had reservations about the Union's seriousness. There was more show than substance to debates and I was irritated by the easy applause of the undergraduate audience for jokes contrived with much burning of midnight oil.

Despite this I shared the general respect for the stars of the Union because, whereas my personality was still developing, their's seemed so complete and fully formed. Robin Day, Godfrey Smith, Jeremy Thorpe and William Rees-Mogg were successively Presidents of the Union through 1950–51. Robin Day, already genial and urbane, was kindly towards those younger members of the Union seeking to make their mark; and the worldly-wise Godfrey Smith was strong on literary anecdotes (those about F. Scott Fitzgerald were his particular favourites) of the sort that enlivened his *Sunday Times* column forty years later. Both were three or four years older than the third Liberal, Jeremy Thorpe, whose act – and his manner was always that of an Edwardian actor-manager – included a convincing impersonation of Winston Churchill. As for William Rees-Mogg, with his owlish glasses, gentle stoop, three-piece suit and gold watch chain, it was difficult to be sure whether he had been born that way or had deliberately contrived to become what in the early 1990s would have been called a young fogey. His deep, slightly sibilant voice spoke perfectly formed sentences which would have sounded pompous from the mouth of anyone less intelligent. Also active in the Union by that time was Dick Taverne, whose boyish enthusiasm, intelligence and eager fascination with ideas was sometimes taken for arrogance (which it wasn't); and Norman St John Stevas, who had come from Cambridge, where he had been President of the Union, to Christ Church to take a further degree. In a gossip column I was writing under the pseudonym of 'Alice', I dared to suggest that Norman was organising an election machine on the Cambridge model to ensure that he won the Presidency of the Oxford Union too. There was a threat of a libel writ (it would never have been sustained) but, like many other such undergraduate follies, the moment quickly passed.

The one speech I made in the Union of which I was pleased was in favour of a motion to expel South Africa from the Commonwealth for racism. But generally I adjourned early from the debating chamber to the Union bar. Rather priggishly, I disapproved of politics as a career fuelled by ambition – for which the Union was an ideal preparation – preferring to believe in it as a vocation inspired by principle. This meant becoming an active member of the Labour Club and of the Labour Party Group, a core body of some 150 Labour Party members, which held Sunday morning discussion meetings usually led by a member of the Group or a sympathetic don like Hugh Seton-Watson from University College, or David Worswick from Magdalen. In Michaelmas Term 1949 I managed to recruit a record Labour Club membership of over 100 in Magdalen and, on the assumption that I possessed some organising skills, was made business manager of the *Oxford Clarion*, the Club's thrice-termly magazine. I persuaded the editor Michael Shanks to let me do a special feature, illustrated by photographs, on what I called 'The Other Oxford', which was the Oxford of mean streets and slum houses in the St Ebbe's district, just off the centre of town, which visitors to the dreaming spires never saw (it is now a shopping precinct and car park). On the strength of this I succeeded Michael as editor, also becoming Chairman of the Labour Party Group. By Michaelmas Term 1950 I was Treasurer of the Labour Club, which under Oxford conventions meant the second most senior officer – in effect, Vice-Chairman.

The Chairman – and the first woman to be Chairman ('Chair' or 'Chairperson' were a generation away) – was Shirley Catlin, with whom I thus began a long working relationship in politics and a close personal friendship. Shirley had already been an *Isis* idol – the supreme accolade of acceptance and success – despite the exclusion of women from the Union and the prominence and publicity that Union activity gave. She was, I wrote in my diary, 'a rare character, a unique combination of mental ability, physical energy, friendliness and ambition, plus a vague element of sometimes straying from the whole truth which she would probably justify as a desire not to hurt anybody'. Amongst her qualities was a marvellously rich speaking voice, seductive in conversation and urgently persuasive on a public platform. Typically, her Chairman's message to the *Oxford Clarion* had been date-lined New York, because during the summer vacation she had been touring the United States in the OUDS production of *King Lear*. What was important for our cooperation was that we shared an emotional response to politics and saw socialism mainly as redistributing wealth and opportunity in what we called a 'just society'. I found her 'soft' on issues that required unpopular decisions (I was left to make them), but too little was ever at stake for a serious row. We were to be friends, allies and occasional rivals for the next fifty years, leapfrogging each other in our political careers.

Amongst members of the Club's Executive Committee in our term of office was Ivor Lucas, later to be Ambassador to Syria, and Maurice Shock, who became Vice-Chancellor of Leicester University and then Rector of Lincoln College. There was also a recent convert from the Liberal Party, Gerald Kaufman. Of the college secretaries, the recruiting sergeants of the Club, two, Richard Marsh and Guy Barnet, were also to be elected Labour MPs (Dick Marsh becoming a cabinet minister before going on to other things); and Robert Andrew was to become my chief adviser in negotiations over Hong Kong twenty-five years later, when I was Minister of State for Defence, before ending his civil service career as Permanent Secretary at the Northern Ireland Office throughout a very troublesome period.

The Secretary of the Club, number three in the hierarchy, was Patrick Hutber, with whom I enjoyed spending time, always in argument, with Pat seeing his role as one of constant intellectual provocation. He had a tetchy, roving mind and became City Editor of the *Sunday Telegraph* and a radical Conservative before his premature death. My intention was to succeed Shirley as Chairman of the Club, for which it was thought I would get the necessary votes, but this was also Pat's ambition. Abandoning his usual adverserial style, he walked me round and round New College gardens explaining that he had set his heart on the Chairmanship, and asking how I could justify standing against him when I had admitted that it mattered less to me. Such was the moral force of his argument (and he made it a moral issue of relative need) that I gave in. He bought me two large glasses of sherry in appreciation and he was elected Chairman of the Club unopposed.

Politics in the Labour Club were an opportunity to meet the leading political figures of the day, often over a drink or dinner following a well-attended meeting. Despite the fight for survival of a Labour Government in decline, ministers seemed happy to escape to Oxford to address undergraduates, although with varying success. Herbert Morrison, then Lord President of the Council, read to a crowded meeting in the Union an unsuitable speech intended to refute the Housewives League, a Tory front organisation of that time. But Hugh Gaitskell scored heavily when asked a lengthy and rhetorical question about Keynesian attitudes to income redistribution by an undergraduate trying too hard to be clever. 'What assumption do you make,' Gaitskell responded, 'about liquidity ratios?' It was a serious enquiry, but Gaitskell's reply deflated his questioner and brought the house down. The Labour Club also held joint debates with the Conservative Association, in one of which I supported Aidan Crawley, then a Labour junior minister, against a Tory MP curiously billed as 'Eric Heath', who turned out to be better known as 'Ted'.

Not all our visitors sustained in private conversation the sense of vision they brought to their public speeches. Victor Gollancz had just given a new and spiritual twist to his publishing reputation as author of *A Year of Grace*, an anthology 'to express a mood about God and Man.' He spoke to a meeting of the Labour Club of an ethical socialism that transcended the sordid compromises of the Labour Party in power. After the meeting Shirley and I, ecstatic and hand in hand like two children seeking Jesus on the front cover of a proselytising tract, accompanied Victor Gollancz to the Mitre Hotel, then the best in Oxford. When he had ordered a drink and lit a cigar, he talked to Shirley about her mother, whose interwar bestseller *Testament of Youth* he had published, and I asked him about the Left Book Club. Why, I innocently enquired, given its influence for more than a decade, had it been wound up when it was most needed to halt the slide of public opinion away from the left? Victor Gollancz took out a pen and wrote two columns of figures on the white linen tablecloth, drawing a line under each. 'That's why,' he said, subtracting one column from another; 'it was losing money'.

There were wider political activities outside the university for those of us who chose to participate. In the general election of 1950, Michael Summerskill led a coach party to Fulham West, where his formidable mother Edith was defending a marginal seat. With our help, or so we liked to think, she held it. In Oxford, I also made my first election speech. It was in the Littlemore Primary School and, after a nervous start, I found myself exhilarated by a captive audience of nearly seventy. I kept the meeting going until the arrival of the Labour candidate Elizabeth Pakenham (later Lady Longford), as handsome in her middle forties as she was reputed to have been when, as an undergraduate, Hugh Gaitskell took her to a Commemoration Ball and all Oxford drank champagne from her slipper.

I found a further pleasure in campaigning in the countryside around Oxford. I would be driven over frosty, mist-enshrouded roads – in memory, it was always winter – to Islip, Stadhampton and villages around the mysterious water meadows of Otmoor. Twenty or thirty people would slowly assemble in an unheated hall, not necessarily out of political sympathy but because any event was welcome for its entertainment value. An aged farm worker would tell me of a similar visit by David Lloyd George before the First World War, which I very much doubted; or that until lately political meetings had been banned by the local landowner, which was almost certainly true. Unlike the towns, which were politically emancipated, there was more than a touch of feudalism in the country areas and only the fact that I was an undergraduate from Oxford – respectable and fairly harmless – prevented attendance at such a Labour meeting being heavily frowned upon. I have no idea what they thought of my jejune mixture of social history, party policies and passion, but they always applauded politely, which was encouragement enough. I have never ceased to enjoy the long drives to patient and friendly meetings associated with electioneering in the countryside, even to address audiences no larger than my Oxfordshire ones. Gladstone would have found such behaviour absurdly trivial in his Midlothian days, and it is not serious politics in the television age. But I find such occasions surpassed only by outdoor meetings, winning an audience with a loudspeaker on the back of a Land Rover in the marketplace at Salisbury or on the streets of Ludlow.

Politics of a more dramatic kind erupted on 4 June 1950. It was a Sunday, and Pat Hutber and I were walking back from tea at Somerville with Shirley and Val Mitchison. Ahead of us, just beyond the point at which the Woodstock and Banbury Roads converge to become St Giles, there was a small crowd surrounding a group of men in military formation. Their only uniform was a grey pullover and a distinctive armband, but beside them was an open-backed lorry in which they had evidently travelled. The fascists, in the shape of Oswald Mosley's Union Movement, had arrived in Oxford for the first time since the war. I pushed my way through the crowd and, as the grey pullovers were now standing to attention, shouted: 'Stand at ease.' This achieved its purpose in provoking some confusion in their ranks, and in a moment I was removing my jacket as one of them lunged at me. A man in a raincoat, whom I took to be from Special Branch, reassured me that everything was under control but, after a further scuffle, I was arrested by two uniformed policemen for helping to cause an affray. The whole episode had lasted for no more than two or three minutes and the grey pullovers were soon back on their lorry, their public meeting having taken place before our arrival, although not without some heckling. Pat Hutber, who was currently deep into Freud, put down my violent intervention to an excess of libido: I preferred to see it as a spontaneous and necessary political protest.

But the University Proctors, responsible for undergraduate discipline, were coolly indifferent either to cause or justification when, on the information of the police, they summoned me to appear before them, together with Monty Johnson, the leading student communist, who had also been involved. They simply said that my behaviour had been deplorable and I would be sent down if it happened again. I defiantly refused to give an undertaking, but they explained wearily that they were not in the business of negotiation. There was just time before the end of term to form an Oxford Anti-Fascist Committee and to decide that on the next occasion we would turn out in force and stop them by ridicule rather than fisticuffs. But the efficacy of our plans was never tested because the Union Movement did not return to Oxford in my time.

Apart from the Labour Club, the only other club to which I belonged for more than a term was the Strasbourg Club, whose thirty members were all by invitation. Its impetus lay in the movement towards European union, and its name reflected the establishment of the Council of Europe at Strasbourg in 1949. Those who want to claim a cross-party conspiracy on Europe, feeding out from the older universities into our national life, need only point as evidence to the membership of the Strasbourg Club at Christmas 1950. Dick Taverne, Peter Blaker, John Sutcliffe and I became MPs; Mark Barrington-Ward, Pat Hutber, Keith Kyle and David Webster became influential journalists or broadcasters; and others found their place in the diplomatic service or the City. I was not yet an enthusiastic European, and some members of the Strasbourg Club no doubt drifted into scepticism or outright opposition. But there was a strong current of support for a united Europe flowing through my generation amongst undergraduates of all political persuasions. Many years later we were to come together again to campaign for Britain's entry to the Common Market.

Despite my continued involvement with the Labour Club I began to work harder in my final year, living out of college in Headington relatively free of distractions. In my first five terms I had spent barely twenty hours a week at my books, but I was now squeezing out up to fifty hours for writing essays and revision. However, I was ill-prepared when 'Schools' (as the final degree examinations are called) began on the last day in May 1951, and greatly relieved when they were over. But five days later my collapse into indolence was shaken by a postcard from Karl Leyser saying that the examiners were unable to read my papers and arrangements must be made to have them typed. I then had the embarrassment of reading them aloud to a typist in the presence of an invigilator, sometimes struggling over the illegibility of my own hand-writing and uncomfortably aware of the shortcomings of most of my replies to the examination questions. I would pause and say, 'I know this doesn't make much sense but it is what I seem to have written'. The invigilator would raise his eyes from his book and give me a wintry smile. Whether the clarity of my papers in typescript helped or hindered me with the examiners I shall never know, but despite being given a longish *viva,* I was never a serious candidate for a First. One certain outcome of the experience was a bill for £10 (or over £150 at today's prices) for typing and invigilation. I wrote at once to my MP, requesting him to ask the Minister of Education to refund it, on the grounds that my maintenance grant had been conditional on my completing my degree, which I could not do unless my examination papers were marked. In turn, my modest grant made no provision for such an exceptional pay-ment. In his patient response the minister, George Tomlinson, ignored the simple logic of my plea and said that he could only pay if I had a physical disability. When I began signing on at the labour exchange I repaid the college out of my dole money.

Oxford had been a happy experience. I had greatly enjoyed the constant stimula-tion of ideas, the precision of discussion between sharp and enquiring minds and the tolerance of individuals otherwise divided by passionate convictions. I had made friendships that I hoped would last and was more confident of my own abilities, as much for what I might have done as for what I had achieved. My dream of being a poet rather than a politician had gone, and I recognised that to be an effective organ-iser might be my lot. At the same time I had found an extraordinary serenity in the cloisters and quadrangles of the colleges, watching Magdalen's deer in the Grove be-hind the New Buildings, or the fish swimming in a tributary of the Cherwell be-neath the bridge that led to Addison's Walk. I was the same person who had walked into the porter's lodge two and a half years earlier, but was less ready to settle for a humdrum life.

What I lacked was a clear sense of direction, an awareness of steps now to be taken towards specific goals. I remained uncomfortable about ambition if it meant ruthless, personal competition and pushing to the front, but I wanted to make the most of myself – believing there was quite a lot there to be stretched and moulded.

For the moment, however, I needed money and it was urgent to find someone to employ me. My father had given me a copy of a biography of C. P. Scott, the great editor of the *Manchester Guardian,* on the occasion of my Exhibition to Magdalen, correctly believing that working for a newspaper was high on my list of career pref-erences. But a job on the *Manchester Guardian* was beyond my expectations at this stage, and I did not fancy starting on the *Garston and Woolton Weekly* (our local paper) reporting weddings and funerals. An alternative offered itself when I learnt that the

Liverpool Post and Echo, which published a serious and respected morning paper and a popular evening one, had started a training scheme for journalists. It was the first in the provinces and highly rated. I telephoned Alan Jeans, the Editor-proprietor, and arranged to see him. I found him cold and formal and he did not much like my politics, although he did not rule me out. But as a safeguard against rejection I answered an advertisement for a post as Assistant Secretary of the Fabian Society and, without much delay, was summoned to an interview.

Travelling from Liverpool to London and back in a day, with someone else paying, gave me the sort of satisfaction that a return journey over the Atlantic by Concorde must have given to a young businessman forty years later. I felt I was valued and had arrived. Apart from the interview, I had time for a brief look at the South Bank, where the Festival of Britain had opened, and to make a visit to Lansbury, a model housing estate, also part of the Festival, at Poplar in the East End.

The interviewing team was Margaret Cole, John Parker, MP for Dagenham, Roy Jenkins, MP for Birmingham Stechford, and the General Secretary (my future boss if I was successful), Donald Chapman. He had lately been selected for a relatively safe Labour seat and was expected to continue at the Fabian Society part-time, hence the need for an assistant. Margaret Cole was the senior and most formidable of my interviewers, a member of the Postgate family and married to G. D. H. Cole, who had been an *enfant terrible* in leftish and Oxford academic circles for a quarter of a century. Her only remark after I had been interviewed was that my hair was too long, but years later she explained that she was sceptical about my suitability because most grammar-school boys were drained of spirit by the effort of getting to Oxford. For whatever reason, I was initially placed second, only to be promoted when the first choice dropped out. On 13 July I received a telegram asking whether I would accept the appointment. I hesitated long enough to contact Alan Jeans to discover whether he could yet give me a positive answer, as a trainee job with the *Daily Post* remained my preference. He made me feel that it was presumptuous even to enquire, so I wired back my acceptance to the Fabian Society. At £450 a year, with an office and a secretary, it seemed a good way to start my working life.

The Fabian Society, founded in 1884 by nine members with a capital of thirteen shillings and six pence, had flourished in wartime when the party truce had given it a virtual monopoly of political activity on the left. John Parker, then General Secretary, working through a network of local Fabian societies in all the main towns and cities, had been instrumental in getting many of its members adopted as Labour candidates, and a number were elected in 1945. These remained loyal to the Society through an awkward post-war period and by 1951, with the Labour Government teetering on the edge of defeat, the Society was again becoming a forum for exchanging ideas on the future of democratic socialism. There was no difficulty in getting the brightest and best of young MPs to speak at its weekend and summer schools, Tony Crosland and (the youngish) R. H. S. Crossman – wholly unlike but frequently confused in name – being particular favourites. Rising academics were fairly easily coaxed into writing research pamphlets, amongst them Brian Abel-Smith of the London School of Economics whose *The Reform of Social Security*, published in 1953, was to be the first serious critique of the Beveridge Report as it had been implemented, and raised some problems unsolved almost fifty years later.

The combination of responsibilities, initially for organising events, and later for running the whole Society, including its research and publications programme, turned out to be well-suited to me, and I was on a constant learning curve. I learnt from Jack Diamond, the Honorary Treasurer, how to consider options, weigh evidence and make financial decisions in the day-to-day running of an organisation, albeit one with a staff of not much over a dozen. I learnt to address meetings – at least one a week – of ten to thirty Fabian members in a draughty Labour Party headquarters or a room over a pub; and what it was like to drive through the mill towns of the West Riding on a wet Sunday morning in November. I learnt the conventional printers' signs that enabled me to edit pamphlets, together with at least a minimum feel for layout and design. I learnt about economics and social policy and launched *Fabian International Review* (nominally edited by Kenneth Younger MP, lately Minister of State at the Foreign Office, but effectively by me). But overall, in joining the Fabian Society when I did, I found myself throughout the 1950s with a ringside seat at the fight for the soul of the Labour Party as three Conservative victories in succession transformed the country's political agenda.

At the end of the 1940s the choice for the party had been characterised as 'consolidation or socialist advance', 'socialist advance' in the 1950 manifesto meaning the nationalisation of sugar and cement. There were also disputes about a 'socialist foreign policy' and over the rearmament of Germany. After Aneurin Bevan's resignation, such disputes merged into the highly personalised and often extremely bitter conflict between Bevan and Gaitskell, with *Tribune* the voice of the Bevanite left. This conflict was not immediately diminished by Gaitskell's election to the leadership in 1955, and the left remained restless even after their partial reconciliation two years later. By the late 1950s, nuclear disarmament was divisive and immediately after Labour's 1959 defeat the future of Clause Four of Labour's constitution became the focus of dispute.

I was not a main player in the events that marked a decade of turbulence, the like of which was not seen again until the 1980s. My role was that of a civil servant, not openly taking sides in personal or ideological disputes where partisanship might vitiate my effectiveness as General Secretary. We claimed with some justice that the hurricane winds that assailed the Labour Party became no more than a gentle zephyr or, at worst, a stimulating fresh breeze when they blew down Dartmouth Street and round my Westminster office. But I was well placed to follow the arguments and form views of my own about the tactical and strategic choices facing Labour. I was also able to observe at close quarters some of those with leading parts in the drama and others newly emerging on to the political stage.

After I had been Assistant Secretary for two years, it was decided that Donald Chapman should resign as part-time General Secretary to allow me to be considered for appointment as his successor. When the job was advertised and the applicants narrowed down, the effective choice was seen to be between me and Peter Shore, who had been a prefect when I was in the fourth form at Quarry Bank and was making a name for himself in the Research Department at Transport House (then, and for many more years, the Labour Party headquarters in Smith Square). As a boy in Liverpool I remembered him as a slight, rather shy figure, but in contacts during my Fabian time I had found him a considerable political operator, with an unfailing device for making points to which people would listen. Pushing back a displaced lock of hair and raising his voice, often with a half-laugh of amused discovery, he would draw attention to an apparent paradox or ask a sharp question. Such interventions won him attention and respect, and I admired his skill while ungenerously resenting the reputation that it gave him for rather greater wisdom than me. Private conversation could be similar, with something tentative about his views and a suggestion of a part of him held back.

Unknown to me, Peter was already what the historian and biographer Ben Pimlott later called 'a one-man Wilsonian fifth column within the predominantly Morrisonian Labour Party headquarters', and he became the candidate of the left for General Secretary, principally supported by Harold Wilson, Dick Crossman, Ian Mikardo and Tommy Balogh, now a Bevanite enclave in a mainstream, soon to be predominantly Gaitskellite, Executive Committee. I had the advantage of being the incumbent and votes did not split entirely on ideological lines, so I won comfortably by a margin of more than two to one. Peter appeared to bear no grudge. After some years he moved up to become head of the Labour Party's Research Department, making a major impact on policy. In the 1960s, when he was at the heart of the Wilson circle, I had nothing to say to him and I was not pleased when, acclaimed by a well-briefed and tame Downing Street press corps as Labour's new whizz-kid, he leapt into the cabinet in 1968 when I was still languishing in junior office. But his opposition to the Common Market, which established him as a formidable debater and very much his own man, restored my respect despite my sharp disagreement with him over the issue and my distaste for the narrow, chauvinist terms in which he increasingly expressed himself.

Gerald Kaufman succeeded me as Assistant Secretary and became a welcome presence around the office, although never taken entirely seriously. He was happiest spending time at the House of Commons and least comfortable at weekend schools in dealing with the domestic problems of guests demanding action on noisy lavatory cisterns or complaining that they were obliged to share a room. On such occasions he was frequently seen disappearing into the middle distance. Other members of my staff included Alan Blyth, who became a distinguished music critic, and, during a summer vacation from Oxford, Tony Howard. He was appointed as a temporary bookshop assistant but spent much of his time working the ancient manual switchboard through which all telephone calls were routed and – so he later protested – wrapping up parcels of dirty washing sent by Gerald Kaufman to his mother in Leeds.

Running the Fabian Society was a full-time job, but it also came to absorb much of my leisure time during evenings and at weekends because it gave me plenty of opportunity for doing what I most enjoyed – writing, talking and organising. I was delighted when the *Manchester Guardian*, under the byline 'From a Correspondent', printed an article of mine of twenty-four column inches – a good, sizable piece – on 'Currents of Socialist Opinion', based on discussions at a Fabian summer school at Broadstairs in August 1952. What I did not report was that as a result of some wild behaviour, which included Geoffrey de Freitas, the large and boyish MP for Lincoln, sliding down the main banister rail and breaking it, we were banned from ever returning to the premises by the owners, Kent County Council. A year or two later I wrote again for the *Manchester Guardian* on the occasion of the seventieth anniversary of the founding of the Fabian Society. I got enormous pleasure from seeing myself in print, finding it infinitely more satisfying than a speech well made. Right at the end of the decade, I was matched with Mark Bonham Carter in a *Sunday Times* leader-page discussion of the common ground between the Labour and Liberal Parties. The starting point was Jo Grimond's call for the realignment of the left, and although it was nearly thirty years before we found ourselves in the same party as Liberal Democrats, Mark and I reached a surprising measure of agreement, perhaps because we were not entirely representative of our parties. I also wrote a Fabian pamphlet, *What Shall We Do About The Roads?*, as much for the exercise and discipline of developing an argument of 15,000 words as for any passionate interest in the subject.

Fabian weekend and summer schools were social as much as political occasions. In wartime, with no opportunity to travel abroad and seaside towns protected from invasion by sandbags and barbed wire, they had taken place throughout August and been over-subscribed. Dartington Hall in Devon had been a particularly popular venue, partly because the management – it was a co-educational school of liberal inclinations – was tolerant of Fabian behaviour, including nude bathing and a good deal more sexual freedom than was then commonplace.

In the sober post-war world the attendance at Fabian schools, although diminished, remained good owing to currency restrictions on foreign travel. Some freedoms had become part of nostalgia, but schools were still places to meet old friends and make new ones, and no political test was required for attendance. One pink-faced young chartered accountant who frequently came to schools became a Tory MP and, as Lord Wakeham, Leader of the House of Lords, before presiding over the Royal Commission on its future. Another, Fred Tuchman, served as Chairman of the Bow Group and became a Conservative Member of the European Parliament. It was in his house that I met Silvia Szulman. She had striking red hair and a disposition to stand up to me in argument, which most of my recent girlfriends had lacked. Our main argument on this occasion was the extraordinarily trivial one of whether train journeys were mainly for talking to other travellers, as she seemed to believe, or for silence and a good book, which was my overwhelming preference. As for politics, lineage and background, she had arrived in England in 1939 a refugee from Berlin, where her mother had run a communist cell and her father had been a tailor's cutter. Both were Polish Jews who had fled Poland when the Berlin of the Weimar Republic was a relatively safe haven. I was sufficiently taken with Silvia to ask her out a few days later to dinner at the Hong Kong restaurant in Shaftesbury Avenue. Eighteen months later, six days before my twenty-seventh birthday, we were married. I doubt whether she was aware of all the ups and downs of political life to which she was harnessing herself, but politics were in her blood.

When, in 1951, John Perkin asked me whether I would like to become Labour's parliamentary candidate in Macclesfield, the answer was 'no', because my new Fabian job came first, although in 1955 I was more tempted when offered Liverpool Garston, then a safe Tory seat, as it was where my parents lived. But it was not until 1957 that I felt I could be distracted from my Fabian duties, and that was to fight a by-election at Bristol West. There were two notable events during it. First, when I was standing on the Clifton Suspension Bridge in the Georgian heart of what was an elegant constituency, an RAF Vampire jet flew perilously under it, only to vanish up the Avon Gorge and explode in flames seconds later. A photograph of me on the bridge was the by-election news that day. Then, second, I fell ill with jaundice which, had I followed my doctor's instructions, would have confined me to bed and put an end to all campaigning. As it was, I canvassed in the morning and then took a press conference in the darkest corner of the darkest room in the headquarters of the Labour Party's regional office so that the real news – that I had gone distinctly yellow – would be concealed from reporters who could hardly see their notebooks. Perhaps they guessed, but respected my privacy because the fifth safest Tory seat in Britain was hardly likely to succumb to me. There was in fact a swing to Labour of five per cent, which was regarded as an honourable outcome. But the ground soon closed over me. There was no one to see Silvia and me off from Temple Meads railway station the next day and life in Bristol West, hardly disturbed by the ripple of the by-election, continued in its comfortable way. The seat was eventually won by Labour forty years later.

I then made three serious attempts to be selected for Labour seats, in anticipation of the 1959 election. When M. Phillips Price, a rich and eccentric landowner whose earlier career as a journalist had involved reporting the Russian Revolution for the *Manchester Guardian*, announced his retirement, I was nominated for Gloucestershire West and put on the short list. My two main supporters told me I was well placed but, on the eve of the selection, calmly announced that they would be absent at a football match. There were about seventy people present on a Saturday afternoon in a hall at Cinderford in the Forest of Dean, and my speech was well applauded. But when the votes were counted, I had six, and there was no solace in learning that Jeremy Bray, a future parliamentary colleague, had received only two and Clive Callman, later a circuit judge, no votes at all. Most of the votes had divided between Charlie Loughlin, sponsored by the shopworkers' union USDAW, who won, and another candidate sponsored by the Transport and General Workers. 'You made a very nice speech, dear,' said a friendly woman delegate afterwards, 'but you see, we need the money.' It became clear that the agent had carefully marshalled the votes of party members, because his salary had been paid out of the pocket of Phillips Price and a trade union-sponsored candidate was now the only hope of keeping his job. Angry at such a frustrating – and pre-ordained – outcome, I walked most of the twenty miles to Gloucester, where I was staying, and telephoned Silvia to say that I had no intention of ever attending another selection conference. My resolution lasted all through a good night's sleep. The following day I awoke determined to beat the system.

This time my attempt was at Grimsby, where Kenneth Younger was retiring to become Director of the Royal Institute of International Affairs, Chatham House. Kenneth had been very friendly towards me in our Fabian contacts, and Silvia and I had dined at his house in Kensington. He was happy at the thought that I might succeed him and, more importantly, I had the support of the local Fabians who were prominent in the life of the town and the leadership of the Labour Party. In this case, I lost honourably to a strong candidate who deserved the seat but who held it by a margin of only 101 votes at the election, too few for me to have been sure to retain. Tony Crosland, with previous experience of parliament and Hugh Gaitskell's clear personal endorsement, won the selection on the final ballot by forty-eight votes to my thirty-two. He later told Silvia that I had made a far better speech, but there were no hard feelings, although I wondered whether I would ever be better placed to win or would have such congenial potential constituents.

My third unsuccessful attempt at selection was a farce, a fix but as it turned out, an

escape. In August 1959, when most people were on holiday, the selection took place
for Birmingham Sparkbrook, in circumstances contrived to give it to a colourless local councillor of no known virtues. It was clear to me in advance that there would be
no real contest, and I so anticipated my defeat that I cannot remember the voting figures nor any emotion about losing. But in the general election eight weeks later, the
Conservatives won Sparkbrook, and the Labour candidate returned to obscurity. For
the 1964 election the local party chose Roy Hattersley, who won it back, but by that
time I was already in the House of Commons.

My sorties to parliamentary selection conferences – an always painful process of
exposure and likely public rejection, which tests the nerve and calls for resilience –
coincided with my election in 1958 to St Marylebone Borough Council. The Labour Party held two multi-member wards in an otherwise overwhelmingly Tory area
and the Labour group on the council was unusual. Apart from me, there were two
doctors, two university teachers, a parson, a barrister, a journalist, the Countess of
Lucan (mother of the 7th Earl, who was later to disappear), and a working man. The
leader, Tom Vernon, was a bachelor accountant in late middle age who wore a pin-
striped suit, looking every inch a city gent, but was believed to be very close to the
Communist Party. Tom Vernon was strong on party discipline. At my first group
meeting we learnt that the controlling Tory majority had decided, as an economy
measure, to do away with the artificial flowers that decorated the Seymour Hall and
Baths. 'You will oppose it,' said Tom Vernon, turning to me. 'But I don't like artificial
flowers,' I replied, assuming this was relevant. 'What's that got to do with it?' he asked.
The Tories were *against* artificial flowers; it followed that we were *for* them. I was not
persuaded by this argument, but four years on the council taught me how to make
the best case in debate on practical, everyday issues and to play a constructive part in
committee work. I enjoyed being an elected representative in the Town Hall on
Marylebone Road and a thoroughly awkward member of the Planning Committee,
objecting to every development that made no provision for car parking. It confirmed
my view, inherited from my father, that local government was an honourable estate,
and I regret that I did not spend more years in it. The main victim of my council activities was Silvia. Early evening meetings took me away from home precisely when
I was most needed to help cope with two children under five, soon to become three,
in a small flat. I don't think she found many compensations in municipal politics.

Amongst Oxford contemporaries who had been prominent in the Labour Club or
the Union, I was alone in the continuity of my political activities. Most, perhaps wisely,
had chosen a specific career. Dick Taverne, Michael Summerskill and Conrad Dehn
had gone to the Bar; Shirley Catlin, Val Mitchison, Michael Shanks, Oleg Kerensky and
Ivan Yates had become journalists. From my office in Westminster it was easy to keep in
touch, and a day seldom passed without lunch with one of them. But apart from my

pleasure in their company, I felt it important to try to prevent them drifting away from politics. I wanted them to remain committed and to consider fighting parliamentary seats. Shirley needed no encouragement, had her own circle of contacts and was the first to do so, at a by-election in Harwich in 1954. Henceforth she fought every general election until 1987, also winning Crosby at a by-election in 1981 in the *annus mirabilis* of the SDP. Michael Summerskill declined to be tempted (perhaps because it is what his mother Edith wished), but Ivan Yates became Labour's candidate in St Marylebone in 1955 and Dick Taverne took on Putney in 1959.

But exchanging ideas and confronting arguments had been amongst the pleasures of Oxford and it was with this in mind that in 1954 Dick and I launched 'The Group'. The Group met monthly for six years and, although the core of its twenty-six fairly regular attenders was of Oxford contemporaries, a minority came from elsewhere. These included Brian Abel-Smith and Peter Shore; Donald Cameron Watt, who became a distinguished historian; Ben Hooberman, loyal family solicitor to many of us for forty years; Ronald Waterhouse, a future High Court judge; and Gordon Borrie, later to become Director of Fair Trading and a Labour peer. Before he died from cancer in 1994, Michael Summerskill painstakingly put together a monograph about the Group, as a footnote to the politics of the 1950s, but I doubt whether our existence or what we said was of much interest to anyone except ourselves. Politically, we were the children of the wartime coalition and the Attlee Government, having in common a belief in what unselfconsciously we called 'socialism' and in the Labour Party as the vehicle for it. We may have welcomed Jo Grimond's election as Leader of the Liberal Party, but with 2.7 per cent of votes in 1955, we did not think much of the Liberals, who were no longer in the big league. Our generation – or so we thought – would help make socialism once again relevant to the people. We did not know that we were exploring a future that we would fail to bring about and that Labour would be in office for only eleven out of the next forty years.

My ringside seat at the Fabian Society was not, however, mainly a vantage point from which to keep in touch with my contemporaries; its unique attraction was as a window on serious political events. For the most part, the 1950s were a decade of Conservative dominance and Labour disarray. The skilful economic management of R. A. Butler, and the emergence of a new generation of clever and mainly liberal Tory ministers in Iain Macleod, Reginald Maudling, Enoch Powell and Ted Heath, contrasted sharply with the Labour Party's slow adjustment to changing times. The 1955 election, called shortly after Anthony Eden had succeeded Churchill as Prime Minister, was so uneventful that I have no personal record of it. But the Government's 49.8 per cent share of the vote was the largest since 1935 and the largest in the second half of the twentieth century. Much the most dramatic event of the decade – and the one with the most far-reaching consequences – was Suez.

The Suez Crisis, as we called it at the time (and about which Keith Kyle was to write a book which gave the best account), burst upon an unsuspecting nation and divided it deeply. The collusion between Britain and France in the invasion of Egypt, ostensibly in support of Israel and to keep open the Suez Canal, but in reality to topple the Egyptian President Colonel Nasser, was shocking in itself and turned out to be a military disaster and an international humiliation. Anthony Eden announced the Government's intention to go to war in the House of Commons on 30 October 1955 and Dick Taverne telephoned me the following morning about a meeting he was helping to convene. The Suez Protest Group which resulted immediately organised a letter to the *Times* and *Manchester Guardian* from some fifteen people, all of them of military age and none of them pacifists, saying they would refuse to fight if called upon. The Group, mainly of professional people including civil servants and Foreign Office officials, represented men and women of all parties and none. Using my Fabian connections, I arranged the printing of 10,000 leaflets which we handed out at tube stations and bus queues; and booked the Friends' House in Euston Road for a mass meeting. I also wrote to my own MP saying, 'I cannot fight in this unjust war' (I was still technically in the Army Reserve). Over the first weekend in November, I attended a Fabian weekend school at Wilton Park in Sussex which was paralysed in its normal programme by BBC news bulletins that chronicled the suppression by Red Army tanks of the Hungarian rising in Budapest as the Soviet Union took advantage of the West's preoccupation with Suez. There was a sense of utter disbelief at all that was happening, together with an underlying fear of the world on the brink of something even more catastrophic.

The time that Dick Taverne and I and many others in the Suez Protest Group put into our activities mirrored a much wider spontaneous reaction through the country against the war. Given the speed of events, even we were too slow but we contributed in a small way to the movement of public opinion which helped to bring about the ceasefire (American sanctions and the loss of sterling reserves being the crucial factors). Within a week the military action was over and a fortnight later Eden departed, a sick man, to Jamaica. In January 1957 he was replaced as Prime Minister by Harold Macmillan.

Suez was to have a major impact on the course of British history, which my own way of thinking and political direction reflected. I had grown up with Empire Day, 24 May, as an occasion to be celebrated at school with a warm show of patriotism together with pride at the many parts of the world coloured red on the map. My father's Canadian cousins had sent food parcels in wartime (also, for some reason, a pair of handsome braces that I wore to support my trousers well into the years of peace) as part of the response of kith and kin in the white Dominions. In the Fabian Society, it was hard to detect any scepticism about the future of what was now called the Commonwealth, the ties of sentiment apparently having been strengthened by the process of decolonisation in Asia and Africa. Before Suez, Britain still felt itself to be an imperial power with the influence and resources to be one. But Suez punctured this confidence and made the possibility of closer relations with continental Europe a major issue.

In the 1950s I saw a good deal of Hugh Gaitskell, although I was too young and untried to be part of his circle. His visit to Oxford and a second meeting with him at a Fabian weekend school established him favourably in my eyes as a man of intelligence and obvious strength of character, who did not talk down to an audience and was straightforward in private dealings. After a conference on economic policy at Buscot Park, the grand Oxfordshire home of Lord Faringdon (it had, I discovered, more pre-Raphaelite paintings than the Walker Art Gallery in Liverpool), I noted in my diary for 2 November 1952 Gaitskell's 'very impressive performance' in the company of a group of academics including Richard Kahn, Nicky Kaldor, Thomas Balogh and David Worswick. He was, I wrote, 'complete master of his subject.' But I presumptuously added that he seemed to lack 'political sagacity' set against Hugh Dalton – 'political sagacity personified' – who was also present. After seeing more of him, I concluded that he had little warmth and carried grudges too far, comparing him unfavourably with Jim Callaghan, whose 'good, lower-deck manner made him the best bet for a future Labour Prime Minister'.

Early in 1954 I was attending another Buscot Park conference, and on this occasion was driven there by Hugh Gaitskell himself in his ageing Rover. It was the weekend of an unsympathetic *New Statesman* profile of him and, although I cannot have been so insensitive to his obvious hurt as to ask the question, 'Have you any friends?', a comment of mine brought an answering response: 'Of course I have friends, there is Patrick, Douglas, Tony and Roy … then there is Dick [meaning Dick Crossman], if he would only behave himself'. He was thus both defensive and vulnerable. When I asked him – and this *was* a question – what qualities were essential to success in politics, he said intelligence, judgement, courage and loyalty, emphasising loyalty. I decided that he had three of these himself, but remained doubtful about judgement. After he had become leader of the party, the Fabian Society published a pamphlet by him on *Socialism and Nationalisation* (virtually the only product of those Buscot Park weekends), which unfortunately contained a number of minor printing errors. When he pointedly drew attention to these at a press conference I was furious, because the blame for them now fell unfairly on me. He telephoned, handsomely, the following day to apologise, but I wondered about his capacity for easy relations with those not close to him.

I mention these things to show that I had no early rapport with Hugh Gaitskell. Despite this, there evolved a growing respect. He might not be skilled in personal relations or the finer arts of political management, but it was precisely the extent to which he was an 'unprofessional' politician that made him ultimately reassuring. Here was a man of intellectual distinction who had reached the top through none of the devious stratagems which so often seemed the necessary route to success. In a crucial way, for me – as for others of my generation – he took the cynicism out of politics.

Of those in the Hampstead Set, as Gaitskell's friends came to be called (he lived at 18 Frognal Gardens, Hampstead), I knew little of Patrick Gordon Walker until he emerged as Gaitskell's chief of staff at the end of the 1950s. Douglas Jay I found mean, anti-semitic and an intellectual snob, although I respected his obvious cleverness. Hugh Dalton, or 'Big Hugh' as he was known in that circle (Tony Crosland sometimes teased him with the title 'Fuehrer', which was a side-swipe at his Germanophobia), flattered me by taking an interest in my future. 'What about coming here?' – his voice boomed through the Lobby – he asked me when meeting at the House of Commons. I hesitated, implying uncertainty about my intentions, aware of the audience that Big Hugh had alerted. 'I don't mean whether,' he continued with volume enhanced, 'but when?' He would take me to lunch at the Little Acropolis in Charlotte Street to pick up the gossip about my contemporaries and to alert me – usually in terms of the state of health of his parliamentary colleagues – to forthcoming by-elections. Hugh Dalton most enjoyed the company of clever, preferably good-looking, public school boys who would tease him and flirt with him. But virtually alone amongst senior politicians of my acquaintance then or since, he showed a genuine interest in helping younger people, whatever their background or style, into parliament. In this respect he was later to play a crucial part in my own future.

The Fabian Society changed its chairman every year, and some were better than others. Not surprisingly from my seat as General Secretary, I liked a chairman who did not interfere in the day-to-day running of the Society but was accessible at all times, helpful with advice when asked and effective in getting committee business through. By these criteria, Harold Wilson and Roy Jenkins were the two who scored most heavily. When I needed his help I would visit Harold Wilson at his office at the timber merchants Montague Meyer (no complaint in those days about Labour MPs having second jobs) and before each meeting of the Executive Committee he would take me to lunch at L'Epicure in Romilly Street, a favourite restaurant of the Bevanites. Frequent Soho meals were clearly one of the fringe benefits of professional Fabianism and they were vastly better than the cold meats served in earlier times by Sidney and Beatrice Webb at Grosvenor Road. But Harold Wilson would sometimes irritate me by his inability to make decisions. Asked to write a short article for a Fabian news-sheet on the eve of the 1955 general election on 'Why you should vote Labour', the Society's President, G. D. H. Cole, turned in a piece which, in its criticism of the party (and strenuous anti-Americanism), clearly said why you should *not*. I felt the Chairman should tell him that we could not publish it and asked Harold Wilson to write. To my surprise this apparently caused him great difficulty and he paced up and down a conference room at the House of Commons discussing for half an hour how he could avoid doing so. Finding no way out, he then said he would postpone writing for the time being because the problem might go away. It was an unsatisfactory outcome to a trivial matter.

As Fabian Chairman, Roy Jenkins was decisive enough to limit Executive Committee meetings to an hour (they had sometimes taken twice as long) and, although I cannot remember any lunches in those years – and Roy became a great luncher – he and his wife Jennifer were hospitable in their invitations to their house at 33 Ladbroke Square. There was even a great party, when we danced to the popular favourite 'Teacher's Pet'. Roy and I occasionally travelled together to meetings of local Fabian societies, and in 1959 he contrived to get me invited for the first time to one of the Anglo-German conferences held at Königswinter on the Rhine. But Königswinter and, more importantly, my friendship with Roy, really belong to a later chapter. It has been different in quality as well as in length from my relations with others in the Gaitskell circle whom I met in my Fabian days.

But it was the victor of Grimsby and the author, in 1956, of *The Future of Socialism* who made the most charismatic impact on my generation. Tony Crosland was a figure of conspicuous glamour. His capacity to reject with contempt a flawed argument presented with bogus authority, or to strip away the sentiment from a conventional political assumption, was greatly admired. So, too – although with awe rather than approval – was his ability to be stunningly rude to women when he was simply bored by them. The combination of high intelligence, a wartime record in the paratroops, matinee-idol good looks and a hint of sexual ambivalence made him immensely attractive to those of us ten or more years younger.

I first met him in 1950, in Uwe Kitzinger's rooms in New College. He had lately been elected MP for Gloucestershire South (he abandoned it in 1955 for a safer seat which he then failed to win), and spoke to a small group of us about economic policy. He was confident and clever, but entirely receptive to ideas from those whose knowledge or experience he valued. These were the qualities that he brought to his politics in the decade ahead, whether jousting with the left in the pages of *Encounter* magazine (no one did it better) or developing his own analysis of current economic problems.

After I had joined the Fabian Society, and throughout the 1950s, I saw him frequently. To my surprise he did not much enjoy parties, at least those with music and dancing. I remember him at New Year 1953, morose and steadily getting drunk in the company of his new and first wife, Hilary, to whom he rarely spoke. But at

Fabian weekend schools he was in great demand, both as a lecturer and as a sociable companion at the bar or on country walks. He was one of a handful of people who could deal with broad ideas in a scholarly and stimulating way, drawing on his wide reading of sociology and political science. He was knowledgeable about Weber and Thorstein Veblen, as well as contemporary American writers like Seymour Lipset, Daniel Bell and David Riesman. But he was ready to find an argument (almost certainly an entertaining one) in the pages of *Vogue* or to illustrate a point from an episode during a trip to the United States, when, as he explained to his unbelieving friends, he spent an evening with the cabaret star Eartha Kitt discussing her speculation in real estate.

The process of 're-thinking' democratic socialism to find an alternative to both consolidation and socialist advance had begun with *New Fabian Essays* in 1952. But, edited by Dick Crossman, this book was uneven in quality, a series of loosely connected chapters by different authors on issues of the time. *The Pursuit of Progress* by Roy Jenkins, published shortly afterwards, was a convincing analysis of contemporary problems but did not take the fundamental debate much farther. Yet a third contribution to 're-thinking' was *Socialism: A New Statement of Principles* from Socialist Union, a group with strong ethical roots led by Rita Hinden and Allan Flanders, whose monthly *Socialist Commentary* was to become the articulate and influential voice of Labour's social democrats in the 1960s. But my own preferred text remained *The Politics of Democratic Socialism*, an essay in social policy (as he called it) by Evan Durbin, published in the early days of the war. Durbin, a close friend of Hugh Gaitskell (to whom the book was, amongst others, dedicated) became a Labour MP in 1945 but died three years later in a swimming accident. I found totally convincing his conclusion that capitalism was not in danger of imminent collapse (*pace*, the Marxists) but in urgent need of restraint; and that the only hope for the future was what he called 'a tolerant party democracy.' In this latter respect he departed from the fashionable left in condemning the torture and show trials of the Soviet Union as readily as the horrors of Nazi Germany. But a book written fifteen years earlier and in very different circumstances could not serve as a text for the second half of the century, and it was into this gap that Tony Crosland stepped with *The Future of Socialism*.

By the late 1950s, this book had become the bible of the revisionists, who rejected both 'consolidation', if it meant inertia, and 'socialist advance', if it meant utopianism. Fundamental to our approval of it was Tony Crosland's analysis of economic and social change and his unusual interest – unusual, that is, for a political writer of that time – in cultural and environmental matters and the arts. A passage on 'Liberty and Gaiety in Private Life; the Need for a Reaction against the Fabian Tradition' was particularly beguiling. The Bevanite wing of the party predictably attacked *The Future of Socialism* as not-socialism-at-all, with a vitriolic review in

Tribune by Will Camp, Chairman of the Labour Club in my first Oxford term and Harold Wilson's press officer in 1970. But there was some confluence of ideas with the editors and authors of *Universities and Left Review*, a thoughtful, younger group, mainly of previous adherents of the Communist Party who had left after the Soviet suppression of the Hungarian rising. Even the Labour Party itself was developing new ideas to match what it reluctantly admitted was, in J. K. Galbraith's title to his much-read book, *The Affluent Society*.

By mid-1959 living standards in Britain, as measured by consumption per head, had risen by as much since 1951 as in the twenty-six years between the eve of the First World War and the start of the Second. For all the attendant problems, including the neglect of investment and the decline of the welfare state, it was responsibility for governing this more prosperous Britain to which Labour, under Hugh Gaitskell, now looked forward. I would not be a member of parliament able to share directly in this adventure, but there could be a place for me somewhere in the machinery of Whitehall. Despite a Conservative budget that had reduced income tax and taken tuppence off the price of beer, it was in that spirit and with such expectations that I threw myself into campaigning when an election was called in September 1959.

Chapter 3

Campaigning

The election of 1959 did not take Hugh Gaitskell to Downing Street and opened up no new opportunity for me. For much of the preceding four years Labour had enjoyed a lead in the opinion polls amounting, at times, to as much as ten per cent, but against all expectations, Harold Macmillan's Government won an overall majority of 100, thus completing a unique series of three successive victories. In these circumstances the question 'Must Labour always lose?' became obvious and urgent.

My own modest contribution towards an answer was to arrange for the publication of a Fabian pamphlet, bearing as its title another interrogative, *Where?* More gramatically, this might have been rendered, 'where to?', because it was concerned with the lessons of defeat for the direction Labour should now take. In the most significant essay, Robert Neild, an economist then on the staff of the National Institute for Economic and Social Research, said, 'The Conservatives won mainly because they could claim that their record in raising living standards was unrivalled'; and concluded that there was no case for further piecemeal nationalisation and that Labour should accept the mixed economy. By themselves, Nield's were hardly revolutionary thoughts, but the tocsin had already been sounded and the battle joined over the future of Clause Four of the Labour Party constitution.

On the day after the election I took part in a preliminary and inconclusive inquest with a group, mainly of MPs, called together by Roy Jenkins at 33 Ladbroke Square. But I was not involved in any of the post-election discussions at Gaitskell's Hampstead home that floated the possibility of dropping the name 'Labour Party', rewriting Labour's constitution and abandoning nationalisation. In a lecture to the Central London Fabian Society, I settled for the 'de-proletarianisation' of the working class (an expression favoured by the *Economist*) as the underlying cause of Labour's malaise, pointing to the steady decline in the number of manual workers amongst voters. I said that Labour's identification with nationalisation and its institutional link with the trade unions caused serious problems, as did the hard-line intolerance of some Labour groups in local government. I concluded that Labour should project itself as a party of committed social reform rather than doctrinaire nationalisation. In all this, I was only reflecting the conventional wisdom of Labour revisionists. Forty years later the analysis stands up tolerably well, although it took most of those forty years for the party as a whole to accept it.

Whether Hugh Gaitskell was wise to choose, without preparation, a frontal attack on Clause Four as the symbol of Labour's old-fashioned and unacceptable image is arguable. What I found profoundly disturbing was the failure of many of his senior parliamentary colleagues to support him against the vindictiveness of the left or on the central issue that Labour could not just carry on as before. I was freer to take a partisan view because I had announced my resignation as Fabian General Secretary and would be leaving the Society at Easter 1960. Shirley Williams (as Shirley Catlin had become in marrying the philosopher Bernard Williams, another of our Oxford contemporaries) was shortly to succeed me as General Secretary, and had made a well-received speech at the Blackpool party conference on the need to get away from nationalisation as the central issue in Labour's future. But for the most part my friends and contemporaries had been bystanders in the debate and they were now alarmed by the shrinking support for necessary change and the isolation to which Gaitskell was being abandoned. I spoke to Dick Taverne and he agreed that we should organise a letter of support for Gaitskell from former parliamentary candidates of our own generation, both to show that Gaitskell was not alienated from younger people and as an indirect reproof to others, more senior in the party, whose nerve and resolution had apparently failed them. We drafted a letter and over a weekend found thirteen other former parliamentary candidates to agree it without much amendment. The text referred to the constructive post-election mood when basic weaknesses in Labour's appeal had been identified and there appeared to be a real prospect that the party would put its house in order. The letter then continued:

> But now this sense of crisis seems to have passed and energies are already being wasted in personal quarrels publicly conducted. We are bound to have disagreements. The signatories of this letter hold differing views about policy. But to disagree is one thing, to divide and weaken the party another. We regard your leadership as settled and look to you to lead Labour back to power again.

The wording of the letter was not particularly elegant and the sentiments now appear trite, but in the prevailing atmosphere what mattered was the fact of any letter at all of this kind. The youngest signatory, Ivor Richard, who had just fought South Kensington, was twenty-seven; the oldest, Merlyn Rees, who had fought Harrow East, was thirty-nine. Others included Gordon Borrie, Bryan Magee and Ronald Waterhouse from 'The Group', and also Shirley Williams. We were seen to be mainstream members of the party with our future before us. In due course, nine of us became MPs (and six of us ministers).

The letter was sent on 1 February 1960 and received good coverage. *The Daily Herald*, in those days still Labour's in-house newspaper, had the neutral headline:

'Stop these rows appeal the 15.' *The Guardian* was more discerning and emphasised the point, made in a preliminary paragraph in our letter, that the Labour Party needed to digest the implications of the economic and social changes that had profoundly influenced the voters. It also repeated, on its own behalf, our concern that the sense of urgency which had followed the election had, in the space of less than four months, largely evaporated. In fact, the situation was more serious than that. The revisionists were now on the defensive because the attempt to change Clause Four had united what Hugh Dalton called 'the Old Believers', both on the Bevanite left of the party and amongst the conservative right and centre, particularly in the trade unions. Despite an imminent compromise on the issue, the future was looking bleak.

This was in my mind when, in my last week with the Fabian Society – Easter week 1960 – and on the eve of joining the staff of the Consumers' Association, Tony Crosland joined me for a lunchtime drink and sandwich in 'The Two Chairmen', a pub in Dartmouth Street, opposite my office. I told him I was convinced that there was a very considerable body of moderate opinion at grassroots level, but if nothing was done to rally it the leadership would look increasingly isolated and unrepresentative of the party as a whole. There was, I said, inadequate liaison between Hugh Gaitskell and his parliamentary colleagues, except for his close friends; and virtually none at all between Gaitskell and his supporters at different levels within the party. This was in sharp contrast to the position on the left, where the weekly paper *Tribune* was remarkably successful as a focus. Able people with broadly Bevanite views were asked to write for it, to sell it in local party meetings and to appear on its platforms. They met leading *Tribune* MPs socially and found each week in the columns of the *Tribune* clear guidance on the line to take in constituency meetings. Was it not possible, I asked Tony Crosland, to match *Tribune* in its organisation and to beat the Bevanites at their own game?

Tony was entirely sympathetic and proposed that a wider group should come together to pursue what could best be done. If I would choose two or three of my own friends, he would bring along Patrick Gordon Walker, Douglas Jay and Roy Jenkins. I decided that my team should be Dick Taverne, Ivan Yates, then with *Reynolds News*, and Michael Shanks, who had become a close friend since Oxford and was Industrial Editor of the *Financial Times*. For this first meeting, Tony Crosland and I had no more in mind than an exchange of views on how the ineffectiveness of the Gaitskellites in the fight to save the Labour Party could be remedied. The defeat on Clause Four – which is what the compromise was – was uppermost in our minds but, as trade unions began their annual cycle of spring conferences, there was also the emerging question of unilateral disarmament.

By the time we met again, Tony had reported the existence of a group in Oxford with concerns very similar to our own. Its moving spirit was Brian Walden, a former President of the Oxford Union with good working-class roots who had put his ideas before Alderman Frank Pickstock, a senior Labour figure on the Oxford City Council. Frank Pickstock had begun his working life as a railway clerk and won a scholarship to Oxford when a stationmaster. Already in his fifties, he bridged the gap between town and gown, being something of a father figure to postgraduate students and others who stayed on at Oxford and played a part in the City Labour Party. But Tony Crosland's own contact with the Oxford group had come through Philip Williams, a Fellow of Nuffield College and a close friend of Tony's since they were political allies – and table tennis rivals – at Trinity College, sharing lodgings before the war. Philip was a great authority on both French and American politics, a member of the Labour Party, liked by everyone and shrewd in his advice to the students who passed his way. The fourth member of the Oxford group was Ron Owen, a colleague of Frank Pickstock's both on the City Council in the 1950s and in adult education. He was a mature student at Queen's College by 1960, and a man of much practical wisdom.

On 26 June 1960 the London group (my four and the four MPs) and the Oxford group came together for the first time. We were joined by Denis Howell, who had lost his seat the previous year as MP for Birmingham All Saints, and was now running a public relations business from his Birmingham home when not refereeing football matches. He turned out to be a staunch ally and an effective political operator. There was much discussion at this meeting about how to go about our purpose, but there was eventual agreement that a manifesto should be published around which opinion could be rallied. It should be aimed, as Philip Williams had put it in a letter to Tony Crosland, at 'non-leftists and non-fudgers' in the Labour Party; those who had drifted out of the party or had been deterred from joining by its present state; active trade unionists who currently played little part in politics; and left-wing Liberals. It would convey some of the impatience most of us felt – and I felt strongly – with the parliamentary leadership, and the signatories would be rank-and-file Labour Party members, not MPs. As for its contents, there would be references to Clause Four (a battle lost) and defence (a battle soon to be joined) but it would go much wider and seek to convey the idea of a 'new look' Labour Party, modernised at every level and leaning towards Europe.

During the three months following our first meeting, the thirteen drafted and redrafted the manifesto. Occasionally we met at the 'Princess of Wales', a pub in Dovehouse Street in Chelsea, but more often at Tony Crosland's flat in the Little Boltons. Throughout, Tony's role was critical. He gave the intellectual lead reflected in the text of the manifesto and, together with Philip Williams, was mostly responsible for its drafting. He also showed a discipline and single-mindedness of which most of us had been previously unaware. When we met at his flat there was no question of a drink until we had completed at least three hours' solid work. Although I was chairman of our meetings, it was his authority that kept us together.

We worked together exceedingly well. There was a harmony of purpose, an excitement and a mutual respect that I had never previously found in politics, and I was exhilarated by the prospect of changing the direction of the Labour Party and saving it from itself. Our plan was to publish the manifesto, hoping that it would have a direct impact on the argument about Labour's future through the publicity it would receive; then, if the response was good, to create an organisation of supporters. We would avoid the formality of membership in order to save costs on administration, to ensure that the control of the campaign remained in our hands and, above all, to avoid censure by Labour's National Executive Committee as 'a party within a party', the Bevanite sin of years ago. As for money to print the manifesto, post copies to the press and supporters and conduct any initial correspondence, there was a whip-round that produced £200 from twenty-five people, and Dick Taverne was appointed Honorary Treasurer.

Our intention was to launch the manifesto at a press conference and hope for extensive coverage to bring it to the attention of party members. We would also compile a mailing list of possible supporters who would receive it simultaneously with the launch. Frank Pickstock's nationwide contacts through his work in adult education, Denis Howell's in the trade union movement and mine from Fabian days yielded nearly 400 names.

There was nothing very new about the techniques we proposed to use. Round robins of the great and the good had played their part in ending capital punishment and were commonplace in CND and satellite organisations of the left. But a campaign from our part of the party would be unusual in itself, especially when it showed unexpected rank-and-file support, 'rank-and-file' being almost synonymous with the militant left in the lexicon of the Labour and trade union movement. The manifesto would also be a more comprehensive and carefully considered statement of policy than most of the quick-fire pronouncements of the left. As for our organisation (if we got that far), we would make it a model in efficiency for what the Labour Party ought to be. There would be nothing of 'a penny-farthing in a jet-propelled age' (Harold Wilson's description of the Labour Party) about anything we set up.

By the end of September 1960, with the Labour Party conference due to begin at Scarborough on 3 October, everything was in place. Frank Pickstock and I agreed that whatever the outcome – whether Gaitskell won or lost on defence – we should go ahead. Ours was not a single-issue manifesto. Nor would a single favourable vote provide more than temporary remission from Labour's current sickness. The constituencies would still be dominated by the left and almost wholly unsympathetic to modernisation. Good, sensible, long-standing members of the party would continue to feel isolated and alone.

As so often in politics, the feel of things after Scarborough could not have been predicted. The narrow vote in favour of unilateral disarmament was offset by Gaitskell's speech which anticipated it. His closing passage, in which he committed himself to 'fight and fight and fight again' to save the Labour Party, raised the stakes and greatly enhanced his stature. Labour's future was now bound up with reversing the Scarborough decision and with Gaitskell's personal survival, and our manifesto and any subsequent campaign must reflect this. On the Sunday after Scarborough, 9 October 1961, the Steering Committee met again. Without much discussion, we added a new opening paragraph in keeping with the heightened mood:

> We are long-standing members of the Labour Party who are convinced that our Movement cannot afford another Scarborough. Rank-and-file opinion must now assert itself in support of Hugh Gaitskell and of those Labour MPs – the great majority – who are determined to resist and then reverse the present disastrous trend towards unilateralism and neutralism.

Nine days later we were on our way.

I took the chair for the press conference at Caxton Hall, Westminster, flanked by Denis Howell and Frank Pickstock. A fortnight short of my thirty-first birthday, I was seen to be representative of the rising generation of university-educated Labour Party members. Denis, just a few years older, was the trade unionist brought up in the tough school of West Midlands politics. As for Frank, he was the steadfast anchor man with impeccable local government credentials and Labour all his lifetime. We were able to announce that we already had the support of former Prime Minister Clem Attlee, of Hugh Dalton and, perhaps most important, of R. H. Tawney, the much respected author of *Religion and the Rise of Capitalism* and *About Equality,* well-known and scholarly texts of ethical socialism.

We had prepared carefully for the press conference, approaching individual journalists beforehand, and our professionalism paid off. The *Daily Herald* published a trailer on the day for 'the first public demonstration of loyalty to Mr Gaitskell since the Scarborough Conference', and followed it up with a half-page spread setting out the main points of the Manifesto under the pointed headline 'We want a party that will win elections.' *The Guardian* ended a leading article in terms that we could not have bettered:

> This manifesto provides a statement of faith in harmony with the traditions of the Labour movement and yet aware of the facts of the modern world. If the moderates in the party take courage from the manifesto and emulate the passion and vigour of the extremists, the Labour Party may yet recover.

The Times gave eighteen column inches to the press conference (we counted them with satisfaction) and printed the manifesto in full; the *Daily Mirror* reported a 'boost to Gaitskell'; and all the national papers and many provincial ones had reports of a kind. The weekly journals, for whose deadlines we had chosen the launch day, followed, as did the Sundays. There was also some radio and television comment. All in all, we congratulated ourselves that, so far, we had pulled it off.

But the publicity was not such good personal news for me. The day after the launch, I was called in by my boss, Caspar Brook, the Director of the Consumers' Association, and sacked. I had been careful to keep my employer's name out of my biographical details to avoid any political colour being attached to them, but my prominence at the press conference and the likelihood that my name would continue to appear, caused alarm. I was told to clear my desk and go.

I had been recruited to the staff of the Consumers' Association by the Chairman, Michael Young, the most remarkable intellectual entrepreneur of his generation. His oblique, self-deprecating manner could give the impression of scholarly remoteness, but this was entirely wrong. He was single-minded and subtle in getting his own way, and the Consumers' Association was one of his many personal inventions, others including the Institute of Community Studies and the Open University. But my appointment had been made without adequate consultation, and I was effectively excluded from the management role I had been led to expect. A rather miserable six months was redeemed only by an assignment to advise on whether the Consumers' Association should acquire from Raymond Postgate the copyright of the *Good Food Guide,* which he had created in 1950 and since edited. This was the first restaurant guide to be entirely free from commercial interests, including advertising. 'Inspectors' nominated by Raymond Postgate obtained no free meals and entries in the *Guide* were generally written by himself or Michael Meyer, the writer and Ibsen translator (whose family owned the timber business to which Harold Wilson was a consultant). Raymond was the brother of Margaret Cole and married to Daisy, the daughter of George Lansbury, briefly Leader of the Labour Party in the 1930s, whose biography he had written. He had been a conscientious objector on political grounds in the First World War and had flirted briefly with the Communist Party before becoming mainstream Labour. He had made his name as a social historian and the author of *Verdict of Twelve,* a highly successful detective novel; and the *Good Food Guide* had developed from a series of articles he had written for *Lilliput* magazine.

In order to prepare my report for the Consumers' Association, I spent days with Raymond at his Hendon home learning about the 'system' by which the *Good Food Guide* was produced (a card index and slips of paper kept in a filing cabinet). I also found the clue to his passion for food and wine – or so I supposed – in his wife's own lack of interest in them. When the time came for lunch, Daisy would go out to the nearby corner shop and come back with boiled ham or fish and chips. These we would wash down with a bottle or two of Chateau Pavis '45 or Cheval-Blanc '43, Daisy preferring gin.

My report to the Consumers' Association was favourable: the *Good Food Guide* was a valuable property, but Raymond Postgate did not have the resources to develop it further. If he continued as editor for some years, the immense goodwill attached to the *Guide* should transfer to its new owners. My recommendation was accepted and the *Good Food Guide* remains with us today. I never learnt much about good wine (and could never afford it) but until Raymond ceased to be editor, I regularly wrote entries for the *Guide,* once doing so high above the Atlantic en route for a ministerial meeting in Montreal.

Initially I was angry at the unfairness of my sacking from the Consumers' Association, but it solved the problem of who would run the campaign. Frank Pickstock was currently handling all the paperwork from his Oxford home and office, but it was a considerable task and advantages were seen in transferring it to London and giving it virtually full-time attention. I was the obvious person to take this on and there was some relief at my availability.

Until my election to parliament eighteen months later, running the campaign was my main activity, although for a day a week I became a consultant editor with the publishers Thames and Hudson, a role I enjoyed. The founder and owner of Thames and Hudson was a remarkable Jewish refugee from Vienna, Walter Neurath, and he had built a successful firm publishing mainly high-quality art books. He had lately signed a contract with an American publisher by which he would acquire the UK rights to a range of books on politics and international affairs. I was to advise on their suitability for the English market and take editorial initiatives of my own. I was offered a full-time job which had the attraction of security and decent pay, but this would have allowed me no time for a major role in our campaign. I have never regretted my brief, part-time foray into publishing and have taken pleasure from the success of a series on the history of European civilisation which I devised, with Geoffrey Barraclough as general editor, and books by both Hugh Trevor-Roper – *The Rise of Christian Europe* (which I bought over the heads of competitors) – and A. J. P. Taylor – *From Sarajevo to Potsdam.* Walter Neurath and his wife Eva generously lent their house near Lucca for two family holidays, and thus began a sequence of annual summer visits to Italy that has since rarely been broken.

Ivan Yates and Dick Taverne in turn provided temporary accommodation in their homes for the Campaign – the Campaign for Democratic Socialism, or CDS as I shall now call it – when it came to London. But in January 1961 I opened an office in two rooms over a snack bar at 27A Red Lion Street, Holborn, with two secretaries, two telephone lines, and office equipment that worked (part of our efficient, new model of what the Labour Party ought to be). Henceforth this was my base when I was not travelling round the country meeting supporters and establishing a local and regional organisation. Denis Howell joined me as a two-day-a-week field organiser, also making local contacts, particularly with trade unionists. Dick Taverne, in and out of the office as Honorary Treasurer, was another member of the day-to-day team.

The manifesto, although of fewer than 1,000 words, set out fully the ideological position and long-term aims of the campaign. We said that the voice of moderate opinion in the Labour Party had been drowned 'by the clamour of an active and articulate minority' and called for a return to Labour's central tradition 'of conscience and reform rather than of class hatred'. The party needed to adapt to the realities of social change to represent 'the new, emerging society and not the society of thirty years ago'. A key paragraph with a direct bearing on the arguments about Clause Four said:

> Recognising that public, cooperative and private enterprise all have a part to play in the economy, we regard the public ownership of particular industries or services as a useful technique to be justified on its merits.

There was much else about political power, education and the freedom of the citizen. The manifesto was deliberately internationalist not only in its argument about nuclear weapons and all-round disarmament but in saying, 'We are convinced Europeans, certain that Britain's destinies are inextricably bound up with those of a resurgent and united Europe'. For all members of the Steering Committee, this was an important statement of position. Hugh Gaitskell was later to complain that he never agreed to these words in the manifesto but, as he was not consulted about the text, the question of agreeing never arose.

Gaitskell was told of the draft manifesto and the impending campaign immediately after Scarborough, and he showed some nervousness about it. But once the launch was over, there was no hint of anything except support. CDS maintained an arms'-length relationship but briefed Gaitskell directly from time to time. On one early occasion he drove Denis Howell and me round and round St James's Park, this being thought to be the only way of ensuring an entirely discreet and confidential meeting; on another, he introduced us to Fred Hayday of the General and Municipal Workers' Union (soon to become Chairman of the TUC) and Bill Webber of the Transport Salaried Staffs Association as contacts at the heart of the trade union movement. Hayday in particular proved invaluable in his knowledge and influence, and became a member of the inner circle of the campaign.

Another key occasion for Gaitskell's intervention was a private dinner at the Cafe Royal in Regent Street given by Charles Forte – a personal admirer of Gaitskell rather than a Labour supporter – early in 1961 to raise funds. Apart from Gaitskell, Patrick Gordon Walker, Fred Hayday and me, those present were professional and business people and £5,000 was promised round the table. Also present was Jack Diamond, the former Honorary Treasurer of the Fabian Society, now MP for Gloucester, who provided the conduit for most of the major donations to the campaign, satisfying himself that the source was an acceptable one and that the money was properly spent. As I found when I visited Eric Fletcher, MP for Islington East and a successful City solicitor, to ask for a donation, raising money was not too difficult. After I had discussed the campaign with him in his chambers he asked me how much I wanted. I pulled a figure out of the air and said, '£500' (over £5,000 at today's prices). 'I didn't think of anything like that,' he said, but he gave me a cheque for £200, which was enough.

But although large donations provided the bulk of our income, we measured the breadth of our support by the very many small donations we received, often unsolicited, including postal orders for 2/6d from old age pensioners. Far-left organisations later claimed that CIA subventions had been accepted, but this was wholly untrue.

As the planning of our campaign took shape, it was clear that our immediate and overwhelming objective must be to reverse the Scarborough vote on unilateral disarmament. If we failed in this, Gaitskell would almost certainly resign and our wider objectives would be that much harder to achieve. Our first task was to rally support by identifying all those prepared to play their part in our campaign; secondly, we needed to brief them on the issues to give them confidence and make them effective. Overall, we had to raise morale and encourage people to believe that they could win. On the morning after the launch, the nature of our task was confirmed by an extraordinary coincidence. Shortly after breakfast Silvia took a telephone call from a member of the Hendon North Labour Party, a safe Conservative constituency on the edge of London of the kind that bred left-wing resolutions. 'Mrs Rodgers,' said her caller, 'just tell your husband that the manifesto has given me courage because in my party I'm on my own in sharing his views'. An hour and a half later there was another telephone call which I took, also from a Labour Party member from Hendon North: 'I'm the only one of this party who supports Hugh Gaitskell but I shall now go on fighting'. When I identified our first caller to our second, she was surprised – 'he never says anything' – but delighted. It was an experience to be mirrored round the country; the moderates had fallen silent, sometimes bullied, often meant to feel out of step, slow on their feet in debate.

But our opponents were a formidable alliance. At their core there were the Bevanites (although Bevan himself had rejected unilateral disarmament in a notable speech shortly before his death) whose views were consistent and predictable and who were the current manifestation of an entirely legitimate dissenting strain in the Labour Party. Wrapped around them were pacifists, again legitimate in the personal exercise of conscience; a substantial number of people who preferred the Soviet Union to the United States; a shifting group of Trotskyists; those who disliked Hugh Gaitskell on personal grounds; and men and women of vague goodwill who went with the crowd. When we attacked the extremists in their own language, we offended those of softer temperament and many members of CND who were honestly, if naively, motivated by the terrible threat of nuclear war. Fighting first on defence gave us a clear issue on which to argue, but it was a gift to the left in uniting them with fringe militant groups and mainly middle-class protesters.

During the early months of 1961 we built up our mailing list. Where we recruited more than two or three members of a constituency party, we chose as a 'whip' someone who we knew from personal contact was level-headed and could be trusted. To our whips we sent more confidential advice on organisation. We even leaked some of our 'confidential' documents when we believed they would alarm our opponents by the success they described. In those parts of the country where we were strong, we appointed regional organisers and held conferences of our supporters.

There was parallel work in the trade unions. We identified the fifty-two members of the National Committee of the Amalgamated Engineering Union, discovered which of them was already committed to one view or another on defence and who might still be open to persuasion. Often these were men with an entirely industrial background who knew little about politics (except if they were members of the Communist Party), although their votes were critical at Labour conferences. We visited them in their homes. In a similar way we identified and talked to key figures amongst the seventy-seven members of the policy-making body of the National Union of Railwaymen. Very often we were approached for help. One day I received a telephone call from someone whose name was entirely unfamiliar, asking me to meet him in the Refreshment Room at Euston Station in an hour's time. He would carry a copy of the *Glasgow Herald* and I would carry a copy of *The Guardian*. When we met he identified himself as Bill Kemp, area organiser in the North of Scotland for the shop workers' union USDAW, whose votes – over 300,000 of them – were finely balanced on defence and were in danger of being cast for the so-called Crossman-Padley compromise, which proposed a halfway house towards unilateralism. Bill Kemp explained that his Aberdeen colleague, Tom Fyffe, had put down for his union's forthcoming annual delegate conference at Bournemouth a model resolution which CDS had earlier drafted. Given that Walter Padley, MP for Ogmore, was Chairman of USDAW and an eloquent old-style orator, should they accept the compromise? I advised them not to, and helped draft suitable speeches for the delegates. The Aberdeen resolution was put to the vote and carried.

We were not always so successful. It proved much more difficult to influence the Transport and General Workers' Union which was tightly controlled by its General Secretary, Frank Cousins. I wrote more than twenty short speeches for their conference delegates, but only three or four were delivered and they made no impact whatsoever. Denis Howell did better with the tiny Metal Mechanics' Union when, over lunch in a Birmingham pub, he persuaded them to reverse their policy on unilateral disarmament and vote in support of Hugh Gaitskell. In a number of unions already firmly committed to what we called 'the proper defence of Britain' and to Gaitskell's leadership, we did no more than provide background material. But I was asked by Sid Ford, President of the National Union of Mineworkers, to write a few paragraphs which would constitute the peroration to his speech to his annual conference, and was then asked to do so by his successors every year for most of the 1960s.

Much of what we did in CDS now seems obvious, but it caused deep resentment on the left, a feeling encapsulated by a conversation I had with Jack Mendelson, MP for Penistone. I had first come across him in 1947 when, as Captain Mendelson, he was a brilliant lecturer at the Army College of the Rhine. But Silvia had met him much earlier, because before the war her mother had been a member of the same communist cell in Berlin as his brother. An active Bevanite during the 1950s, Jack had been a vigorous opponent of German rearmament and his East European connections were widely held to make him a security risk. We had a relationship of wary tolerance and, in a chance meeting with him at the House of Commons, we exchanged views about CDS. 'Why do you object, Jack?' I asked. 'It's what you and the Bevanites have long since done.' 'It's not fair,' he replied, 'because you are doing it better.' It was a curious definition of 'fairness', but the left was incensed by our intrusion into what they believed should be their exclusive campaigning territory.

At an early stage *Tribune* condemned CDS as 'a paper army without a soul and without an effective argument', and tried to ignore us. Later they found our arguments persuasive enough to require answering, and by August we were 'a squalid little conspiracy' smelling of 'the pitch and brimstone of the Inquisition'. The ultimate accolade came from Michael Foot when, in a *cri-de-coeur* in *Tribune*, he declared that if the left was successfully to reassert its dominance in the Labour Party. 'it must learn to think more deeply, to speak out more boldly, to organise more effectively'. The biter had been bit.

We were certainly mischievous when it served our purpose. Immediately after Scarborough, the left launched an umbrella group called 'Conference Must Decide' to assert the sanctity of party conference decisions against the long-standing convention that the Parliamentary Labour Party could not be instructed. I discovered that this group had held a meeting in the precincts of Carlisle Cathedral at which two Labour MPs had spoken, with Canon Holtby, a prominent local member of CND, in the chair. I wrote to the Canon asking for equal facilities for a meeting, given that we, too, were in favour of nuclear disarmament – *multi*lateral disarmament – and he had been reported as attacking Gaitskell's Scarborough speech. When he refused – as I guessed he would – I released our correspondence to the press as a matter of legitimate public concern. The story covered many column inches in *The Guardian, The*

Times and the *Daily Telegraph*, earned a leading article in the *Daily Express* and caused much disarray in Carlisle. It was a scoop for CDS.

Our confidential – and not so confidential – letters to supporters reminded them of the importance of standing for election to the General Management Committees of constituency Labour Parties and told them how they might actively support the campaign. In January 1961 a confidential letter of mine, which was helpfully reported by John Cole in *The Guardian*, included the draft resolution which eventually found its way onto the USDAW conference agenda. But our main vehicle for communication with both supporters and the press was *Campaign*, a monthly broadsheet covering four sides of A4. An old Oxford friend, Christopher Cooper, worked for his family's printing firm in Clerkenwell and this is where it was produced to a high quality, again a model for what the Labour Party ought to do. I edited *Campaign* and we included a running total of our declared supporters. By the end of April 1961 these numbered over 3,000, a third of them holding local Labour Party office, almost a half serving as aldermen and councillors and over 200 having been parliamentary candidates. But we were also strong on young people. In the Sheffield Hallam constituency, our 'whip' was the promising young Roy Hattersley whose mother, a major figure in the Labour politics of Sheffield, was 'whip' in neighbouring Hillsborough. Amongst our younger Clydeside supporters was one John Smith, a law student at Glasgow University who was already winning a reputation as a robust and persuasive debater. But not all of those attracted to CDS carried forward their political loyalties. My diary for 7 March 1963 shows a meeting with Michael Howard, newly down from Cambridge, and I saw him again a fortnight later. When I next met him he was about to become Home Secretary in a Conservative government.

What was said in *Campaign* represented the views of CDS as a whole and there were no bylines for its contributors. Philip Williams wrote something almost every month and Tony King, Bernard Donoughue, Michael Shanks and David Marquand were frequent contributors. Every issue contained some message that was picked up by the newspapers, and thus reached a much larger audience than those who received it in the mail. But our most successful promotion of CDS came as a result of an off-the-record press conference held at Red Lion Street early in April 1961. I had arranged for a large map of the United Kingdom to cover most of one wall in our offices, and into this we had stuck coloured pins to show the location of our supporters, and particularly our organising whips, who now numbered nearly 250. Francis Boyd of *The Guardian*, David Wood of *The Times*, Harold Hutchinson of the *Daily Herald*, Victor Knight of the *Daily Mirror* and Bernard Levin, then writing for the *Spectator*, were amongst those who attended. I gave them a detailed account of our activities and let them see the files. I did not hide our shortcomings or exaggerate the prospect of success, but they were impressed by a busy office and so many coloured pins. There was a marked increase in favourable press comment and when by mid-June Gaitskell looked like winning, we were given credit for much of what had been achieved. The decision of USDAW had been a portent of other trade union victories soon to come; and in those constituencies where CDS was active, there was clear evidence of a shift of opinion towards the leadership. When in October 1961 the votes were counted at the Labour Party conference (this year at Blackpool), the official policy was carried by almost three to one, and a unilateralist resolution moved by Frank Cousins was defeated by a margin almost as large.

CDS was to continue for three more years, although with a reduced budget and a slightly lower scale of operations. From the beginning of 1962 our main organisational focus was on parliamentary candidates, and our main policy concern, growing arguments about the Common Market.

There was anxiety that supporters of *Tribune* and CND would dominate the selection of parliamentary candidates for the general election. We advised our supporters of the importance of vigilance but, in the absence of any coordination, they found themselves dividing their votes between several good candidates while the left plumped for one. The Labour Party had long used an eliminating ballot in the selection of candidates, a form of proportional representation whereby voting continued until the winning candidate had more than fifty per cent of the votes, as the least successful candidate in each ballot dropped out of the running. This was a safeguard against a minority candidate, but there was still much scope for manipulation in compiling the shortlist and approving lists of delegates. Hugh Gaitskell was concerned about the trend in selections and asked Patrick Gordon Walker to convene an informal meeting of the Chief Whip, Bert Bowden, Fred Hayday and myself, to see what could be done. Bert Bowden brought news of impending selections, Fred Hayday tried to get agreement within the trade unions on suitable candidates, and I obtained for the group from CDS supporters what information I could about names being considered.

It is difficult to judge how successful our group was in influencing the choice of candidates: CDS supporters on the ground probably did more by their own alertness, asking for advice if need be. But I was an early victim of our sifting process. The Member for the Lancashire mining constituency of Ince, conveniently near Liverpool, declared his intention to retire and I was nominated to succeed him. But when Fred Hayday discovered that the National Union of Mineworkers wanted to retain the seat for a candidate of their own, my name was withdrawn and Michael McGuire, the miners' nominee, received our blessing. In a personal arrangement between the two of us, I also abandoned my interest in a by-election at Lincoln when it appeared that Dick Taverne had a better chance of winning the nomination.

But my own chance soon came. On 6 December 1961 I had a telephone call at home from Hugh Dalton. 'Bill,' he said – and his voice reverberated around a house almost empty of furniture, into which we had lately moved – 'will you come to tea?' I was aware of bookshelves awaiting completion and bare walls needing paint, but he continued, 'I want you to meet George Chetwynd, who is giving up. There will be a by-election.' It was clear that Hugh was matchmaking, because George Chetwynd had been MP for Stockton-on-Tees since 1945 and, for a time, Hugh's PPS. I said 'yes' to tea and turned up at 4.30 that afternoon to Hugh's flat in Ashley Gardens, off Victoria Street, behind the Army and Navy Stores. I felt that Chetwynd was detached rather than enthusiastic about my succeeding him, but he proposed that I should travel up to Stockton in a fortnight's time and accompany him to the annual prize-giving at the Blytheholme Working Men's Club, where I would meet the officers of the Stockton Labour Party. Fortunately one of these, Michael Fitzgerald, a schoolteacher of roughly my own age, 'adopted' me and, henceforth, his determination to get me chosen became a personal mission. He was locally born, a Roman Catholic in a constituency with a considerable Catholic influence, and active in the Cooperative Movement; and he became a good and loyal friend. I rode around the constituency on the back of his motorbike as he introduced me to potential supporters, most of whom were deeply rooted in the working-class life of the town. By the selection conference on 1 March, I was on a shortlist of six, with ten minutes to speak and fifteen minutes to answer questions. The three local candidates seemed unlikely to win, but Maurice Foley, who had signed our candidates' letter to Hugh Gaitskell two years before, was a serious contender; and the candidate of the left was Renée Short, the tough and uncompromising voice of everything to which CDS was opposed. I won on the third ballot, getting most of the second preference votes of the local candidates and of Foley.

Although Stockton-on-Tees had been Labour since 1945, there was no assumption that it was a safe seat at a by-election. George Chetwynd had been a popular and hard-working Member and there was much talk of a personal vote. On the doorstep, I learnt to smile generously when told that no new MP – meaning me, if elected – would be able to match him. The Conservatives chose an able candidate in Gerald Coles, a young barrister, but from 14 March, when Eric Lubbock swept to a stunning by-election victory in Orpington, the main threat was seen to come from the Liberals. The Conservatives, alarmed that they might be pushed into third place, took an unprecedented step and brought in the Prime Minister to rally the faithful. Harold Macmillan thus returned for the first time since his defeat in 1945 to the constituency which he had represented in parliament during his formative years when he had written *The Middle Way*, advocating Keynesian economic planning to solve the misery of unemployment. My own response to the danger of being swept away by the post-Orpington tide in a constituency where voters over the age of fifty could still remember a Liberal MP for Stockton, was to show an unbending confidence and to predict that I would have a majority of 7,327, 'a foolish forecast,' as Tony Howard told Silvia.

I had a good agent and we fought a hard campaign, much of it to the accompaniment of 'Billy Boy' ('where have you been all the day?') played through a loudspeaker. I was up at 6.00 A.M. to canvass the queues as men waited for the fleet of buses that took them to Haverton Hill, the last shipyard on the Tees. I visited a score of small engineering works dotted about the town, including foundries where workers manually extracted white-hot ingots from open furnaces. I enjoyed outdoor meetings when I had to win the attention of an audience, at a factory gate or from amongst busy shoppers, but also arranged two or three indoor meetings each night on housing estates and in middle-class districts.

On the evening of polling day, the votes were counted in the Corporation Hall, a rather bleak space of indeterminate purpose. On this occasion there were trestle tables on which the ballot boxes were opened, and, in the centre of the room, a series of long trays with divisions, rather like extended cutlery boxes. These were set at an incline so they could be readily seen, and into them were put the bundles of votes cast for each candidate, giving the impression of a race as one pile lengthened and pulled ahead of the others, only to fall back again and be overtaken. When Silvia and I arrived at the count about an hour after it had begun, a white-faced Oliver Walston greeted us with the news, 'You've lost,' and pointed to my pile of votes which was distinctly shorter than Gerald Cole's. I was quickly told that the first ballot boxes to be opened had come from the safest Tory wards, but I did not enjoy the count.

In Stockton, the routine of these occasions was well-established. Once the count was complete and the candidates had been told the result (and there were no mobile phones in those days with which to pass on the news), the room was sealed, allowing only the candidates, their families and agents to leave and be driven in a fleet of police cars all of 200 yards to the Town Hall. This was an early eighteenth century building, and against it a wooden platform – looking rather like a scaffold – had been erected. The Mayor in his robes and chain was waiting for me and around the platform, filling the High Street, was a crowd of several hundred. There were a substantial number of party workers and an outer ring of those who had taken advantage of extended licensing hours. As I arrived there was a roar and, for a moment, it looked like an occasion out of Hogarth. When the microphones had been switched on and the crowd had fallen silent, the result was announced as:

Rodgers	19,694
Coles	12,112
Mullholland	11,722

Thus on a poll of 81.5 per cent, I had a majority of 7,582, all I had hoped for. The

Liberal, John Mulholland, had been forced into third place and his disappointed supporters, led by a young Edinburgh student called David Steel, booed my result. Those were days before the arrival at by-elections of television, so I gave my first interview to Robert Kee, then representing BBC Radio. It was 5 April 1962 and, in parliamentary terms, I had arrived.

But constituents can chasten a young, newly elected MP. As I walked around the centre of Stockton on the Friday morning, glowing with success, I found life remarkably normal and no queue of people waiting to shake my hand. But one woman, carrying her shopping basket, stopped me. 'Mr Rodgers?' she enquired, and I smiled warmly. 'I just want you to remember that yesterday more voters wanted someone else as their MP than wanted you. Good morning.' She was, of course, right. With 45.2 per cent I had less than half the vote. I was not really the toast of Stockton after all.

In my early weeks as MP I went in search of traces of Harold Macmillan to discover how mutual had been a relationship with the constituency to which he had attached much sentiment. I went to dinner at the 'Black Lion', a grillroom he had patronised. 'Which was Mr Macmillan's table?' I asked, having in mind to sit there. The waiter's face was blank. I pressed the point until it became clear that memories of Mr Macmillan had long since gone. I called at the haberdashers from which the Member for Stockton had bought his shirts (although Turnbull & Asser and Jermyn Street were surely more his style) and asked whether they could match one for me. But no memory was stirred in the ancient shop assistant. Amongst councillors and leading Conservatives, the Prime Minister was certainly remembered in his Stockton days, and they were about to make him a Freeman of the Borough. But there was little in their comments to show more than strictly appropriate respect.

Harold Macmillan was to pay tribute in his memoirs to his wife, Lady Dorothy, for her canvassing skills, adding that she was always received with courtesy and had been remembered with affection. I raised the question with some older women in one of Stockton's working-class districts: did they remember her? Yes, they remembered her but not with affection. They would tap on the windows of her car and, when she wound them down, they would spit on her. For all Macmillan's love affair with Stockton and his own position on the radical left, a Tory MP in Stockton during the Depression, especially one from London, was an outsider representing a party that was unsympathetically governing Britain.

I was to serve as Member of Parliament for Stockton-on-Tees (or for the larger part of it, given boundary changes) for longer than Harold Macmillan or any other MP since the constituency was established in 1868. I enjoyed the constituency work, dealing with problems at my 'surgeries', winning 'cases', visiting factories and promoting industrial development which would prevent a return to the bad old days. At an early stage I established with the Labour council – following a row about the death of a child in a house which the council had only half demolished – that I would not give it my uncritical support; and with my local party – whose last-minute summons to a routine meeting I refused to accept – that I would not take instructions about parliamentary matters. In the 1960s and even later, Stockton did not have the acute problems of urban decay of many inner cities, and my first battle with authority – again with the Labour council – was over the philistine redevelopment of the High Street as a result of the activities of the architect John Poulson, who later went to prison, and the gullibility (and probable corruption) of local aldermen. I would sometimes visit Stockton even when I had no significant business simply because I liked being there. But I did not enjoy Sundays, except on Armistice Day when I read the lesson in the fine Parish Church and joined the Mayor in taking the salute as the Royal British Legion marched past.

The centre of Stockton, with its broad High Street, open market and jumble of shops, suggested a country town. The village of Norton, with its Norman church and comfortable Georgian houses, was also in the constituency. But Stockton had been a considerable port, with its own customs house, trading with the Baltic and northern Europe before being engulfed by the Industrial Revolution; and ship-building, steel foundries, marine engineering and the arrival on the Tees of Brunner-Mond chemicals in the 1920s, had resulted in a tough working class and a strong trade union movement. This in turn had produced the Stockton Labour Party, dominated by the Transport and General Workers' Union, the engineers and the boilermakers. My patron, Michael Fitzgerald; Alan Moses, another schoolmaster who, with his wife, hospitably put up all my family in his house from time to time; and Maurice Sutherland, a locally born solicitor who was on my selection short list, were the only active middle-class members of the party. Nor were there any small businessmen or tradespeople, a few of whom usually gravitated towards Labour. This was in contrast to the London constituency parties I had known, and places like Gloucester and Grimsby. Most of the members of the Stockton Labour Party would have said they belonged simply 'because it is the party of the working class'.

The Stockton Labour Party did not have much passion or breadth of vision. It was narrowly based and rooted in hard times. But I gave it my attention, and this ensured a tolerant reception on occasions when my views might otherwise have resulted in serious disputes. A minority on the left may have been relieved to see me go when the break came in 1981, but most were hurt and puzzled rather than angry.

Stockton was only part of my life as a new MP and, once the by-election was over, I set about combining attendance at the House of Commons with picking up the reins again at CDS. As defence receded as the issue of fiercest dispute in the Labour Party, the question of Britain's future relations with Europe emerged. Welcoming as I had done the Government's announcement in July 1961 that it would make a formal application to accede to the Treaty of Rome, in my by-election I had been cautious about raising it when there was little public interest. But when a two-day House of Commons debate on Europe was announced I decided to make my maiden speech, and did so on 7 June 1962. I followed the convention by referring to my constituency and argued that membership of the Common Market would be good for local industry and thus for jobs. But I also called for an act of faith that Britain's future role in Europe would prove compatible with retaining its distinctive identity.

From the summer of 1961, *Campaign* regularly began to give space to opinion in favour of Britain's membership of the European Economic Community. We accepted the official party policy of not endorsing entry irrespective of the terms and emphasised the Opposition's duty to scrutinise them. But in refuting arguments against entry on the grounds that they were deliberately misleading, unfounded on fact or based on sheer prejudice, we were nailing our colours very firmly to the mast. In July, Roy Jenkins wrote: 'We agree with Hugh Gaitskell that to go in on good terms would be the best solution. But we believe that the starting point for the Labour Party's examination of the terms should be a strong desire to find them acceptable, accompanied by a lively awareness of the dangers of staying out.'

The reference to Gaitskell made the position plain: there was now a perceptible and, we feared, growing gap between his thinking and ours. In a further article for the Brighton conference issue of *Campaign,* under the headline 'Common Market Crisis', Roy Jenkins sharpened our perception. 'We do not ask the party, or the leadership, to follow our commitment,' he wrote. 'But if the leadership continues the process of pulling the party into an outright anti-European position, the result may be irreparable damage to Labour's future.' In the context of previous support for Gaitskell, these were strong words. My personal position was also hardening, more because I found the opponents of entry shrill and unconvincing than for any new arguments in favour that had arisen. I joined the Labour Common Market Committee – the lobbying group for Europe – and went with Tony Crosland (who had also just joined) to see Gaitskell. It was an amiable enough meeting but there was no sign that he was open to persuasion.

The Labour Party conference at Brighton opened on Monday 1 October 1962, and the Common Market debate was scheduled for the Wednesday. On the Tuesday evening, at a trade union dinner, Fred Hayday, who had remained close to CDS and was a strong supporter of Europe, came over to me. 'It will be all right,' he said. 'I've just spoken to Hugh. There will be nothing we can't endorse.' But the following morning it was not all right, in his eyes or mine or any of the pro-Europeans. Gaitskell's speech was long and closely argued, but it was a passionate statement of opposition to Britain's entry. He particularly attacked the idea of a federal Europe which would mean 'the end of a thousand years of history'; and his peroration was an uncompromising declaration against joining except on the most exacting terms. Conference rose to its feet – and standing ovations were rare in those days – as Gaitskell's former enemies applauded ecstatically and most of his friends bit their tongues. I was outraged by the speech – particularly the chauvinism of 'a thousand years of history' – folded my arms and sat tight.

Gaitskell was soon aware of the damage he had done and agreed to come to my home at 48 Patshull Road to meet a number of younger people I had invited who had been profoundly shocked by Brighton. But he did nothing to reassure us. He said that privately he found the whole matter a bore and a nuisance but as late as July had thought that he might need to bring the party round to supporting entry. The recent White Paper had changed all that because it had made clear that the Government's aim was now to enter Europe whatever the terms and despite all the undertakings previously given, particularly to the Commonwealth. We would be crying for the moon if we believed that Britain would get reasonable terms. In any case, the problem of Europe was a parochial one compared with the great issues dominating the world.

This was a bleak response, giving nothing to his friends. 'I knew it was bad', said Bob Mitchell as he left early to catch his train, 'but not as bad as this'; and Mitchell, later MP for Southampton West, was far from being an uncritical Europhile. Gaitskell was asked a direct question about whether he would prefer a unilateralist anti-Common Market parliamentary candidate to a multilateralist pro-Market one. Although implying a reluctant preference for the latter, he gave no direct reply. I felt that he was in an inflexible mood and, having made his speech at Brighton, would not let previous loyalties stand in his way. CDS had chosen to become European without consulting him; so be it, the consequences were our affair.

The following day, in an addendum to a record of his remarks which Silvia had made, I wrote: 'In the earlier part of the meeting he was lively and seemed anxious to listen. As the evening wore on he gave the sense of an increasing weariness.' I had no idea that this weariness was consistent with a worsening medical condition of which he knew nothing, although symptoms had begun to emerge in the summer. In a generous act of propitiation, Silvia and I were invited to a congenial Monday lunch at Frognal Gardens on 10 December, but it was the last time I saw him. At the end of that week he went into the Manor House Hospital for investigations and later, having been discharged and readmitted to the Middlesex, he died, on 18 January 1963. He had been struck down by lupus erythematosus, a rare disease of the tissues, difficult to diagnose and impossible permanently to cure.

The private funeral was followed within ten days by a memorial service at Westminster Abbey. It was far too soon for this to be a celebration of his life, as memorial services are supposed to be, rather than an occasion for national, and international, mourning. Roy Jenkins wrote to me from Washington that Hugh's death was totally shattering and he found intolerable the idea of coming back to an England without him. As for Tony Crosland, I have an indelible memory of him, long, dark coat flying behind, striding off alone and in deep distress along Victoria Street. Their right to grieve was so much greater than mine that I felt presumptuous the extent of my own bereavement. Despite the shadow cast by disagreement on the Common Market, and my experience of a rather spiky personality, my sense of loss was great.

A year after his death I edited and published a short volume of essays by people who had known him from his earliest days – including John Betjeman at the Dragon School – to his years as Leader of the Labour Party. I wanted to have their thoughts on record before Gaitskell's life disappeared from view, as I feared it would, put away like a rarely opened book in a dark corner of a dusty shelf. While his death was deeply traumatic to my section of the party, others had no interest in continuing to evoke his name. It was sixteen years before Philip Williams' exhaustive biography of Hugh appeared (dedicated to Tony Crosland, himself now dead) and a dozen more years before it became acceptable in the Labour Party to speak of Gaitskell as a leader tragically lost at a crucial time. Denis Howell and I formed the 1963 Club in his memory, at which like-minded MPs dined together once a month for more than a dozen years. But this was seen as a source of troublesome dissent and even conspiracy by those who preferred to forget Gaitskell altogether.

Unrestrained by grief or sentiment and not above welcoming the opportunity now presented to them, the left and centre-left of the party began their campaign to make Harold Wilson the new leader almost as soon as the seriousness of Gaitskell's illness became apparent. We were not so quick off the mark or so united. When I re-turned to London from Stockton on the Sunday after Gaitskell's death, I telephoned Tony Crosland and discovered that he had called a meeting at his flat the following evening to decide what to do. Denis Howell, Dick Taverne and Jack Diamond were amongst those present, together with Fred Hayday, John Harris and Jennifer Jenkins, representing Roy. No firm view emerged. There was some support for Jim Callaghan and some for Patrick Gordon Walker. Fred Hayday said that the trade unions thought that Frank Soskice, the Shadow Home Secretary, would be a good candidate but, fail-ing that, would support George Brown. Denis Howell and Jack Diamond were firmer than others for Brown, but John Harris strongly warned us that Gaitskell had found him a difficult deputy, liable to tantrums and with a drink problem. There was unanimity only on not wanting Harold Wilson.

But even that began to fray a little the next day at the second meeting, held at Jack Diamond's Westminster flat. Only MPs were present and Christopher Mayhew, who was very much against George Brown, reminded me that I had said, 'I suppose it will have to be Wilson', in a casual exchange on the eve of Hugh's death. John Strachey was firm for Brown but George Strauss and Douglas Jay rejected both Brown and Wilson. In the end, it was agreed to meet late the following day after the House rose. On this occasion over twenty of us were present, including George Thomson, Tom Fraser, Willie Hannan and Dick Mabon, from the important group of Scottish Labour MPs; and Alan Fitch, a Lancashire mining MP, and another much-respected Lancashire member, Ernest Thornton, leader of the cotton workers. We could not claim to be representative of the whole Parliamentary Labour Party although we were no longer just a circle of friends. But it soon emerged that the meeting was quite divided between the respective merits of Brown and Callaghan. On the question of who could beat Wilson in a straight fight, the balance was in favour of Callaghan but there were serious doubts whether he would get sufficient votes on the first ballot to have a chance of doing so.

On the morning of the Monday – now 28 January – eight of us met at Jack Diamond's flat, hoping that we could agree on a single name to put to a larger group that evening. We could not. Five of us – Jack, Denis Howell, Patrick Gordon Walker, Sydney Irving (the Labour and Cooperative MP for Dartford) and I were for Brown with varying degrees of firmness, but Tony Crosland, Douglas Jay and George Thomson were for Callaghan (George Thomson's wife, Grace, and Silvia both wishing that Denis Healey had been senior enough to be a candidate). I wrote that afternoon to Roy Jenkins. I said it would be a very close thing between Wilson and Brown. My own view was that Brown would win by a majority of fewer than ten votes, although the consensus in the parliamentary party favoured Wilson. My current estimate was 105 votes for Wilson on the first ballot, with 95 for Brown and 45 for Callaghan.

The report we received that evening was broadly in line with this. It was clear that Wilson would lead on the first ballot and that Callaghan had no chance at all of winning. But in view of the strength of feeling and the sharp division of loyalties, it was agreed that we could not ask for a collective decision for Brown that everyone would be expected to follow. Thus we had lost a whole valuable week of campaigning for our preferred candidate and had then failed to agree on who it should be. Meanwhile, Dick Crossman, George Wigg and Leslie Plummer could be seen ticking off names on their lists and building support for Wilson in the certain knowledge of who their candidate was. When the nominations of Wilson, Brown and Callaghan were announced at the parliamentary party meeting at 6.30 P.M. on Thursday 31 January, Wilson already had a solid body of committed support, but the former Gaitskellites were divided roughly two to one between Brown and Callaghan. On the first ballot Wilson got 115 votes, Brown 88 and Callaghan 41. For Wilson it was plainly a winning position, and on the final ballot he beat Brown by the comfortable margin of forty-one votes.

My personal doubts about Wilson stemmed from my Fabian experience, and my political reservations from his equivocal attitude to Gaitskell in his Bevanite days and, more recently, over Clause Four and defence. He had stood against Gaitskell for the leadership in 1960 as a bogus unity candidate, and the only principle he seemed to live by was 'Harold Wilson first'. Where Gaitskell was straight, Wilson was tricky; where Gaitskell had vision, Wilson was the super-tactician. But looking back, I now think that, like a child confronted by a step-parent, I felt a resentment towards Wilson simply because he took Gaitskell's place. This gave me a low level of tolerance in all my future dealings with him.

CDS was in a difficult position. Gaitskell's death made holding the line on defence and promoting conscience and reform against ideology even more important. In so far as the left had made Wilson their candidate for the leadership, both against Gaitskell and to succeed him, he could now hardly become our man. But Wilson had been chosen in an open and democratic way by the parliamentary party and we would serve no purpose if we appeared to sulk. An election was not far off and we should do nothing to threaten the handsome lead in the opinion polls that Gaitskell had bequeathed to his successor. The message to our supporters in *Campaign* was written by Philip Williams: we congratulated Wilson on his election, welcomed what we called – with some sleight of hand – his endorsement of Gaitskell's policies and said that no supporters of CDS should object 'if a different voice makes them more acceptable to some sections of the party'. It was what our supporters wanted to hear. They were mainstream, not sectarian; loyal, not fractious.

On the first anniversary of Gaitskell's death I wrote a short article, explaining that we had tried to cement to his successor the natural loyalty of the key rank-and-file members of the party of whom CDS was composed, and readily conceding that Harold Wilson could hardly have had a more successful year. In remembering our loss, we could look forward to a Labour government that very shortly would embody the values for which he stood.

When in the autumn of 1964 the election was eventually called, the winding up of CDS began. By the end of October 1964 the office was closed and the files deposited in the attic at 48 Patshull Road. In the absence of any buyers for the office furniture, I took home a table to serve as a desk. I am sitting at it now. CDS was never revived. Its papers and card indexes were locked away until PhD students began to ask for them. It had served an exceptional purpose at an exceptional time. The circumstances that led to its establishment and success were not to occur again.

The Trotskyist *Newsletter* called CDS 'a right-wing faction ... its aim – to disrupt the Labour Party'. Others with more claim to be heard occasionally cried 'witch-hunt'. But we did not call for expulsions and were careful about references to 'fellow travellers', a pejorative term for those who supported the Soviet line without being

Communist Party members. However, faced by the Soviet Union at the height of the Cold War (the Berlin Wall was built in 1961), we were – and were plainly prepared to say it – on the same side as the United States, believing that neutralism (towards which unilateral nuclear disarmament was the first step) was incompatible with Britain's freedom. We pointed to the hypocrisy of those who urged the West but not the Warsaw Pact to disarm, and said that Labour policy should be made only by Labour Party members and not influenced by paid-up members of the Communist Party voting as they did in their trade unions on resolutions for the Labour Party conference. For my own part, I could never accept the aphorism 'better red than dead'. Such a choice, with its false antithesis, had been meaningless to all those who had died in show trials and the gulags, or disappeared after 1945 in Eastern Europe. If CDS appeared at the time to be a clinical operation to save the Labour Party, there was in all of us a passionate conviction that the things we fought for were central to democratic socialism. Contrary to *Tribune*'s claim, CDS had a soul. Without a soul, there would have been no campaign.

Following Hugh Gaitskell's death and in the last year or two of CDS, I continued to find my feet in the House of Commons. Between my election in April 1962 and the general election of October 1964 I made only ten speeches. I felt no compelling need to speak more often when getting to know my colleagues in the lobbies, corridors, bars and tea-rooms and absorbing the atmosphere of the place seemed the more important part of learning. My most deliberate act was to choose one area of policy – transport – which was specific enough for me to make a mark. I read all the documents I could find, asked obscure questions about research and secured two late-night adjournment debates on traffic problems and the criteria for road building. I attended meetings of the parliamentary party's transport group, which was dominated by Members with trade union or constituency interests (Stockton, despite its distinctive place in 1825 in the development of railways, was not a railway town like York, Crewe or Carlisle). By the summer of 1964 my identity was sufficiently well established to secure a flattering front-cover of the *Sunday Times* colour magazine as a serious candidate for junior office in the Department of Transport should a Labour government be formed.

My other parliamentary activities were mainly in support of George Brown. Following his defeat for the leadership, he remained Deputy Leader and was persuaded that he should widen his sphere of interests. He had spoken brilliantly in favour of the Common Market in winding up the Brighton debate which Gaitskell had opened by invoking a thousand years of history, and was also knowledgeable about defence. But he had a serious gap in industrial and economic affairs, and matters which today would be covered by the Department of the Environment. I agreed to become his *chef de cabinet* and recruited Oliver Walston, who had been active in

CDS as a Cambridge undergraduate and whose father – one of the first life peers – was a close friend of George Brown, as a speechwriter. I introduced George Brown to rising stars like Michael Shanks, whose book *The Stagnant Society* was an eloquent testimony to Tory failure; and Peter Hall, author of *London 2000,* and geographer extraordinary. George was desultory rather than diligent in his studies, but learnt fast and generally impressed those called upon to advise him. It was an opportunity for me to widen my own knowledge, and gave me the experience of dealing with the unpredictable and sometimes irascible figure that George Brown had already become.

As the Parliament drew towards its statutory five-year limit and an election in the autumn of 1964 became a certainty, I had enjoyed an invaluable two-and-a-half year apprenticeship. I had never previously thought that I was clubbable but I liked the House of Commons, its fabric, its people and its ways.

A House of Commons day was busy but not often strenuous. Even if I was sitting in committee, there was no need to arrive before 10.30 A.M.; and without a committee, which was most of the time, before 2.30 P.M. In fact, there was no need to arrive at all because I was self-employed and on a fixed salary, and was not obliged to clock in. I would spend time in the House of Commons library, reading the day's papers, or in the tea-room, gossiping. These were essential parts of the parliamentary process and, mixed with visits to the Chamber for Question Time and debates, they lightened the day. Even when I spent twelve hours in the House, which might occur two or three times a week, this would be broken by meals and other congenial occasions. I certainly did not think that I worked harder than most professional people of my age. I had obligations – to my constituents and to my party – and I wanted to make my mark. But late nights did not bother me and I found no evidence that the House of Commons would be a wiser, less adversarial place if it adopted a more normal working day.

It was easy for some London and Home Counties Members to support the idea of getting back to their comfortable homes for dinner. But most of my colleagues from the North-East and many other Labour MPs could not afford a flat or a house in London, and stayed at cheap and lonely hotels. They had nothing to gain if the House rose regularly at 6.00 P.M. As for the argument that the hours were difficult for women Members, no job gave greater freedom to make decisions for yourself than being an MP. It offered, as Silvia said, the ultimate in flexi-time. There were serious problems about how to balance a parliamentary career with bringing up a family, but such problems were common to every profession.

Nor were they exclusively the problems of women. When I was first elected, we had three children under five. I saw too little of them when they were growing up and now, with families of their own, they complain about my failure. I took them to school most mornings and persuaded myself that this proved I was a good father, despite seldom helping with homework and rarely being there at bedtime. What was more damaging than my absences at the House of Commons was my escape, when at home, into my own capsule of quiet space, keeping the children at a distance. But here again, there was nothing unique about the need to recover from stress and excitement. At least my children were able to enjoy tea on the Terrace and other outings to their father's place of work.

My salary when elected was £1,250 a year, there having been no increase in parliamentary salaries for eight years. But soon after, it leapt to £3,250, or more than £35,000 at today's prices. This seemed a reasonable salary for a public servant, which is what I was. On my election I had no office or desk of any kind, and my locker was not even large enough to take my briefcase; and after I had been seven years in the House my secretarial allowance stood at £500 a year. My constituency had neither as many social problems as inner-city areas like Hackney or Liverpool Walton, nor as many articulate voters as Hampstead or Oxford, so I may have had less correspondence than some Members. But I managed through twenty-one years in parliament with Margaret Wallington, my part-time secretary, who I usually saw only two or three days a week. I had no difficulty in preparing my speeches with the help of the House of Commons library, and I have no idea how I would have employed a personal researcher, which MPs now take for granted as part of their 'office costs'. In the 1970s, the payment of expenses rose by a factor of almost ten, while MPs' salaries barely kept pace with inflation. This was because governments allowed themselves to be bullied by newspapers that made a fuss about MPs' salaries but tolerated a compensating increase in expenses.

Compared with my by-election in Stockton, the general election of 1964 was dull. For three weeks I felt isolated from important events outside, following them on radio and in the newspapers. I had few visiting speakers because mine was regarded as a safe seat. In fact, I won with a slightly smaller majority but just over fifty per cent of the vote. Now more of my constituents – 457, to be precise – wanted me to be their Member of Parliament than preferred someone else.

Chapter Four

Into Government

Polling day in the 1964 election was 15th October, a very wet day. Alec Douglas-Home had extended the 1959 Parliament almost until its final constitutional date in the hope that he might pull back the Conservative deficit in the opinion polls and win. He almost succeeded. But instead of a narrow margin of his own, he bequeathed an overall majority of four seats to Harold Wilson and a Labour government.

My votes were counted on Thursday night and, after spending the Friday morning in Stockton, Silvia and I had an early pub lunch and drove back to London. When we left Stockton, the returns from the Tory shires were almost complete, and Labour had lost the substantial lead it had achieved in the boroughs overnight. But by the time we reached London, Harold Wilson had been to the Palace to kiss hands and six cabinet appointments had been announced. George Brown was First Secretary of State and head of the new Department of Economic Affairs; Jim Callaghan was Chancellor and Patrick Gordon Walker had been appointed Foreign Secretary, despite having lost his seat in Smethwick in a poor-white backlash on the racial issue. Shortly afterwards there was a telephone call from Jennifer Jenkins: would we come over to supper as soon as we liked? I had a short conversation with Roy, but he had heard nothing since returning from Stechford, although he had spoken to Patrick to express his sorrow. We drove over to Ladbroke Square, sat down at table and had reached the cheese when the telephone rang. Coming back into the dining room, Roy said, 'I am to become Minister of Aviation – cabinet rank, although not in the cabinet – and you are to join George as his Parliamentary Secretary in the new department. That was George, he wants us to go over.' We assembled at the Brown flat at Marble Arch sometime after 10 o'clock, and also present was Tony Crosland – in carpet slippers – and Susan. Tony was in a black mood because he did not wish to become Economic Secretary at DEA and George's Number 2, least of all when Roy was to have a department of his own. George was quite unfairly bullying him for having discussed his appointment with Jim Callaghan. I said little. It was sufficient to have confirmed by George that I was to become a junior minister in his department, thus entering government just before my thirty-sixth birthday. I was immensely lucky, after only two and a half years in the House. Roy had been first elected in 1948 and Tony in 1950. They had had to wait many years for the good fortune that now was mine.

But confirmation was delayed. Three full days elapsed before the telephone call from Number 10. It came with all the halting courtesy of an invitation to lunch with the vicar: 'The Prime Minister wonders whether you could call on him later in the morning, say, at 11.30?' It seemed almost appropriate to plead a prior engagement or suggest another time. But I was there at 11.30, sitting alongside the cabinet table with Harold Wilson saying, 'George has asked for you — Patrick did as well — I hope you will go to his new department and concentrate on regional planning.' I thanked him, murmured how pleased I was and asked where I was to go. 'Turn right outside, down the steps into the Park and then turn left. Storey's Gate is the address.' So I turned right, down the steps and then left in search of the Department of Economic Affairs.

I could not find it. I discovered that Storey's Gate was a short stretch of road I had known during my Fabian years, but had not identified by name. It ran from the Park down to the Methodist Central Hall, having on one side a bombsite, once designated for a new Colonial Office, now abandoned and rich in purple willowherb and wind-blown rubbish, and on the other an anonymous row of Victorian offices and the 'Red Lion'. I went into the pub and asked the barmaid where the Department of Economic Affairs was. 'Never heard of it, love, not round here.' I nosed into the office buildings and scanned the list of occupants. In the end, I returned to Great George Street, where the Treasury had a reception desk open to the public.

'Can you tell me where the Department of Economic Affairs is?' I enquired. The woman looked sceptical, picked up the telephone and repeated my question. She paused and looked again at me.

'Why do you want it?'

'Because I've just become a minister there.'

'Gentleman says he's just become a minister', and there were some further discussions on the telephone.

'Well', she said, 'its address is Storey's Gate, but it isn't in Storey's Gate at all. It's in the Park, at the other end of this building, was the Ministry of Defence.'

And so, half an hour late, I climbed the monumental steps, past lavatories still marked 'Officers' and 'Men', and was taken to an office which I was told was mine. I had arrived, I was a minister, but what was I supposed to do?

I had not previously set foot in a government department, except briefly to visit my Oxford contemporary David Lane in the Resident Clerk's flat at the Foreign Office for a meeting of 'The Group'. All my backbench representations to ministers had been made to them at their rooms in the House. Those few friends who had become civil servants had rather pompously distanced themselves from me because of my involvement in politics. I had met senior civil servants from time to time — some at a lunch club in Romney Street — but their rank and role was rather a mystery. There was a Whitehall series from the publisher George Allen and

Unwin, in association with the Institute of Public Administration, in which retired Permanent Secretaries gave a historical account of the department's evolution and described its responsibilities. But the processes of government – how it really happened – were hidden from the reader. What was the interaction between ministers and civil servants? At what level, and by whom, were decisions made? It was a world of unexplored possibilities. The best flavour of it all, and the flavour to me was good, had been in the three volumes of memoirs of Hugh Dalton, *Call Back Yesterday, The Fateful Years* and *High Tide and After.* But the wartime years had brought into the civil service a wide range of talented men and women from academic and business life – Gaitskell had been amongst them – committed to winning the war and then to post-war reconstruction. Times had been abnormal and relationships presumably closer and more personal. Even Herbert Morrison's *Government and Parliament,* an invaluable guide (there was no other to such matters), was more than ten years out of date. There were no Whitehall correspondents in 1964, digging behind the front page story to reveal the secrets of cabinet committees and no 'Yes, Minister' to describe all too acutely how ministers and officials got on with each other. So I was now walking the corridors of Whitehall, wholly untutored despite some minor responsibility for the government of Britain.

I was to be a minister from 1964 to 1970 and, after an interval in opposition, from 1974 to 1979. Of, perhaps, 200 Labour MPs who were in and out of government at one level or another during those eleven years, only a handful served as long, and none served, as I did, in six different departments. It was a unique opportunity to witness the process of government, which could be as absorbing in its contrasts and challenges as the politics of party and parliament.

But the Department of Economic Affairs was no ordinary Whitehall ministry and was under no ordinary political control. There are differing views about its precise origins. Legend has it that the idea of a new department had emerged in the course of a short taxi journey Harold Wilson and George Brown had taken from St Ermin's Hotel to the House of Commons. Wilson had seen it as a way of containing his deputy in a department with no executive responsibilities; Brown had grasped at the opportunity of creating a power base of his own. In practice, the potential for such an economic planning ministry had been discussed within the Labour movement for many years, building on the role of the Central Economic Staff under Sir Edwin Plowden and the Economic Section of the Treasury under Sir Robert Hall during the Attlee Government. At the Fabian Society I had published as early as 1954 a research pamphlet on *The Machinery of Economic Policy,* by Robin Marris, a Cambridge don; and the Labour Party had formulated its own case for a Ministry of Production Planning, and its manifesto referred to it. By 1964, with an early election inescapable, informal discussions were taking place between senior members of the Opposition and Sir Lawrence Helsby, Head of the Civil Service, about how the department might be set up. On 25 May, after Silvia and I had spent an evening with George and Sophie Brown, I noted in my diary:

> George was talking of plans for a new Production Ministry. He hoped to have Roy as his No. 2, but Roy had declined, hoping to get a Ministry of his own. But other plans are going ahead. Eric Roll, currently our Economic Minister in Washington, is designated as Permanent Secretary. A man called McIntosh, a Balliol friend of Roy's, will be high up. Donald MacDougall will be economic adviser. Tommy Balogh will be in and out of the office (although, happily, mostly in Harold's). Battles are being fought. Sir Lawrence Helsby doesn't like it at all (and George doesn't like him).

I added:

> George was at his most engaging: relaxed, outspoken, good-humoured, quick. Altogether his ability is outstanding and an incoming Labour government would need his talents desperately. This is one reason why we must save him from himself – if we can.

As I arrived at Storey's Gate, the Department was still assembling, with more people treading the corridors than there were desks and chairs in their offices. Eric Roll, installed as Permanent Secretary, was to be one of a policy troika, together with Sir Donald MacDougall, who would be in charge of economic planning, and Fred Catherwood, a businessman-accountant recruited from Tube Investments (and later a Tory MEP), who was to head a team of industrial advisers. The administrative civil servants comprised two divisions formerly in the Treasury, concerned with economic coordination at home and overseas and led respectively by Douglas Allen and William Neild (who had started his working life in the Research Department of the Labour Party), both Deputy Secretaries; and the Regional Development Division of the Board of Trade. This was now led by Arthur Peterson (himself from the Home Office), whose habit of drawing slowly on his pipe before giving a considered reply to a question from the Secretary of State caused George Brown much irritation. There was also a job lot of unattached officials, the result of a trawl round Whitehall and consisting of some high talent and some obvious misfits. Ronald McIntosh had arrived, promoted to Under-Secretary, and his laid-back confidence and innovative mind made him popular with George. Further down the line, and at every level of seniority, there were men and women of ability and promise, some sceptical and drafted into the Department against their will, others volunteers committed to the whole concept of new-style planning. John Groves, straight from No. 10 and Alec Douglas-Home, never seemed at home in the Department as Head of Information, but served it conscientiously. Douglas Henley, cool, clever and unsmiling, was a master of public expenditure and later became Comptroller and Auditor-General. Derek Mitchell, expelled from No. 10, where as Principal Private Secretary he had increasingly found himself at odds with the kitchen cabinet, passed through en route to a future in the City. Altogether, eight career civil servants in the Department were later to become Permanent Secretaries, and others were to achieve major distinction elsewhere.

At its peak, the Department had an establishment of not much over 500, which compared with three times that number at the Treasury, which was itself a small department (there were nearly 10,000 at the Board of Trade). The diverse members of this irregular team were to react in very different ways to the roller-coaster of events, from the excitement and vision with which the Department started to its ignominious extinction five years later. In the meantime, they were obliged to deal with the idiosyncratic behaviour of a demanding Secretary of State with immense drive and energy, but unsettling habits and an underlying insecurity. For most of them, living with George Brown was an experience not to be missed but, hopefully, never to be repeated. Life in the DEA was more, not less, colourful than the newspapers came to describe it.

On the day of my arrival, Eric Roll put his head round my half-open door. 'I am ready to brief you just as soon as you ask for me.' It was an informal but meticulously appropriate greeting from a Permanent Secretary, although someone whom I had first met in the company of David Marquand and his father, Hilary, some years before. He proved to be a wholly sympathetic man, to whom emollience came more readily than conflict. He had a wide circle of friends, stretching back to childhood in Vienna, through a period as Professor of Economics at Hull when still in his twenties, to service as Ted Heath's negotiator on agriculture in the course of Britain's first application to join the European Community. He needed all his skills to propitiate (and sometimes comfort) his own diverse team of administrators and establish a good working relationship with the economic section and the team of industrial advisers.

George Brown had his favourites amongst officials. He valued intelligence, constructive ideas and a quickness of mind, all qualities characteristic of a good civil servant, but usually present in unequal quantities. An ability to stand up to him and answer back was also essential, and this came less easily even to experienced officials. George would listen to and often heed advice against adopting the unconventional action he proposed, but had no time for those who instinctively hung back from any bold and uncharted course. The Department itself was without precedent in peacetime and a gamble. Those who worked in it were expected to enjoy what was inevitably a rough experience.

George worked on incomes and prices with a close team of three, for which he had a respect and liking. Evan Maude, the Under-Secretary, was a Treasury official in his middle forties, of a steady, undemonstrative intelligence and with an immense capacity for producing endless high-quality paperwork. On the incomes side, he was assisted by Fred Jones, who had worked in the TUC Research Department and reached the DEA via the National Economic Development Office and finished his career in the Treasury. Fred understood the intricacies – and illogicalities – of trade-union attitudes and could speak on personal terms to most trade-union leaders. He was a fine example of how the civil service could benefit by attracting to its ranks outsiders in mid-career with a background very different from the Administrative Class recruited straight from university. Finally, of the three, there was Anne Mueller, a contemporary of mine at Oxford, sometimes self-effacing in her reticence, but calm, thorough and endlessly hard-working. For nearly two years, these three served George Brown far beyond what would normally have been their expectations of duty in the most exacting and publicised of the Department's activities. Much of what he achieved, ephemeral though it turned out to be, was to their credit. In turn, George was, at least in private to me, deeply appreciative of their endeavours.

Elsewhere to the Department, if not at the beginning then soon after, came a great variety of individual talent, sometimes to be driven hard within their experience and sometimes to be neglected and unhappy in positions never made for them. There was my old friend Michael Shanks, recruited from the *Financial Times* to be Fred Catherwood's deputy and eventual successor; and Sam Brittan (brother to Leon), also from the *Financial Times*, who sat uneasily in the Press Office. Amongst the temporary civil servants and those arriving in Whitehall for the first time were a number with Fabian connections. I had first met Humphrey Cole, a statistician and son of G. D. H. and Margaret Cole, playing cricket at a Fabian summer school. Denys Munby, a transport economist, was the author of Fabian pamphlets, and John Grieves Smith, another Fabian, was an expert on steel. John Jukes, formerly of the Atomic Energy Authority, also had a Fabian connection (and many years later became an SDP Councillor in Sutton, Surrey). Amongst the recruits to Donald MacDougall's team were Wilfred Beckerman and Roger Opie, two Oxford economists who had occasionally advised the Labour Party; and Dick Sargent, a Professor of Economics at Warwick University and yet another Fabian. Very few of these were recruited by ministers, and all went on to distinguished further careers.

Amongst the permanent, administrative civil servants I recognised a Fabian in Jim Vernon, whose wife was a member of the London County Council. But it never occurred to me then or later to enquire about the politics of those civil servants who worked for me, and I would have recoiled rather priggishly from any one of them who had offered me the knowledge. If I had guessed, it was that they were representative of the traditional middle-class professions, inclined to be right of centre, but with a good sprinkling of social democrats. There is a chance that a majority of them voted for a Labour government in 1964, if only to break with the monotony of thirteen Tory years, but a larger proportion voted for Ted Heath in 1970, welcoming a meritocratic Conservative leader when the Labour Government had frittered away its inheritance of goodwill. Whatever the case, the DEA had more than its fair share of men and women who wanted the Labour Government to succeed and gave something of their hearts to the professional task they were called upon to perform.

For the first time I came across a key figure in the apparatus of government: the Minister's Private Secretary. Mine had been released from the Ministry of Agriculture, and had none of the obvious tact called for in this role. He was the conduit that conveyed my day-to-day wishes to the Department and, in return, informed me of their views. His intentions were wholly good and his loyalties fierce, but I often wondered whether he gave me a reputation for unreasonableness that I did not entirely deserve.

Coming to government for the first time, or arriving in an unfamiliar department, a minister must rely upon the guidance of his private secretary. He must be entirely frank with him, even to the point of indiscretion. In turn, the private secretary must know how to keep confidences entrusted to him (or her) while filtering through essential messages to the Permanent Secretary and other senior officials. Ten years later, when I was newly appointed Minister of State for Defence, Sir Michael Cary, the Permanent Secretary, came casually into my office one day and said, 'I have a feeling you are not yet quite happy here. Can I help?' He had received a message through my excellent Private Secretary, David Young, although I was quite unaware of what impression I had been creating. But although a good private secretary enables the minister to learn the necessary conventions of a department, there are few rules that a senior minister cannot break and should not from time to time challenge.

George Brown, preoccupied with economic policy, left me with a free hand to formulate the terms of reference of the new Regional Planning Councils and Boards. In order to obtain the formal agreement of some other departments about what was now proposed, I wrote amongst others to Dick Crossman, the Minister of Housing and Local Government, whom I had known since my Fabian days. When, a week later, no reply had come, I enquired about what was happening. A message was received from Crossman's office that a reply was on its way, but to George Brown because it was not appropriate that a cabinet minister should reply to a minister of lesser rank. Years later I teased Crossman about this pomposity. He opened his eyes widely and put on his innocent, startled look. 'But I was told by my Private Secretary that I wasn't allowed to write to you.' When I came to read his fascinating diaries, I reflected on his strictures about the rigidity of the civil service in the light of his own willingness to take 'No' for an answer on such a trivial matter.

It was the Principal Private Secretary to the First Secretary of State who had easily the most demanding job in the Department, in day-to-day proximity to George Brown, often for twelve unrelenting hours. Tom Caulcott, a tough and wiry Treasury official, survived for three months, resigned, was persuaded to stay on, was sacked and reinstated and then resigned again. Caulcott was no respecter of persons and not a man to be bullied. He had a great aptitude for running a busy Private Office, dictating a memorandum and waving a member of his staff to a new duty while conducting an important telephone conversation. He kept the business of George Brown's office moving through the hectic first months of the Government while the Department sought to establish its role in a sceptical Whitehall. His successor, a man of greater patience and much inner strength, was John Burgh, who survived the ups and downs of fortune and eventually George Brown himself. On one occasion, taunted beyond endurance by George at the end of an exhausting day, John Burgh threw an apple core in his direction. When George put out his tongue and quickly disappeared towards the exit from the building, he hurled himself across the room as if to follow until I flattened myself against the closed door and held him back. It was a stormy relationship, with the fault wholly on George's side. John Burgh was an able and devoted civil servant, who later became head of the British Council and then President of Trinity College, Oxford. He has remained a warm and valued friend.

The Principal Private Secretary can do much to determine the extent to which a junior minister is drawn into policy-making at the highest level, and he is privy, day to day, to the fast-moving events around the Secretary of State. The Secretary of State has little time to pause and seldom looks in advance at the list of those who may be attending a meeting in his office. Dealing with the Prime Minister and his cabinet colleagues, and enjoying the company of men of power outside the government circle, his junior ministers may slip to the bottom of his memory. This is not incompatible with a little jealousy towards a younger man and a suspicion that one day your chair may be his. The Principal Private Secretary can offset the Secretary of State's neglect and persuade him to use his junior ministers to advantage. Although my relations with George were always close and I could elbow my way into a meeting even when not invited, John Burgh did much to ensure that I was always in the mainstream of Departmental events. When George had been succeeded by Michael Stewart and I was losing interest, John urged on me the extent to which I might determine the direction of the Department in a major way, given a new Secretary of State with little experience of its affairs. It was not his fault that my response to this invitation was half-hearted.

Only once in my years as a junior or middle-rank minister did I have a serious clash with a Principal Private Secretary. Roy Jenkins had brought with him to the Treasury from Aviation and then the Home Office an outstanding Principal Private Secretary in David Dowler. When I arrived at the Treasury as Minister of State, they had worked together for almost five years. There was a close understanding and David Dowler knew Roy's mind on virtually every issue. With the authority of the Chancellor behind him, he had come to take for granted a certain freedom of action over junior Treasury ministers which was certainly not to be constrained by a late arrival such as me. As a matter of course, I was happy to discuss with him the Written Answer to a difficult Parliamentary Question and to settle on a suitable form of words. What I found intolerable was that he changed the Answer without reference to me after our agreement and put it into *Hansard* in my name. I was very angry, and we had a row, and our relations remained cool until his premature death.

Within a short time of my arrival at the DEA, I had two salutary experiences. There were a number of able women civil servants in the Department, including Jennifer Forsyth, later an Under-Secretary at the Treasury (and, after her retirement, a Labour councillor in Chelsea), June Bridgeman, who also became an Under-Secretary, and Phyllis James from the Board of Trade. I was determined to set up without delay a major seminar on aspects of regional planning and to invite to it outsiders from the universities and industry. This was regarded as precipitate in advance of the Department forming its own view, but I asked Phyllis James to draw up a provisional list, look for a convenient date and come back to me with detailed proposals within forty-eight hours. She failed to do so, saying that she was not sure whether the views I had expressed were my final word and whether the Secretary of State had been consulted. I made clear to her that this response was unsatisfactory. She was entirely free to argue the case against outsiders, but not to hesitate once I had decided. As for the Secretary of State, if she was doubtful about my authority, she should discuss the matter with the Permanent Secretary, who would then discuss it with me and George Brown if he so wished. There was no further delay. The conference took place, and I came to value Phyllis James as a sometimes awkward but entirely competent official. In retrospect, it was not surprising that she wondered whether the brash new Parliamentary Secretary knew his mind and whether the First Secretary would endorse it. If I had been wiser and divined the depth of her initial doubts, I would have suggested that she might like to take the Permanent Secretary's advice from the beginning. On the face of it, there had been a failure of loyalty on her part. In practice, although it was a warning to me, there were extenuating circumstances for her.

In the five departments in which I served as a junior or middle-rank minister, my relationship to the Secretary of State was a crucial factor in my dealings with officials. They were anxious to discover whether I was prepared to argue my case and stand up to him; and whether, in turn, he was susceptible to my advice. Once that was determined, an appeal to the Secretary of State never took place, although I occasionally suggested it when officials looked uneasy about my decisions. Increasingly, the process went the other way. 'Let me try this out on you, Parliamentary Secretary ...', a senior official would say, and the case was made for a particular course of action which he had in mind to recommend to my political boss. If I was unconvinced by the proposal, I seldom heard anything more, but if I approved it, I was made an ally in advocating it to the Secretary of State when the time came.

In the absence of specific duties, a Parliamentary Secretary could become a departmental dogsbody, active in the House, making visits round the country, but having no decisions of his own. Herbert Morrison, mindful of the problem at a time when much smaller Whitehall ministries were very centralised, proposed a Charter for Parliamentary Secretaries to enable them to escape boredom and exclusion. The problem is compounded for a Parliamentary Secretary by the sense of having become a political eunuch, bound by collective responsibility but with no share in major policy making at the cabinet level. In Morrison's time it was customary for senior ministers to appoint their own Parliamentary Secretaries with no more than a nod of approval from No. 10. This, at least, ensured compatibility. But no Prime Minister today is willing to delegate this patronage, and the result may be a misfit and an absence of mutual confidence and trust. I was lucky with all the senior ministers I served and found that my own standing with officials – and thus my influence – was enhanced as a result.

My second, early, lesson came as a warning about departmental boundaries and jealousies. As a matter of principle, George Brown wanted the DEA to be represented on virtually every cabinet committee and on its equivalent matching committee of officials. We were to be as pervasive in our influence as the Treasury. As George strictly limited his own regular attendance, a heavy burden fell on Tony Crosland (later on, his successor, Austen Albu), the other Parliamentary Secretary, Maurice Foley (who had been unsuccessful on my Stockton shortlist but had won another parliamentary seat), and myself. In a short time, I became an expert (of a kind) on broadcasting, defence dispersal and farm prices. As for officials, they were soon serving on some eighty inter-departmental committees (covering everything from the road programme to overseas development), sometimes with as many as five senior people attending a single meeting. The idea was simple. Almost every area of policy had economic or public expenditure implications which required a Treasury view. But the Treasury was always governed by short-term considerations, and the DEA had been created, amongst other reasons, to take a long-term strategic view. It was thus the role of DEA ministers and officials to offset the Treasury in discussion.

The Treasury, not unnaturally, resented our presence, but in the first year or eighteen months of the DEA our agreement or disapproval of any course of action carried equal weight with theirs. If we backed the Ministry of Health or the Ministry of Labour against the Treasury, we won; if the Treasury backed the department against us, we lost. There was rarely any attempt on either of our parts to take the matter further, ultimately to cabinet. This often made for frayed nerves and short tempers but, on balance, better decisions were made as a result of a third perspective and the authority that

My father and mother at their 1918 wedding. I was born ten years later.

A very determined child on Southport sands. But holidays were mainly taken at boarding houses on the North Wales coast and in the Isle of Man.

A rough lot: Squad 10, E company in basic training; I am third from the left on the back row. Illiteracy was common amongst National Servicemen; later I taught English to my Sergeant-Major.

A Fabian cricket team in 1954. Roy Jenkins is next to me in the back row. The scorer, in a blazer, is Gerald Kaufman, and the youngest player, sitting on the grass, is Michael Cockerell, the future television presenter.

With Harold and Mary Wilson in 1955. As Chairman of the Fabian Society, Wilson was helpful, but I resented him becoming Labour Leader on Gaitskell's death.

The Anglo-German conference at Königswinter on the Rhine, 1959. I am leaning forward on the left of the table, Patrick Gordon Walker and John Strachey are nearer the camera on the right. Königswinter conferences marked stages in my life for almost thirty years.

With Hugh Gaitskell and my local party chairman in Stockton.
Gaitskell had only nine months to live.

Canvassing in Stockton-on-Tees with Alderman Allison, leader of the council. The pattern of industrial dereliction in the North and economic over-heating in the South has changed little.

Winning the Stockton by-election. Did I ever again wear a three-piece suit?

Family, 1964. Silvia then, clockwise, Juliet, Rachel and Lucy.

Shamefully recruiting my children, but with a willing wife, to increasing my majority in 1966.

Silvia, by Oliver Walston. On many occasions we have enjoyed staying with Oliver and Anne Walston at Triplow Farm, near Cambridge.

The young minister, learning about government and how to survive with George Brown as his boss.

At sea with the Royal Navy, one of the compensations of life at the Ministry of Defence.

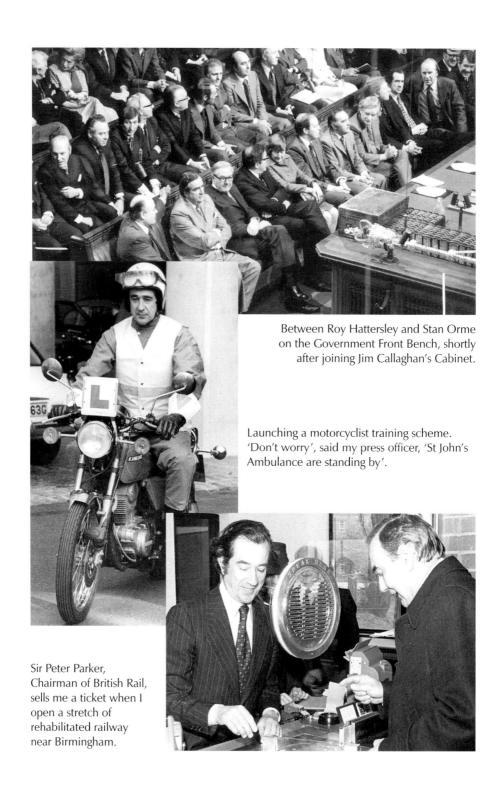

Between Roy Hattersley and Stan Orme on the Government Front Bench, shortly after joining Jim Callaghan's Cabinet.

Launching a motorcyclist training scheme. 'Don't worry', said my press officer, 'St John's Ambulance are standing by'.

Sir Peter Parker, Chairman of British Rail, sells me a ticket when I open a stretch of rehabilitated railway near Birmingham.

flowed from George Brown as First Secretary of State. This was particularly the case in decisions affecting the economic and social development of the regions, because regional planning – including what used to be called 'distribution of industry policy' when it belonged to the Board of Trade – was one of the DEA's major responsibilities. It was from this that my uncomfortable lesson stemmed.

During the relatively calm two or three parliamentary months that followed the Queen's Speech but preceded major legislation, a half-day debate was arranged on Northern Ireland. When cabinet allocated speakers for this – it was before the more recent Troubles – George Brown insisted on the locus of the DEA, arising from its responsibility for industrial development in the regions. The Home Office (which had looked after the affairs of Ulster since the 1921 Treaty), and particularly George Thomas, the Parliamentary Secretary whom I squeezed out of the debate, resented this intrusion. As for my own officials, they had quite enough to do without offending their Home Office colleagues and doing research for me into tiresome matters outside their competence. It was predictable that Hugh Delargy, the Labour Member for Thurrock, a radical in Irish affairs, should use the opportunity to speak against the division of Ireland and to provoke the Ulster backwoodsmen. In turn, he was entirely justified in complaining when I failed to reply to the points he had raised, lamely pleading insufficient time. The fact was that not only had my own officials provided me with an inadequate brief but the Home Office civil servants in the official box failed to pass me any notes of advice on political matters raised in the debate with which I was not familiar. It was one of my two worst speeches in the House, although I doubt whether anyone except Hugh Delargy and George Thomas much cared. Delargy was understanding of my dilemma, but when, almost twenty years later, I made my first speech for the SDP, I thought I saw a sly smile on the lips of Mr Speaker Thomas (as George Thomas had become) as he failed to protect me from a rowdy House.

But the division of labour with the Treasury was at the heart of the DEA's – and the Government's – problems. Apart from the question of personalities (and there was no natural good will between George Brown and Jim Callaghan) and the routine business of cabinet committees, there were central questions of economic policy to be confronted. Either these would be solved through 'creative tension' – a euphemism for rows that nevertheless ended in agreement – or the outcome would be postponed or fudged. It was important that there should be a clear understanding about the relative tasks of their departments between the First Secretary and the Chancellor of the Exchequer, and this was embodied in a written document.

The Concordat, as this was called, was being discussed as the DEA moved into Storey's Gate. But ten days later it still required the Prime Minister's final approval, and its existence was being denied even to the rest of Whitehall. It was an awkward compromise designed to emphasise cooperation in a relationship made for conflict. The functions of the two departments were to reflect 'the unity in diversity of economic policy'. Both departments would be 'centres of coordination', and each would consult the other before proposing any substantial departure from agreed policies. The DEA would be 'primarily responsible' ('primarily' was underlined in the typescript) for long-term aspects of economic policy and the Treasury 'primarily responsible' (also underlined) for short-term. But, to make the position doubly clear – or doubly opaque – neither distinction was 'absolute'. Primary concern or responsibility did not mean either 'only' or 'exclusive'.

The Concordat continued in much the same vein, emphasising that short-term and long-term aspects of policy tended to merge together and that most considerations concerning the allocation of resources were inseparable. But when it came to setting out the division of actual functions, the Treasury list, although shorter, was of more substance. It would retain its responsibility for public expenditure, including the Budget; and for home and overseas finance, including monetary policy, the balance of payments and exchange control. As for the DEA, its main tasks were to formulate a National Plan for economic development and to supervise its implementation, and to coordinate external economic policy (important for future relations with the European Economic Community). Beyond that, the First Secretary and head of the DEA would be Chairman of a cabinet committee on economic development and Chairman of the National Economic Development Council (NEDC), previously the Chancellor's task.

The roles assigned to the First Secretary and the weight George Brown carried as Deputy Prime Minister were far more relevant to the potential influence of the new Department than the constraints of the Concordat. The reluctant but well-intentioned efforts of Sir Lawrence Helsby and the irresistible force of George Brown had given a logic of a kind to the DEA. But there was uncertainty about how it would now perform. This uncertainty was increased by the decision, reached within twenty-four hours by Harold Wilson, George Brown and Jim Callaghan in most secret conclave, not to devalue the pound. Henceforth, in a charade reminiscent of a nursery game, even the word 'devaluation' was banned from conversation throughout Whitehall. In the DEA, any oblique reference amongst ministers was accompanied by index finger to the lips and a prolonged 'shhhh ...' The word itself was never mentioned. Although George had been (and remained) in favour of devaluation, he had not fought for it with the vigour he brought to other issues. As a result, the Government embarked upon three wasted years and the DEA had an uphill struggle from the beginning.

For, above all, the DEA was meant to be the department of 'growth', coming to grips with and reversing Britain's long-term industrial decline, hidden throughout the post-war period, but now visible in all the economic trends. To the DEA, 'growth' meant the planned growth of the stagnant sections of Britain characterised by high and persistent unemployment, inadequate infrastructure and poor social provision; and the growth of new industries and the modernisation of old ones encouraged by government intervention and helped by government money. The theme was of indicative planning, or planning by agreement, carried forward on a tripartite and voluntary basis.

I moved fast to set up Regional Planning Councils and Boards in pursuit of policies which built on initiatives taken by Ted Heath as the minister in charge of the regions in the closing months of the previous government. From his office as President of the Board of Trade, Douglas Jay opposed virtually everything we proposed on the grounds that the distribution of industry policy of the Attlee Government was the last word on such matters. There was also opposition of a different kind to the original suggestion that the new regional structure should be of 'Planning Councils' rather than 'Economic Planning Councils'. I believed that economic growth in the regions depended on infrastructure and land-use planning as well as industrial incentives and restraints. But land-use planning was strictly for local government, and local government came under Dick Crossman. There was a protest from his office, and shortly afterwards he shambled in to see George Brown, accompanied by the redoubtable Dame Evelyn Sharp (whom many years later, following her retirement, I came to know better when she took the SDP whip in the House of Lords). Dick was sheepish and unsure of his brief; Dame Evelyn was clear and firm.

There was to be no crossing of boundaries: 'planning' was well understood to be the sort of planning that stemmed from the Town and Country Planning Act of 1947 and similar legislation and, as such, was her responsibility and not the DEA's. Without a ruling from the Prime Minister, a Statement to Parliament and a further transfer of responsibilities, she was strictly right, so George agreed that 'economic' should be inserted. As it turned out, this decision, impossible to resist without a pitched battle because it had not been considered before the election, was a grave error. I had hoped that nominated councils, which is what in the short run they would have to be, would evolve into elected regional government. At that stage I had no considered view on how this process would be achieved, but the successful intervention of Dick Crossman's department killed that prospect.

For the moment, l pushed ahead with deciding the form and powers of the Councils and Boards and looking for people to serve on them. The Boards were to comprise civil servants representing the main Whitehall departments in the regions, with an independent chairman at Under-Secretary level who would become a member of the staff of the DEA. In Tom Beagley and Philip Chantler we found two able Board Chairmen, and the remainder performed their task perfectly well, despite some very recalcitrant members, especially from the Board of Trade. It was to the composition of the Councils that I gave my main attention. I was determined that their membership would not be nominated directly by interest groups, as had become the custom, and that we should retain the freedom to get the best available talent and mix. We would invite the CBI and the TUC to make several proposals and choose between them; we would select our own local government representatives; and a final third of the membership would be drawn widely from the universities, the professions and the social services. It was a successful formula. Into the third category I slipped many men (alas, too few women) whom I knew personally from Oxford or Fabian days and who were emerging into public life. One was Jack Goldberg, a classical scholar from Magdalen, a Manchester solicitor and prominent in North West Arts. He proved an excellent member.

It was important to get a fair political balance, but there were sensitivities in regions like the South-West where Labour was thin on the ground. Should we appoint the Headmistress of Cheltenham Ladies' College, who was an active Conservative but who would be a very acceptable member? We did. Should we appoint, in the North-West, the veteran Alderman George Eddie of Blackburn, who was being urged upon us by Barbara Castle? We didn't. I was particularly keen to appoint younger people and, with an average age of something over fifty, we did not do too badly. Finding chairmen was difficult, given the need both to appoint the best available candidate in each region and to show a reasonable balance of talent and experience overall. One of my best appointments was of Professor Charles Carter (another Fabian contact) in the North-West. In three cases I found it impossible to come up with a confident choice of my own or to agree with George Brown on his. In the Northern Region, there was much talking behind cupped hands about Dan Smith, and I did not like him. But he was an outstanding leader of Newcastle City Council and had been led by George, during pre-election discussions, to expect a major role in government. George appointed him out of guilt as well as on merit, and he performed well until corrupt practices caught up with him and he ended up in prison. In East Anglia, George appointed the merchant banker, Kenneth Keith, who never had his heart in it, and in the South-East his own brother-in-law, Maurice Hackett, who did not have the capacity for the job. Despite this, the machinery we set up in the regions worked remarkably smoothly and survived long after the DEA had disappeared.

But the core of the DEA's work lay in the National Plan, and most of the excitement and publicity in the Department's responsibility for prices and incomes policy. In both these respects it took tripartism – government working closely with both sides of industry – to its apotheosis and with very mixed results. The National Plan, a White Paper of nearly 500 pages, was principally the product of Sir Donald MacDougall and his staff, but with a major input from the Department's industrial advisers and prepared in close consultation with both the CBI and the TUC. The opening sentence of the National Plan set the tone: 'This is a plan to provide the basis for greater economic growth'. It went on to announce the growth target as a twenty-five per cent increase in national output between 1964 and 1970, based on an annual rise in industrial productivity of 3.4 per cent. The National Plan was launched in September 1965 with a popular edition, 'Working for Prosperity' (price one shilling), and a massive campaign to win understanding of its detailed analysis of the needs of separate sectors of industry. But in July 1966 it quietly perished, after a short period of uncertain life, in a sterling crisis and a tough set of deflationary measures. My direct involvement in the National Plan was slight, but I gained some experience in advocacy by making speeches around the country to audiences increasingly sceptical about its relevance to the deteriorating economic situation that the Government appeared to be ignoring.

Once the major decisions had been made on regional policy, I became restless. In the absence of executive responsibilities for the Department, which would have generated both desk and parliamentary work for ministers, there was too little for me to do. I told George that I was getting bored and persuaded him to transfer junior responsibility to me for prices and incomes policy. As this was central to the Government's programme – and to George's own interests – I would have limited discretion of my own, but at least I would be in the firing line.

The Board of Trade had long been the 'sponsoring department' for industry, and the President of the Board of Trade was the usual route for access to government for manufacturing industry, except when representations on the Budget were made to the Chancellor. The trade unions had access mainly through the Ministry of Labour, particularly over industrial relations and health and safety. The creation of NEDC by Selwyn Lloyd in 1961 had brought both sides of industry into closer contact with government and each other. But the DEA went further, for it offered access at the highest level, and to a department specifically charged with industrial policy in its broadest sense. George Brown was in regular (sometimes, it seemed, continuous) contact with George Woodcock, General Secretary of the TUC; and the bringing together into the CBI of the hitherto separate employers' organisations enabled its first Director-General, John Davies (later to become a member of Ted Heath's cabinet), to be available in a similar way. If George Woodcock or John Davies had not been summoned to Storey's Gate at least once during the week, they would telephone plaintively on Friday morning to discover why they were out of favour. They might weary of the First Secretary's strenuous style, but they welcomed inclusion.

But for the Government consultation – and cooperation – was essential to its anti-inflationary prices and incomes policy. On 16 December 1964 – within two months of the Government coming into office – the tripartite 'Joint Statement of Intent' was signed beneath the chandeliers of Lancaster House with all the pomp and ceremony of the Treaty of Versailles. It was later printed, as if on parchment, to hang on walls in offices and workshops around the country, although it is doubtful whether this was the purpose to which it was always put. In the House of Commons, George said that the agreement provided the foundation on which a fair and an effective policy for prices and incomes could be developed 'without which our economy cannot become strong'. The statement was a major personal achievement for him, into which he had put a unique combination of energy, persuasion and threats.

But without devaluation and a moratorium on new public expenditure, the economic situation was becoming increasingly grave. From the voluntary agreement of December 1964 until the compulsory policy of July 1966, a great deal of the time of ministers and officials went into winning support for essentially short-term measures. I found myself advising George on everything from the BBC licence fee to railway pay and laundry charges, either summoning to the Department the employers and trade unions to persuade them to adopt a moderate course or considering whether a reference should be made to the National Board for Prices and Incomes, which was set up early in 1965 under the former Conservative cabinet minister Aubrey Jones. I spent half a day in the West London bakery of Joe Lyons and Company and another half day with Garfield Weston, investigating the weekly baking cycle and the possibility of reducing overtime and using equipment more intensively. I discovered how often negotiations between the trade unions and employers went on without any understanding of the effect on prices or any attempt to improve productivity and absorb increased costs. It was a remarkably unsophisticated world and very far from Lancaster House, the National Plan or textbook accounts of collective bargaining. All in all, the learning process was more valuable to me than my own resulting contribution was to government policy-making.

The really demanding moments came in the summer of 1966. A number of weaknesses had emerged in what had begun as an entirely voluntary policy, and it was decided to take statutory powers to require early warning of proposed pay and price increases. Following the election in March, which gave the Government an overall majority in the House of Commons of almost 100, and as the economic crisis mounted, the Department prepared a Prices and Incomes Bill. When the time came to introduce it, I discovered, greatly to my surprise, that despite more than twenty years in the House, George Brown had virtually no experience of handling legislation. He had never been responsible for a Bill, nor had he even sat on a Standing Committee. At the Second Reading on 14 July, the Opposition mustered its maximum vote on a three-line whip and, led in committee by Sir Keith Joseph, intended to fight the Bill all the way. Terence Higgins, an able young Conservative who later served at the Treasury under Ted Heath but was unfairly neglected by Mrs Thatcher, was to be his number two, and Norman St John Stevas and John Biffen, both members of the committee, would no doubt amuse their colleagues and delay proceedings with some style. On the Labour benches would be Frank Cousins, again in charge of his union, having resigned from the cabinet over the compulsory powers in the Bill. Advising him from the sidelines, in the first row of the public gallery, would be an assistant from the Research Department of the Transport and General Workers' Union, Norman Willis. George Brown, who at his best could be dominating in the House, was apprehensive of leading in committee, and the Lord President, Bert Bowden, warned that we would only get the Bill by sitting until 26 August, long after the normal commencement of the recess, which would be intolerable to Members on both sides but doubly awkward for Labour Members with children on holiday from state schools.

George had a further problem. He had opposed the deflationary package announced on 20 July and argued again for devaluation. But he had lost the argument in cabinet, despite support from a group as diverse as Roy Jenkins, Tony Crosland, Barbara Castle, Dick Crossman and Tony Benn. A consequence was that the Bill would now have to be strengthened by a new Part IV which would make its passage doubly difficult.

On the Labour membership of the committee I negotiated with the Chief Whip, John Silkin. In addition to Frank Cousins, he wanted to add Eric Heffer amongst Labour opponents of the Bill, saying, with all too typical casuistry, that he would extract from both of them an undertaking not to vote with the Opposition in any circumstances. I opposed this, and Eric Heffer was dropped. But George was still difficult to pin down on either the details of the Bill or how it would be handled, showing a lack of enthusiasm even for briefing the Labour members of the committee. Finally it was settled that, as far as possible, I would lead, assisted by Shirley Williams, now a junior minister at the Ministry of Labour, and, occasionally, by the Solicitor-General. Following convention, George would be absent for cabinet business and, in practice, for rather longer intervals. When all-night sittings began, I worked out a schedule whereby Shirley and I would cover the hours from midnight until 8.00 A.M. and also certain mornings. But George could not keep away and spoke more in committee than the Solicitor-General, Shirley and I put together. He rose all too readily to the bait the Opposition threw him that his presence was essential to progress on the Bill. The reality was that Keith Joseph only had an incentive to delay progress (and make news) when the First Secretary of State was present. George trusted Shirley and me to look after the Government's interest, but hoped that we would not do it so well as to manage without him. The sittings on the Prices and Incomes Bill proved the longest since the Gas Bill of 1947, twice lasting through the night and once for over twenty-four hours. The Chairman was Harold Lever, who earned the praise of both sides of the committee way beyond the normal courtesies and was later presented with a copy of the committee proceedings bound in leather.

The passage of the Bill through committee was seen as a triumph for George, but in the anticlimax of completion he felt only the anguish of defeat. The DEA, the department of planning, had been stopped dead in its tracks by short-term measures of economic expediency. The National Plan had gone, and so had a voluntary incomes policy based on cooperation with both sides of industry. He had fought twice for devaluation and lost both times. In the last resort – as he admitted to Barbara Castle during the July crisis – the Prime Minister would always win, if only because he, George, was not an acceptable alternative. George would often throw open the door to the Private Office and shout, 'Get me Burke' when he could not or would not speak to the Prime Minister about an alleged slight. The Secretary of the Cabinet, Sir Burke Trend, would then come to the telephone and explain, usually successfully, that there was no cause for alarm. On Europe, where George's strong personal commitment was matched by the DEA's responsibility for external economic policy, he had seen the Prime Minister soften in his opposition to joining the Community. In other circumstances, this alone might have been a sufficient justification for soldiering on, even in adversity. But this was not George's temperament. Often suspicious, strangely insecure, he could imagine slights where none were intended and count as failures what others would call success.

In the conduct of cabinet and departmental business his mind was quick and creative, and he could master a difficult brief in a very short time. The richness of his voice added force to his advocacy, especially when he was persuading reluctant businessmen and trade unionists to support the Government against their better judgement. He had the vision to grasp big ideas and the coruscating energy to pursue them. And he was enjoyable company if you could stand up to him and did not constitute a threat.

He was a genuine egalitarian in being unaware that his own authority and status made unequal a relationship which he treated as equal. At its most extreme, he shouted indiscriminately at anyone, including members of parliament and civil servants, if he thought they warranted it. Early in the 1964 Parliament, I was accosted in the Members' Lobby of the House by Eric Heffer, an assertive left-wing MP, who threatened me with physical injury as proxy for George Brown, whose junior minister I was. The cause of this outburst turned out to be the rudeness of a cabinet minister towards a newly-elected backbencher. I taxed George with this, and he was surprised. It had not occurred to him that he had caused offence, as he had dealt with Eric Heffer no differently from the way he dealt with Harold Wilson.

The task of soothing relations between George and backbenchers normally fell to Willie Hannan, his PPS, an admirable sixty year-old Glaswegian who gave steady and thoughtful support on all major issues. But I was also a two-way channel of communications between George and the Parliamentary Labour Party, conveying encouragement – and warnings – to George and rallying support for him from time to time. On the afternoon of 20 July 1966, following a morning cabinet and the Prime Minister's Statement on public expenditure cuts and a pay and prices freeze, George sent a letter of resignation to No. 10, having engaged for most of the previous twenty-four hours in a semi-public agonising about what to do. No announcement was made, but his behaviour around the House of Commons soon made clear to everyone that he was, at the least, half in and half out. When I caught up with him he was maudlin, determined to register his dismay at the harshness of the Government's economic measures, but reluctant to let go. I was convinced that his resignation would be a disaster for the Government at a critical stage in its life, and a personal tragedy for George. My task was to persuade him that his friends in the House wanted him to carry on and that he had not lost their confidence. I decided to launch a round robin and, finding the precincts of the House busy with MPs in the feverish mood of late July, quickly collected a hundred or so signatures. A few of his cabinet colleagues, battered by him in the past and resentful of his emotional self-indulgence, would have been happy to see his resignation stand, but there was general relief when, by midnight, it was withdrawn. I know of no precedent for such a petition. It also established in the minds of MPs a greater personal commitment on my part to George than was in my interest, carrying with it the implication of less independence of mind and action than was good for me.

But George's departure from the DEA was not long postponed. A little before noon on Wednesday, 10 August, I was told that the First Secretary would like to see me in his room at the House of Commons. The Prices and Incomes Bill was going through its final stages, and at last the House would rise for the summer recess. George was slumped at his desk with a half-empty bottle of sherry in front of him. 'Have a drink?', he offered. 'No thanks, George, not at this time of day.' There was a pause. 'I'm leaving', he said. 'Leaving? Not leaving the Government now, after all!', I exclaimed, and he told me that he was not moving out, but to another department. Then began a game, with George insisting that he was sworn not to tell me where he was going, but urging me to guess. At the third attempt, having tried to reconstruct Whitehall to create another department in his image, I hit on the Foreign Office, and he put his finger to his lips and nodded. I was surprised and pleased and began to say so, but he stopped me:

'I'm over the hill, Bill, I'm over the hill.'

'But you're not and you needn't be if … you look after yourself better.'

He sat up in his chair, alert. 'What do you mean by that? Come on, say it, what do you mean by that?'

'You know very well what I mean.'

'Say it, say it!'

'Stop being awkward, George.'

'Say it, say it.'

'All right ... you've just got to stop drinking.'

He subsided, the bottle of sherry now practically all gone. He had teased me into making my point explicitly, but made no complaint about the substance of my message. After a while we went on amicably to discuss what he could do in Europe and the importance of an early renewed bid for entry to the Common Market. He clearly felt some pleasure at the prospect of the Foreign Office, although his perspective on his political life did not change.

That night I wrote an obituary of his time at the DEA and reflected on the future:

> He will shake up the Foreign Office, which will be no bad thing, but how long he will survive is anyone's guess. He managed two years at the DEA when some people would not have given him two weeks. For the moment he is happy, and success would do him a world of good: withdrawing from East of Suez; into the Common Market. The sad thing is that success in foreign policy is even more difficult than in home. You can't bully, bribe, charm and outwit the world's leaders and give them a drink at the end.

As for being over the hill, that happened effectively when he lost the leadership. Since that moment, at best he had been on a plateau, and now it would be all downhill, slowly or fast as the case might be.

The new Secretary of State for Economic Affairs was Michael Stewart, reluctantly swapping the Foreign Office with George. I had first met him as a visiting speaker at Oxford and saw something of him through the 1950s when his wife, Mary, served on the Fabian Executive Committee. He was a quiet man, but with a sharp and orderly mind and a strong sense of principle. I respected his seniority, but found it impossible to have with him the open and vigorous discussions that I had long enjoyed with George. His own restraint was inhibiting, especially as my confident knowledge of the Department inevitably exceeded his. I fell to sending him long memoranda on policy and keeping out of the way when visitors from the CBI and TUC arrived. On occasions when I was present, I became only too aware that a classical education and a period as a schoolmaster had made him too reliant upon rational argument. By an inexorable process of ratiocination, he would lay bare a complex problem of industrial relations to reach an inescapable conclusion that bore no relation to reality. Businessmen and trade unionists found him a relief after George, but they were baffled.

I had been spoilt. Working with George had been an exhilarating introduction to the process of government. His departure from the DEA was bound to leave me rather flat, especially as I was ready for a change myself.

Chapter 5

Vicissitudes

When the change came it was the least welcome of the moves I made through Whitehall departments in the next three years. It brought with it all the mean and unworthy thoughts that reshuffles inspire in those who are disappointed by them. On Friday 6 January 1967, I was standing by the reception desk of the Queen's Hotel in Stockton when the telephone rang and, once answered, was passed to me. 'Mr Rodgers?' The question was followed by only a moment's pause. 'The Prime Minister.' I had no chance to take the call in a more private place and was soon involved in an uncomfortable dialogue. After a muffled voice had crackled down a bad line, I was obliged to say, to the surprise of Silvia and several casual listeners, 'Please speak up, Prime Minister'. This time I heard him clearly. 'I am making some changes and I hope you will be prepared to go to the Foreign Office.' A pause on my part, then, 'What as, Harold?' 'Sideways, as Parliamentary Secretary at this stage.' I struggled with the disappointment while collecting my thoughts. I said that I had hoped to move up to Minister of State and enquired whether anyone else was moving. The Prime Minister confirmed that they were but made some soothing remarks and asked whether I would like to reflect and call him back. An hour later I did so, accepting, and a few days later I was installed in a room overlooking the Horseguards Parade, far grander than my rather bare cell at the DEA.

But I was not happy. Two years earlier, when Tony Crosland had moved from the DEA to become Secretary of State for Education, I had been within a hair's breadth of succeeding him as Minister of State, with Bruce Millan from the Scottish Office lined up to take my place. I was then blocked by Tony, presumably piqued by the circumstances of his own move (to a post that Roy Jenkins, Wilson's first choice, had declined) and inspired by a curious petty jealousy that occasionally ruled him in his relations with some younger men. I would have been very lucky at such early promotion and had no complaint whatever when the vacancy went to Austen Albu, a long-serving MP with appropriate industrial experience, and a friend. But when Tony Crosland gratuitously boasted of his action at a dinner party, it was hurtful, especially when he claimed that he had had no ambitions at my age, which was nonsense.

There had been another missed opportunity when Jack Diamond, the Chief Secretary to the Treasury, was invited by Harold Wilson to become Minister of Aviation.

On this occasion I was congratulated on my impending move by David Watt of the *Financial Times* who had just come from a briefing at Number 10; and by my Private Secretary, who had heard the news on the Whitehall grapevine. But the Chancellor of the Exchequer, Jim Callaghan, prevailed upon Jack to stay at the Treasury and my own promotion – to Financial Secretary – was aborted.

In these circumstances it was not surprising that to move sidewards after over two years in the most junior ranks of government inspired me with no delight; and for some weeks I wondered whether I would be better off on the back benches. I might have been wise to ask to see the Prime Minister to talk over my future as others apparently did, but I found the idea of such an approach distasteful. If I was to make progress in his government, I told myself in uncompromising terms, it should be on obvious merit, not as a result of crawling to him.

In January 1967 Harold Wilson might have been prepared to treat me even-handedly; eighteen months later, deeply worried about conspiracies against him, and with Roy Jenkins now Chancellor, his motive in at last promoting me was different. The circumstances again involved a telephone call rather than a meeting, on this occasion to Patshull Road at lunchtime on a Sunday. David Best, my old friend from Quarry Bank, had arrived with his young family from Israel and I had not listened to the one o'clock radio news. Harold Wilson's opening words were, 'You will know about Ray Gunter,' and, without waiting from me to say 'No,' explained the consequential changes which would take me to the Board of Trade as Minister of State. I was too unprepared to say anything more than 'thank you,' and joined Silvia and our guests for lunch, totally mystified by this extraordinary turn of events. Later I learnt that Gunter had resigned from the cabinet and, later still, that the Prime Minister had panicked, believing quite wrongly that this was the first stage in a plot to replace him to which I was privy. In time-honoured style, promoting me to Minister of State was a way of buying me off.

My third and last move in the 1964–70 Government came about in a very different way. In August 1969 Silvia and I rented a house at Le Castellet, near Toulon in the South of France, and Roy Jenkins and his family were staying a few miles away. One evening, as we sat on our terrace with a drink, Roy asked me if I would like to move to the Treasury. Harold Lever was shortly leaving (somewhat to Roy's relief) on promotion to the cabinet and Dick Taverne would replace him as Financial Secretary, leaving a vacancy for me. Eighteen months earlier I would have jumped at the chance of joining Roy, Dick, and Jack Diamond, who was still Chief Secretary, but now my reaction was guarded. The Treasury team had fought its crucial battles; and this Parliament was almost over. What could I contribute at this late hour? Had he thought, I asked, of David Owen as an alternative if the Prime Minister was unwilling to promote David Marquand from the back benches? Roy was not put out by my hesitation, asking only that I should let him know my answer when I returned to London. Silvia's views were hard-headed and decisive. The Treasury was the elite department in Whitehall and experience in it, even for a short time, would be a distinction for the future. As for the Board of Trade, if I was serious about my political career, enjoying myself visiting lighthouses in small boats in rough seas and planning new airports, which I did as Minister for Shipping and Aviation, was neither here nor there. I gave Roy the answer 'Yes', and on 13 October I entered what were quaintly called 'the Treasury Chambers', not by the Great George Street entrance where I had made my enquiries five years ago, but from Whitehall.

Serving in three departments during three and a half years meant that my knowledge of each of them was superficial. There was also a disadvantage in not being identified as an expert – if only a parliamentary one – in any area of policy. But for anyone interested in the processes of government, the experience was fascinating. The DEA had been a new and unstructured department without executive powers. But the Foreign Office and the Treasury were powerful voices in Whitehall, and the Board of Trade was long-established, even if its influence had diminished.

At first the Foreign Office had to bear some of my resentment at moving sideways, and officials were puzzled that I was not obviously pleased to be there. It also took me some time to adjust to a culture and pace somewhere between an Oxford college and a gentlemen's club, where departmental meetings took the form of leisurely and well-mannered conversations, and relationships between the most senior officials and junior ones were rather like those between father and son. Officials seemed to cope with George Brown with greater success than those in DEA, as if a sense of history and long experience of managing men made them relaxed about another ministerial bird of passage. In the DEA ministers had taken the initiative and run things: without them the department would not have existed. But for the most part the Foreign Office ran itself, and ministers had to intervene positively if they were to change the direction of policy. In the DEA, a paper would land on my desk with a recommendation and a request for a decision; in the Foreign Office, such papers would arrive informing me of decisions apparently taken, leaving me just time before implementation to query them.

My fantasy, close to experience, was for an official to come into my room shortly before one o'clock. 'I mustn't delay your lunch, minister, but I thought you would want to know that we shall be declaring war on Ruritania about tea-time today.' 'Oh, thank you for letting me know, Sir James,' I would respond; then, as an afterthought, 'But could you tell me why?' And war would be postponed until after lunch when officials would patiently explain the matter before agreeing, with some reluctance, that the Foreign Secretary himself ought to be consulted.

On two occasions in particular I was sharply faced by stopping a process already begun. I was responsible, amongst other things, for consular affairs, and at six o'clock one evening, as I was leaving for the House of Commons, my Private Secretary, Richard Samuel, asked if I would see a senior official about an urgent matter. The Under-Secretary was wearing a long, grey coat as if already halfway across St James's Park to the Athenaeum. His message was that a British citizen was to be executed in Nigeria the following day unless I sent a telegram asking for a pardon. He listened impassively as I said that I was against the death penalty and that a British citizen could not be allowed to die, only then asking about his offence. 'He is a mercenary,' was the reply. 'He went into a bar and brutally attacked the Nigerian barman. When another mercenary intervened, he shot him through the head.' There was a stillness in my room. 'What will happen if he is pardoned?' I asked. 'They will put him on a plane with a ticket to his native Glasgow.' More silence until I asked, 'What then?' 'He will walk off the plane and on to the streets.' For half an hour I talked round the question as much to myself as to anyone, in the end suggesting that we send a telegram asking for a stay of execution until some enquiries could be made about the prisoner's criminal record in this country. Dutifully my instructions were carried out. Next day I learnt that he had been pardoned and deported – not to Glasgow but to Kinshasa.

A different challenge to intervene arose from the Government's wish to maintain commercial relations with Greece while doing nothing to give comfort to the Junta of colonels who had taken over the country. 'You will want to know,' said my Private Secretary one morning, 'that an official of the Royal Mint is flying to Athens today to sign a contract'; and he explained that for a hundred years the Royal Mint had produced coinage for Greece. This certainly appeared to be a commercial transaction wholly consistent with policy, but I felt uneasy. The formula, 'You will want to know,' was often a means by which officials covered themselves on the margin of their responsibilities. It could be a warning that they were up to something. Protocol and caution were the watchwords on Greece in the Foreign Office and, as a result, I had seen Andreas Papandreou, the socialist leader of the opposition Centre Union (and later Prime Minister for many years) in a private room at the London School of Economics because it was thought too provocative to receive him in Whitehall. Accordingly, I now asked for details of the proposed contract and said – and my Private Secretary pulled a long face – that the official of the Royal Mint should be stopped at Heathrow until I had cleared his trip. Two hours later Richard Samuel brought in the relevant papers and, more importantly, the design that the Royal Mint had agreed to execute. It was for a commemorative medallion dated 21 April 1967, with a phoenix rising, to celebrate the first anniversary of the Junta coming to power. I vetoed the trip without hesitation. Our Ambassador to Greece was the only one to protest, but he did not try to evoke the Foreign Secretary's authority against me, and, having first sent me an angry telegram, he later called to apologise.

George Brown could easily have been prejudiced against Foreign Office officials, whose casual hauteur and social background seemed to have changed little over the years, but he valued most of them for their intelligence and honest advice. He had his favourites and those he mistrusted – he sent Roger Jackling as Ambassador to Bonn in preference to the more deserving Con O'Neill – but these could not easily be predicted. Soon after my arrival he pointed out to me Patrick Hancock, currently his principal adviser on European affairs and later Ambassador to Italy. Hancock wore a black undertaker's jacket and pin-striped trousers and had the superior manner of the old school. 'Don't underestimate that man', said George, 'forget the style, he's good', and by 'good' George meant the source of high-quality advice and the capacity to stand up to him in argument.

When George Brown had the opportunity to appoint a new Permanent Under-Secretary he joyfully announced to me, 'I'm appointing an engine driver'. This seemed far-fetched, and so it proved to be. Sir Denis Greenhill had been a managerial apprentice on the London and North Eastern railway before the war, but this was after Bishop's Stortford College and Christ Church, Oxford. He had curiously unformed, almost childish, handwriting, which belied his complex nature. He reminded me of Beatrice Webb's description of Hugh Dalton as 'a subtle, wily man with a certain peculiar charm'. Denis Greenhill had spent much of his time close to the Secret Intelligence Service, and when talking to him I sometimes felt myself in a hall of mirrors, where nothing is quite what it seems. But he was always fair to me, the most junior of ministers; and I liked him, and Silvia liked his wife Angela, who wrote poetry, which was far from true of all Foreign Office wives she met.

In this I shared her mixed opinions. I felt sorry for Foreign Office wives in so far as they were traditionally shackled to their husbands' careers, thus denied one of their own. But abroad, in an ambassadorial role themselves, they often seemed to lack any knowledge of life in the United Kingdom outside their own narrow circle. When they discussed education, it was the public schools; when they talked about where to live, it was invariably about London and the Home Counties (except Kentish Town, where we lived, which generally rendered them speechless). The superficiality of their conversations could be excused by the need to find common and non-controversial ground with people they never expected to meet again. On closer acquaintance and after I had ceased to be a Foreign Office minister, I discovered wives who were studying with the Open University, had taught in state schools or had been social workers. But these were generally of a younger generation, and amongst wives as a whole there was a good deal of plain snobbery, not easily detected in their husbands, nor ever, in my experience, in the wives of home civil servants.

Together, Foreign Office officials made up a formidable team, but I never found them difficult or obstructive, or doubted their competence. I stayed for a few days with Sir Anthony Rumbold, a scion of a well-known Foreign Office family, in Bangkok. The Ambassador's house, with its walled compound, was a fine example of nineteenth-century colonial architecture. Over dinner he consulted me about the impending visit of Jack Diamond who, on behalf of the Treasury, was looking for savings in Britain's overseas representation. Should he serve good wine to please his guest or show prudent economy with something cheaper? I advised the best in his cellar and be damned, which I am sure was his independent way of doing things.

On the Sunday of my visit, we took the ambassadorial Daimler and drove twenty-five miles north-east to where the old summer palaces of the Kings of Siam were to be found. There we embarked on a broad-beamed boat to return in leisurely fashion by river to Bangkok. As we lunched off Thai delicacies, washed down by champagne, I recalled to myself the aphorism of the 3rd Marquess of Salisbury that the aim of British foreign policy was 'to float lazily downstream, occasionally putting out a diplomatic boathook to avoid collisions'. It was the opportunity for a question that I enjoyed asking officials: 'Why did you join the Foreign Office, Ambassador?' Sir Anthony waited a while, as a benign sun blessed our gentle progress, before replying: 'Because I like Abroad'. It was the only possible response.

My own Private Secretary and many Foreign Office officials had an Intelligence background, and MI6 operators were often indistinguishable from career diplomats in our embassies (occasionally in places like Ulan Bator in Mongolia, they were the Ambassador himself). Early in my time at the Foreign Office on a visit abroad when I was accompanied by Silvia, our hostess, the Ambassador's wife, promised that dinner would be an informal occasion 'for family and friends'. When twenty of us then sat down round the candle-lit mahogany table, I sought some explanation, given that the Ambassadress did not appear old enough to have contributed significantly to the numbers. I then learnt – what I should have guessed – that 'family' meant members of the Embassy staff; and – something quite new to me – that 'friends' were members of MI6 attached to the Embassy. The generic description 'the Friends' for those who worked in the Secret Intelligence Service was soon familiar to me in the day-to-day language of the Office.

One of the reasons why George Brown had asked for me to be transferred from DEA – and thus connived in my failure to be promoted – was his wish for someone he trusted to look into the fringe Intelligence activities of the Foreign Office. He believed that amongst those receiving low-level Intelligence briefing were a number of Conservative MPs, and that others were on the payroll. This indeed proved to be the case, but I was also surprised to find at least one prominent Labour Party official who had been recruited to Intelligence in his student days. But my probing into dark corners came to a sudden halt when there was a message from Number 10 that the Prime Minister had decided that further access to Century House (the headquarters of SIS) should be denied to me. As I was not a Privy Councillor, it was 'inappropriate'.

I experienced the mystique of the Privy Councillor's oath – convenient to Prime Ministers and senior officials alike and cherished by incumbents – with reverse consequences when I became a Privy Councillor eight years later as Minister of State for Defence. On the morning my appointment was announced, the Department's Chief Scientific Adviser, Sir Herman Bondi, came into my room with a broad smile. He congratulated me on becoming a Privy Councillor and then explained that it had solved a problem. There was a dispute between the scientists and the Naval Staff about an aspect of Chevaline, the updating process to put more nuclear warheads on the missiles carried by Polaris submarines. This was a Top Secret agenda, but now I had become a Privy Councillor he was authorised to ask me to take the chair to resolve the matter. The idea that I was more trustworthy than the day before or when I had first signed the Official Secrets Act was absurd. But I had crossed into new territory and was a different man.

But my main task in the Foreign Office was making it more sensitive to the House of Commons and more accessible to MPs. I changed the officials dealing with parliamentary business to more sympathetic ones and brought MPs into the department for regular briefings, which had never occurred before. I also organised 'planted' Parliamentary Questions from friendly Labour MPs. George would say, 'Why do I always have to face hostile questions on Europe and Vietnam?'; and when I conveyed this message to backbenchers they would respond, 'If you will draft questions for us, we will put them down'. It was a game everyone played, despite complaints from the Opposition and an occasional reprimand from the Speaker. It is still played today.

But I genuinely wanted greater participation of MPs in the making of foreign policy, and hoped to get agreement on the appointment of a Select Committee on Foreign Affairs. When I first made the suggestion officials were very uneasy, but after lengthy discussions, Sir Paul Gore-Booth (Denis Greenhill's predecessor as Permanent Under-Secretary) reluctantly agreed that greater openness and better informed MPs could be to the advantage of the Foreign Office. When I put the proposal to George Brown, he at first gave it a cautious welcome; at least it would surprise Dick Crossman who, as Lord President of the Council, was finding great difficulty in persuading cabinet colleagues to accept cross-party select committees in their areas of responsibility. But then he asked whether he would be able to appoint its members, and I explained that although the Chief Whip would have the major say, the Commons itself would ultimately choose. 'Does that mean that I would have to have Jack Mendelson?' and there was a fierce inflexion in his voice. 'Not necessarily', I replied, 'but you couldn't count on it'. That was the end of the matter. George was beyond persuasion, and officials sighed with relief. It was a dozen or more years before a Conservative government, to general approval, did what I had wanted to do.

Despite my reservations about moving to the Foreign Office, I look back at a period full of incident and variety that I rather enjoyed. On the occasion of Trooping the Colour, when the Queen took the salute on the Horseguards Parade and the Household Cavalry and the Brigade of Guards wheeled and counter-marched in all their ceremonial glory, Silvia and I held a party in my splendid room. Our guests were our friends, especially those with children, and the Foreign Office carpets were well spread with discarded nuts and broken potato crisps. But one potential guest was absent. The day before I had been telephoned by one of George Brown's secretaries. 'The Foreign Secretary wonders whether you would like a distinguished American visitor at your party.' 'Why?' I asked and, as an afterthought, 'Who is he anyway?' 'Well, he wants to see the ceremony and' – there was a hesitation – 'his name is Richard Nixon'. My reply was an immediate 'No!' Nixon's reputation in the days of senator Joe McCarthy's communist witch-hunt and then as Vice-President had been quite enough to put me off. All that came later and led to Watergate was predictable in his character long before he reached the White House. I never regretted my failure to entertain a future President.

One central issue of policy, the European Community, and particularly de Gaulle's veto on the Labour Government's first bid to join, resulted in my becoming leader of the UK delegation to the Council of Europe, a post usually reserved for a senior backbencher but involving sybaritic trips to Strasbourg, especially at asparagus time. Another, Anglo-American relations, took me to Vietnam at the height of the war.

The British Ambassador, Sir Peter Wilkinson, seemed like a courteous diplomat of the old school and just a bit unworldly. But he had served in pre-war Berlin and won distinction on a mission behind the lines in Austria during 1939–45. When he drove round Saigon in his Austin Princess wearing a straw hat, it was not a sign of eccentricity but of defiance. He took me to see General Westmoreland, then commanding the American forces. As we left, he asked me what I thought of 'Westy'. 'Not much, Sir Peter,' I said – I hope with some diffidence – and expected to hear diplomatic dissent. But the Ambassador had an acute understanding of guerilla warfare and could distinguish between his hopes for an American victory and the prospect he saw of defeat. His telegrams to London were marked by great critical shrewdness about the ebb and flow of battle. Several years later, when I had returned to publishing, I asked him to write a book about his wartime experiences. He declined. What had been to him, he said, 'the excitement of a Point-to-Point' had been to millions a cruel matter of life and death.

Later in 1967, I contrived a freelance non-ministerial trip that took me to a number of universities on the East Coast of the United States and in the mid-West. Although in Labour terms I was a hawk on Vietnam, I found myself something of a dove on the campus, where faculty members were more concerned about how the Americans could extricate themselves than the merits of the war itself. Inconclusive discussion, even with academics unrepresentative of the general public, can sometimes convey a message about how opinion is moving, and I formed the view that American bombing of North Vietnam, then a feature of the war, would come to an end. Shortly after I had returned to London I wrote a memorandum to the Prime Minister (my one and only direct communication with him in that Parliament) warning that the Government should not get too far out on a limb in support of a controversial policy. 'It is their war, not ours; we don't condemn particular acts but nor do we necessarily defend them.' I predicted that the bombing of the North would stop in the following spring. Five months later, on 31 March 1968, it did.

These were the days of the Cultural Revolution in China. Anthony Grey, the Reuters' correspondent, had been locked up in Peking and other British citizens were under arrest. The British Embassy had been attacked by an organised mob; and the Chinese were doing everything they could to destabilise Hong Kong by riots and intimidation, as they had already done successfully to the neighbouring Portuguese colony of Macao. The Governor-General's political adviser was a Foreign Office official, T. A. K. Elliot, whose name (and initials) I remembered from my Fabian days when he contributed to the funds without formal membership. Anthony Elliot turned out to be an old Balliol friend of Roy Jenkins, and whether or not his understanding of British politics helped, he was an outstanding success in holding the line against the breakdown of civil order in Hong Kong. My infinitely easier task was to hold the line in the House of Commons, where there was angry frustration at Britain's apparent inability to protect its own citizens in China.

On one occasion the Chinese Chargé d'Affaires asked to see me, Chinese counter-protests to the British government being at least as frequent as ours. I sat behind my desk — a much more formal and distancing position than usual — and he sat in front of me with his interpreter at his elbow. Behind them both, a little to their left, was the head of the Foreign Office China desk, John Denson, who was my interpreter. As I had anticipated, the Chargé was soon attacking 'the running dogs of imperialism' and falsely accusing of spying those British citizens they had detained. I stopped him and said that I would listen to any message from his government but not to abuse. If he was unwilling to use civil (by which I meant diplomatic) language, I would refuse to hear him. But 'running dogs' were part of his script and he had no intention of departing from it. After a minute or two more, I got up and left the room. My abiding memory, as I turned back briefly in the doorway, is of a scene that might have been painted by Magritte. The sunlight shone brightly through the windows, casting in silhouette the backs of three heads as one of them continued to address, both in Chinese and in translation, my conspicuously empty chair.

The Foreign Office looked after its ministers. A trip abroad would be smoothly arranged with immediate passage through Customs, a splendid car and, if need be, scheduled aircraft delayed. Even at home the object was to minimise the burdens of office, not only with creature comforts but by restraining importunate visitors. A regular duty was an evening schedule of two or three cocktail parties. When I was first in the Foreign Office, Silvia would usually accompany me, but she later decided – quite rightly – that this was a waste of time, diverting her both from her children (at bedtime) and a career of her own. However, foreign ambassadors – whether paying courtesy calls on their arrival and departure or with important messages to impart – were not easily admitted to the presence of even a Parliamentary Secretary. 'The Thai Ambassador has asked to see you,' my Private Secretary would say, 'and I've offered him twenty minutes next week'. And twenty minutes it would be, some days later.

I had been conditioned by this protection when I moved to the Board of Trade and had come to take for granted that it was the way of the ministerial world. 'I've just had the Town Clerk of Manchester on the telephone', my new Private Secretary said soon after my arrival there as Minister of State. 'He wants to bring an urgent delegation about the airport.' 'What about half an hour, say a week today?' I suggested. My Private Secretary radiated disapproval. 'But Minister, they want to come tomorrow and they'll expect at least an hour, which is what they usually get.' I woke up. I was back in the real world of domestic politics: my Foreign Office cushion had gone.

For me the Board of Trade meant something of a *Boy's Own Paper* life flying round the country in one of Air Traffic Control's 125 Jets and spending time with the coastguards and going aboard ships. These were just as romantic to me as in my Liverpool days, thirty years before. I had a curious fencing match with the new Permanent Secretary, Sir Anthony Part, who let it be known soon after my arrival that he was waiting for me to call on him. Had it not been put that bald way, I might have done so. But Eric Roll and Paul Gore-Booth had, of their own volition, called first on me, which precedence strictly required, so for more than three weeks we did not meet. Then we found ourselves together in the President of the Board of Trade's office, and mutual introductions ensured a drawn game.

In the Board of Trade, as in my previous departments, I enjoyed Parliamentary Questions and encouraged my friends to put down questions for oral reply in my area of responsibility so that I would have a fair share of opportunities to appear at the dispatch box when we were top of the House of Commons' Order Paper. I took a lot of trouble to redraft the rather formal replies put before me by officials and sometimes changed the wording while I was on my feet. I had sandwiches in my office on the day and worked through lunch to master the replies I might give to supplementaries and to get the adrenalin flowing. One of my most persistent questioners on aviation was a former BEA pilot on the Opposition back benches called Norman Tebbitt. Despite his uncompromising and sometimes rancorous manner, I liked him, a feeling I have never quite been able to overcome.

The popular view is that Parliamentary Questions are a charade involving no check on the arbitrary actions of governments, and even bringing the House of Commons into disrepute. This may have been true of the then twice-weekly gladiatorial exchanges between the Prime Minister and the Leader of the Opposition, but it was not the case with questions to departmental ministers. When an oral question appeared on the Order Paper, I would often say, 'We must get a move on and make a decision I can announce', thus accelerating the department's work. On other occasions, when by a narrow squeak I had avoided disaster, I would go back to my office and say, 'Never again. I saved the day but didn't deserve to.' And steps would be taken to put things right. When MPs on my own side of the House were involved, I would later admit to them that their question had successfully prompted action. But Opposition MPs remained unaware that they had been much nearer to scoring a point than my confident reply led them to believe.

Tourism was one of my responsibilities within the Department. Its growing balance of payments importance to Britain was recognised in a Bill that I took through the Commons. Under it, grants were to be offered to encourage the building of new hotel rooms; and the old, rather ineffective, British Travel Association was to be replaced by a new quango, the British Tourist Authority. The original intention was to incorporate within it the English Tourist Board, while granting independence to the tourist boards for Scotland and Wales. But in Standing Committee I was convinced by the arguments put forward by back-bench MPs that I was wrong and that England needed a separate tourist board; and, despite initial resistance by Harold Lever at the Treasury, got agreement to amending the Bill. When it came to making appointments I asked around on an informal network for names. Raymond Postgate and Jennifer Jenkins came up with useful suggestions and so did Harry Evans, then in his early years as Editor of the *Sunday Times*. As he and I swam together in the open-air pool on Hampstead Heath, I explained the sort of people I was looking for and we pulled ourselves up on to the floating platform to discuss names. 'Why not Jean Robertson?' he asked, referring to the paper's travel editor. It seemed a good idea, so in due course she was appointed. In such casual ways were ministerial appointments made by ministers.

I was more uneasy about the role of ministers in being able to award licences for airlines to fly on often lucrative routes. On one occasion when a decision was pending on a licence to fly to Malta, Silvia found herself sitting next to the applicant, a buccaneering airline operator, at a concert at the Albert Hall. 'Where do you get your pheasants, Mrs Rodgers?' he suddenly and obligingly asked her. 'From Sainsburys,' she replied. Her neighbour was not so easily rebuffed. 'But wouldn't your husband like a weekend's shooting in Yorkshire?' This time she was able truthfully to reply that I had never shot a bird in my life and would not want to start doing so now.

The question of licences was one of the issues examined by Sir Ronald Edwards in a report on the reorganisation of civil aviation. This required major decisions to be embodied in a White Paper, approved by the cabinet and implemented through legislation. The handling of the Edwards report enabled me to see the President of the Board of Trade, Tony Crosland, in action for the first time as a senior minister.

Tony Crosland had not been entirely pleased by my appointment. He was candid in admitting that he was anxious to extend his political support on the Labour benches beyond the Gaitskellites, who had been his natural allies, by offering patronage to a wider circle on the centre and centre-left. But he was very good to work for as he readily delegated responsibility in what became almost a federal department.

Civil Aviation he generally left entirely to me, but the Edwards Report needed his personal attention. Before the first of a series of meetings, I held discussions with officials, from which it emerged that I did not share their preference for new arrangements for air traffic control, while they did not share my enthusiasm for a Civil Aviation Authority. Tony Crosland was told about this and invited me to open the meeting with my comments on the proposals of officials. But when, two hours later, the meeting broke up, we were no farther forward, with Tony demanding more detailed information with which to make up his mind. Sir Max Brown, the Second Permanent Secretary, asked if he could come to my room. 'We didn't get very far', I volunteered, and he said that was exactly his worry. He then suggested that progress might be quicker if the two of us could agree a possible compromise.

At the next meeting Tony Crosland opened by saying that he knew I wanted an independent Civil Aviation Authority, so he would like officials to make their case against. 'President,' said Sir Max, 'we have certainly had reservations and there are details to be settled, but after further consideration we believe that the Minister of State's proposition is basically sound'. Tony was surprised, perhaps disappointed, but could get no alternative view from the other officials present. He then returned to the business of the previous meeting, only to find that I was now ready to acquiesce in the views of officials. A third meeting then came to a relatively quick conclusion on all outstanding matters. Tony must have guessed there was collusion, but said nothing.

When it came to determining the location of a third London airport, in the face of strenuous opposition to the development of Stansted from the residents of rural Essex, Tony Crosland appointed a Royal Commission under Mr Justice Roskill to consider possible sites. Never had any previous Royal Commission had such a quality of advice from geographers, town planners, economists, engineers, sociologists, agroscientists and (or so it sometimes seemed) water-diviners and astrologers. Every assistant professor at the Massachusetts Institute of Technology must have been consulted. But in the end all the recommendations of Roskill in his report were abandoned and many years later, as a result of a simple political decision, Stansted became the third London airport after all.

It is too easy to ridicule a process that brought real professionalism to areas of government where it had previously been lacking. Tony Crosland was right to recruit the best brains from outside the civil service to the solution of complex problems. But he was just too painstaking and lacked a confident instinct for decision.

With my colleague at the Scottish Office, Dick Mabon, I hoped to find a quicker solution to the problem of a major airport to serve the Lowlands, given that Edinburgh had a badly-aligned runway, Glasgow's airport was on the wrong side of the city, and the international airport at Prestwick was miles from anywhere. In the meantime I wrote to the Treasury to sound out the prospects of financial assistance for short-term ameliorative measures or for something bolder. It proved the only occasion in my life when I have replied to a letter of my own. Within a week of sending it, I had become Minister of State at the Treasury with responsibilities, under the Chief Secretary, for expenditure on aviation. I ensured that my letter to my successor at the Board of Trade – my reply to myself – was encouraging, but the project was later killed off by the Secretary of State for Scotland, Willie Ross, who argued that electoral considerations required immediate largesse for Edinburgh and no further nonsense about the longer term. Scottish ministers were very good at getting their own way as election time approached. Their gloomy messages in cabinet about the loss of seats and the advance of Scottish nationalism guaranteed reluctant support for a new motorway or bridge or further railway electrification.

Arriving at the Treasury I was now amongst old friends, although I had seen none of them at close quarters in their ministerial roles. But I had received an inkling of Roy Jenkins' style as Chancellor of the Exchequer from a conversation with Sir Douglas Allen shortly after his appointment as Permanent Secretrary to the Treasury. Douglas, whom I had known since the DEA, intercepted me at a party to ask more than half seriously whether I had any advice about how he could make personal contact with the Chancellor, who was proving remarkably elusive when it came to discussions within the department. My only suggestion was that he should sit next to Roy on a transatlantic flight, and a few weeks later he told me that he had done just that. During seven hours with his prisoner, en route to Washington, Douglas had made up triumphantly for lost time. But the serious message was that Roy Jenkins preferred informal contacts with his officials. He made his decisions and then conveyed them through his devoted Private Secretary, David Dowler. Perhaps the department as a whole took on the colour of the Chancellor because, with one notable exception, I can recall no meetings round the table of the kind that had been routine in my ministerial life elsewhere.

On the whole, Treasury officials were as clever as those in the Foreign Office but with less style. They were St Paul's and Manchester Grammar School (and, I like to think, Quarry Bank) rather than Eton and Winchester. They were also more inclined to acknowledge the necessity of having ministers to make decisions, even if serious policy-making was for the Chancellor alone. What they had in common with their Foreign Office counterparts was a belief that the issues dealt with by their department were bigger than the careers of transient politicians. To officials in the Foreign Office, a bad speech in parliament, even if it led to a ministerial sacking, was of no great consequence provided that nothing was said to offend our NATO allies or create a diplomatic incident. In the Treasury, no speech was a bad speech – at least, one that mattered – unless it led to a fall in the sterling exchange rate or a dangerous loss of reserves. Alas, I cannot claim that as my excuse for making, as a Treasury minister, what was my worst speech in twenty-one years in the House of Commons.

Major decisions on the decimalisation of the currency – from 240 pence to the pound to 100 new pennies – had been made three years before and the final details were now being settled. Decimalisation left no obvious place for the old sixpenny coin, which would have inconveniently become two-and-a-half new pennies, and the Government decided to abolish it. But 'Save Our Sixpence' suddenly emerged as a cross-party campaign and a gift to the Opposition. My own preference would have been to phase out the sixpence slowly, letting it die a natural death. But the decision had been made in cabinet and had been frequently spelt out in answer to Parliamentary Questions.

Not surprisingly, the Opposition decided to take a Supply Day for a debate when Iain Macleod would propose a critical motion, and the task of replying fell to me. The debate was set for 19 February 1970, and in the preceding days there were newspaper rumours that the Government would announce that the sixpence was reprieved. I was sufficiently worried by this to ask Roy Jenkins to raise in cabinet that morning whether the decision stood firm. At about 12.30 P.M. I received a message that it did, and then put the finishing touches to a difficult speech when there would be critics on the Labour benches behind me as well as a full turn-out of confident Tories in front. But to my horror, when the latest edition of the *Evening News* (then London's second evening paper) was delivered, the headline ran, 'The Sixpence is Saved'. Underneath, the story was worse. Lena Jeger, a Labour MP campaigning for the sixpence, had been to see the Prime Minister at lunchtime and he had agreed to a reprieve. Pressed by me for urgent clarification, Number 10 were vague about the conversation, although claiming that no such undertaking had been given. But the damage was done. By the time I went into the debate, a majority of the Members who packed the Chamber believed that a change of policy was about to be announced.

Iain Macleod was at his mischievous best. He welcomed signs of surrender by the Government and said that if I confirmed the *Evening News* leak, he would not press his motion to a division. He made a virtue of a short speech so I could tell the House without delay what it was hoping to hear. I could do no such thing. Furthermore, I was obliged to defend the policy without calling Lena Jeger a liar (which she was not) or holding the Prime Minister personally responsible for the muddle (which he was). I spoke for nearly forty minutes – far too long – giving way to angry interventions on over a dozen occasions. My speech was a disaster; *The Times*, in calling it 'gloomy and convoluted', was generous. I had been put in a corner and had not fought my way out. In that evening's Parliamentary Party meeting, I was attacked by Lena Jeger for failing to follow the lead the Prime Minister had given her at lunchtime; and although my friends defended me, they were puzzled by what had happened. Later, when the truth emerged, my predicament was well understood. The speech, however, had been made; there was no taking it back.

My only worthwhile contribution to affairs of state during my eight months at the Treasury, where I was rather under-employed, also arose from decimalisation, in this case the hope that it would not lead to inflationary price rises. The Budget Committee was the formal meeting place of ministers and officials – a series of meetings Roy Jenkins could apparently not escape – that reached conclusions about the contents of the Budget. The Treasury was a hierarchical and centralised department – Roy had warned me that I would have a less clearly defined ministerial role than I was accustomed to – and the Budget was certainly seen to be the Chancellor's own. The contribution of officials was unusually tentative. Their principal function appeared to be to advise on the dire consequences of any policy initiative and make any decision of the Chancellor a very personal one. It was not surprising that there was disapproval when I suggested that instead of raising the 2d stamp duty charged on every bank cheque to one new penny (an increase of forty per cent), we should get rid of it altogether. It would cost the Exchequer £11 million in a full year (about £100 million at today's prices), more than officials wanted to give away. Sir Arnold France, the head of the Inland Revenue, spoke strongly against it as inconsistent with his priorities; and he was supported by Jack Diamond, who doubted whether it would be popular. Roy Jenkins did not reach an immediate decision and this allowed me to show that, with decimalisation not due until February 1971, ten million people with bank accounts should be pleased by such a gesture at a cost of less than £1 million in the current financial year. That settled the matter, and the abolition of stamp duty on cheques was announced in Roy Jenkins' Budget speech.

The Prime Minister's behaviour over the 'Save-the-Sixpence' campaign, although minor in itself, was a symptom of much that had been wrong throughout several years of government. When George Brown eventually resigned in March 1968, his criticism of the Prime Minister's style – to which he attributed his resignation – was lost in memories of his own erratic behaviour. But for many of us there had been too much slithering and sliding in Downing Street. The Prime Minister's well-remembered television broadcast of November 1967 about the 'pound in your pocket' was only the most public evidence of self-deception sometimes flowing over into falsehood. During the long saga of Rhodesian sanctions I had seen the secret telegrams concerning the British naval patrol which was trying to enforce the blockade of oil supplies through the Mozambique port of Beira. Despite the Prime Minister's claims to the contrary, sanctions were *not* working. In the spring of 1966 I had been aware of how seriously the economy was deteriorating, which he declined to admit or act upon. It was not surprising that in the lobbies and corridors of the House of Commons there was criticism of Harold Wilson's performance, and that this was strongest amongst junior ministers who could neither speak out in public nor play any part in policy-making in cabinet.

Prime Ministers should take in their stride intermittent rumbles of criticism amongst their supporters, and the discussion of possible successors. But Harold Wilson's jumpiness about criticism of his performance as Prime Minister turned into self-fulfilling paranoia. The more he conceived of plots against him – without confronting face to face those supposed to be plotting – the more plot-like discussions became. The tendency towards counter-conspiracy was heightened by a kitchen cabinet at Number 10 apparently reporting to Harold Wilson whatever he wanted to hear. I described it to Silvia as a Borgia court.

The court jester was Colonel Wigg (as he preferred to call himself), Member of Parliament for Dudley and Paymaster-General for three years from October 1964, a bumbling figure who would have been hard to take seriously had it not been for his access to the Prime Minister. George Wigg had played some part in unmasking John Profumo's affair with Christine Keeler in the dying days of the Macmillan Government and had acquired a reputation – at least with Harold Wilson – as a security expert. I had two experiences of him that convinced me that even a court jester could be a menace.

I had spent the day at home in bed with 'flu, when at about 10.45 P.M. the telephone rang and George Wigg announced himself. 'I just want you to know that I shall be reporting the remarks you made in the lobby tonight to the Prime Minister.' Astonished, I asked him what remarks he had in mind. 'Oh, you know, about Harold, I shan't repeat them now.' 'But,' I said, 'I wasn't in the lobby, I didn't vote; I've been ill in bed all day.' There was only a moment's hesitation. 'I'm sorry,' he said, 'mistaken identity, it must have been Hattersley,' and he put the phone down. Quite apart from the ridiculous error, Roy Hattersley now presumably became the victim of George Wigg's one-man KGB.

The second occasion was even more bizarre, again involving a telephone call to my home. 'Bill?' a voice enquired. 'George Wigg.' And before I could respond, he continued, 'You will remember what we discussed. Well, it's on but I can't tell you more over an open line.' 'But what have we discussed, George?' I asked. A short silence followed. 'Is that Bill?' 'Yes, it is.' 'Which Bill?' 'Bill Rodgers.' At which point he said, 'Wrong Bill', and rang off. Again the whole episode was laughable, except that here was a man whose role was to whisper in the Prime Minister's ear.

The first suggestion of problems in the parliamentary party came by a different route and was directed at a different target. In June 1966 the Chief Whip, Ted Short, asked me to call on him and then said that the left wing of the parliamentary party had become troublesome, implying the Prime Minister's personal concern. Could I do anything by way of discreet organisation to swing the balance the other way? I was cool about the idea, not seeing the need for any such action. Nor in the absence of a personal message from the Prime Minister himself did I want to be the victim of a plague-on-both-your-houses admonition of the kind of which Harold Wilson was a past master.

But by later in the year, the Prime Minister's enemy within had become what in conversations with the kitchen cabinet and ministerial friends he called 'CDS'. This was the 1963 Club of mainly younger MPs who had been supporters of Hugh Gaitskell and now met for dinner at the House of Commons once a month. Roy Jenkins and Tony Crosland were, in effect, the senior members of it, and others who attended regularly – apart from Denis Howell and myself as convenors – included Dick Taverne, Roy Hattersley, Brian Walden and Ivor Richard; and, from the intake of 1966, David Owen, David Marquand and Donald Dewar. We had no fixed agenda but enjoyed each other's company and the usual gossip that was commonplace wherever two or three MPs gathered together. When the economy was in trouble (which it was, most of the time) we asked who was to blame and what should be done; when by-elections were lost (and fifteen Labour seats were lost in that Parliament) we considered why. We talked about the shortcomings of the Prime Minister and who might replace him. If nothing else, given the opinion polls, sheer survival was enough to prompt the discussion of a Harold-must-go campaign.

In this we did no more than mirror the thoughts of Jim Callaghan, Roy Jenkins, Tony Crosland, Denis Healey and other members of the cabinet who were just as aware of Harold Wilson's failings as ourselves. The questions for them – and therefore for us – was which of them would become leader if Harold Wilson was replaced, and by what device could a change be accomplished. For a short period early in 1968, when he was newly installed as Chancellor and support for the Government had reached its lowest level since opinion polls began, Roy Jenkins might have successfully engineered a *coup d'etat*. But by the spring of 1969 Jim Callaghan had sufficiently recovered his influence to be able to block Roy, who was supporting Harold Wilson and Barbara Castle over the reform of the trade unions and *In Place of Strife,* which Callaghan cleverly and unscrupulously opposed. In a long conversation I had with Roy Jenkins on 9 May, he made it clear that he would not be prepared to serve under Callaghan as Prime Minister, a course that David Owen had advocated. Further, Harold had said that he would not give way to an older man (he was fifty-three and Callaghan fifty-seven), which was consistent with an earlier, expansive moment when he had stretched out his arm towards the cabinet room and said to Roy Jenkins: 'One day this will be yours'. Roy was not against his friends keeping the pot gently boiling, but he cautioned against a long, drawn-out and bloody leadership fight that would be very damaging to the party and the country. Earlier in the year when I had reported to her a discussion in the 1963 Club, Silvia had said, 'The Labour Party has had it ... we'll have a party led by Roy and Jo Grimond'. But that was not a prospect I took seriously and I doubt whether it was yet in Roy's own mind.

There were times in those difficult years when many of the younger Gaitskellites wished that Roy Jenkins, Tony Crosland and Denis Healey could sink their differences, sideline their ambitions and learn to work together. Here were three men of similar age and outstanding talent who could save the nation. There was no great ideological gulf between them and, if it came to the point, they ought to be able to agree on who should replace Wilson. But this was naive. Denis Healey was a loner, immersed in the Ministry of Defence and not a sure and instinctive judge of the political mood. As for Roy and Tony, their long competitive friendship was an impediment to cooperation. In addition, there had been a shift in the balance of power between them, in which Tony had been the loser.

A majority of young, newly-elected Labour MPs of 1964 and 1966 – at least, those who called themselves Gaitskellites – admired Tony Crosland for *The Future of Socialism,* his tough intellectual arguments with the left and his insouciant glamour. Roy Jenkins, although he had reformed the laws on obscenity and was strong on Europe, was a relatively unknown quantity. But when they saw Tony at close quarters, he seemed to have lost some of the fearless, visionary independence of his earlier years. He was more calculating in his political judgements, often making the opinions supposedly held by his working-class constituents in Grimsby the touchstone of his own. At first this populism was an engaging affectation, but later it became an excuse for being awkward. In the 1963 Club he could become petulant; and whereas he had been the strongest advocate of group loyalty in CDS, he now found it increasingly difficult to accept decisions that went against him. Relaxed and with a drink, I found him the Tony Crosland of old – warm, irreverent and stimulating. But in influence, he had been decisively overtaken by Roy Jenkins both in government and around the table at our 1963 Club dinners.

Although Tony Crosland had been first into cabinet, Roy Jenkins had been a great success as a liberal Home Secretary before becoming Chancellor of the Exchequer, the office that Tony most coveted and seemed best equipped to fill. Roy was loyal to his friends and attentive to their interests. His historical sense helped to make him a confident judge of contemporary politics and he had shown himself courageous in government and a formidable debater in the House of Commons. As Tony Crosland failed to stay in the running, he became our obvious candidate for the future leadership of the party.

This was a reversal of fortunes that Tony found both hurtful and puzzling. He complained to Roy Hattersley that the 1963 Club dinners had become a cheering club for Roy Jenkins; and in deciding whether or not to attend, he was torn between jealousy if Roy was to be present and fear of missing out. In her deeply affectionate biography of her husband, Susan Crosland chastises a number of us (and me in particular) for heavy-handedness towards Tony over the position he adopted a year or two later on the Common Market. She has a point. But in a tense and critical situation, we were applying to Tony the standards of mutual support and collective loyalty which we had learnt from him. In the autumn of 1969 there was speculation that Tony would be sacked from the cabinet. This would have been a cruel fate and would have dismayed us all. We valued and admired him, despite the view we had reached that he was not a future leader.

The autumn reshuffle of 1969 marked the end of speculation about the leadership. But Harold Wilson continued to infuriate many Labour MPs by finessing difficult decisions and blaming all the Government's misfortunes on the press. After a meeting of junior and middle-rank ministers where he had lectured us like a schoolmaster on our errant behaviour, oddly holding up our Scottish colleagues as a model to us all, I found Edmund Dell, Merlyn Rees and Shirley Williams as fed up as I was with Harold Wilson's patronising triviality. But it was clear that there would be no change of leader before a general election which we still hoped that Labour might win.

The Government had reached the low point of its popularity in the first half on 1968, and then in June 1969 had been forced into retreat over its plans for trade union reform. But by the spring of 1970, Labour was miraculously recovering in the opinion polls and the local election results were good. When an optimistic Harold Wilson announced a general election, there was just time to take a truncated Finance Bill through the House of Commons. On 27 May I moved Clause 33, which abolished the stamp duty on cheques, and two days later Parliament was prorogued.

But the voters were not sufficiently pleased by Roy Jenkins' cautious budget, or impressed by the more stable path on which the Government now appeared to be settled. The Conservatives under Ted Heath won a comfortable overall majority of seats, and Labour gained its smallest share of the popular vote since 1935.

Chapter 6
Marking Time

The election had been fought in the most glorious weather; and when a few days later defeated Members of Parliament came back to clear their desks, they looked as if they were returning from a long Mediterranean holiday. Sadly, amongst them was George Brown, who had lost at Belper, thus ending twenty-five years in the House of Commons. Defeat also brought to an end his ten-year deputy leadership of the Labour Party, and this vacancy had to be filled quickly.

No deputy leader had hitherto succeeded to the leadership, but there was no doubt in my mind that Roy Jenkins should run. On 25 June, a week after polling day, a small group, including David Owen, Bob Maclennan and myself met at Dick Taverne's house to consider the campaign. We agreed that it should be discreet and that with the exception of Tom Bradley, Roy's PPS, his closer friends should stand back, leaving the business of counting heads and persuading colleagues to a wider spectrum of Labour MPs. The forty new Labour Members were more of a problem because they had not seen Roy in action as a minister and we did not know where their loyalty lay. On 30 June Silvia and I gave a small party for a number of these, including Bruce Douglas-Mann, an old Oxford friend, Phillip Whitehead, soon to become our neighbour in Patshull Road, and John Smith, newly elected for North Lanarkshire. Roy arrived late, but just in time to shake a few hands and, I hoped, influence a few votes. My guess was that he would win on the first ballot by an overall margin of about twenty votes, although others regarded this as optimistic. In the event, he obtained 133 votes against 67 for Michael Foot and 48 for Fred Peart, the centre-right candidate. The old Gaitskellites, it seemed, were coming back to power. If Roy could work reasonably well with Harold Wilson, he would become his successor.

Within less than two years, in an extraordinary transformation of fortunes, this expectation fell apart. Roy resigned as Deputy Leader and a fissure opened in the Labour Party over Europe which was almost to swallow it up. A centre-right coalition of Fabian intellectuals, trade unionists and what might be called the schoolmasterly class had long run the party, keeping the left at bay and in a minority. There had been ups and downs and Harold Wilson himself had come from the left. But for the most part, the spectrum of opinion represented by Jim Callaghan and Roy Jenkins – and, for that matter, Fred Peart – had held together. Now it became seriously fractured at a moment when disappointment with the failures of the 1964–70 Government and electoral defeat had given an impetus and opportunity to the left. Europe was not the sole cause of Labour's decline, but for almost a quarter of a century being pro- or anti-Europe became a defining characteristic of Labour MPs, creating tensions between former friends which inhibited them from working comfortably together.

Initially, however, there was no hint of the forthcoming drama. Before the House rose for the summer recess I stood for the Shadow Cabinet for the first time and received a reasonable vote without being elected; then spent a whole month in the Italian sun with my family, during which I saw much of Roy and also arranged to return to part-time publishing; and soon found myself as Labour spokesman on aviation supply under Tony Benn. This was not an entirely congenial experience. Tony Benn was still mainly in his boyish phase, but his energetic pursuit of the limelight coloured his relations with me. The collapse of Rolls Royce and the Government's announcement that they would nationalise the larger part of it in order to save 100,000 jobs (and a main defence contractor) created a political storm. When new developments over the weekend justified a further government statement, I decided to put down a Private Notice Question. As a matter of courtesy I telephoned Tony Benn but he was against my doing so and I reluctantly agreed to accept his verdict. Not long afterwards he telephoned back. 'Bill, I've been thinking of what you said. I'm now convinced you're right, so I've put the PNQ down – in my name.' So at my expense he got credit for political acuteness and the opportunity for a good parliamentary performance. I wondered at the time whether this was an untypical example of a lack of generosity quite unlike anything I had experienced with the ministers I had served in government. But when Eric Heffer resigned as Minister of State for Industry four years later, ostensibly over the Common Market, he told me he was fed up with working for Tony Benn because he always denied him a chance to shine.

My other new parliamentary role was more satisfactory. As Leader of the House of Commons, Willie Whitelaw had decided to replace the long-standing Estimates Committee with a new Expenditure Committee which would, for the first time, be expected to scrutinise aspects of departmental policies. This was a bold move for which he has received less credit than he deserved, because it was to be overshadowed by the setting up of a comprehensive list of departmental committees almost ten years later. The government in which I had just served had shown great reluctance to give parliament increased powers of scrutiny (George Brown had scuppered my own attempts in the Foreign Office), but I was responsive to David Owen and David Marquand when they urged that I should become chairman of one of the six virtually autonomous sub-committees, which would deal with trade and industry matters.

It was a decision I did not regret. Between 1971 and the end of the Parliament we conducted three enquiries: into the role of private money in the public sector (then a central question of industrial policy); the effectiveness of regional development incentives; and the wages and conditions of African workers employed by British firms in South Africa. All were politically sensitive, but my four Labour and four Tory members produced unanimous reports.

I took the view that a cross-party select committee should not be used as an instrument of parliamentary warfare. Indeed, the whole idea of a select committee was to get away from the adversarial nature of exchanges in the Chamber of the House (which was one reason why Michael Foot, amongst others, disapproved of them). There were extravagant hopes for select committees, in part because of a failure to recognise that Senate and House committees in the United States operated within a very different constitutional system where the writ of political parties ran much less strongly. When a select committee, usually in the person of its chairman, has tried to mimic – in the tough cross-examination of witnesses – a committee on Capitol Hill it has generally looked ridiculous and done harm to the system. As a result, the reforms of 1970 and 1979 have made less impact on parliamentary control of the executive than they might have done.

My own most public inquiry was not, however, directed at government and was only undertaken by some stretching of the terms of reference of the Expenditure Committee. Early in 1973, Adam Raphael of *The Guardian* had written a dramatic series of articles from which it appeared that British firms investing in South Africa often employed their workers in intolerable conditions. This immediately became a major political issue but one about which the Conservative Government and the Labour Opposition were cautious, as it appeared to concern the internal affairs of a foreign government. When I made a bid to consider it in my committee, both the Leader of the House, Jim Prior, and the Shadow Foreign Secretary, Jim Callaghan, saw this as an easy way out.

It proved a fascinating inquiry and it achieved results. I did not – I hope – conduct it as an inquisition or play to the gallery of press interest (there was then no televising of parliament). But we asked for evidence of their behaviour from all public companies operating in South Africa and summoned a number of their best-known chairmen before us. There was a great deal of apprehension about such an appearance. This was partly due to anxiety about the substance on which they were to be examined, and partly because witnesses feared they would be out of their depth in the unfamiliar environment of a select committee. One chairman eventually persuaded us to excuse him from appearing by sending a psychiatrist's letter explaining that he was under treatment. Lord Kearton, of Courtaulds, successfully claimed constitutional immunity as a peer from appearing before members of the lower house. When we invited Sir Isaac Wolfson, Chairman of Great Universal Stores, to give evidence, his family and his solicitor pleaded that he should be excused on the grounds of age and illness. I was ready to agree until I saw that he had taken the chair at the annual general meeting of his company. There was apprehension amongst his friends that Sir Isaac would put his foot in it, but he was a great success, speaking without notes and in a very straightforward fashion.

The companies that gave evidence occasionally protested that South African law prevented them from improving the wages and conditions of their African workers. This was almost always not the case. But my committee was focused on the performance of British companies and did not allow itself to be dragged into discussion of either the policies of the South African government – little as we liked them – or the argument advanced by the ANC for banning all further British investment in South Africa. Despite this, when I called on the South African ambassador to sound him out about the possibility of arranging a visit to South Africa by my committee he said that any application for visas would be refused.

The report was published in March 1974 and our main recommendation was for a new code of practice that should govern the conduct of British firms employing African workers. This dealt with industrial relations and the payment of minimum wages above the poverty line. We said that a company's wage structure should be determined by job evaluation and not according to race; and that everything should be done by way of education and training to ensure the advancement of Africans into more qualified and better-paid jobs. It was, in the context of the time, a radical document. A number of firms that had clearly been exploiting their African workers – often with the London main board of the company turning a blind eye to local management – felt under threat. Others, with a better record, reviewed their procedures and rates of pay. Adam Raphael's original highly critical articles put firms on their guard and, by the time my committee took evidence, some were able to point to very large increases in pay. Others began a process of careful monitoring with regular inspections by senior personnel from the United Kingdom. Within two or three years the code, with few amendments, had been adopted by the European Community as guidelines for all EC companies operating in South Africa.

As my committee reported in the week in March 1974 in which Harold Wilson squeaked back into Downing Street, it is not surprising that its achievement was largely missed. But our report made a direct impact on the lives and welfare of tens of thousands of people. Of all my activities in my years in parliament, chairing that committee must easily have done the most for humanity.

By Easter 1971, when my committee was progressing comfortably into its first inquiry on the financial aid provided by government to the private sector of industry, it became clear that a serious row about Europe was about to break out in the party. The Government's Industrial Relations Bill had inflamed feelings on the Opposition benches, although it partially implemented Barbara Castle's (and Labour's) own *In Place of Strife*. On one occasion when the 'guillotine' prevented any further debate after midnight, the Opposition divided on every remaining amendment until the dawn. With a full chamber of MPs, voting on each amendment took sixteen minutes, and Dick Taverne and I passed the night by walking out of the Palace of Westminster, turning left into Millbank, over Lambeth Bridge, along the embankment in front of St Thomas's Hospital and back over Westminster Bridge between divisions, then drinking half a pint of bitter between the next. But staying up all night was a fruitless exercise and it fed a mood in the parliamentary party that the Government should be opposed on everything irrespective of its merit. There was militancy abroad.

Despite Hugh Gaitskell's 1962 Brighton speech, Labour in government had moved steadily towards closer relations with Europe. In May 1967 it had decided to apply for membership of the European Economic Community, and in the House of Commons only thirty-five Labour MPs had voted against the motion to approve the application. From the junior ranks of government I had seen all policies in every department begin to take account of what was now regarded as Britain's European destiny. President de Gaulle's veto did not change matters. It was taken for granted that Britain would eventually join, and every subsequent step taken by the Labour Government was designed to show its European commitment. My own brief ministerial leadership of our delegation to the Council of Europe was one small token of the Government's good intentions; and by early 1970, with de Gaulle gone, a second application to join had been launched. This would have been pushed forward to success had Labour won the election, with Roy Jenkins as Foreign Secretary overseeing negotiations conducted by George Thomson who was already in the cabinet as 'Minister for Europe'.

Since the early 1960s Roy had been the undisputed leader of Labour's Europeans; and Shirley Williams' well-informed commitment made her a powerful voice in the shadow cabinet and the National Executive Committee. Amongst backbenchers, John Mackintosh was a courageous and effective platform speaker. There was a wide range of pro-European views amongst Labour MPs; these extended from a mild conviction that there was no alternative to joining the Community to a passionate federalism. I saw myself as somewhere in between, quite certain on both economic and political grounds that Britain should join but hazy about the speed and direction in which the Community should develop.

I was, however, uncompromising on one point: that as a decision on Britain's entry would mark an historic change in our foreign policy, it was above conventional party politics and ought not to be trivialised by the usual antagonisms of parliamentary life. If I sometimes seemed passionate about the matter, it was through irritation that my party showed no such sense of history and was unable to rise to the occasion. A Labour government under Harold Wilson, of which I had been a member, had sought to take Britain into the Common Market. The brief that George Thomson would have taken to Brussels was the one now in the hands of Geoffrey Rippon; and it was inconceivable that the outcome of negotiations would differ much from the one that a Labour government would have asked parliament to endorse. It hardly made me a Euro-fanatic to believe in a consistent approach to a great issue.

I had taken every opportunity to ensure there was no misunderstanding about my views in my local party in Stockton. This was particularly important when revised constituency boundaries were bringing new activists on to my management committee. For the most part, there was goodwill even when my views were disapproved. I attended the Cooperative Women's Guild, for a meeting made up entirely of women mainly in late middle age and presided over firmly by a former mayoress. After I had spoken and answered questions, she summed up: 'Ladies,' she said, 'we've heard our Member of Parliament about the Common Market and we don't much like it.' She paused and there were appreciative murmurs around the room. 'But,' Mrs Clough continued, 'Mr Rodgers is very well informed and we shall support him whatever he does', at which there was loud applause. It was the clue to how I should proceed. I would try to persuade my party members of my views, but not browbeat them. I would recognise their right to differ from their MP, while expecting in return their acceptance that I would vote in accordance with my conscience.

At the inaugural meeting of the Labour Party in my enlarged constituency (I had 30,000 new voters) on 15 April 1971, I presented a written report on the previous year, with some reflections on the future. I acknowledged that there were firm opinions both in favour of and against entry to the Common Market and that neither side was likely to budge. There was, I concluded, 'no need to divide the party and cause bitterness over the most important decision this country must take this century'. My formula for avoiding such a conflict was a free vote in the House of Commons. Early in February I had written an article for the *Daily Telegraph* in which I said that most Labour MPs would happily settle for a free vote. I also had in mind that Bob Mellish, the Chief Whip, had volunteered that a whip would be imposed, in his own words, 'only over my dead body'. In my article I said that there were forty Labour MPs ready, in extremity, to defy a three-line whip but perhaps sixty more who would join them in a free vote.

At that time there was still uncertainty about the way in which Harold Wilson would choose to lead the party over this issue, but by Easter he was clearly moving to reverse Labour's position when in government, even if two steps forward were generally followed by one step back. In these circumstances there was now little chance of a free vote unless he (and, for that matter, Mellish) believed that the alternative was a substantial number of Labour MPs ultimately prepared to defy a three-line whip against entry, come what may. A group of up to forty MPs, led by Roy, would be significant, but fifty or sixty who would stand firm on the night in any circumstances would make a damaging three-line whip less likely. And if the attempt failed to come off, there would be comfort in being in a group too large to be disciplined. Either way we would have done something for Britain's standing in Europe by avoiding a division wholly on party lines. In fact, we might have done something more, as there was bound to be at least a handful of Tory rebels to make the final vote without us a close-run thing. I decided to set myself the task of finding at least fifty, giving them confidence in what they were asked to do and the knowledge that they were not alone. From May until October this occupied much of my time.

My task was complicated by an advertisement, signed by 100 Labour MPs, that appeared in *The Guardian* on 11 May. This was a wholly admirable attempt to show that the signatories continued to believe in Britain's membership of the European Community. But otherwise it was bland and carried no implications whatsoever about voting, least of all if there was a whip. As a result, in the weeks ahead it was easy for Bob Mellish to claim that our support was declining as one by one the signatories were approached and a number of them promised to support the party line (in fact, twenty-one of them eventually voted against entry). It was not until the autumn that the Chief Whip conceded defeat and acknowledged that *The Guardian* list was never relevant to the exercise I was conducting.

This exercise was limited and simple. Initially, it was hardly more than a patient canvass of opinion, with names recorded on a slip of paper kept in my pocket. I was not interested in whether my parliamentary colleagues were in favour of the Common Market or even wanted to vote for entry. My only question was whether they would be prepared to do so against a three-line whip. In today's marketing terms it was, I suppose, a very 'soft sell'. I would enquire as to how they saw current developments on Europe and express the hope that there would be a free vote. Only then did I test them on voting against a three-line whip. I tried to avoid arguing the case either on the main issue or even on the vote itself. This led David Marquand, although amongst the staunchest of supporters, to tease me with the accusation of 'moral blackmail'. He meant by that that I allowed them no way out from personally confronting the choice. But my colleagues were responsible MPs who were following the debate in all its nuances, and their broad commitment to Britain's membership of the Common Market was already well established. How they would vote in extremity was all I wanted to know.

There was another consideration. Every MP had a different, complex series of pressures upon him which might affect his or her own future. A new Member, elected in 1970 with a difficult constituency, faced much greater risks than one soon to retire, with a constituency party firmly committed to Europe. There were also domestic and family factors, different in every case. It would have been quite wrong for me to push Members to vote against their better judgement. Nor would it have worked. My list, as it grew longer, was of colleagues whose determination I was sure about given mutual support at a later stage. If I persuaded anyone to say 'Yes' when in their heart they remained anxious or doubtful, they would change their mind later and undermine the credibility of the whole exercise. In fact, on more than one occasion I counselled a colleague against giving a firm promise when I suspected he had not fully thought through the personal consequences of voting for entry.

Alan Fitch, a Lancashire miner in his fifties, and an ally in all good causes, confessed that he was worried about deselection and felt that he might have to vote against his convictions. Later, he said that his wife had agreed to come out of retirement as a teacher and support the family if he lost his seat. Jim Tinn, MP for Redcar and thus a parliamentary neighbour of mine, said that he would vote for entry if I would feel isolated on Teesside but preferred to be released in view of heavy constituency pressure. With no hard feelings on my part, they both eventually abstained.

I had great sympathy for back-bench MPs tortured by conflicts of loyalties and physically affected by their anxieties, but none towards Tony Crosland. He tried to diminish the importance of the argument by saying that Europe was not an issue that caused excitement in the clubs and pubs of Grimsby. These tergiversations came sadly from the adventurous Crosland of old and won him no respect. In the parliamentary party even those Labour Europeans who were not themselves prepared to defy a whip expected something more robust from him. When a year later he stood for the deputy leadership of the party, a number of us pointedly declined to support him. But we could not determine the outcome of a secret ballot and, when Tony received only sixty-one votes, it was a measure of how he had brought upon himself his poor showing. We were angry with him, but others were just disappointed.

Meanwhile, as spring turned to summer, activity became more intense, with much essential 'networking' amongst the Labour Europeans. My diary records a lunch on 18 May, in the embassy-style splendour of Harold Lever's Eaton Square flat, to discuss strategy, at which Roy Jenkins, Shirley, Roy Hattersley and Douglas Houghton, the pro-Europe Chairman of the parliamentary party, were present; and meetings with supporters in the country at Yeovil, Edinburgh, Loughborough, Oxford and Margate. A news item in The Times on 9 June, following my briefing of David Wood, said that thirty Labour MPs were rock-solid for Europe come what may; and the day after, I called together for the first time those back-bench members on my list. Nineteen attended, which was a good number for a Thursday without much parliamentary business, and they showed none of the hesitations that had been worrying Roy Hattersley (although he was entirely firm himself) or that David Marquand and I had momentarily detected in David Owen. Allowing for absentees who had apologised for their absence, members of the shadow cabinet and some senior members I felt it better not to approach yet, I recorded that the 'rock-solid' thirty were now at least forty-five.

What I did not tell the meeting, or the press, or even Roy, was that I had written to the Prime Minister on 3 June to make the case for a free vote across all parties. This was wholly consistent with my promise to those whose support I canvassed that a free vote remained our strongest preference. I made it clear that I was writing on my own account and said that a free vote on the Government side would make it impossible for the Opposition to impose a whip. In turn, this would ensure a much larger majority for entry, and something close to even support for Europe across the main parties. A free vote would also go some way to meet the criticism that parliament was acting arrogantly in the face of hostile public opinion. 'It would be,' I said, 'an unusual act of statesmanship to match a historic decision'.

Ted Heath replied almost at once, saying that no decision had been made on the arrangements for deciding the issue but reminding me that, in Opposition, the Conservatives had imposed a three-line whip to support the Labour Government's application to join the Community. It was a fair point. My own calculation was that over 100 Labour MPs would vote for entry on a free vote, even if Harold Wilson came out for a vote against; and that Tory rebels would number about fifty. Ted Heath was eventually persuaded by his own senior ministers to concede a free vote once he had squeezed down the Tory rebels to a minimum. But it was too late for Labour to change course.

On 24 June I went to Bob Mellish's Bermondsey constituency to debate with Peter Shore, losing by thirty-two votes to seven. Mellish's view about a three-line whip had now changed. He said the issue required a clear party line. If the special Labour conference called for 17 July came out against entry – or the autumn conference did – the parliamentary party would have to follow. This meant a three-line whip.

July was a feverish month. Initially the special conference was a source of great anxiety. Roy was not allowed to speak, as he was a member of the National Executive Commitee which determined who should speak on its behalf. We discussed tactics and I lunched with Derek Gladwin, a member (and later Chairman) of the Conference Arrangements Committee, to ensure his help in avoiding a vote. Fred Hayday, a key trade union figure since Gaitskell's days, agreed to speak, and we held a briefing meeting at St Ermin's Hotel (five minutes from the House of Commons and a favourite meeting place for Labour Europeans) to settle tactics for the day. Our particular anxieties about the conference were the influence that Jim Callaghan might exert, now that he was outflanking Wilson as an anti-Common

Marketeer, and the role of Ian Mikardo, a leader of the left who would be Chairman of the conference.

Passing along the corridor from my House of Commons room one day to a lift, I came across Peter Shore, Jack Mendelson and Brian O'Malley, all committed anti-Marketeers. 'What's this, a little conspiracy?' I asked cheerfully, as they were otherwise friends of mine. They looked a bit sheepish, but denied it. Then the door of Fred Peart's room opened and through the smoke – with a dozen other conspirators in the background – emerged Ian Mikardo. As we got into the lift I said: 'What's the Chairman of the Labour Party doing with all these anti-Marketeers?' He snapped back: 'Can't I meet anyone I like?' But then I asked, more than half in provocation, whether it was true that Jack Jones, the anti-European leader of the Transport and General Workers' Union, had threatened to withdraw trade union sponsorship from all MPs who did not toe the line. 'It's a lie, you know it's a lie and you keep on repeating it!' Mikardo shouted; and as we reached the principal floor, he stalked off angrily. I turned to O'Malley and Shore and asked what on earth had got into him. Both of them were laughing. It seemed that there had been a row and Mikardo had lost the argument. Despite this, he proved a fair Chairman of the special conference, calling speakers from either side; and although Wilson made his firmest anti-Market speech to date, it passed off better than expected.

But tensions were mounting. When Roy spoke at a meeting of the parliamentary party on the Monday two days later, his speech was interrupted by fierce applause; and at the end of it, there was a sustained banging of desks, an unusual form of self-expression on such occasions. It was a strong, powerfully-argued speech and the response was an entirely spontaneous expression of defiance and frustration from pro-Marketeers who felt they were being pushed into a corner by an inexorable process. But Harold Wilson saw things differently. To him, Roy's speech was a deliberate challenge and the response a carefully contrived demonstration. It made him feel insecure and, as so often in the past, he tried to reassert his authority by implicating Roy's supporters – or CDS, as he continued to call us in private – in some trivial wrongdoing. The result was a quite unnecessary row that dominated the newspapers for the rest of the week.

On the Tuesday, in what The Times called 'a remarkable outburst' to the PLP, Harold Wilson attacked parliamentary spokesmen in the Jenkins camp who 'can find it in their hearts to sully their purity by continuing to sit on the front bench at my invitation'. It was an extraordinary choice of words and a very curious sentiment, given that we were in the course of an open debate. It was also typical of Harold in that no names were named, leaving the innuendo to do its unspecific damage. In fact, the newspapers fastened primarily on my name and Roy Hattersley's. Our alleged offence was in leaking to the press, with unflattering comments and ahead of its delivery, the text of the leader's speech to the special conference. The whole idea was farcical. Neither of us had seen the speech, despite Harold Wilson's claim that a copy of it had been circulating at a lunchtime meeting of the Labour Committee for Europe which we had both attended. But in any case, the speech was released to the press by Harold's staff in the early afternoon and no damage had been done by premature disclosure.

I was pretty fed up when this became the front-page story on Wednesday morning, although the general tone of editorial comment was astonishment at Harold Wilson's remarks. At lunch that day I was sitting at the 'cabinet table' in the House of Commons dining room – a table for seven that was usually occupied by the Labour Chief Whip and other senior Labour MPs – when Harold Wilson came in and was obliged to occupy the only vacant seat, which was next to me. After a few tense moments that Bob Mellish tried to fill with chit-chat, I abruptly asked Harold, 'Do you want me to resign from the front bench?' He mumbled something to the effect that there was no need to do so if I hadn't seen the speech, before Mellish intervened, saying, 'No arguments, now'. I then asked Harold if he would see me that evening to discuss the matter, and he agreed.

Passing through the Members' Lobby, where MPs and journalists meet, I was accosted by Bob Carvel, who had already written the lead story for the *Evening Standard* under the banner headline 'Who Told Whom About This Speech?' He asked me about developments, and I told him of my lunchtime exchange with Harold Wilson and of the meeting that had been agreed. Not surprisingly, the next edition of the paper said: 'Mr Rodgers has asked for a showdown interview with Mr Wilson. He wants the Opposition leader to speak plainly and say precisely what action by colleagues he is complaining about.' This was a fair rendering of the position, but Harold immediately sent me a note to say that he was not aware that our conversation had been 'on that basis or that the press were to be informed before it even took place'. This really meant he was annoyed that I had been ahead of him in announcing the meeting, which he would have preferred to describe as the result of a stern summons from him. He told me that the meeting was therefore postponed and would now take place in the presence of the Chief Whip and the Chairman of the parliamentary party.

Postponement meant only that the story dominated Thursday's newspapers. The *Guardian* had a big piece about 'the letter row' and *The Times* gave it four columns on its front page. Bob Maclennan and David Owen were now implicated in the leaking of the speech and there was much – a little too much to make me entirely comfortable – about my wanting 'a straight talk' with Harold Wilson. But at one o'clock I received a message from his office that he would see me at 2.30 and I could bring anyone I liked. It was difficult to round up a team in little over an hour but, in the end, I took Dick Taverne, David Owen, Denis Howell, Dick Mabon and Roy Hattersley. Hattersley was at first reluctant to join me, then relented, although he was anxious that I should not deliver an ultimatum and wanted to speak first. But I opened by saying that we were all concerned with the unity of the party, worried by the events of the week and wanting to cool it. We had been smeared by innuendo which could be particularly damaging to us in our constituencies. We needed to know precisely where we stood on campaigning for Europe. Was he saying, for example, that I should stop counting heads as I was quite openly doing? All my colleagues were outspoken and firm; Douglas Houghton was helpful in supporting the view that Harold's Tuesday remarks had been ill-judged; and even Bob Mellish offered us support by telling Harold that he should summon the offender to see him, as he claimed he knew who he was. Harold then justified his Tuesday statement as needed to steady the party, but exonerated all of us from being guilty of the leak. Further, there was no need for any of us to resign, or curtail our European activities, at least – and here he was a bit vague – until the party finally decided its position at its autumn conference. This was game, set and match to us but we avoided any triumphalist comment and were content for the story of our meeting to appear next day as 'peace all round'. The row had not been of our making and we were glad to put the whole matter behind us. We were certainly not conspiring against Harold as Leader; we wanted merely to continue to campaign and to rally our troops on the merits of the issue.

On 4 August, with the recess imminent, we met at Roy Hattersley's to consider a programme of meetings in the country intended to secure good press coverage to offset the anti-European campaign – of which Jim Callaghan had emerged as the leader – now being organised by the National Executive Committee. I was worried by complacency in our camp about the impact of this but Roy Jenkins, Shirley Williams, George Thomson and Harold Lever committed themselves to a series of meetings, with Hattersley and I filling in a few gaps.

Earlier that day I had taken to a further stage my own main activity of gathering the names of those who would vote for entry against a three-line whip. Jim Wellbeloved, a mainstream, back-bench Labour MP with whom I shared a room, had tried to persuade me that a mass abstention by European-minded Labour MPs would be better than a smaller number voting for entry. I did not dismiss the idea out of hand but asked him to bring me the names of those who, in those circumstances, would join us in abstaining rather than vote against entry. I first agreed that twenty such names would be significant but, as his fruitless search continued, every day reduced the numbers we needed to produce. In the end, Jim admitted defeat. He could find no-one prepared to play his game. He would abstain himself but support the principle of maximising the vote for entry. He hoped that when the Chief Whip was convinced of our numbers, he would relent and advise Harold Wilson that a free vote was the only sensible course.

I had intended to collect signatories for a letter to the Chief Whip when the House returned in October. But Dick Buchanan, the respected Labour Member for Glasgow Springburn, urged me to start doing so before the recess. Accordingly, I went to my room and typed out the formula:

> We feel that you should know that we are amongst those who intend to vote for entry to the Common Market on the terms which have been negotiated.

I put it on the noticeboard for John Smith, who had agreed to collect the signatures of Scottish Members, and it was soon returned with eight names, a good beginning. The final step I took before the House rose was to collect holiday addresses from all my potential voters, putting them on notice for a meeting in the last week week in September, on the eve of the Labour Party conference.

In fact, the House of Commons was unexpectedly recalled for two days during the recess on Northern Ireland business, and our meeting took place on 22 September. I was able to collect more names for the Mellish letter, allocate responsibilities for approaching any waverers (they would be best canvassed by close friends) and lay plans for the crucial three weeks between the end of the Brighton conference and the vote on the principle of joining the European Community which would follow a unique, six-day debate.

The vote at Brighton took place on the Monday and, predictably, was five to one against entry. But our Labour Committee for Europe rally the previous evening attracted an audience of 800 and the issue kept running all week, not wholly to our disavantage. On the Tuesday, in his annual leader's speech, Harold Wilson predictably called on pro-Marketeers to come into line, but this received a cool reception even from those MPs who intended to vote with the party. There followed a private press briefing to the effect that there would be no disciplinary action against us if we behaved ourselves after 28 October, but this olive branch was then withdrawn under pressure from Ian Mikardo. In the face of such blowing hot and cold, we maintained the initiative with a clear and determined line. On Tuesday my round robin to the Chief Whip made news; and on Wednesday a Labour Committee for Europe manifesto resulted in a complaint to Roy from Harold Wilson that it had upstaged reports of his own speech. Roy was welcomed to the rostrum for his speech on economic policy by long applause, which was a measure of the intensity of support for him in the conference. By the end of the week, and much against expectations, the pro-Europeans had come out of it all rather well.

But there was a danger of overplaying our hand. James Margach's lead story in the *Sunday Times* was a rather nasty piece under the headline 'The Jolly Rodgers flies over Brighton'. When I saw Roy at East Hendred, he was worried about excessive publicity and expectations being raised too high. The question of whether he could remain Deputy Leader unless he gave an undertaking always to vote with the party after 28 October was also being discussed.

Two days later, on 12 October, a carefully chosen delegation joined me in a meeting with the Chief Whip. I left out David Marquand, David Owen and other young Turks and took Carol Johnson, a former full-time official of the PLP, Arthur Palmer, who had first been elected in 1945, Ben Ford, sponsored by the engineering union, and Dick Mabon, representing the Scots. These would be seen as solid and fair-minded men who would not readily rock the boat. When we saw Mellish we emphasised the representative character of the dissidents on my list who included twelve members of the trade union group. I showed him the letter with its fifty-seven signatures, saying that I believed he should expect between sixty-five and seventy to vote for entry. He then asked how we intended to vote on the Bill which would implement the Treaty of Accession. I replied that most of us would vote with the party while hoping that legislation would not be fought line by line, night after night as Michael Foot was threatening. Mellish was generally conciliatory, accepting our numbers and even hinting that if there were 100 votes for entry at the party meeting a free vote was still a possibility.

Getting 100 votes was not as easy as it sounded. Not all of those on my list would turn up for a party meeting; and those who had now decided to vote with the party had little interest in making it easier for the recalcitrants. When *The Sunday Times, The Times* and *The Guardian* all said that the Government could only win on Labour votes, the pressure on us was intense and the idea of a free vote increasingly unacceptable to the majority. Despite this, a motion in favour of a free vote was defeated only by 140 votes to 111. But Mellish's hint came to nothing. Now he accepted the recommendation of the parliamentary party as a decision. There was little left for me to do but hold my troops against final attempts to demoralise and dislodge them and to prepare for the debate that would begin on 21 October and conclude on Thursday 28 October, my forty-third birthday.

As the shadow cabinet chose the speakers to represent the party's official point of view, Roy was again in the ridiculous position of not being allowed to speak in the debate. George Thomson, Shirley Williams and Harold Lever were similarly placed as part of the minority in the shadow cabinet. In the circumstances I asked to see the Speaker, Selwyn Lloyd, to discuss the names he might call to represent our point of view. Over a very large pre-lunch gin he was most helpful and asked for a list, which I provided, with the days and times when they would prefer to be called. I decided to speak on the first day to leave me free thereafter to look after my group through a period of increasing tension. Unlike many well-trailed debates which fail to fulfil their promise, there was a sense of a great occasion. The attendance of Members was steady, with good support for speakers representing minority views in their parties. For the first time I had the experience of Members coming into the Chamber to hear me, with about sixty on the benches when I started and 150 sitting and standing when I finished sixteen minutes later. I was heard in silence, and there was a good House of Commons shout of approval at the end. The *Daily Telegraph* described it as 'a dignified performance' involving 'polite defiance of the party line'. That is what I had aimed at, because there was no point now in rhetoric of a kind that might put off any waverers.

In view of the arguments about Europe that were to continue for many years and rack the Conservative Party in the 1990s, with the antis arguing that the political consequences of joining were never taken fully into account, it is worth recalling what the *Daily Telegraph* reported of the debate:

> Continuing a trend, MPs turned more and more to talking about the issue of sovereignty and tended to be rather brief on economic topics. It has now got through to a lot more MPs that sovereignty is a vital issue.

The House of Commons was making up its mind through almost forty hours of continuous debate, following ten years in which the issue of joining the Common Market had been at the top of the national agenda. The antis were entitled to deplore the outcome, but they could hardly claim, then or later, that the argument over sovereignty had not been heard.

While the debate continued in the Chamber, there were agonising discussions outside it about whether Roy and shadow cabinet members intending to vote against a three-line whip should first resign. When I called on Roy that evening he mentioned sleepless nights. Harold Lever wanted to go and Shirley Williams said that five out of six middle-rank shadow ministers said they all should do so. But Roy had been both surprised and fortified by a pledge of support from Ted Short, who had said: 'We hardly know each other, and didn't get on in government, but I have the highest regard for your stand and will do all that I can to help'. I was joined at dinner by Dick Crossman, who was as perverse as ever, arguing that if too many Labour pro-Marketeers voted for entry it would be damaging to Roy who would then be challenged for the deputy leadership by Willie Ross. This did not seem to me an intimidating prospect, and I concluded that Crossman was simply up to his usual mischief.

On the Friday morning I travelled to Stockton to meet members of my party's Management Committee. Most were friendly, even those who were not happy about what I proposed to do. I concluded that the following weekend I would ask for a vote of personal confidence on a motion I would draft, but would not seek positive endorsement of my action. I returned to London by sleeper and saw Roy three times over the weekend. The crisis about early resignation seemed to have passed and his thoughts were turning to the post–28 October situation.

On the Monday I declined to appear on a *Panorama* programme about Europe, feeling that all my time and energy should go into holding the troops through the remaining few days; and on 25 October I sent a note to all those on my list of Labour MPs committed to vote for entry. It began:

> A determined effort is being made to undermine our strength. The whips see it as their duty to do so. Their method is to imply hesitation in others and to quote the example of colleagues whom we have never expected to vote with us.

It concluded:

> But the facts are simple. There is still overwhelming evidence that over sixty of us will be in the lobby voting for entry on Thursday night.

By Wednesday I had my final tally: allowing for the notional loss of three supporters at the final hurdle, I believed that I could count on sixty-six. I told David Wood, and he was sufficiently convinced that it was the most authoritative available figure (the whips were still talking down our expectations) for it to appear in *The Times* the following day as the likely outcome.

At that stage I had only a vague idea of how many Tories would vote against entry, but on the morning of the 28th I walked down the corridor from my room and called on Sir Gerald Nabarro, the colourful MP for Kidderminster, who would certainly be one of them, to get his view. He told me there would be thirty-six Tory rebels, which I accepted.

With little else to do, it was now time for a flutter. I telephoned Eldon Griffiths, who was running a sweepstake, and put £1 on an overall majority of 111. Then I found Ian Mikardo who, as usual, was keeping a book. He offered me odds of five to one against a majority of over 100: I put on £5. Finally, I walked up Whitehall to Ladbrokes, entering a betting shop for the first time in my life, to put £3 on a majority of between 110 and 115. Meanwhile Silvia, taking advice from Peter Jenkins – who was protectively sceptical about my forecast – spread her bets around my figure.

In the evening, Ron Brown (George's elder brother) was threatened with being beaten up by a trade union delegation from his constituency and decided to abstain, but I had no wind of any other slippage. In fact, when the division had been held and the votes counted, we had lost one but gained four, to give a vote for entry of 69 Labour MPs with 20 abstentions and an overall majority of 112. It was, by any measure, a highly satisfactory outcome given that the free vote we wanted had been denied to us. As for the winnings, mine amounted to £95, while Silvia collected £70. Thus was virtue doubly rewarded.

That Sunday I went back to Stockton. There was some reluctance to pursue the matter of how I had voted in the division, but I insisted that a confidence motion should be discussed. I asked not for approval but an acknowledgment of my right, as

Member of Parliament for Stockton, to vote according to my conscience on a great historic issue after I had discussed it fully with both my constituents and my local party. The motion was carried by thirty-four votes to none, a highly satisfactory result which left my position in Stockton secure.

What turned out to be not so secure was my position as the party's front-bench spokesman on civil aviation. Despite previous hints from Harold Wilson that there would be no recriminations, Roy was certain he would sack me, which seemed to be confirmed by some typically oblique remarks about my being the public relations officer for the pro-Marketeers. I wrote to Harold to ask at what point my counting of heads had become unacceptable, given that it was always in the open and he had confirmed in July that he had no objection to my doing so, but he did not reply. Meanwhile I was nominated again for the shadow cabinet (with Roy Hattersley, amongst others, standing down at the request of Roy Jenkins to allow me a clearer run) and received eighty votes, putting me within six places of election and usually quite sufficient to ensure a decent front-bench job. But it was not sufficient on this occasion. Walking through the Division Lobby I was approached by Bruce Millan. 'I hope', he said, 'that there will be no hard feelings if I accept the job of shadowing civil aviation Harold has just offered me?' This meant I had been sacked, although I had heard nothing whatsoever from Harold himself. So it was my mischievous pleasure to ask for confirmation and tell the press of the round-about way in which Harold had taken his revenge.

Five others were dropped from the front bench. Four of them were a rather odd selection of junior spokesmen who had voted for entry – David Marquand but not David Owen, for example, nor Roy Hattersley – but the most inexplicable dismissal was of Cledwyn Hughes, a former cabinet minister who had only abstained on 28 October. If there were to be any reprisals I was an obvious target, and I could not reasonably complain about being sacked although Harold Wilson should have done it face to face, taking me to task for my behaviour. As it was, the circumstances of my fate even gave me a few bonus points for character amongst my parliamentary colleagues.

But in the flow of great events, these were minor incidents. Far more important was Roy's future as Deputy Leader. In November he was re-elected and, although his lead over Michael Foot was narrow, it was a considerable achievement to pick up between 50 and 70 votes (to give a total of 140) from amongst those who had voted against entry. It was just possible that the party would now settle down without any further damaging upheaval, but by February the exhilaration of 28 October had been replaced by the depressing experience of voting against the European Communities Bill. We claimed that the vote of October was a vote of principle which justified our decision to defy the party whip but that the Government should not require our support to get its own legislation. But there was no logic or moral justification in this. We were simply coming back into the fold out of loyalty to the party and anxiety about where continued dissent might take us. I was ashamed and in tears when I went through the Division Lobby against the Second Reading on 17 February (Harold Lever was physically sick), and erratic in my attendance at its further stages. But there was no such escape for Roy, least of all when the shadow cabinet narrowly voted to support an amendment to the Bill in favour of a referendum.

Now, a quarter of a century later, the idea of a referendum is not shocking. But in the early months of 1972 it was seen as much as a device to humiliate Roy and put the pro-Marketeers on the spot as a constitutional innovation to be considered on its merits. It was calculated to divide the party in a way that the long debate on Europe since Hugh Gaitskell's time had never entirely done. The right approach would have been to bind up the wounds of 28 October and let the healing process take its course.

In February, after the Second Reading vote, I told Roy that I believed he should resign. By Easter, six weeks later, I was much more reticent, although aware of how deeply unhappy he had become. The best comfort I could offer – and it was not much comfort – was that in resigning he would win his freedom. But although I believed he was still five-to-one favourite to succeed Wilson, he would be no better than evens after resignation. I was, I think, torn between a cool assessment of the right political course – to stay – and my instinct, reflecting my own emotional turmoil, that Roy would be so obviously miserable that he would lose authority and be open to defeat by Michael Foot if challenged again for the deputy leadership. On 2 April I noted in my diary: 'If I was in Roy's shoes I would resign', but when I wrote to him five days later I fell short of translating that view into a firm conclusion. I said that the initiative was slipping from the Europeans as our sense of direction became less clear, but although resignation would create a new situation, it might not be to our advantage. But for all the conflicting advice his friends gave him, the decision was Roy's alone, and on 10 April he resigned, together with George Thomson and Harold Lever, although not Shirley (nor, less surprisingly, Roy Hattersley).

This was a momentous event, but I did not foresee its full significance, which was that from now on Labour Europeans were to be outsiders in the party. Those who kept their heads down and subordinated their European convictions to strenuous party loyalty on every other issue were forgiven. But others of us, particularly those close to Roy, were regarded almost as if we were a different species. Perhaps there was some initial justification in that we found it hard to conceal the contempt we felt for our party having stood on its head over Europe. But if a wariness towards us – occasionally mixed with guilt – was understandable, the tendency to treat us as outsiders weakened the party's ability to resist the dangerous drift to the left during the 1970s.

The vote of 28 October 1971 and Roy's subsequent resignation had rearranged the pieces on a chessboard of the Labour Party, separating the European knights from the anti-European bishops of the right and centre. It took a long time to put them together again.

The period from Roy's resignation until the general election of 1974 was gloomy. I enjoyed chairing my select committee, spent time usefully in Stockton and wrote a controversial column for the monthly magazine *Socialist Commentary*, but much of the pleasure had gone out of politics. Dick Taverne had been less fortunate than I in his constituency party, and was soon embroiled in a bitter dispute which led to his resignation as Labour MP for Lincoln, and a by-election in March 1973 which he fought – and won – as a Democratic Labour candidate. I did not share his view that he was merely anticipating an inevitable split in the Labour Party and, much as I wanted him to win, I could hardly campaign for him against the official Labour candidate. The compromise was for Silvia to go to Lincoln in the by-election (although as much from her own choice as on my behalf); and, in order to be even-handed, to spend some days in the Chester-le-Street by-election in support of the Labour candidate Giles Radice, where polling would be on the same day. I was delighted to welcome Dick back to the House of Commons and, to be fair to my Labour colleagues, they did not expect me to treat him other than as a friend with whom I would associate as freely in the bars and tea room as in the past.

But it must have been assumed that my own future was uncertain – if only because the Labour Party might be uncertain about me – for I received two unexpected offers, one of which would have taken me out of politics altogether. The first was to become a director of Securicor, which was emerging as a leading security firm with a negotiating agreement with my own trade union, the General and Municipal Workers. But I was uneasy at what looked like private-enterprise policing, and turned it down. I took much more seriously an approach from a head-hunter from Ward Howell International, who asked me if I wanted to become Director-General of the Office of Fair Trading that would be established under the bill currently passing through the House of Commons. Here was a chance to run a new organisation in an area of great interest to me and with a salary of £15,000 – four times my parliamentary salary and well over twice my total earnings (I was now doing some management recruiting and head-hunting myself). I would have a clear role, giving scope for measurable achievement, and a degree of peace after the turbulence of politics. For ten days I turned the matter over. Roy Jenkins was shaken that I might consider leaving the House but felt – perhaps because of the uncertainty about his own future – that he should not influence me. Others were similarly cautious, aware of the attraction of the job and that Harold Wilson would not reappoint me as a shadow minister. But in the end it was Silvia and my daughters who, in a family conclave, declared that politics was my life and they could not seriously believe that I would be happier out of it. If I left the House of Commons now, I would always regret it and there were more important things for me to do in the next few years than protecting the consumer. I telephoned the head-hunter to decline, and the possibility that I might have voluntarily left parliament disappeared quickly behind me.

Outsiders in the party we might be, but with Britain's entry to the Community on 1 January 1973, Labour's Europeans had achieved their central purpose. George Thomson was installed as a Commissioner in Brussels and, although a great loss to our ranks in the House of Commons, kept in touch with us on his frequent visits to London. In George's place, I became Chairman of the Labour Committee for Europe and, at its annual general meeting early in 1973, said that we should now accept as inevitable the renegotiation by a Labour government of the terms of entry, even if this was a preliminary to a referendum we were still against. I was personally optimistic that Harold Wilson and Jim Callaghan – lined up to become Foreign Secretary – would want renegotiation to be a success. Meanwhile, Labour Europeans should organise discreetly and keep their powder dry. John Roper and David Marquand wrote a pamphlet on 'A Labour Britain in Europe'; visits were arranged to Brussels for party activists and trade unionists; and a widening circle of personal contacts was established. I had regular lunches with Shirley, to keep her involved; and Roy Jenkins readily made himself available for meetings.

But in the course of these preparations for any change of government as the date for a general election drew closer, there was, perhaps for the first time, a difference of emphasis between Roy and myself about the future. As Roy has subsequently written, for four years as Deputy Leader he had held the lead position on the inside track to succeed Harold Wilson. Now, without that advantage, he had to run faster to retain any chance of winning. But for all he might do to husband his credit on the European and international wing of the Labour Party and to campaign loyally round the country, especially at by-elections, he was unlikely to succeed unless Labour lost the next election. Not-wanting-Labour-to-win thus became part of his mind-set.

He never made this explicit when we talked together, either because it would be very damaging if he became identified with such a point of view or – more likely – because he thought I would disapprove. But it was not so much a matter of disapproval on my part as of being unable to accommodate myself to the idea of not wanting to win. That Labour did not deserve to win, given its behaviour on Europe and the inflationary Social Contract it had agreed with the trade unions, I did not doubt, and said as much in a *Sunday Times* article which questioned the party's institutional links with the unions and was critical of the role of Hugh Scanlon and Jack Jones. But wanting to lose went too far. There was also more than a vague irritation tucked away inside me that Roy and his generation – meaning mainly Crosland and Healey

– had somehow failed us and that Shirley and I and our contemporaries should not be deprived of having our chance in cabinet. I still very much wanted Roy to become Leader of the Labour Party and believed that if he showed a fighting sense of purpose and reminded Labour MPs of his great parliamentary and ministerial skills, he could still re-emerge as Harold Wilson's natural successor. After all, Jim Callaghan had returned from the dead despite his failure as Chancellor in the 1960s. I saw no reason why Roy should not come storming back finally to outpace him even without a Labour defeat.

In September 1973 I wrote a position paper, sending a copy to Roy. 'Apart from illness', I said, 'there is no chance whatsoever of Wilson giving up the leadership this side of the election. Nor is there any chance of beating him in a ballot.' It was possible that he might be challenged by a maverick candidate of the left like Eric Heffer, and it would be a bold and clever gesture for Tony Crosland to rehabilitate himself in the top echelon of the parliamentary party by standing but, on balance, I was against Roy doing so. I then turned to what might happen after a general election:

> If we win, the question answers itself and I wouldn't be surprised if Wilson survived to the end of that Parliament. If we lose, I do not take for granted that Wilson will resign. With the left well entrenched in the trade unions and the NEC, he will lean over to them. The PLP will have lost perhaps twenty of its most doughty fighters and the new Members will not be immediately eager to ditch the man who presided over an election that returned them to parliament for the first time.

I concluded that either way, looking to whether we won or lost, Roy's strength would be greatest if he returned to the shadow cabinet and was seen to have played his full part in the election.

For the time being, all went to plan. Roy stood for the shadow cabinet, was elected near the top, and then shortly before the House rose for the Christmas recess was at his devastating best in virtually destroying Anthony Barber's reputation as Chancellor of the Exchequer in a single, dramatic winding-up speech. The problem was that despite this excursion into economic affairs, in returning to the front bench he had been obliged to become Shadow Home Secretary. This was not calculated either to arouse his enthusiasm or to ensure that he was well-placed to win any leadership contest. Earlier in the year a small group of Jenkinsites, who met regularly for lunch to discuss the political scene, had concluded that if Roy returned to the front bench in government it should only be as Chancellor. But Roy baulked at the idea which he saw as fraught with difficulties and unpleasantness, especially – although he did not say this – as he did not have his heart in fighting to win the election.

On 6 February 1974, with the assumption that polling day would be on 28 February or soon after, the same group met for lunch at Bob Maclennan's, with Roy,

David Marquand, David Owen, Patrick Gordon Walker, John Harris and Betty Boothroyd, newly elected to parliament, amongst those present. Roy discovered unanimity on two points: that if Labour won, he should insist on becoming Chancellor; and if Labour lost, he should challenge Wilson for the leadership without delay. Given a small Tory lead in the opinion polls, the expectation of a miners' strike and a 'Who Governs Britain?' theme for the campaign, the prospect was that he would be faced with the second course. But we spent more time discussing the first and Roy, despite his triumph over Barber which had put Denis Healey's claim to be Chancellor in the shade, was as uncomfortable with the idea as he had been six months earlier. We shared with him the view that the election could have no outcome that would raise our spirits but, with the huge advantage of not having the burden of choice before us, we assessed the options with detachment.

The election was announced the day after our meeting, allowing a campaign of precisely three weeks. My constituency had been sufficiently redistributed to make comparisons with 1970 difficult, but a majority of 12,371 on 75.2 per cent turnout was good enough. In the country, the revival of the Liberals, who won six million votes, and came second in 146 seats, was the most significant factor and evidence that the two-party system was breaking down. As a result, the question was whether the Conservatives, with only 38.2 per cent of the vote, would remain in office or be displaced by Labour, with only 37.2 per cent.

On the Friday after polling day I made my usual victory tour around Stockton, then left with Silvia for London. As we listened on the car radio, the results from the Tory shires were declared, eroding Labour's initial majority of seats and making the outcome uncertain. When we arrived at Patshull Road just before seven, there was a message from Jennifer Jenkins, so I telephoned. I spoke to Roy and he said would we go over to Ladbroke Square, although there wasn't much to eat. Silvia, who had felt car sick, was disinclined, so I went alone, arriving about 8.30. There certainly wasn't much to eat – cold meat and rather mangy salad and a bit of cheese and some wine. Roy was very tired and depressed and had drunk a fair amount. At first the conversation was desultory, about how we had fought the election and his experience of it and mine. Roy took the view that Enoch Powell had certainly influenced the result in the West Midlands. We then talked about what would happen if Harold Wilson did form a government. I repeated the view I had taken before the election: that the Treasury was the one job that really mattered and it was where Roy was needed.

This clearly didn't fill him with any greater pleasure now than previously but he said, 'Well, I suppose so if it is only until the autumn', which I took to mean until a further, early general election, which seemed inevitable.

The following day was full of predictable telephone conversations, and some surprising ones. With John Roper I agreed that if a Labour government was to be formed, Labour Europeans must be part of it. And I rejected a suggestion from David Owen that Roy might become Leader of the House, seeing that as a role for Jim Callaghan, whose parliamentary skills and wheeler-dealing would be required with a tiny government majority. It would also free the Foreign Office for Denis Healey, thus conveniently making room for Roy at the Treasury.

One surprising call was from Tony Benn. Despite recording in his diary two years earlier that I was 'an intolerable man', he had twice invited me to his home in Holland Park Avenue for a political *tour d'horizon*. Our conversation now took a similar form, although he was mainly keen to persuade me that there should be no coalition with the Liberals or prior agreement on the contents of the Queen's Speech. He sounded rather less hysterical than usual, but I did not risk any discussion about Roy's future, especially because I thought he was probably taping our conversation.

When Roy spoke to me on Sunday he was a good deal more cheerful than thirty-six hours before. He was also conciliatory to the extent of telling me, with a certain rabbit-out-of-the-hat relish, that he was preparing a memorandum for Harold Wilson which would open the door to the possibility of his becoming Chancellor of the Exchequer again. This was good news and, as Harold could hardly risk forming a government without him, I began to persuade myself that victory had been won. But next day we had our greatest disappointment since Roy became the acknowledged leader of the former Gaitskellites.

The group of us who had met at Bob Maclennan's on the eve of the election had agreed to meet again, this time at Harry Walston's apartment in Albany, on the Monday evening after polling day. As we assembled, on this occasion some twenty strong, we learnt that Ted Heath, having failed to persuade Jeremy Thorpe's Liberals to support a continuation of his Government, had resigned. Harold Wilson had been to the Palace and would shortly return to Downing Street. We were excited by these events but apprehensive of where we, the Jenkinsites, would now stand. We waited anxiously for Roy and the news he would bring.

When he arrived he said without delay that he was to become Home Secretary and the only remaining question was whether he would also take on Northern Ireland. This was greeted with dismay. Patrick Gordon Walker typically suggested that it might all be for the best, and David Owen untypically went along with him, although he had hoped that Roy would become Chancellor. But I said that it was defeat and there was nothing more to talk about, cruelly adding, 'How many votes are there in prison reform?' With an accusing bitterness and remembering his previous reluctance I demanded: 'Did you make clear you wanted the Treasury?' Roy now became as angry as I had ever known him to be, replying that unless you were Prime Minister you could not make such decisions about your own future. He then threatened to walk out if we persisted in this pointless questioning. Later he apologised for being petulant but he had every cause to complain. I was so immersed in my own disappointment that I failed to see the depth of his anguish or the extent of his exhaustion. Later we all talked more calmly about the future, with Roy making the point that as none of us had ever really believed in Harold Wilson, why should we expect more from him now? On that wry note, we dispersed.

After a good night's sleep, I felt better the following day. My sober assessment remained that in the hierarchy of the government, Roy was now below Callaghan, Healey and Michael Foot. He would recover some lost ground through his ministerial performance, but there was no question that he had suffered a huge defeat. David Owen and David Marquand telephoned to say how awful the previous evening had been and I particularly recalled the face of Cledwyn Hughes, most unkindly treated two years earlier and most let down now. I also became aware that my own ministerial future was in doubt. If there was to be another Labour government I preferred to be part of it but, as appointments were announced from Downing Street, this seemed increasingly unlikely.

On the Wednesday morning I had a press conference to launch my South African report and bought champagne for my select committee, which we drank on the Terrace. Then I met Roy by chance and he took me to Brooks's for lunch. He was still pretty low and, although our friendship was entirely restored after the events of Monday night, I did nothing to relieve his misery when I said that I had never expected him to return to government without my doing so. From a distance of many years, this seems to have been another heartless remark, but it arose out of a low-keyed assessment of where Roy's future now stood and the consequences of the promotion to the cabinet of Merlyn Rees, Jim Callaghan's close colleague and aide. In the past, Roy had been thoughtful and assiduous in nurturing the interests of his younger friends. For once, deeply preoccupied with a turning point in his own career, he had failed to do so. Apart from John Harris, who would go to the Lords and join him as Minister of State at the Home Office, it looked as if all of us might be left out.

What precisely passed that afternoon when Roy went to see Harold Wilson again I do not know, but on the Thursday evening I received a summons to Downing Street for the following day, as David Owen and Bob Maclennan subsequently did. It was almost too late, as I had conditioned myself to being out of government and a free spirit on the back benches, very much my own man.

Perhaps this contributed to a remarkably relaxed, even friendly conversation with Harold Wilson, during which I said that my main concern was that my select committee's report on South Africa should be implemented. I thanked him, without resentment or irony, for offering me a job and he suggested I might like time to consider whether to accept. Leaving Number 10, I felt dejected by the decision I was faced with and talked for advice to almost anyone I could find, including Bill, the policeman who was 'Back of the Chair' at the House of Commons, who said, 'Take it, why not?' But even Silvia was uncertain. Those, like David Owen, who were joining the Government, inevitably said 'accept', while David Marquand, who looked like being left out, said neither one thing nor the other. Roy was quite clear that I should accept; and indeed it would have been very strange, in view of our Wednesday conversation, had I not done so. So two hours after my first visit I went back to Number 10 and said, 'I've thought about it, Harold, and the answer is "Yes".' He said, 'I'm glad', and seemed relieved, emphasising how important the job was and that it would be paid at the top rate for a full minister outside the cabinet. So as I left I asked, 'Does that mean I'm a Privy Councillor?' and, hesitating for a moment, he replied, 'Yes, it may mean that'. I wasn't pressing hard but I thought that if other senior ministers were Privy Councillors I might as well become one. Meanwhile I had become Minister of State for Defence.

Chapter 7

Dancing to Beethoven

With Labour pledged to renegotiations and a referendum, Britain's future in Europe would again be the main issue in the new parliament and I saw preparations for fighting the referendum as my main extramural activity. But for the moment I had to find my way around a new department. Like the Foreign Office, Defence looked after its ministers well. Sergeant Dave Bourne, my driver – civilianised into mufti for security reasons – was happy to be available day and night. He assumed that taking Silvia shopping was part of his duties, and had to be persuaded that the rules governing the use of ministerial cars were rather stricter than those applying to senior officers. He knew where a leg of lamb was to be had at a bargain, and supplied me with Ordnance Survey maps free from an unspecified source when I announced that I intended to buy them at Stanfords in Covent Garden. My Private Secretary, David Young, was always in command of business, keeping me in line if I was in danger of confusing my ministerial and party roles. David Young was a grammar-school boy from Sheffield and I detected in him values very like my own. Years later I tried unsuccessfully to recruit him as the first Chief Executive of the SDP and thus lodged in him the idea that the civil service might not be his only career. When I met him again he was Deputy Chairman of the John Lewis Partnership.

Managing the private office was a specially sensitive job at Defence, given three services all jealous of their own interests and with officers of every rank to match their civilian counterparts. If in my previous departments I had a particular point I wanted to discuss I would ask to see the principal who had immediate knowledge of it. But at Defence, if it was an inter-service matter, the Army, the Navy and the RAF would want to be represented at the meeting, although not by anyone as junior – and unversed in the tricky politics of Whitehall – as a colonel, junior captain in the Navy or group captain in the RAF whose ranks, to my surprise, were classified as equal to that of a principal. In no time at all I would find myself with an assistant secretary in support of the principal, thus enabling each of the services to match him with a Whitehall warrior of more senior rank and sophisticated experience. A short meeting with a single adviser had now become a much longer one with eight participants. No wonder my office overlooking the river was equipped with enough chairs for a public meeting.

The Permanent Secretary was Sir Michael Cary, son of Joyce Cary, the novelist; a gentle, courteous man, much concerned that I should be happy in the department. He was matched – and more than matched – on the service side by the Chief of the Defence Staff, the formidable Field Marshal Sir Michael Carver, who had a rigorous intelligence and sometimes a wounding tongue. Under pressure, he developed a slight stammer. I found it difficult to judge whether this was the result of irritation at the stupidity of his opponents or of trying to suppress the suspicion that they might be right. He had a strong political sense, not in accommodating to the whims of ministers but in independently recognising the full strategic consequences of Britain's diminished resources.

In the spring of 1974 I was sent off to Malaysia, Singapore, Australia and New Zealand to consult, as part of another defence review, about Britain's final withdrawal from East of Suez. I had an RAF VC10 at my disposal and a small staff, and I enjoyed my trip. In Kuala Lumpur I talked to the Defence Minister, who preferred to avoid comment on decisions he believed had been taken. In Singapore, Lee Kuan Yew, not yet the authoritarian Prime Minister he was later to become, said that the decisions were wrong, but that he was relaxed about withdrawal as it had been anticipated in Denis Healey's White Paper of 1968.

But the mood was different in Canberra and Wellington. The Australians said they would close their own air force base in Malaysia if Britain left; and in New Zealand I found a dependency culture that assumed Britain would still guarantee security in South-East Asia. Descending to Wellington through fluffy white clouds, and avoiding the dark mountain peaks that emerged from them, I was captivated by what still looked like a colonial settlement with brightly coloured wooden houses dotted about the steep slopes that rose from the bay. Perhaps that contributed to my wish to salvage some minimum comfort for those whom I had been sent to consult, because high over the Indian Ocean on my way home I devised a plan to keep a communications unit in Singapore at what was, in terms of defence spending, the knock-down price of £12.5 million. The admiral who was my military adviser joined enthusiastically in the drafting and, by the time my VC10 arrived back at Lyneham in Wiltshire, I had a memorandum I believed Roy Mason (Secretary of State for Defence) and the Overseas and Defence Committee of the cabinet would accept.

But I did not allow for Mike Carver. He shot down my memorandum in flames. He did not dispute the practicality of what I proposed or that my communications unit would serve some purpose. But the policy of successive governments was to put all available resources into NATO. Spending even as little as £12.5 million in Singapore would be a frivolous departure from our central purpose. His conclusion – a political one – won the day, and my mission to far-away places marked one more predictable stage in the ending of Empire.

Following the early departure from office of the Army Minister, Colonel Brayley – the owner of a glass-blowing factory in Canning Town who had been elevated from anonymity to the House of Lords as a reward for making generous donations to the party – there was, for the first time since 1945, no minister in the department with war-time military experience. Denis Healey's role as a beachmaster at the Anzio landings in 1944 had stood him in good stead as Secretary of State; at least he had seen war and understood military realities. Neither Roy Mason, who was a Yorkshire miner before entering parliament, nor I could set any such knowledge to advantage in discussions with the chiefs of staff. If the head of one of the services claimed that the potential human cost of failing to buy new defence equipment might run into thousands of lives lost, it was a brave minister who did not weaken. The choice was seldom put so brutally, but the chiefs were determined in getting their way and only tough ministers stood up to them. They also had the privilege of direct access to Number 10 and an active speaking role, equal to that of ministers, in the relevant cabinet committee. On the whole I enjoyed their robust advocacy and, with help from my civil service advisers, could tell when two and two failed to make four, even in arcane areas of defence procurement. They tended to expect an easier passage from their representations to Roy Mason, so I learnt the art of the pre-emptive strike by which I would get his endorsement of my decisions before they had a chance to challenge them.

But they were not easily defeated. When I arrived in the department I discovered that early decisions had to be reached on the purchase of four new guided-missile systems. I insisted that they should be taken together as a 'package', as I was sure they would raise the usual difficult question of whether we should buy American or British. The chiefs of staff generally preferred to buy American because the equipment had been successfully developed, was cheaper and would be compatible within NATO. But ministers were under great pressure to buy British to support advanced technology, especially avionics, and jobs in the defence industries, even when the risks of escalating costs and reduced performance were high.

When I received the first submissions from the chiefs of staff, I discovered that three of the recommendations – to buy the Franco-German Milan, the American Sub-Harpoon and the British Sea Skua – were not seriously in doubt. But in the fourth, finely balanced case of an anti-tank helicopter system, the chiefs came out in favour of Tow, an American alternative to the British Hawkswing, while I thought that the margin of advantage was so narrow that British industry should be given its chance. At the end of an appropriately long discussion with the Secretary of State, Roy Mason came down on my side, perhaps because he had already taken informal soundings with the Prime Minister about what he preferred. The decision – to buy all four new systems – then went to the Overseas Policy and Defence Committee of the cabinet and was approved.

But that was not the end of the matter. A few weeks later, the summer parliamentary recess intervening, I received a memorandum. The chiefs of staff, it said, had taken the opportunity to review the urgency of their needs for new equipment against the defence budget and had decided that some replacements should be postponed. This meant that it was no longer necessary to proceed immediately with a decision on a new anti-tank helicopter missile. In effect the chiefs were saying that if they could not have the American system Tow, they would not take Hawkswing. When the announcement was finally made on 23 September 1975, 'financial pressures' were given as the reason for deferment and the development of Hawkswing was brought to an end.

The chiefs of staff were far too intelligent to deny that there are two sides to every question, but the military mind found it difficult to admit doubt, presumably because an army seeks to advance or is forced to retreat and cannot be seen to be dithering in between. But intellectual 'dithering' is part of the process of decision-making and ministers might have benefited from a more open exchange of ideas with their service advisers.

Ministers were particularly vulnerable when senior officers were joined in their representations by Sir Lester Suffield, Head of Defence Sales. He had spent most of his life in the motor industry, lately with British Leyland, and I found him a hard, sharply-focused man who resented any political restraint on the selling of defence equipment to any willing buyer. These were the days when the Shah of Iran was a favourite in Whitehall, both as one of the West's few friends in a strategically important part of the Middle East and as a valued customer for British goods. The Navy was eager to win ministerial approval for what was known as a through-deck cruiser, a mini-aircraft carrier with a complement of helicopters and jump-jet Harriers. But within the defence budget it was impossible to sanction development on operational grounds. The case was then promoted, with the naval staff and the Head of Defence Sales singing in chorus, for buying the through-deck cruiser for the Navy, as it could then – but only then – be successfully sold to the Shah. When I raised the question of whether the Shah had any need for such a fighting ship, this was regarded as seriously irrelevant. As for Iran having the personnel to operate a highly complex and sophisticated piece of equipment, for Britain to offer the necessary expensive training was seen as yet another export opportunity. At that stage the through-deck cruiser did not go ahead and the Shah disappeared from the scene long before one could have been delivered. But on many lesser occasions there was intense pressure on ministers to agree to purchase additional equipment for the three services because of the export potential once it had become operational. Sir Richard Scott's report of 1996, on arms for Iraq, was a commentary on the continuing hazards of defence sales – which also present problems for Tony Blair's Government, given the ethical dimension to its foreign policy.

When the chiefs of staff came forward with a joint submission, it was difficult to prise them apart to discover the conflicts of opinion that had preceded what was almost certainly an inter-service deal. Ministers were no longer faced directly with the internecine service rivalries that had been commonplace in the past, but this made it harder to tease out the options necessary to an informed discussion. The independent advice of civil servants – the civilians in the department – became especially valuable, including that of the Chief Scientist, Sir Herman Bondi. Professor Bondi looked like a caricature of a Whitehall boffin, with thick glasses, stand-up hair and a wide mouth; he later became head of Churchill College, Cambridge. Another source of sound advice was the Head of Defence Procurement, Sir George Leitch, a mathematician by training and a wartime expert in operational research. When I became Secretary of State for Transport, I persuaded him to become chairman of a committee to assess the case for building new trunk roads. Long after he had retired, the criteria laid down by the Leitch Committee still commanded wide acceptance.

The career civil servant of whom I saw most was Arthur Hockaday, who had briefly been Denis Healey's Private Secretary. He was the Deputy Secretary in charge of planning and policy, which put him close to those Foreign Office officials concerned with the strategic consequences of the Cold War. He was always intellectually stimulating and could hold his own with the defence analysts of the Pentagon and the Brookings Institute. Off duty, his passion was for railway timetables and interesting ways to travel, and when I decided to visit the long-running arms reduction talks in Vienna, he suggested that part of my journey should be by Danube steamer. Arthur, Silvia and I, together with a small staff, caught a train at 12 noon from Victoria to Dover, crossed to Ostend, then joined the train that would take us to Passau on the frontier between Bavaria and Austria. This part of the journey was a great disappointment, as I had imagined a combination of the Orient Express and the Blue Train, those symbols of pre-war luxury and romance. Instead the food was pre-packed, the compartment utilitarian and the sleeping car a creaking survival from better times. But twelve hours on the Danube, accompanied by some Wagnerian weather, redeemed it all, as our boat weaved its way along the river, stopping to collect and set down passengers for whom this was their daily means of routine transport. At Vienna we straggled up from the pier, together with a troop of boy scouts, and carried our luggage to where four black Mercedes were waiting, our military escort and diplomatic reception committee led by Clive Rose, head of mission, looking vaguely disapproving of this unconventional form of ministerial arrival. Arthur Hockaday loved it all.

The whole trip was one of those which ministers allow themselves from time to time. It served a purpose in showing the commitment of the United Kingdom Government to the success of the negotiations and enabled me better to understand the obstacles to agreement. But it was also a thoroughly enjoyable visit to one of the great cities of the world which still confidently showed much of the bourgeois opulence and baroque grandeur of the Habsburgs. We stayed at the Hotel Bristol, walked in the Vienna Woods, called at the Spanish Riding School, enjoyed dinner with the head of the Russian delegation, with whom Silvia got on famously, ate cream cakes and drank hearty Austrian white wine made from the characteristic grüner veltiner grape. Such are the occasional perquisites of office which I, like every other fortunate minister, was happy to enjoy.

Another trip took me to Hong Kong and, this time, to the opulence of the late twentieth century. Here my relaxation was limited to a day at the races in the Governor's box during a pause in negotiations for a new defence agreement. The Governor of Hong Kong was Murray MacLehose, who had been George Brown's Private Secretary when I arrived in the Foreign Office. He had the physical presence and natural authority for his imperial role. Although appointed by the Queen on the recommendation of her ministers, as head of the Hong Kong Government he was expected to defend the interests of the colony as much from Whitehall as from the encroaching Chinese. This meant resisting any cuts that might put its security at risk. I went with a tightly drawn brief approved by the Treasury, and it was assumed that I would ask the Chief Secretary for some relaxation of it when stalemate was reached. But I was determined to settle the matter without reference back to London. I was fortunate to have my Oxford contemporary Robert Andrew as my chief adviser and also that the commander-in-chief was General Bramall, who saw all the advantages of finding a solution on the spot. Together, we worked out a deal by which the release of some of the land held by the military, desperately wanted by Hong Kong for housing, would offset hostility to the reduction of the already modest naval forces that patrolled coastal waters. Murray MacLehose recognised that my offer was a good one and at the end of a week's negotiations we signed a new defence agreement. I was able to return to London with more than I had been expected to achieve, and his standing was in no way diminished.

On my return journey from Hong Kong I called at Diego Garcia, the former coaling station, far out in the southern Indian Ocean, that Britain had leased to the Americans as a naval base. It was a coral atoll, which made conventional burial impossible, and the tombs of the sailors who had died there a century before were spread out over part of its surface like excrescences on the face of the moon. The Americans had all the home comforts their forces expected, including fillet steak for lunch, and the facilities of an operational command. The British, anxious only to assert their continued sovereignty, had left on the island one petty officer and six men with nothing much to do but keep fit. I was accompanied by both the petty officer and an escort of Americans on my visit to the cemetery which, apart from an old wartime Catalina flying boat wrecked on the shore, was virtually the only 'sight' a visitor might enjoy. Suddenly I felt a sharp jab in my arm, and a large, black hornet rose and flew away. At the best of times I was allergic to insect bites, which could produce grotesque and uncomfortable swelling, and a hornet was something to take seriously. The Americans moved fast, and soon an ambulance, stretcher bearers, and a doctor with an injection of serum were on the scene. But the petty officer moved faster. He took my arm, put his mouth to the bite and sucked hard, spitting the poison on to the rocky ground. I cannot say which prophylactic saved me, but I would like to believe it was the devotion to duty of the Royal Navy.

But despite my trips abroad, I was not greatly stretched in Defence either in the weight of my responsibilities or demands on my time. I received relatively few letters from MPs, because most of their constituency cases went to the separate service ministers. My main parliamentary task was to hold the line on defence spending and nuclear questions against the Labour left. In terms of meaningful debate this was easy enough, because most back-bench critics showed no interest whatever in policy analysis, but were simply against defence spending on pacifist or political grounds. They were not prepared to set out the case for a credible non-nuclear option based on transferring expenditure to conventional forces, or to propose a different 'mix' between the army, navy and air force in making our contribution to NATO. The exception was the new, young MP for Edinburgh Central, Robin Cook ('self-contained, unemotional and difficult to know', I noted), who had given serious thought to problems of arms control and who looked hard at vulnerable points to attack in the details of our policy. But even he stopped short of an intellectually honest critique, often preferring to dig into an issue only one spade down when he suspected that the unacceptable truth (unacceptable to him) lay one spade deeper.

In the day-to-day work of the department, out of the gaze of parliament, I was involved in decisions both ridiculous and – I hesitate at the description, 'sublime' – of critical importance. In the first category was a request for me to authorise expenditure for the 'stretching' of twenty Ford Granada cars, needed, so I was told, for senior officers in full ceremonial dress and carrying swords. After much argument, I was persuaded to agree to the purchase of ten, although I had a feeling that my successor would probably be asked to sanction the remainder. In the second category was my involvement in the decision to 'update Polaris', which was the bland parliamentary description for the Chevaline programme, which substantially increased the number of nuclear warheads carried on submarine-launched missiles. The policy – set down by the Prime Minister – was the less said the better, which conveniently brought together his wish not to upset left-wing Labour MPs with Whitehall's traditional secrecy. As a result there was far more to be discovered about missile technology openly in Washington than there was classified as suitable to tell parliament in London.

Somewhere in between these two extremes of gravity was the so-called 'Cod War', early in 1976, when Iceland's gunboats ran rings round the expensive and sophisticated frigates of the Royal Navy when they were called upon to defend British trawlers in their traditional fishing grounds. My task in this case was to give ministerial cover to operations control in London and to resist the bellicose calls of Roy Hattersley, Minister of State at the Foreign Office, for an even larger commitment of naval vessels and manpower.

But Roy Hattersley and I were on the same side, with differing degrees of emphasis, in the major event of the Parliament around which both our departmental careers were wrapped. In its manifesto for the second election in 1974 – which gave the Government a (slender) majority – Labour made much of its renegotiation in Brussels of the terms of Britain's Common Market membership, and promised the British people 'the final say through the ballot box' on whether to stay in or come out. Although the word was delicately avoided, this meant an early referendum and, as there was no point in arguing further against the principle, Labour's Europeans now had to ensure that it was won. This meant fighting our case in the party through the Labour Committee for Europe but also, in the view of most of us, full participation in whatever cross-party organisation was formed to campaign for a 'Yes' vote. In the autumn of 1974 I was approached by David Marquand and John Roper, who asked whether I would be willing to become director of this umbrella campaign as preliminary soundings had indicated that this would be widely welcomed. For several weeks I seriously considered the possibility, but when I spoke to George Thomson he advised against. If I resigned from the Government – as I was bound to do – I might not be taken back; and, short of organising the campaign, there would be lots of scope for a significant role. I saw the wisdom of this and the advantage of having a wholly neutral figure in charge, preferably one with contacts and influence in a wider circle than mine. Sir Con O'Neill, a distinguished former diplomat (not one of George Brown's favourites) was eventually appointed and did an excellent job. I became a member of the Steering Committee for the campaign and Chairman of the Final Stages group which worked out the policy and tactics for the last fortnight up to polling day on 5 June 1975.

The Steering Committee for Britain in Europe was one of the best committees on which I have ever served. It worked fast and there was no dead weight. Hard things were occasionally said and tempers became frayed. But discussion was open and decisions were quickly and firmly made. Perhaps there was an underlying deference to the opinions of others in a mixed political group whose unity was critical to our endeavour. The Tory network was complicated by Ted Heath's replacement as leader early in February 1975 by Margaret Thatcher, Willie Whitelaw becoming the key bridging figure between the two. Whitelaw campaigned around the country, often in harness with Roy Jenkins, who became President of Britain in Europe, and was a regular attender at the Steering Committee during the last four or five weeks. Otherwise the most active Tory members were Geoffrey Rippon, a veteran of the 1971 negotiations to join the Community, Douglas Hurd, a close link with Heath, Tony Royle, a former junior minister in the Foreign Office, and Geoffrey Tucker, Heath's press officer when he was at Number 10. David Steel, with whom I worked for the first time, was the principal Liberal at our meetings, while Jeremy Thorpe, then still the Liberal Leader, travelled the country.

Apart from myself, John Roper and John Harris made up the core of the regular team. John Harris, Minister of State at the Home Office, was a key player. He was one of nature's insiders and had been close to Roy Jenkins for a decade, filling a vital role as adviser, particularly in dealings with the press, and as a go-between acceptable even to Marcia Williams at Number 10. Roy valued him highly but I had not known him well. In Britain in Europe he played his part brilliantly and his judgement was almost always right. The success of the campaign owed more to him than to many of the more readily identified political stars.

John Harris was one of the so-called 'principals' who began to meet regularly for breakfast at the Dorchester Hotel well in advance of the formal campaign. It was not the time of day I most enjoyed for business, but he persuaded me to attend because it was an important meeting point in what was a complex network of cross-party contacts. It was also a new and not unwelcome experience to discuss high politics in warmth and comfort. Britain in Europe was nothing if not well-heeled; Earl Grey with lemon and the best hotels was a world away from ill-lit and draughty Labour committee rooms and the milky-brown concoctions that passed for tea. But what impressed me when the organisation got under way was its sheer efficiency, and this was not only a matter of money. If a new photocopier was required by Con O'Neill, it would be delivered the same day; if a member of the staff was falling short, he or she would be quickly bypassed or told to go. Ernest Wistrich, the cautious Director of the European Movement, complained about the Americanisation of the campaign and not only because John Harris and Geoffrey Tucker had hired Charles Guggenheim, a clever film-maker from Washington, to produce our television commercials. But Britain in Europe was not so much slick as highly competent.

Con O'Neill's number two was Peter Thring, whom I had known first as a Tory parliamentary candidate on Teesside and then as head of ICI's public affairs department, run from Millbank. At first I was doubtful about this appointment, but his business background neatly complemented Con O'Neil's diplomatic skills. It was later said that the experience of working together with representatives of other political parties in the referendum campaign gave a number of us – particularly Roy Jenkins – the taste for cross-party politics which led to the SDP. I certainly came to know better, to like and respect some of those with very different political views than mine. But my most enduring impression was of a formidable fighting machine, fashioned in this case for Europe but of a kind that in those days won elections for the Conservative Party.

For me, one of the curious by-products of the referendum was an easing of my hitherto tense relationship with Harold Wilson as some of my long resentment of him began to drain away. Once or twice a week I would lunch at the big table in the Members' dining room of the House of Commons, at which I had had a row with him four years earlier. I usually arrived about 1.30 P.M., late given the eating habits of most MPs, and Harold Wilson would often arrive soon after. As other members completed their lunch and departed, we were left alone, and we talked about the renegotiations and the forthcoming referendum. A note in my diary for 2 December 1974 tells me that we discussed the movement of opinion in the constituencies in favour of Europe and the scope for developing a European policy for regions of high and persistent unemployment. He asked whether I had any thoughts about solving the sovereignty problem, adding in a rather surprising explanation of his question: 'You, like me, have been the chairman of a select committee of the House'.

On another, later, occasion, shortly before the outcome of the renegotiations was to be put to the Parliamentary Labour Party, we were joined by Stanley Clinton Davis, a soft-left anti-Market junior minister who liked to stand well with his leader. In answer to a question of mine, Harold Wilson replied, 'I can't imagine any minister outside the cabinet will feel they can vote against the terms – abstain, yes, but not vote against'. Poor Stanley's face went white and he dropped his knife and fork with a clatter. 'I wish, Harold,' he protested, 'you had made that clear earlier', and his voice trailed away. Harold went on eating, leaving Stanley Clinton Davis to hurry away to reconcile his loyalties. But Stanley knew how to survive, and a decade later he was one of Britain's Commissioners in Brussels, and took his place again in government for a short while after 1997.

Throughout February and March there were regular meetings in Roy Jenkins' room at the House at 6.30 on Wednesdays. These were primarily intended to coordinate activities in cabinet and between cabinet and the campaign outside. They were attended by Shirley Williams and Edmund Dell, amongst others; and Roy Hattersley, who, until the terms were known, generally reported on the negotiations in Brussels. We had lunch together occasionally and our contacts were friendly. He voted the right way on all major occasions on Europe, but a strong personal declaration of his European commitment was sometimes a prelude to sentiments of compromise. Perhaps he was wiser than me.

The campaign advanced by stages, accumulating energy which would be fully released once the Referendum Bill had been through parliament. But the Anglo-German Königswinter conference of 1975 was the point at which the excitement of the pro-Europeans began bursting out. When I had first visited Königswinter in 1959 (the conference was then in its ninth year) our discussions were still preoccupied – as I was – with German guilt and rehabilitation, the Germans being mainly the recipients of British patronage and advice. By the 1970s this had changed completely, with the British now learning from the Germans the secret of their economic success and how best to benefit from membership of the European Community. The 1975 conference was not wholly concerned with Community matters. Ted Heath – returning to the public arena after five weeks in retreat following his leadership defeat by Margaret Thatcher – joined with Roy Jenkins in giving a graphic account of how to stand up to terrorist blackmail, the Germans having recently failed to do so. But the forthcoming referendum was on everyone's mind. On the Saturday night we enjoyed a great party at the home of the British Ambassador, Sir Nicholas Henderson, which overlooked the Rhine. This was an event later described by Roy Jenkins as 'combining something of the atmosphere of the Duchess of Richmond's pre-Waterloo Ball with that of Wellington's battle-planning headquarters'. The music on the turntable may have been the Rolling Stones, but we were dancing to Beethoven as the echoing triumph of his choral symphony prepared us for the decisive weeks of campaigning that lay ahead.

Meanwhile I had one relevant departmental responsibility. This was how to enable the Services to vote in the referendum. The rules for service voting had been changed in 1969 as the result of a Speaker's Conference. Instead of a once-and-for-all registration, servicemen (and their wives, when abroad) were obliged to put their names on the register of voters every year. Given the circumstances of Service life, this gave a registration of only twenty-five per cent of those entitled to vote. As the referendum approached, the pressure from within the Services to make special arrangements grew. I agreed on the merits of the case, but also took the view that service voters were likely to be marginally more European. In the end I was given four days to come up with a scheme of my own which cabinet would find it difficult to refuse. I gave instructions that there should be direct balloting in units, and asked for the ballot papers to be got back to London in twenty-four hours, using the RAF, so that the count would not be delayed. Cabinet found it impossible to resist these proposals, which showed that the Services could run a viable scheme on an acceptable timetable. In due course I had the experience of speaking first on the Committee Stage of the Referendum Bill to move the Government's own amendment to give the Services a vote. It was a small triumph which gave me disproportionate pleasure. My only regret was that this was the day when Silvia launched *HMS Newcastle* at Swan Hunters on the Tyne, an event which I had hoped not to miss and which came to mean a great deal to her.

The referendum campaign was fought mainly in the media and at meetings. There were almost 1,500 present at the opening rally of Britain in Europe at the Free Trade Hall in Manchester (not at all the historic building I had expected but rather like an Odeon cinema). Such occasions were not gatherings of the faithful whipped in by the political parties. They were men and women, generally sympathetic to the platform, who listened carefully as if they hoped to be persuaded. Roy Jenkins, Willie Whitelaw and Jeremy Thorpe spoke at the Manchester rally, with Vic Feather, late of the TUC, brilliant in the chair, and this was a team that attracted large audiences all around the country. But there were many smaller meetings and I spoke at eighteen in twenty-one days, usually returning overnight on the sleeper in order not to miss the Steering Committee.

What the campaign lacked, and marked it off from a general election, was any canvassing. Despite the claim that there were some 300 branches of the European Movement functioning around the country, there was little evidence of activity from most of them. In any case, their members probably had little experience of canvassing, which is an art requiring a little political skill and much resilience. The result was that some strong supporters of Britain in Europe had no outlet for their energies and were fed up with the lack of local activities. One of these was Silvia, who had a fair capacity for becoming impatient at what she saw as complacency or sloth. Not long before polling day she discovered that despite a nice office in Finchley Road, nothing was being pushed through letter boxes in the London Borough of Camden where we lived. So she found some willing helpers, and leaflets were delivered to almost 10,000 homes.

When the campaign was over, and the referendum had been won by a majority of two to one, I wrote a long account of it for my personal records. It contained references to over fifty people who had played a significant part in events. As I read it now, one missing name is Tony Crosland's, but I see from my diary for Tuesday 4 March 1975 that I called on him in his room at 9.30 P.M. for a drink. He was friendly and welcomed a chat after a long gap. I told him about the campaign and he was glad to know it was going well, although he was not prepared to speak on any cross-party Britain in Europe platform. I noted that he would even require a bit of coaxing to speak for the Labour Committee for Europe. He then said, rather ruefully, 'I made a mistake four years ago. You must decide what side you're on and stick to it.' It was the first time that he had spoken to me about the run-up to the vote in the House of Commons in 1971 when his behaviour had alienated him from many of his friends without enhancing his standing with Labour MPs as a whole.

With the referendum over and decisively won, I felt rather flat. The government of which I was a member was struggling with an increasingly restless party, a small majority and inflation rising to an annual rate of twenty-seven per cent. But at Defence I was in a backwater, with little to do except bide my time and speculate on my own future. We went on holiday early, not this year to Italy but to Cucuron in the Vaucluse. Shortly before I left, Leo Pliatzky, an Oxford friend of Roy's and a Second Secretary at the Treasury, told me that in discussing the appointment of chairmen to nationalised industries with the Chancellor, Denis Healey, he had asked, 'Why not Bill Rodgers?' But Denis had dismissed the idea, saying that I would not be interested because I'd be in the cabinet when Harold Wilson went. This was not much comfort to me because Harold looked like going on forever and I counted seven or eight others who he would find reasons for preferring.

Another future I speculated upon was Shirley Williams'. She too had talked to me shortly before I left on holiday, but on quite a different matter. For two or three years I had kept a folder in my filing cabinet labelled 'The State of the Party' and this was beginning to bulge with speeches (some of them my own), articles and press cuttings. Now, late at night and over a bottle of wine in my House of Commons room, Shirley had put it to me that I should organise the fight to restore the balance against an increasingly militant and encroaching left. For Shirley Williams to raise such matters was itself unusual, because in the past she had chosen to stand a little aside from the roughness of internal troubles. But she was incensed by the behaviour of the National Executive Committee, on which she sat, and was finding problems in the constituences – including Stevenage, her own – where she had once been sure of a wholly friendly welcome. I could only agree with Shirley's analysis, but said that I was reluctant to do more on my own because it needed the authority of a cabinet minister to organise any effective fight-back. I would play my part, but on this occasion she must raise the standard.

On my return from holiday I made a strong speech about the state of the party which provoked, amongst other things, a letter from Miss Enid Lakeman, the doyenne of electoral reform, reminding me that the use of the single transferable vote in multi-member constituencies would make it easier to resist a take-over by the left. I sent a courteous reply, saying that I did not exclude the possibility of proportional representation but was not yet convinced that the existing system had irredeemably broken down. Otherwise the autumn of 1975 slipped away until the grey of winter matched the mood of politics.

I failed to recognise the first hint of a change. Soon after Christmas, on a day when Silvia and I were lunching at East Hendred, Roy Jenkins asked whether I thought there was any possibility that Harold Wilson might soon resign. I dismissed the idea out of hand and almost forgot the question, so implausible did it seem. When, on 16 March, his resignation was announced, I was taken by surprise. I was also horribly afraid that even if Roy Jenkins' supporters had been properly prepared, this was not the time for a leadership contest that he could win, given his low-key second term at the Home Office. Harold Wilson had decided to abandon an apparently sinking ship. The economy was in crisis and the party was demoralised. Labour MPs were looking for comfort and security, which meant the populist and unifying Jim Callaghan – escapist though this might prove – rather than the demanding challenge of Roy Jenkins. From the beginning it was an uphill struggle to put Roy in a winning position. John Roper was tireless; Giles Radice emotional; David Marquand caring; and Ian Wrigglesworth busy and practical. Roy himself did everything he could, but more than once found himself accepting the sad apologies of old friends and allies who felt that on this occasion they must vote for Callaghan.

On the first ballot – with six candidates – I hoped for 75 votes for Roy, predicted 68 and felt in my bones that it would be 65 or lower. In the event, 56 was simply not good enough, with Foot on 90 and Callaghan on 84. Tony Benn with 37 votes, Denis Healey with 30 and Tony Crosland with 17 were clearly also-rans, but there was no chance that on further ballots their votes would sufficiently transfer to Roy to enable him to overtake Callaghan. There was also the fear that unless Callaghan was not firmly backed as the front-runner to beat Michael Foot, Foot might just stay ahead and become the winner. I believed then and believe now that Roy Jenkins was right to accept defeat and withdraw from the contest at that point.

The vote was announced on Thursday 25 March, and when I dined with Roy at Brooks's on the following Tuesday I found him, as I wrote in my diary, 'three-quarters gone to Brussels'. I had not previously known that Harold Wilson had raised with him the possibility of becoming President of the European Commission and, in the shock of learning this, I did not urge any alternative course. But when, the following Sunday, Silvia and I went for lunch at East Hendred it was an emotional occasion. Silvia was in tears and, from my deep affection for Roy and not wanting this parting of our ways, I urged him to think again about leaving British politics, at least if he were to become Foreign Secretary. Roy was clearly distressed by the extent to which he had been abandoned in the leadership vote by old friends whom he liked and respected. Perhaps he warmed to the thought that he was still wanted, knowing I spoke for others besides myself. The following day I wrote him a letter, again urging him to stay while not wanting to press him unreasonably if Brussels was what he really preferred.

At that stage I did not seriously doubt that he could have had the Foreign Office if he wanted it but on Tuesday, after he had discussed the prospect with Callaghan, I learnt otherwise. On Wednesday the news was the same and on Thursday 8 April, when I was sitting at my desk in the Ministry of Defence, a message came that the Home Secretary would like me to go over to see him. I walked across Whitehall to the Home Office, arriving just before 5.00, and stayed with Roy until 6.30. He told me at once that the new Foreign Secretary was to be Tony Crosland and all that was left was the public announcement. On his desk, propped up against an inkstand, was a letter to Giscard d'Estaing, the French President, accepting the Presidency of the European Commission. It was still unsealed. But when the BBC Six O'Clock News announced the new Callaghan Cabinet, with Tony Crosland at the Foreign Office, Roy fastened the envelope down. It was a symbolic ending to his ministerial career.

I was telephoned that evening by John Horam and David Marquand, who said that they hoped Roy would remain Home Secretary and stay in the Commons. That was the view of a majority of Labour MPs. But I knew there was no point in trying to persuade him and my instinct told me it was better for him to go. The verdict of the parliamentary party mirrored both the deep wounds of the long controversy over Europe and the growing momentum towards the left. More than one Labour MP, afraid of being out of line with local activists about who should be leader, admitted giving his ballot paper to his constituency chairman to mark. Roy Jenkins had won significantly more votes than Tony Benn, but outside parliament Benn's star was rising and Roy could have done little to diminish it. He had no great taste for narrow party politics or the messiness of internal party warfare. If the Labour Party was fast becoming ungovernable, Roy, as a potential leader, was already out of time.

Jim Callaghan, with whom little love was lost with Roy, said to me later that Roy lacked the will to fight. On his record, this was grossly unfair. But the integrity and generosity of spirit that so commended him to his friends was matched by a moral fastidiousness when an ability to stomach uneasy compromise or to be ruthless might have served his interests better. I would greatly miss Roy in the House of Commons, and not just for the excitement of high occasions. I would miss congenial dinners when we were joined by other friends and cleared the cellars of Chateau Gloria before going benign into the Chamber for a vote at 10.00 P.M.; and the occasional breakfast on the terrace by the Thames on a soft summer morning after an all-night sitting. The House of Commons was a place of deep affections and loyalties as well as of cruel moments. For fourteen years Roy had been part of my pleasure in being there.

But I was staying in parliament, and shortly I had to answer my own summons to see the Prime Minister. My experience of him had been different from Roy's and I felt none of the resentment that had characterised my earlier feelings about Harold Wilson. But when Jim Callaghan suggested that I should move sideways to become Minister of State at the Home Office, I refused. I reminded him that I had served in five departments and said that I now wanted either to move up into the cabinet or out of the Government altogether. As for the Home Office, there was no point in going there for the remaining few months of Roy's tenure. Jim took this well, hinted that my time in cabinet would soon come and asked whether I would be prepared to stay at Defence. I agreed and later in the day, in an exchange of letters, he confirmed his understanding of the position. My best guess was that when Roy Jenkins left the cabinet in the autumn, I would join it.

Meanwhile there was time for a family holiday, and we planned to return to NuoglaVecchia, near Livorno. I had booked a house for the whole of August, expecting that the recess would begin by the end of July. But parliamentary business dragged on, and twice I postponed our departure on the long drive through France, Germany and Austria (we were going via the Brenner Pass). In the end I decided to leave, anticipating no further critical votes. But when, three days later, we arrived, I was hardly out of the driving seat when I was given an urgent message to call my Private Secretary at Defence. On doing so I was told there was a three-line whip for the following day and he had been unable to persuade the government business managers to let me pair. I then telephoned the Chief Whip Michael Cocks, and spent twenty minutes setting out all the good reasons why it was nonsense for me to return. At the end he said, 'Bill, I understand and returning from the sunshine of Tuscany will be a wrench. Why not telephone the Prime Minister at Chequers and explain?' At that point discretion became the better part, as I had no wish for Jim to reconsider his half-promise of the spring. So I telephoned British Airways and Alitalia, only to find that all direct flights to London were booked and I would need to go first to Rome. But my flight to Rome was late, I missed my connection to Heathrow and an alternative flight via Milan was delayed by mechanical trouble. I eventually dashed through customs at Terminal One just before 9.15 and reached the House of Commons five minutes before the division. It was won by six votes – a comfortable majority for those precarious times – but I had a strong feeling that had I stayed away it would have been mysteriously lost. The round journey had cost me a couple of hundred pounds – the rules, quite properly, did not allow me to claim it – but I hoped virtue would be rewarded.

It was, as on 10 September I had another summons to Number 10. The Prime Minister had been due to leave for Canada but had delayed his departure because of a threat of a seamen's strike. Having nothing better to do, he brought forward his reshuffle. Now I was in the cabinet as Secretary of State for Transport, with Roy Hattersley as another new entrant. Jim Callaghan later said that at that point he believed either Hattersley or I would one day become the Leader of the Labour Party. But despite the long years he was to serve as deputy, Hattersley had no more chance than I had in the political climate that was to prevail for the next fifteen years.

Mine was a re-created department carved out of the Department of the Environment into which it had been merged in 1970. This meant that I had no departmental staff to inherit. I had hardly returned home from Downing Street when Sir Douglas Allen, now head of the Home Civil Service, telephoned with congratulations and, more importantly, names from which to choose my Permanent Secretary. He made it clear that his favourite candidate was Peter Baldwin, a Second Secretary at the Treasury and former Private Secretary to Jim Callaghan when Chancellor and, very briefly, to

Roy Jenkins. As I had known Douglas Allen during my time at both the DEA and the Treasury, and trusted him, I accepted his recommendation without further enquiry. By the afternoon Peter Baldwin was at Patshull Road to discuss the future. I agreed that we should share common services with Environment to minimise disruption and maintain career prospects for officials. Asked where I wanted my office in the Marsham Street building we should also share with Environment, I took a mischievous pleasure in choosing the eighteenth floor, as it would put me one above Peter Shore, Environment's Secretary of State. In fact, I saw no problem in a good working relationship with him, as strong differences on Europe had not erased the mildly respectful goodwill I had felt towards him since schooldays. In any case, I believed that transport should be closely integrated with land-use planning and other environmental matters, and had no intention of being uncooperative.

But the prospect of running a small department did not feel like a difficult challenge. My two best-known predecessors had been Ernest Marples and Barbara Castle, both of whom had scored with the public on showmanship. I would not try to match them but believed I could make it a well-run department, free of disasters and of good standing in the eyes of my parliamentary colleagues. The real test for me – the one by which I would judge myself – was whether I could make a significant contribution in cabinet. This was territory I explored with Peter Baldwin that afternoon, remembering the cabinet briefs I had seen at the DEA and the Treasury enabling ministers to speak with authority on every item on the cabinet agenda. If I failed in this, it seemed pointless being in cabinet, except for the status. I would also become a fairly silent member, as there were relatively few transport issues that called for a cabinet decision. Peter Baldwin was receptive to my thoughts, saying that he would try to get Treasury briefs for me, drawing on his contacts. He also proposed a special unit in the department to help. All this I found satisfactory. I liked Peter Baldwin's slightly understated manner and detected in him humanity as well as competence, which ought to be the formula for a successful time together.

A further matter to be settled was who would become my junior minister. I had an out-patient's appointment for minor surgery at University College Hospital the following day and, as the surgeon was explaining his intentions, an excited nurse announced that the Prime Minister wanted me on the telephone. The staff at Number 10 were being over-zealous in tracking me down, but the Prime Minister said that he wanted to settle my junior minister, and what about Bob Cryer? 'Good God, Jim,' was my startled reply. 'So you don't want him? I know he'd like to join the Government.' I hesitated to say that applied to almost 200 other backbenchers but suggested that if he wanted someone on the left, Robin Cook had debating skills and a sharper mind. Meanwhile, I'd like Giles Radice. 'Everyone likes Giles, but not this time', he responded. 'So you won't have Cryer?' 'No, Jim.' 'Then I'll think again.' The result was that I got John Horam, an entirely acceptable choice, and Cryer went to Industry where he lasted two years before resigning.

My team was not completed until a couple of months later when I recruited Roger Liddle to be my special adviser. Special advisers to cabinet ministers – some highly expert, others primarily political operators – had first become commonplace in the 1964 Wilson Government. But they were still controversial in Whitehall; civil servants were suspicious of them while some cabinet ministers believed they had nothing to offer a senior politician who knew his stuff. My own experience had convinced me of the need for confidence and mutual trust between ministers and officials, and I did not like the cloak-and-dagger enthusiasm of some of the younger political advisers who seemed over-eager to promote their minister's cause irrespective of the wider interests of the government.

However, after three or four weeks in office, I changed my mind. In Tony Goldman, son of Sir Sam Goldman, one of the great Treasury mandarins of the 1960s, I had a conscientious Private Secretary. But he was busy with the day-to-day management of the business that passed through my office and seemed to have little time to give me advice on policy. What I needed was another pair of hands, someone without executive responsibility in the Department and having political nous. This meant an outsider, and thus the special adviser I had first intended to do without. I consulted Frank Pickstock, and he recommended Roger Liddle who, like me, had read history at Oxford and, at twenty-nine, had already served as Deputy Leader of Oxford City Council. I had recently heard Roger proposing a toast at a wedding and such are the consequences of casual encounters that I asked an eloquent best man to transform himself into a wise adviser. This he did to great effect. Roger Liddle became a friend and a close colleague in all my causes. He briefed me on ministerial papers, kept in close contact with other political advisers in Whitehall and provided liaison with the party, especially with Labour councillors in local government who would be affected by many of my decisions. The rule I made was that my Private Secretary and senior civil servants in my Department would always have access to the written advice he gave me, and Roger or I would report to them any relevant conversations where they were not themselves present. This openness seemed to work, especially when civil servants discovered that through his own experience and his contacts in the party, Roger Liddle was able to contribute to a dimension of knowledge not available to them and to ensure that decisions, once made, were better received than they might otherwise have been. Roger's advice to me was no alternative to finding my own solution to problems. But I benefited from discussions with him, and a personal commitment beyond what civil servants could always offer.

Chapter 8
Cabinet and Catastrophe

Arrival in cabinet had not come as a surprise. It was like the ending of an over-long journey. I was pleased to have made it rather than excited. The outlook for the Government was bleak, but I was no longer on the sidelines. At my first two cabinets I did not speak at all and was thoroughly fed up with myself. Then at my third I spoke on one departmental matter and one other, enjoying my initiation; and at my fourth I spoke to a paper of my own and felt I had arrived. I even wrote in my diary, with the naivety of a boy remembering his first adolescent kiss, 'I caught the attention of cabinet and my intervention was decisive'. But every diary is egocentric and no doubt half of those who contributed to the discussion felt that they had articulated the winning argument.

As a junior minister I had attended cabinet a number of times, but with a specific brief, leaving after the matter had been discussed. Only now was I able to observe how cabinet functioned in dealing with all the items that filled its agenda, routinely for two and a half hours on a Thursday morning. Being an effective member of any committee – and cabinet was no more than a rather grand committee – depends on the shape of the table, the number of people present and where you sit. A small, round table gives everyone equal access to the chairman and makes it easy to intervene. But the cabinet table was long and narrow, with room for two members on one narrow end (two civil servant note-takers sat at a small table at the other) with the remaining twenty-one members of the cabinet, plus the Chief Whip and the Cabinet Secretary, seated at the two long sides. All places were allocated: the Chancellor of the Exchequer sat opposite the Prime Minister, with the Foreign Secretary, the Home Secretary and the Lord Chancellor flanking him. They were in his immediate vision and could easily catch his eye. Much worse off were those sitting on the Prime Minister's own side of the table. Except for his three or four immediate neighbours, they could only be seen by the Prime Minister if he made an effort to identify them. In their case there was no point in a raised eyebrow or a half-opened mouth as a signal that they wished to speak.

For my first few months in cabinet, as a new member I was well down the opposite side of the table but, as the Prime Minister tended to glance towards both ends from time to time, I found no great difficulty in being called, although it was impossible to join in the quick exchanges of a closely-argued discussion. But when Joel Barnett arrived in cabinet as Chief Secretary, he took my place and, although I moved up slightly in the hierarchy, I was now on the wrong side of the table. At first I tried to catch at least the corner of the Prime Minister's eye by turning almost at right angles in my chair and looking directly towards him. But here I faced the problem of the body movements of Sir John Hunt, the Cabinet Secretary, who sat next to the Prime Mininster, and Harold Lever, who sat nearer to me on Sir John's other side. Whenever Sir John leaned forward in his seat, Harold Lever leaned back, and whenever Sir John leaned back, Harold Lever leaned forward, thus at all times blocking my line of vision. Eventually I found a way of turning my head towards the left, with my chin almost on the table and showing an obvious restlessness supplemented by an attention-seeking 'Prime Minister ...' in rather over-urgent tones. It was far from satisfactory and my position at the table remained inhibiting.

As I walked out of Number 10 with Tony Crosland after one of my early cabinet meetings, I plainly showed my disappointment about how things had gone. 'You're not surprised, are you,' he asked, 'at the unsatisfactory nature of cabinet?' I had already noticed that his own contributions to discussion were often thin and inconsequential, but Tony had a habit of dismissing as unimportant matters that he did not want to understand or that presented him with an awkward political choice. What I had not previously recognised was that much routine cabinet business involved only four or five ministers and a good deal of boredom for the rest. To pass the time I learnt to decorate my cabinet agenda with the most elaborate and complex designs, all inviting rather obvious Freudian analysis, although the objects of my frustration were the events around me. A more lasting by-product was my first pair of glasses, when I found that in raising my eyes from a sustained piece of doodling I could not easily focus on the other end of the cabinet room. Half-moons, which I continue to wear today, suited my purpose admirably, especially when an exchange of frivolous notes with Joel Barnett became an alternative way of passing the time. But except in the closing months, frustration rather than exhilaration marked much of my time at cabinet meetings and I often returned to my office in Marsham Street to lie flat on the floor to unwind, assisted by my favourite drink, an outsize gin and Italian.

It was soon clear to me how Jim Callaghan had balanced his cabinet and intended to run it. The key was in cutting down Tony Benn to size and isolating him from his erstwhile allies. This meant deference to both Michael Foot, Deputy Leader and symbol of the old, Bevanite left, and Peter Shore, who had once been one of Benn's close circle of friends. Jim Callaghan plainly did much to square Michael Foot in advance of cabinet, while Foot's loyalty rested on the belief that this was almost the last chance to save a Labour government. As for Shore, he worked hard, occasionally raised his voice in histrionic advocacy of a rather poor case, but often came up with a compromise and was never tied to the brief he carried as Secretary of State for the Environment. Shirley Williams, now graced with the additional title of Paymaster-General and chairing several cabinet committees, was also treated with a certain deference. But the emotional force she brilliantly brought to a public platform was not always effectively deployed, and she seemed a little trapped by her responsibilities at Education. My own role seemed to be as the compleat social democrat and a foil to Tony Benn. I found myself on cabinet committees as diverse as Europe, industrial democracy and broadcasting, as much a part of a balancing act with the left as for my departmental interests.

Harold Lever, never usually lost for words, said less than I expected. The talkers were Stan Orme and David Ennals, on almost anything; and Merlyn Rees, radiating muddled concern and goodwill. The Prime Minister had least time for John Silkin, whom he listened to with impatience verging on contempt; and Edmund Dell, whose expertise he would have respected more had it taken account of political realities. I enjoyed Edmund's laconic interventions. He was an intellectual heavyweight and never gilded the lily of unpopular advice. But apart from the Prime Minister, the man who really mattered was Denis Healey, arrogant and flippant in turn and not much given to listening to the views of colleagues. Soon after my arrival in cabinet, his became the key role in the Government's survival.

There are at least seven published accounts of the IMF discussions that dominated cabinet for much of November and December 1976, all differing in emphasis and detail. But the broad outline of events is not in dispute. Faced with a growing balance of payments deficit, a rising Public Sector Borrowing Requirement and a falling pound, the Prime Minister and the Chancellor decided there was no alternative to asking the International Monetary Fund for a substantial loan. But the IMF set hard terms, the practical effect of which would be severe public expenditure cuts on top of those the Government had already made in July. The first question for cabinet was whether a practical alternative existed to an IMF loan; the second, whether a lesser cut than the £3 billion for which the IMF was asking might be negotiable.

The events of 1976 were only one of many battles fought over the years to save the pound as it dropped from £2.80 to the dollar in 1964 to £1.60 today (and very much lower in between). As for expenditure cuts, these became endemic in the system of economic management when Labour governments struggled to fulfil their social aspirations against an economy which stubbornly failed to yield steady growth. But many such economic crises involved only the Prime Minister, the Chancellor and a handful of senior colleagues, with decisions reached in some secrecy. On this occasion, eight meetings of the full cabinet were needed to settle matters; and alternative courses of action were explored in a process closely followed by observers outside parliament. It was open government by accident.

From the beginning, two things seemed to me inescapable. The pessimistic Treasury forecasts and the gloomy IMF assumptions might turn out to be wrong (as Tony Crosland was soon to argue), but the crisis of confidence that had sent the Government to the IMF would not easily go away; and, in the end, the Prime Minister and Chancellor would have to agree on the necessary measures, because the Chancellor's resignation was unthinkable. As for my own departmental budget, if the issues were grave enough I would concede whatever cuts the circumstances required, taking care to choose them myself rather than allow the Treasury to dictate.

Although the IMF negotiating team had been in London for more than a fortnight, the cabinet marathon began on 18 November, with a sober statement from the Prime Minister and a somewhat avuncular promise that he would keep us fully informed of the progress of the negotiations. Denis Healey then followed, saying that he and the Prime Minister would agree on the quantum of the cuts early in the following week; EQ – the cabinet committee dealing with economic strategy – would then consider the options; and, finally, cabinet would decide how to present them. David Ennals was first to speak but I followed, saying that it would be wrong for the substance of these matters, if they were as grave as the Prime Minister implied, to be settled by anything less than full cabinet. This was plainly the mood of the meeting and, on procedure, the Prime Minister was content to disagree with his Chancellor.

The following Monday, at about 6.00 P.M., Harold Lever walked into my room at the House of Commons and said that at the special Tuesday cabinet we should reject the IMF terms which were now emerging. They made no sense and the Prime Minster should speak to President Ford in Washington, saying that he could not carry his cabinet. Later, David Ennals knocked at my door, warned me of an urgent minute he had sent to the Prime Minister and said that he too would oppose the package. Later still, Ennals, Shirley Williams and I joined Roy Hattersley and we agreed to oppose any attempt to get a final agreement the following day because time was needed for alternatives to emerge. In this we were encouraged not only by the Prime Minister's promise of a full discussion but by a strange message conveyed through Shirley that he did not entirely agree with the recommendations the Chancellor was about to make. In my diary I wrote, 'What game is he playing?', concluding my entry for the day with the single word: 'messy'.

At cabinet the following morning, 23 November, Denis Healey presented his proposal for meeting the demands of the IMF for cuts amounting to £3 billion, of which £1 billion would be in public expenditure. It was a take-it-or-leave-it, perfunctory performance and I was not impressed. Tony Crosland followed with a more closely argued case, saying that the July measures (savings of £1 billion) were working and any further cuts would result in higher unemployment and could not be defended on any reasonable grounds. There followed an unfocused general discussion. Two members of the cabinet, Edmund Dell and Reg Prentice, were firm for Healey and six or seven others would probably have given their assent if pressed. Tony Benn was out on his own, outlining a full siege economy. Peter Shore was the most articulate on the left for rejecting the IMF package in favour of tight import controls; and he appeared to carry Foot, Albert Booth and John Silkin. There remained what was emerging as the Crosland–Lever group, which included Shirley Williams, Ennals, Hattersley, Bruce Millan (the Scottish Secretary), and myself. But I was not a fully paid-up member because I needed to be persuaded that the Crosland analysis could be sold to the IMF, thus ensuring the loan without the strings.

Cabinet on Thursday 25 November started in euphoria, perhaps encouraged by the apparently relaxed mood of the Prime Minister, his promise that there was no need yet to reach conclusions and the report of another friendly conversation with President Ford. Tony Crosland came forward with his proposals, offering the IMF a quarter of the cuts they had asked for. I spoke last in an hour's discussion, saying that while Crosland had carried me all the way in his critical analysis of the Chancellor's package, the key question was how to restore confidence, and in that sense the IMF were only the intervening institution. I saw Sir John Hunt nod, in an unusual departure from his studied neutrality, but my effort to bring what I saw as a degree of reality to the proceedings only left my colleagues in gloom.

At 10.30 p.m. the following Tuesday evening, on the eve of yet another cabinet, there was a meeting in Tony Crosland's room at the House. Apart from Tony there were Harold Lever, Shirley, Ennals, Hattersley and myself. Tony and Harold Lever were tense and hardline. They said that the Healey package remained quite unacceptable and Harold added that for him it was a resigning matter. They then went further than before, Tony saying that if the IMF refused to settle on our terms – Crosland's and Lever's – the Prime Minister should make a statement to the House of Commons saying that we were withdrawing British troops from Germany and Cyprus. This would put irresistible pressure on both Ford and Helmut Schmidt who had so far resisted the Prime Minister's request to tell the IMF to agree a less stringent loan. It would be, Harold Lever said, a gigantic game of bluff which we would certainly win if we kept our nerve. Ennals and Hattersley went all the way with this. But Shirley was reserved and I was sceptical, arguing that if this was the alternative to Healey's proposal, our bluff would be called. In Britain's own interest there could be no question of abandoning our NATO obligations and if we threatened to do so it would be a further blow to confidence. I was sorry, but if this was all there was on offer they could no longer count on me.

On Wednesday morning in cabinet, the Chancellor, Crosland, Benn and Shore all spoke to their papers. Tony Benn's on 'the alternative strategy' had obviously been written by Francis Cripps, one of his political advisers, and he did not seem to understand it. When he referred to the present crisis being like 1931, the Prime Minister said, 'nonsense', he had lived through it. Whereupon Benn counter-claimed that his father had been in cabinet at the time, which provoked Fred Peart to say that his father really knew the score because he had been the agent for the Labour candidate at Seaham Harbour when Ramsay Macdonald had fought as the leader of the National Government. All this was good-humoured but quite irrelevant, and produced one of Crosland's familiar scowls of disapproval. What was striking was Benn's inability to answer questions about his paper. On the instructions of the Prime Minister, for whom he worked at Downing Street, Bernard Donoughue had telephoned me, as he may have telephoned other ministers, to encourage questions to Tony Benn. I simply asked what were the employment consequences of his proposals, and got a waffling reply and no figures whatsoever. Another question provoked the response, 'You can't really expect me to know the answer when I don't have the Treasury computer at my disposal'. It became a game that no-one took seriously, as Benn's proposals were stripped bare of credibility.

Peter Shore spoke next to his paper, making a much better case for imposing import controls for eighteen months, knowing the answer when asked to explain the consequences of such measures, even when these would be unpleasant. Tony Crosland seemed subdued and only said a few words, following the lines of his intervention in the previous week that further public spending cuts of £1 billion would be disastrous. Lever spoke once without great effect and was attacked by Edmund Dell, also below his best. Roy Mason, Elwyn Jones and John Morris were pro-Healey and Bruce Millan pro-Crosland, but I had the feeling that some of the excitement was draining out of the arguments. The Prime Minister had no difficulty in summing up by ruling out both the Benn and the Shore versions of the alternative strategy, although he rather carefully did so 'on behalf of the majority of the cabinet' – and saying that we should settle the quantum the following day.

This time Denis Healey carried authority, and his deflationary package was only half what he had originally told cabinet the IMF was asking for. If he had been unconvincing a fortnight before, I now found him persuasive. Crosland, whose passionate wish to protect public expenditure I shared, had lost me on the impracticality of his game of bluff with the IMF. But in any case he tamely said that as the Prime Minister had now declared his personal support for the Chancellor's package, he would come into line. Lever, rather less precisely defining his reason, said the same and so did Ennals, Shirley Williams – whose last-minute proposal of a compromise had been dismissed – and then Hattersley, in a long, somewhat tortured and self-justifying speech that produced some wry smiles. Thus did the revolt of the moderates come, rather ingloriously, to an end. I was not clear whether the Prime Minister had encouraged Crosland in the hope that he would come up with a better package than Healey's – as he implied – or just to give him a run for his money. Whatever the case, he had been left somewhat stranded. As for the Prime Minister, he had handled cabinet with skill and good humour, giving everyone an opportunity to submit papers and to speak and, so far, had avoided any resignations. It was, I thought, a considerable performance.

Three cabinets in the following week agreed on where the cuts should fall. I accepted my share, despite it being larger than expected. In so doing I protected one important scheme that cabinet might have axed. The Newcastle Metro was an imaginative plan to run a light railway on existing lines north and south of the Tyne, with a new bridge across the river and an underground section under the centre of the city. In my few months as Secretary of State it had caused me much trouble, as costs escalated and road transport workers and ASLEF argued bitterly whether bus drivers or railwaymen should drive the trains. My civil servants were inclined to despair, seeing no end to the industrial dispute, but I was determined to give the scheme a chance. I went to Newcastle, threatened to withdraw funding and talked to local MPs about how serious the situation had become. I gave the unions and management until Christmas to sort things out. My ultimatum worked, and the County Council agreed to a strict financial regime and the unions to calling a truce. When I wrote to the Treasury for prompt authorisation of the next tranche of spending, they jibbed at it in the post-IMF mood. But they had no case for requiring more expenditure cuts from me than those which the cabinet had already accepted. The money was paid and the Metro went ahead.

When Denis Healey announced the outcome of the IMF negotiations in the House of Commons on 15 December, it was one more blow to the morale of the Labour MPs, even though it had been foreshadowed. The loss of two safe Labour seats at Walsall North and Workington in the autumn had made the Government's survival even more precarious. On such occasions, a party is more likely to divide into factions than rally to its leadership. In Labour's case the steady advance of the left was a growing threat. Tony Benn might be in a minority of one in the cabinet, but amongst party activists his writ ran large.

The Parliamentary Labour Party had witnessed the first organised attempt to stem the left-wing tide in 1974. When the veteran left-winger Ian Mikardo had been elected Chairman of the PLP through the neglect of a majority of Labour MPs, the Manifesto Group had been born. My only contribution – as a minister I was excluded from formal membership – had been to suggest its name, in the belief that the future held far worse things than *Let Us Work Together,* the manifesto upon which the recent election had been fought. The Manifesto Group had quickly restored the balance in the PLP, but its members were now deeply worried about developments in the constituencies and believed that the Group should be matched by an organisation outside parliament.

The situation was different from a year ago, when Shirley Williams had tentatively suggested that I should take an initiative and, later, when I had turned down an approach from John Cartwright and Ian Wrigglesworth to convene a meeting to launch a new CDS. I was now in the cabinet, giving me the authority the occasion needed. More importantly, Jim Callaghan was Prime Minister and he was happy to see a role for Tom McNally, his personal assistant, in whatever we chose to do. In the light of these circumstances I agreed to take the chair at a meeting at Central Hall, Westminster, on 20 February 1977, to launch the Campaign for Labour Victory, or CLV as it came to be known. This name, like that of the Manifesto Group, genuflected towards a purpose to which no-one in the Labour Party could take exception. At the same time the germ was contained within it that Labour would become permanently unelectable if its left wing took over.

Shortly before the date of the meeting, Shirley Williams made a brave speech aimed at the Militant Tendency, of whose activities she had become increasingly aware as a member of the National Executive of the party. She challenged the democratic credentials of the Trotskyite left, asking for evidence that they believed in freedom of speech and ruled out violence as a means of achieving their ends. If they could not give unequivocal answers to such questions, she said, they did not deserve to belong to the Labour Party. In the mood of those times, this was strong stuff.

My own speech at the meeting of 20 February was on a parallel theme. I said that many people had the impression that the main opposition to the Labour Government came not from the Tories but from the National Executive Committee of the party. Then I referred to Militant resolutions passed in the closing minutes of protracted constituency meetings, often accompanied by intimidation. But my remarks were mainly addressed to the supporters of *Tribune,* which that weekend was celebrating the fortieth birthday of the foundation of the paper. Having referred critically to the hard left, I said:

> The legitimate left is a different matter. The legitimate left has been an essential element in the coalition of the Labour Movement from the earliest days. We may disagree with it but we respect its right to exist. But the legitimate left has an obligation. It must not be a Trojan horse for the wreckers. It would betray its own form of radicalism if it provided a way in for those with whom we have nothing in common. The Labour Party is the party of Bevan as well as of Gaitskell. The heirs of Bevan – the legitimate left – have their role to play in saving the party.

My speech was well reported and much approved by a majority of Labour MPs. But the legitimate left, in the description I had coined, failed to acknowledge that they had more in common with Shirley, myself and our friends than with the Trotskyites and other factions of the hard left. Neil Kinnock's Bournemouth speech, denouncing Derek Hatton and the Liverpool Militants, was still more than eight years away.

Arguments with the legitimate left were not only about 'entryism' and organisation but also about ideas, particularly about how democratic socialism could be made relevant to the voters in the closing decades of the century. Three months later, in a lecture given in Stoke-on-Trent under the title 'Socialism without Abundance', I set out my own views. I said few people now believed that the public ownership of industry was the key to democratic socialism; and that most voters wanted more money to spend on themselves as much as better social services. I was in favour of giving men and women more control over their own lives, and referred to the brutalising consequences of tower blocks and massive council estates without public transport or community facilities. 'Socialism without Abundance' was later published in full in *Socialist Commentary*, and it reads well enough today. But the mood of 1977 was different, and *Tribune* gave a whole page to Neil Kinnock to reply, under the banner headline: 'Panic in the face of socialism's oldest enemy'. Kinnock also put down a mischievous parliamentary question to the Prime Minister, asking if my lecture represented the policy of Her Majesty's Government. What I had said about listening to the voters was, he declared, 'a confession of bankruptcy, a tired grab at populism', and my ideas should be strenuously opposed. It was a predictable response, good-tempered on this occasion, but showing an inability to escape from *Tribune's* ideological time-warp or to recognise the threats to Labour from disappearing voters and unrepresentative party activists.

My Stoke lecture was in memory of Tony Crosland, who had died in February of a massive heart attack. A few days before his fatal stroke, I had had a drink with him in his room at the House, which is how we generally kept in touch outside the course of government business. As always, I came away warmed because the old, disrespectful, iconoclastic Crosland often re-emerged on such occasions. I had ceased to see him as a future leader of the party, and he had long since dropped me from his inner circle. But this did not diminish my personal affection for him, or erase the memory of everything that had made him such an exciting figure when I first met him at Oxford in 1950, and for a dozen years after.

Until a by-election provided the voters of Grimsby with a successor to Tony Crosland, the Government's hold on the House of Commons was even more tenuous and, when the Opposition put down a no confidence motion for Wednesday 23 March 1977, there was a real prospect of defeat unless allies could be found from amongst the smaller parties. At lunchtime on the Saturday before the critical vote, I received a telephone call from Peter Jenkins of *The Guardian*, who had traced Silvia and me to East Hendred, where we were visiting Roy and Jennifer Jenkins who were over for the weekend from Brussels. He wanted me to know that David Steel might be interested in a deal. I telephoned Steel at his Ettrick Bridge home to confirm this, and found myself discussing possible terms. He wanted an overall agreement that could be sustained until the autumn of 1978, and a formal liaison committee between the two parties. The Government would have to promise direct elections to the European Parliament, with proportional representation in a regional list system, and progress on devolution for Scotland and Wales. These were quite specific terms, but I said that all of them were practical, although there would be no agreement if he was pressing for PR at Westminster which, he assured me, he wasn't. In my view – and I thought this would command the majority in cabinet – an agreement with the Liberal Party would be infinitely better than a deal with the Ulster Unionists, which was also being canvassed as a means of saving the Government. I then spoke to Jim Callaghan at Chequers. He knew through Cledwyn Hughes, the Chairman of the PLP, that the Liberals were showing an interest, but the proposals I put to him were the first he had received and he did not think them unreasonable. He asked me to tell Steel that he would see him at Downing Street on Monday morning.

Jim Callaghan telephoned me on Monday evening and said that everything appeared to be going smoothly. But when I came back from lunch on Tuesday I was told that David Steel wanted to speak to me urgently. 'We are in danger of coming unstuck on one point,' he said, 'direct elections. Everything else is negotiable but not this.' He was expecting a draft minute of agreement from Number 10 at any moment, but he had made clear to the Prime Minister that he needed more on Europe, because without it he couldn't carry his colleagues. I was sympathetic but said I did not think it within the Prime Minster's power to deliver the whole payroll vote for regional PR, the idea of which was very new even to those who would support it. Peter Shore was against direct elections and few of the other members of cabinet were keen. The most I thought he could ask was for the Government to give regional PR a fair wind (to use the familiar Whitehall phrase) in the House of Commons. David Steel seemed mollified by this, recognising the limits to which the Prime Minster could go. After ten minutes of discussion, it looked as if he would sign.

In cabinet the following day, 23 March – now on the eve of the confidence vote – the Prime Minister said that he had started with high hopes of an agreement with the Ulster Unionists. They had wanted a Speaker's Conference on the representation of Northern Ireland in the House of Commons and some progress towards self-government in the province. These points would be followed up, but meanwhile there was the prospect of an agreement with the Liberals, which would not, of course, 'compromise the integrity of the party'. Michael Foot joined in the Prime Minister's endorsement, saying that without it, 'Mrs Thatcher will celebrate May Day round this table'. On direct elections, the agreement was acceptable because the device of a free vote – whatever the Government's recommendation – would protect the rights of every member of the party. Peter Shore led the opposition, but when the Prime Minster went round the cabinet table collecting votes, he was joined only by Tony

Benn, Stan Orme and Bruce Millan. Cabinet had voted for the Lib-Lab pact and the no confidence motion was defeated by 322 votes to 298.

I welcomed the pact, and not only for the stability it gave to the Government, eventually for two years. In cabinet, the Prime Minister's hint, 'as much as I might like it, the Liberals wouldn't agree', occasionally provided him with a welcome excuse for not pursuing a course advocated by the Labour left. But Liberal activists around the country were very uneasy about the pact, and David Steel was under constant pressure to point to results. In turn, most Labour ministers were reluctant to admit, at least in public, that the Liberals were influencing policy. As for civil servants, they were unsure how to deal with the sometime maverick partnership between their minister and the Liberal spokesman who now had access to his office and expected to be consulted. I liked David Penhaligon, the MP for Truro, who was attached to me at Transport, but his disorderly ideas and methods of work did not fit in easily with my own style. He influenced me more than he imagined, especially on rural questions, although I did not shout this to the rooftops. Labour's 1974 manifesto had envisaged the nationalisation of all the ports. I had no intention of proceeding with this, but in extremity I could have called in aid Liberal opposition to it. Overall, nothing in my dealings with the Liberals during this period persuaded me that a coalition, although this was far short of one, would not work to the advantage of the country. As for David Steel, he had proved himself an astute leader with a strategic view of politics and the courage to seize an opportunity. Whatever some cartoonists may have claimed – as they were to claim later of his relationship with David Owen – he was not in anyone's pocket.

Running the Department of Transport was not particularly onerous. As I had anticipated, success often depended on presentation. Once, I was persuaded by my assistant press officer, who did not like me, and hoped I would fall off, to ride a motorcycle round the windy forecourt of our Marsham Street tower block for a photograph – I looked like a lugubrious spaniel – to promote a government training scheme. Another photograph was taken on top of the Severn Bridge as part of an exercise to reassure MPs that the bridge was not about to collapse, as it was closed so often to traffic. What the work of the department lacked was an obvious coherence. For all the talk of 'an integrated transport policy', issues as diverse as lorry drivers' hours, the wearing of seat belts, concessionary fares for pensioners and the future of the vehicle road tax were not easily pressed into a single mould. Much time seemed to be spent in crisis management, advising the Chairman of British Rail to avoid a strike of engine drivers in January when stocks of coal for the power stations were at their lowest; or preventing the escalation of protests about road building to the point that no roads at all could be built.

Much as I deplored the disruption of properly constituted public inquiries into road building and the intimidation of inspectors that sometimes went with it, I believed that some of the grievances of protestors were justified. After discussions with the Council on Tribunals, I took steps to distance the inquiry process from the Department in order to emphasise its independence; and a committee under Sir George Leitch came up with a formula for assessing the economic benefits of a new road that was widely accepted as fair. As a result, for more than ten years there was relative peace between the road builders and the environmentalists.

In arguments about road building, some MPs were not above being on both sides at the same time. There had long been a proposal to build a road linking far-from-prosperous North Devon with the M4 motorway, although it was not in any immediate programme. When Robin Maxwell-Hyslop, Jeremy Thorpe and Edward du Cann, the MPs most affected, asked to see me, I listened carefully to their arguments and was sufficiently impressed to agree to give the road a higher priority. 'It will be a relief to build a road that everyone wants', I said, 'and to know you will give it vigorous support.' Maxwell-Hyslop and Thorpe, delighted at their unexpected victory, readily assented, but du Cann adopted his suavest manner (and that could be very suave indeed). 'Minister, may I say how immensely grateful I am to you for listening so sympathetically to our request and for making such a brave decision. I am absolutely delighted and of course I support you all the way. But you will understand that I have some constituents who don't want the road, and on their behalf, from time to time, I shall have to deplore the approval to it you have given.' In the end the road was completed, and I drive along it today with some satisfaction. As for Edward du Cann, master of the smoothest double-talk, he eventually fell out with his business partners, his party and his constituents, so it was a pin-prick for him to fall out with me.

But the balance between road and rail and between the private and the public sectors of the industry was at the heart of transport policy, and I decided to publish a White Paper which would be a formal declaration of government policy. In my experience, the discipline of setting down arguments on paper was always salutary and, in this case, would oblige officials to take a longer-term view of their everyday tasks. If we were not to have an integrated policy we might at least have a balanced and coherent one within post-IMF resources. I wanted nothing in the White Paper that was self-consciously ideological, so it defined the objectives of transport policy as contributing to economic growth, securing for everyone a reasonable level of personal mobility and minimising the harmful effects on the environment. But, the White Paper said, we needed to decrease our absolute dependence on transport. Housing and employment had become increasingly separated; larger hospitals, schools, shops and offices served wider areas and meant longer journeys, and the costs of transport had not been taken into account. The grand sweep of transport policies meant little to most people; what mattered was how transport impinged upon them in their daily lives. In one of the paragraphs I wrote myself, sitting at home in front of my Imperial 'Good Companion' typewriter, I said:

> Complaints are familiar and are widely shared. The bus that is full or late or does not come at all; the train that is crowded or slow or does not run on Sundays; the delays and frustrations of motoring; most recently, the rising costs of all travel. The heavy lorry brings goods to the High Street and serves the factory and the farm, but is disliked almost wherever it goes.

These were prosaic sentiments, but nothing that has happened in twenty years has invalidated them. The main thrust of my White Paper was towards strengthening public transport and limiting new road schemes to those that most met economic and environmental objectives. Nothing has invalidated that either, and, indeed, it was the basis of John Prescott's 1998 White Paper.

Not that my transport policy pleased everyone. At the Labour Party conference I was attacked by a delegate for inadequately financing South Yorkshire County Council and making it difficult for Sheffield to honour a pledge not to increase its bus fares before the end of the century. Yorkshire stubbornness, when injected with left-wing militancy, was hard to overcome. At the other extreme, the Chairman of West Sussex threatened to take me to court for cutting the county's grant for road building because West Sussex refused to subsidise its buses. Both were good examples of the tension that characterises the relations between central and local government. The Government had decided that public transport should have priority within the limited resources available. It could only implement its policy by using its allocation of grant money to get local authorities to do its bidding. Thus the financial dependence of local government on Whitehall inevitably constrained its freedom.

My White Paper referred to the European dimension of transport policy and the need to work within the Community on noise and pollution problems. On my second day in the Department I summoned the Deputy Secretary in charge of external policy to tell him where I stood. 'You need to know, Mr Lazarus', I said, 'that I am a strong European and I want the department's policy and actions to reflect that'. There was a slight pause, then Peter Lazarus pronounced the fateful words, 'Yes, Minister', with his eyes slightly averted from mine. I recognised the warning. It was not easy to be a good European, particularly in a government that had no great enthusiasm for Europe despite the outcome of the referendum.

During a period when Britain's presidency of the Council of Ministers created opportunities for European initiatives, I prepared a policy statement on the lines of my own White Paper. Peter Lazarus and his team of officials played their part and I was helped by Ray le Goy, who was now in charge of transport in the Commission, having been one of my civil servants at the Board of Trade. At an early meeting of European transport ministers, with myself in the chair, I presented my policy statement with a flourish and invited discussion to begin. But there was silence. Only after some coaxing of those ministers I had specially briefed in advance did I get a minimal response. I realised then that this was not like a cabinet or a cabinet committee which started from common assumptions and was able to reach decisions without reference back. These ministers were accustomed to dealing with practical questions, mainly concerning harmonisation, and only after extensive preparation by officials and with a negotiating brief approved by their governments. I also became aware that if any of the ministers from the other eight member countries knew of my own personal convictions about Europe – and the German and Dutch ministers did – that carried no weight whatsoever, given the overall reputation of the British Government for coolness towards Europe.

On one occasion I was required to negotiate with the French deputy transport minister. He had known Philip Williams – Gaitskell's biographer, of Nuffield College, Oxford and CDS – when Philip had done research in his le Mans constituency, and quickly grasped my European credentials. But he combined his transport portfolio with responsibility for fish and, after a fruitless night spent negotiating with John Silkin, my anti-Market colleague and Minister of Agriculture, he was not disposed to make any concessions to me.

But my most difficult European challenge was on tachographs, and here I lived more by my political wits than by principle. The tachograph was a mechanical device for recording the hours and speeds at which a lorry was driven. The European Community had laid down maximum drivers' hours in the interest of road safety, and harmonisation of the law was consistent with fair competition. Our partners in the Community had adopted the tachograph as the means of ensuring that the rules were kept, but in Britain the road haulage industry was strongly opposed to 'the spy in the cab'. Some fiercely independent lorry drivers genuinely resented the intrusion of the tachograph, while others feared that it would reveal how often they exceeded the speed limit or took time off to visit girlfriends. The industry had been told, perhaps with the intention to provoke, that it was all the fault of Brussels and, within weeks of my arrival in the Department, a strike was threatened, led by the Transport and General Workers' West Midlands region, which had a reputation for industrial militancy and having the employers in their pocket. Any such strike would spread quickly to the whole country, leaving no obvious way out for the Government except a war of attrition. It would become a matter for the Prime Minister and the cabinet and would play into the hands of the anti-Marketeers, who would rather enjoy my failure, humiliated by the Europe I so much supported.

I decided to play it long, taking the heat out of the immediate crisis and relying on the European Court of Justice to deliver a verdict on the case for Britain retaining logbooks as an acceptable alternative to the tachograph. I knew we would lose, but I would then yield with good grace and the union would abandon its strike, knowing the Government had no room for manoeuvre. My tactic worked and the tachograph was eventually introduced without incident. But I had a letter from Roy Jenkins, as President of the European Commission, chiding me for failing to introduce the tachograph sooner. There was also a piece by Bernard Levin in the *Times,* combining wit and vitriol, that ridiculed my position and claimed that I had given in to the unions. I wrote him a long reply in my defence, arguing that there were good, rational grounds for the approach I had adopted. In so doing I half convinced myself, perhaps because it was uncomfortable to be seen to be dragging my feet. But the disruption of a strike would have been damaging to the Government and the country and, once again, the European Community would have become the whipping boy. No-one was seriously disadvantaged by the delay.

One of my more constructive achievements was my Green Paper proposing to extend concessionary bus fares for pensioners nationwide – they were currently available only in the districts where they lived; another, my announcement in November 1978 that Vehicle Excise Duty would be abolished. An end to VED was a major change of policy, and cabinet agreement to it involved persuading the Chancellor that savings in administrative costs and fairness as between motorists – those who used their cars a lot and those who used them little – justified transferring the tax to petrol prices. In a message to my civil servants I said, 'We shall all have a small place in history, having abolished a tax'. But my confidence was premature. Abolition was to take place in stages and be completed by 1983, but an incoming Conservative government reversed the decision.

Seat belts and whether their wearing should be compulsory was another half-completed issue I inherited. A government bill had been introduced into the House of Commons in the 1975–76 parliamentary session, but had made slow progress against the official Opposition, led by Norman Fowler, and back-bench dissidents on both sides who claimed that it was a restriction of personal freedom. When the House returned in October 1976 for tail-end business, I had the choice of insisting on several all-night sessions but with no hope of getting the Bill; or abandoning it and trying again at a future date. The second seemed a feeble course, but the Bill was not mine and had been poorly handled, and there was nothing I could do to rescue it. My decision to abandon the Bill brought a demand – it was more than a request – for a meeting from Dr Havard, the leader of the BMA, who criticised what I had done in uncompromising terms. I promised him that I would introduce a new bill as soon as possible.

This proved harder than I expected. As the Government soldiered on, a bill on seat belts was seen to have no electoral advantage and I had great difficulty in getting it on the cabinet agenda for approval. When at last I achieved this in October 1978, the omens were not good. On the evening before the item was to be taken I was called to Number 10 to discuss a possible rail strike. On the way out of the cabinet room I said to the Prime Minister, 'We have seat belts tomorrow. I hope it will go through.' 'Ah,' said Jim Callaghan, 'seat belts, yes ...', and his voice trailed away, which was a plain warning that he didn't see it going very far, especially as he had put it last on a full agenda. When we reached item eight the following morning it was ten minutes to one, and the mood was for a prompt ending. I abandoned my prepared script, referred to the public expenditure savings that would follow from fewer accidents and reminded cabinet that the principle of compulsory seat belts had already been agreed three years before. David Ennals, as Health Minister, supported me and there were a few murmurs of approval round the table but no major contributions. 'I think', said the Prime Minister, summing up, 'that the cabinet is not persuaded'. But Harold Lever, intervening at a point when the Prime Minister was usually heard in silence, said, 'Are you really sure ... ?' 'Well', said Jim Callaghan, 'we'll see', and he went round the table asking everyone for a 'Yes' or a 'No'. 'Congratulations, Secretary of State, you've won by two to one', was his magnanimous verdict. But there was a sting in the tail. 'Now you must negotiate with the Leader of the House a date for Second Reading. If on a free vote it gets a good majority, we'll take it from there.' The sting was that no-one was more opposed to seat belts – on libertarian grounds – than Michael Foot. Second Reading eventually took place on 22 March 1979 and was carried by 244 votes to 147, with Foot voting against it, together with Dennis Skinner, Enoch Powell, Norman Tebbitt and the shadow transport minister, Norman Fowler. But six days later the Government was defeated on a no-confidence motion and it was Norman Fowler, doing an abrupt about-turn when he succeeded me, who put compulsory seat belts on the statute book.

Apart from inheriting my seat belts policy, Norman Fowler also inherited my newish and outstanding Private Secretary, Genie Turton. Shortly after the change of government I met her walking down Whitehall, looking pleased with herself. I asked what had happened to put her in such a genial mood. 'I've just written a really good speech for Norman', she said, 'attacking all your policies as Secretary of State'. I may have winced and I certainly teased her. But such are the ways of our system of government that make it necessary for civil servants quickly to transfer their loyalties. Whatever their personal feelings, the great majority do so successfully and without losing the friendship of former ministers with whom they have closely worked.

Occasionally I had to talk to the Prime Minister about appointments or industrial relations, but how I dealt day to day with the nationalised industries for which I was responsible was very much a matter for me. Tony Benn saw his nationalised industries as an adjunct to his department, closely under his control. Edmund Dell appeared to come to a similar conclusion by a different route, arguing that there was no point in having a publicly owned sector of industry unless it was managed by ministers together with the rest of the economy. At the Board of Trade under

Tony Crosland I had dealt with the nationalised airlines, and at Defence with the publicly owned ordnance factories, where I had appointed, first, Michael Shanks, and then Alastair Morton as non-executive directors. This experience had brought me to a different conclusion, that the original conception of Herbert Morrison was right and nationalised industries should be held at arms' length by ministers who should not try to interfere in management. Their role was to appoint the chairman and, after discussion, the board, and let them get on with it, although this should not preclude advice or gentle pressure from time to time. It was not a relationship that could easily be defined, and it depended on a degree of mutual trust. Nor was it easy for a Labour minister to maintain, given the differing views of his colleagues and intense parliamentary and public interest in how the industries performed. Nevertheless, I tried to apply it in respect of certain publicly owned ports, including London and Liverpool, for which I was responsible; the National Bus Company, that dominated the long-range coach business; the National Freight Corporation, which was the major road haulier; and British Railways.

Railways were daily in the public eye, mainly due to their shortcomings, particularly rising fares and poor industrial relations. Here the chairman was Sir Peter Parker, whom I had first met in the several photographs of him that had adorned Shirley Williams' room in Somerville College. At Oxford he had been Chairman of the Labour Club and President of the dramatic society, and had played rugby for the university. In every way he had been a star. He was a man of effervescent and restless charm, with an instant capacity to make you feel that no-one in the world mattered to him more than you. In this he had much in common with Shirley, and he matched her in his energy.

Peter Parker became Chairman the day I joined the cabinet, and he immediately identified himself with what he called 'the railway community', embracing in that phrase both management and unions; and decided that some confrontation with the Department of Transport on rail subsidies would do his leadership no harm. But, as we both learnt, a long history of decline had bred cynicism amongst battle-hardened railwaymen about what any chairman or minister might achieve. The National Union of Railwaymen, who represented most railway staff, and ASLEF, the engine drivers' union, were at each other's throats and not ready to change their style. Nor, in the aftermath of the IMF visit, would there be much more public money for the railways, even if the shift foreshadowed in my White Paper were achieved. In the industrial and economic climate of the times, all too often the purpose of my meetings with Peter Parker was to ask what he was doing to prevent a threatened rail strike or to urge that an increase in fares should be consistent with the Government's anti-inflationary policy. It was an intolerable straitjacket in which to live for any businessman, especially when the rail unions – representing his employees – had easy access to ministers. Occasionally I would call Peter Parker and the rail unions – almost certainly fighting between themselves – to a single meeting in the hopeless endeavour of knocking their heads together, thus enabling me to report to an anxious House of Commons that I was doing all I could to avert a strike. This must have been pretty difficult for Peter Parker, but he was too much of a politician himself seriously to complain. During seven difficult years (the larger part after my time) in what often seemed a thankless and impossible job, he did as much as any chairman could do to improve efficiency on the railways and make them attractive to passengers.

One appointment which fell to me was of Sir Arthur Peterson as Chairman of the Mersey Docks and Harbour Company. As a young minister ten years earlier, I had visited the Liverpool docks where my Uncle Harold had spent all his working life. They were introducing new computer-controlled traffic equipment and better aids to navigation on the river, and the future looked bright. But trade had collapsed dramatically, partly through the switch to freight containers for which traditional dock facilities were unsuited, partly through the rise in importance of continental ports like Hamburg, and partly through chaotic industrial relations. I had known Arthur Peterson as a civil servant in DEA and he had later been Permanent Secretary at the Home Office. I appointed him because I thought the port needed a chairman quite untainted by the past. On a visit to Liverpool, he invited the trade unions to meet me for lunch in the Dock Board offices, one of the three great buildings at the Pier Head which gave the skyline its special character. The unions told me that it was their first-ever invitation to such a social occasion. It was a tough industry with hard men on either side, and the ship-owners who had run the port for many years were Victorian in their attitudes to management.

It was the events of the winter of 1978 which both brought my ministerial career to its climax and sent the Labour Party spinning into opposition for a generation. The industrial disruption of Britain extended from lorry drivers to gravediggers, and was etched deeply on the public mind. The Government was seen to be helpless in the face of trade union power and, at the crucial moment, even unaware of a situation already out of control. There is no record of the Prime Minister speaking the fateful words: 'Crisis! What crisis?' on his return on 10 January 1979 from a summit meeting on the West Indian island of Guadaloupe, but the sentiment was there. It was the third serious misjudgement Jim Callaghan had made in six months, despite all the skills he had shown during his first two, difficult, years in office. In November 1978, in the run-up to the main events, opinion polls showed the Government to be only one per cent behind the Opposition in popular support, a gap which a general election might easily have closed. By the end of February 1979, it had widened to an unbridgeable nineteen per cent.

I had not been much involved in strategic decisions on pay policy aimed at bringing inflation down from the horrendous twenty-seven per cent a year it touched in 1975. The Prime Minister had, rightly, seen this as his personal responsibility, but when he told cabinet on 13 July 1978 that five per cent should be the guideline for future settlements, I was amongst those who said it was unrealistically low. The following week he formally asked cabinet approval for the figure, and now there was more than a tremor of unease. I put it to the Chancellor that even if the trade unions reluctantly accepted a five per cent norm, in practice it would result in settlements of at least 7.5–8 per cent. 'Would it not be better', I asked, 'to settle for a higher norm than risk five per cent as too low to be taken seriously?' In fact, the Treasury's own estimate of likely wage settlements was nearer 10–11 per cent, but in a notoriously leaky cabinet, Denis Healey declined to admit any drift above the level the cabinet might agree.

If the cabinet acquiesced too easily, it was partly in the belief that five per cent would be a good campaigning slogan. As we cleared our desks, we assumed an autumn election with nine-tenths of major wage claims to be settled after it. Under the pretext of pre-holiday drinks, I gave what was understood to be a farewell party for my own departmental staff; and discussed idly with Peter Baldwin which office of state I might next occupy. In turn, he reminded me of the long-standing rules about what decisions were inappropriate for a minister once the date of a general election had been announced.

As we assembled for cabinet after the holidays in the lobby outside the cabinet room, we might have been a Cup Final team waiting to take the field. Elbows were grasped in self-conscious greeting and slightly nervous jokes eased the tension. At the TUC earlier in the week the trade unions had overwhelmingly rejected five per cent, but when the Prime Minister's speech had alerted them to the political battle ahead, they had rallied to give him a standing ovation. In advance of cabinet, Jim Callaghan had canvassed individual views and I took for granted this had shown a clear majority for an early election. As the Prime Minster described how he had been to see the Queen that morning, then rehearsed to cabinet his Government's achievements, this seemed the prelude to a formal announcement. When he said that, to the contrary, he proposed to carry on, we almost rose from our chairs in astonishment. 'May we consider for a moment the economic consequences?' asked Peter Shore. 'You may', came the reply, 'but I have no intention of making a second visit to the Palace today with a different message'. Shirley Williams also tried to intervene, but the Prime Minister brushed her aside, saying that he would like to turn to cabinet business. And that was that.

But all too soon it became clear that the Government faced a winter wages war. Free from the restraint of an impending election, trade union criticism of the five per cent norm became universal and there was evidence that the Transport and General Workers' Union was using a strike of Ford workers to demonstrate its implacable hostility to pay policy of any kind. The new General Secretary, Moss Evans, had neither the will nor the authority to provide effective leadership, and the TUC as a whole proved resistant to the blandishment of private dinners with the Chancellor and arm-twisting behind the scenes. By early December, industrial action was disrupting services on British Rail's Southern Region; the bakers were moving towards a fourteen per cent increase at the end of a five-week strike; British Oxygen had severely broken the guidelines in a major pay settlement; and Shell, Esso, Texaco and BP tanker drivers were threatening to strike.

Then, on 22 December, a 12.5 per cent pay increase was awarded to BBC staff. In normal circumstances a BBC pay settlement would hardly have been significant. But television had already been hit by overtime bans and early closedowns and the prospect of a total blackout over Christmas was thought to be real. The Government's pretence that the settlement was tolerable was an admission that it feared the political consequences of the dispute; and that five per cent, even for the well-paid, had become a joke. For a moment there was relief but most ministers departed from Westminster tired by their efforts and depressed by their failure.

It was Tuesday 2 January 1979 before the business of government resumed. During the holiday, I began to worry seriously about the breakdown of pay policy, the loss of resolve amongst colleagues and the extent to which matters were falling apart. There was gossip that ministers had tipped the wink to the BBC about the use of arbitration to get a quick decision at whatever price. In addition, my departmental responsibilities as Transport Secretary gave me a special role if there was industrial action by lorry drivers.

Early on 2 January, I dispatched a letter to the Chancellor, copying it to the Prime Minister and senior ministers, warning that a road haulage stoppage was imminent. 'The long-term effects of a strike could obviously be very serious', I wrote, 'but it would be wrong to put any pressure on the Road Haulage Association to improve an offer already so far beyond the guidelines'. I then sent a message to the Chancellor that I wished to see him urgently on wider issues. When I called on him at Number 11 Downing Street that evening, I found him unusually subdued. 'I'm very worried, Denis', I said. 'Morale in the party is at rock bottom and the Government is seen to be drifting dangerously. I think it is.' He readily agreed. Since the defeat in the House of Commons before Christmas on sanctions to back up pay and prices policy, he had not known what next to do. We would just have to pick up the pieces and try again.

In the light of this disappointing – if understandable – response, I now decided on an initiative of my own. I would express my concern publicly and try to stiffen the Government's resolve. For the Thursday evening I prepared a strong speech in defence of pay policy for a meeting I was to address at Hutton Rudby in North York-shire. In the event, heavy snowdrifts prevented the speech being delivered. But on the basis of a press release, the morning papers reported it as a sharp attack on those who broke the Government's guidelines and an attempt to rally colleagues and reassert pay policy.

I was aware that the escalating road haulage dispute could turn out to be devastat-ing for the Government. A year earlier I had discovered the complete inability of the RHA to stand up to intimidation by the Transport and General Workers' Union. A loose grouping of a large number of mainly small firms, the RHA lacked a tradition of strong leadership or sophisticated industrial relations skills. Nevertheless, when in November I discussed the latest round of negotiations with the Chairman of the RHA, I was told they hoped to keep within the guidelines, and I reported accord-ingly to Number 10. But as 1979 opened, the RHA jumped to thirteen per cent in a clumsy attempt to get a quick settlement. They were quite unprepared for a long struggle and were eventually to succumb through their inability to counter a steady flow of union misinformation and propaganda designed to persuade their members that other firms were giving in. On 3 January, when the road haulage strike began, 15,000 men came out in Scotland in support of their claim. By the following Mon-day, the strike had spread to all parts of the country, panic food buying was reported, essential supplies were in danger and the prospect was being discussed of up to two million men and women being laid off work.

The loss of jobs turned out to be much less than expected and there were few serious shortages of food. But from the first days of the strike, the sense of mount-ing chaos was acute. The ugly and arbitrary action of pickets framed against a bleak, winter landscape showed that the Government had lost control. On his return from Guadaloupe, the first task of the Prime Minister was to restore public confi-dence. Whether the nation faced a genuine crisis might be a matter of opinion. But the crisis for his Government was beyond dispute.

The easiest course was to seek a quick end to the road haulage strike at whatever cost. But all hope of salvaging anything like five per cent in the public sector would be utterly destroyed if private road hauliers were encouraged to surrender to indus-trial action and settle at will. Only one practical course was available; an open attack on the irresponsibility of the TGWU, and the spinelessness of the TUC, coupled with an unqualified determination to keep supplies moving. At every stage since the summer, the TGWU had fought a holy war against five per cent. The new leadership of the union was not popular and lorry drivers enjoyed earnings well above the na-tional average. The union had chosen to confront the Government. My view was that the Government should respond in kind.

By the time cabinet met on Thursday 11 January, newspaper headlines were describing Britain as browned-off and battered, and lacking in leadership. The Prime Minister's complacency at Heathrow the previous day was now seen as irresolution. A fly on the wall would have confirmed that cabinet was no better. Ministers were told that Moss Evans was unwilling to appeal to lorry drivers to return to work and would soon make their strike official. As for the TUC, it was frozen into impotence by divisions. Some cabinet colleagues urged the Prime Minster to appear on television to steady the nation, but I was sceptical and he was not sanguine about what he could say. Tony Benn was not the only one of my colleagues who clearly saw any criticism of the unions, even in the privacy of cabinet, as an act of treachery. It was an inconclusive and infuriating meeting.

My own personal responsibilities, however, provided an opportunity to show that the Government was not entirely helpless. After consultation with colleagues, a list of priority supplies was compiled and put to Harry Urwin, Assistant General Secretary of the TGWU (the only union official to show a sense of reality during these events). On the next day this list was telexed by the union to its regional secretaries. At the same time I revived the regional emergency committees of my department and instructed their chairmen to establish contact with the TGWU in an attempt to resolve bottlenecks locally and to provide a fast and reliable channel of information to my office. But it soon became clear that the TGWU headquarters at Transport House had only *recommended* priorities for essential supplies, and local strike committees had been given the list 'for action at their discretion'. This was to be a source of constant friction and, coupled with aggressive picketing, the main cause of public anger.

For the Government as a whole, from Saturday 13 January the task of dealing with the consequences of the road haulage strike and for preparing for the worst in other disputes fell to the Civil Contingencies Unit (CCU) of the cabinet, with Merlyn Rees, the Home Secretary, in the chair and Sir Clive Rose of the Cabinet Office, whom I had first met during my defence trip to Vienna, at his right hand. Ministers and officials met daily and received reports from both myself and other ministers, especially the Minister of Agriculture, John Silkin, who was concerned with the availability of food.

It was inevitable that the CCU would have in mind the possibility of bringing in the army to move supplies. But the armed forces are reluctant to be called upon to perform civilian tasks. At best, they see it as interfering with training schedules, pre-empting leave and reducing their numbers in operational theatres. There is also a strong wish to maintain political neutrality and foster goodwill on all sides of the community. Ministers of Defence (and I had been one of them) are adept at demonstrating insoluble logistical problems about the deployment of troops. When, on this occasion, I urged the need to move vital medical supplies out of Hull docks, defence ministers were adamant and bland. 'It will take days to put a suitable convoy together', they said. Nor did they have available detailed plans of the docks to tell them where to go. The Home Secretary, advised by the Cabinet Office, was no more eager for the risks involved. The declaration of a state of emergency had been considered by the Prime Minister but rejected by cabinet, and it was to be considered and rejected again. Although a hawk in other respects, I was amongst those doubtful about the advantages of a state of emergency. Troops could be used on a limited scale quite legitimately without one.

It was a symptom of disarray that the cabinet met, unusually, on a Monday for a long session on pay policy. The House of Commons was about to return from the recess for an immediate debate on the industrial situation. I reported that there was no end in sight to the lorry drivers' strike. In addition, there was now little chance of avoiding a national rail stoppage, provoked entirely by a dispute between Ray Buckton and ASLEF and Sid Weighell and the NUR. Cabinet was also told of the risk of a nationwide official strike of water-workers, which would pose a grave threat to health. This time strong views were expressed about feeble TUC leadership; the balance had swung too far in favour of the unions, and secondary picketing had become a serious threat. But for a second time there was no practical outcome to the cabinet's deliberations, and in the House of Commons the following day Mrs Thatcher launched an effective attack on the Government, whose paralysis was plain.

Jim Callaghan was deeply depressed by the behaviour of the unions, which was quite outside almost fifty years of his experience of the Labour movement, during which he had courted a special relationship with them. He was now a man divided within himself, his mood swinging between an instinct to be tough and a fear of where that would lead. He knew that the public was increasingly outraged by the sight of pickets on the television screens. But he was unwilling to denounce openly the abuse of trade union power. A three-hour meeting with Len Murray and Moss Evans at Downing Street was confirmation that beer and sandwiches remained a Labour Government's only formula for industrial peace. As it took place, television sets at Number 10 were tuned to Mrs Thatcher building on her previous day's success with a virtuoso performance unusually free from party rancour.

By default, a new policy was emerging. There would be a long haul to another voluntary agreement with the unions, and the Government would hope meanwhile to minimise the worst consequences of the strike and save the tattered remnants of pay policy. It was not easy. In making the strike against the RHA official, the TGWU claimed that it would enable them to restrain such secondary picketing. But on the evening of 16 January, I had to complain to Alex Kitson, who was coordinating the strike for the union, that nothing had changed. The following day I sent him a shopping list of some forty road haulage depots where action was being taken in defiance of apparent instructions. Pickets were blocking materials for the manufacture of penicillin; preventing the collection of propane gas required to de-freeze railway points; and refusing to allow the movement of chlorine for water purification. Even where the regional and district officers of the union were granting dispensation for certain products, local strike committees were insisting that they countersigned the documents. There was a laborious delay in dealing with emergencies.

In an unprecedented move, a national liaison group had now been established, with Sir Clive Rose representing the Government and Ron Todd the TGWU. But when, later that week, the TGWU finally issued a code of practice for picketing, it was inadequate. At the meeting of the CCU on 23 January (also the 'day of action' of 1.5 million council workers) I reported that the new code had made only a limited impact on secondary picketing. Agreed priorities continued to be ignored by strikers and there was very little movement through the ports. It was crucial to tell the TGWU that either essential pharmaceutical and medical supplies were freed immediately or the Government would use its own resources to move them.

That evening the Prime Minister hastily convened a meeting of all cabinet ministers involved in dealing with the spreading industrial disruption. The idea of a state of emergency was still in his mind, and he seemed unable to grasp my alternative solution of using the army to move supplies without one. In desperation I threw across the table to him – unlike in full cabinet, I was sitting almost opposite – a list of priority supplies that needed moving urgently. I said that we should now deliver an ultimatum to the TGWU that if it was unable to act then the Government would find its own solution. This the Prime Minister accepted. On his instructions, Moss Evans and his deputies were summoned to an immediate meeting with the Home Secretary, the Employment Secretary, Albert Booth, and myself. Merlyn Rees welcomed them far too generously, with an apology for calling them to an evening meeting; and Albert Booth was strangely tongue-tied on the issue itself. I was happy to be left to tell Moss Evans that in future detailed lists of specific cases in which essential supplies were being blocked would be delivered regularly by hand from my private office in Marsham Street to his in Smith Square, less than five minutes away, where they would be signed for.

There remained the strike itself, how to settle it and consequences for pay policy. On this, the key decision had been taken a week earlier and had found me among the minority in cabinet. On Thursday 18 January, the question had arisen in cabinet of how long the strike should be allowed to continue, given any influence the Government might have on its duration. Had the time come to suggest to the RHA that they should settle for twenty-two per cent? The obvious way was for the Government to decide not to restrict rates and charges in the road haulage industry. The wage settlement could then be passed on to the customer (and in inflation). This course was favoured, amongst others, by Roy Hattersley, the Prices Secretary. I was strongly opposed to it because it looked like abject surrender. The cabinet's policy, I said, was beginning to be 'give in, give in, give in'. But although I had a number of allies, I lost the argument.

When cabinet was over, I sent my official car away and walked back from Number 10 to Marsham Street through St James's Park. I summoned Genie Turton, my Private Secretary, and Roger Liddle, my special adviser, and telephoned Silvia. 'I'm about to resign', I announced. 'I've had enough'. My colleagues had no stomach for a fight, even when the Government's only chance of survival lay in strength of purpose. But my theatrical mood did not last. The practical problems of dealing with the strike were too absorbing. At five o'clock I was back at yet another meeting of the CCU; and later that night enjoyed a blinding row with Alex Kitson in a BBC television studio, with Robin Day barely holding us apart. By the time I was called to Number 10 the following day to discuss my threat of resignation with the Prime Minister, my mind had already moved on to limiting the damage of the cabinet's decision and to continuing the struggle.

At the end of January, when the battle was over, I made a speech in Stockton-on-Tees, stating the case for a pay and prices freeze as an alternative to the policy of muddling through. I failed to clear it in advance with Number 10 as protocol required, irritated cabinet colleagues, especially Roy Hattersley who, despite his bluff exterior and responsibility for prices, had never been prepared to fight, and gave Mrs Thatcher and Labour backbenchers an opportunity to attack the Prime Minister in the House of Commons for allowing me to say such heretical things. But there was no word of reproach from him.

The cabinet decision had not ended the strike. Another fortnight was to pass before a private arbitration in Bristol allowed a settlement of over twenty-two per cent to spread throughout the country. Even then, the greater part of February was to be occupied by strikes in the health and municipal services, some of them more immediately painful to the public than the action of the lorry drivers. But the cabinet decision was taken to be a symbol of the Government's whole conduct of industrial affairs. The trade unions had defeated the Labour Government and opened wide the door to Mrs Thatcher. They had also defeated themselves, because a Conservative government would ensure that they were never the same again.

Without a parliamentary majority, abandoned by the Liberals, humiliated by the unions and defeated on devolution to Scotland, the result of the election was never in doubt. Shortly before it was called, I made a speech in which I said, 'Mrs Thatcher will be a one-woman disaster area for Britain', only to be rebuked by nervous ministerial colleagues who thought this was over the top (not through fears that it might be regarded as sexist). Whatever the government of which I had been a member had done – or failed to do – I was certain that Mrs Thatcher was bad news. I had not felt this about Ted Heath in 1970 and I respected a number of front-bench Tories like

Willie Whitelaw and Jim Prior. But Mrs Thatcher represented the unsympathetic side of suburban middle England that I had known in my Liverpool childhood.

I spent most of the campaign in Stockton, occasionally venturing out into other parts of the North-East and to speak for friends elsewhere. I was never worried about my own seat, which I held with a majority of over 11,000, but more than fifty of my Labour colleagues lost theirs and, at 36.9 per cent, Labour's share of the vote was the lowest since 1931. While Mrs Thatcher, the new Prime Minister, improbably quoted St Francis of Assisi on the steps of Number 10 on Friday 4 May 1979, it was beginning to look as if only a miracle could now save the Labour Party.

Chapter 9
A Painful Parting

With the election over and arguments concerning Labour's future about to intensify, the battle in parliament, where Margaret Thatcher was secure, was likely to be irrelevant for a year or two. But when the House resumed for the Queen's Speech and a short session before the summer recess, I did not anticipate the speed of events; and the idea of starting a new political party never occurred to me. In Stockton I had more than fifty per cent of the vote, and forthcoming boundary changes would probably strengthen my position. I had no difficulties with my local party and anticipated none that would be unmanageable. I stood for the Parliamentary Committee, as the shadow cabinet was formally called, and was elected in the middle order, to my chagrin several places behind Roy Hattersley, although a few places ahead of David Owen. I would have preferred an economic or industrial portfolio and, when offered education by Jim Callaghan, declined, not wanting to find myself in conflict with anything Shirley had done as Secretary of State, and not enthusiastic about facing endless lobbies by teachers' trade unions, when greater issues would be at the top of the political agenda. Jim was irritated and threatened to give education to Neil Kinnock, if that was my final decision. It was, and I settled for defence as an area where it would be important to hold the line in opposition, especially against unilateral disarmament. Neil Kinnock, who had not been elected to the shadow cabinet, thus got his feet on the first rungs of the ladder to the leadership.

I took a strategic view of my new defence responsibilities, concerning myself almost wholly with the question of whether Britain should proceed to build new Trident submarines armed with advanced nuclear weapons and allow medium-range cruise missiles (a kind of sophisticated flying bomb, whose characteristics first came to the attention of the general public years later in the Gulf War) to be located on British soil. I believed that we could not afford, and did not need, Trident submarines to replace Polaris as an independent deterrent, but that our NATO obligations justified accepting cruise missiles. They were an essential part of the NATO modernisation initiated by Helmut Schmidt to emphasise America's continued commitment to the defence of Europe. I wrote articles and a pamphlet to this effect, made speeches in the country, gave a lecture to the Royal United Services Institute and visited Washington to meet American defence chiefs. But in the House of Commons I relied heavily for support on John Roper, whom Jim Callaghan agreed I should bring on to the front bench as my number two. John was already deeply versed in the sophistications of defence policy and well connected with the academic defence establishment abroad. His acute mind and tireless enthusiasm were a great strength to me, as was his loyalty and friendship throughout the traumatic years that were to follow.

Defence had traditionally absorbed much of the Labour Party's limitless capacity for internal wrangling, and steady pressure from the left continued to commit the party to unilateral disarmament and withdrawal from NATO. I was firmly excluded from a party political television broadcast on defence devised by the NEC and masterminded by Robin Cook, and only the most strenuous representations from Jim Callaghan prevented it being overtly unilateralist. There was an outcry by the left at my *Yes to Cruise, No to Trident* pamphlet, and a well-organised group of nine constituency parties carried identical resolutions calling for me to be sacked as defence spokesman. But the majority of my parliamentary colleagues had no complaint, although an exception was Neil Kinnock who supported a unilaterist motion in a defence debate, a predictable gesture by the left but aggravated in his case by his new role as a senior front-bench spokesman. I went to see Jim Callaghan in his Leader of the Opposition's room in the House of Commons to ask what he proposed to do. After a preliminary discussion, he walked to the window and glanced out over New Palace Yard. 'You know, Bill,' he said, 'we had a rally at Cardiff Arms Park a week ago. The speakers assembled, I was one and the other was Neil. We were late and the crowd became impatient.' Jim paused and turned back to face me. 'You know who they started calling for, you know what the chant was?' I shrugged. 'It was: "We want Kinnock, we want Kinnock." Not me, Bill, but Kinnock.' There was silence, and then he asked: 'You want me to sack him?' 'No, Jim,' I replied, 'but let him know he can't vote against a three-line whip on defence with impunity.' I heard no more and did not enquire about the outcome. But I reflected that Jim knew authority had slipped from him.

He should have made way for a successor as soon as the formalities of the new parliament had been completed. To be fair to him, the immediate post-election mood in the Parliamentary Labour Party was good tempered and there was a willingness to re-elect him leader without a contest. But the lesson of his last nine months in office was plain: his avuncular bonhomie and native shrewdness were no longer sufficient to control a turbulent party moving steadily to the left. Jim Callaghan certainly does not bear the primary responsibility for the events of the following eighteen months that made the Labour Party unelectable at the polls for a generation. But his decision to stay as Leader when Denis Healey was waiting in the wings proved a fatal error. He was no longer up to the role in which he was cast in the coming struggle for power.

The shadow cabinet which met for the first time in the middle of June 1979 contained most of the same faces, and few members of it were seized of an impending crisis. We were all tired after five years in government and realised that our defeat had been deserved. We still thought mainly in terms of the mood in the parliamentary party and in varying degrees failed to appreciate the force of the attack that Tony Benn and his allies had been preparing and were now about to mount. Its spearhead was a three-pronged thrust for the election of the leader by an electoral college, the reselection of MPs by constituency parties and NEC authorship of the party's election manifesto. The place of battle was to be the party conference at Brighton.

I first met Tony Benn in the 1950s, when I persuaded him to become a member of the Executive Committee of the Fabian Society. He was fresh and open in his manner and full of ideas, although easily carried away by enthusiasm into political naivety. He took me to lunch at the House of Commons shortly after the resignation of Sir Anthony Eden as Prime Minister, and graphically described how Rab Butler would shortly emerge as his successor. But later that afternoon it was Harold Macmillan I watched arrive at Buckingham Palace to kiss hands. Tony Benn spoke in my Bristol West by-election and wrote a piece for me about modernising the Labour Party – not a word of ideology – after Labour's 1959 defeat. When he found himself excluded from the House of Commons as Lord Stansgate, following the death of his father, it was my friends Dick Taverne and Ivan Yates who played a major part in helping him divest himself of his unwanted peerage.

For a short time in 1970–71, I dealt with civil aviation as part of his team of shadow industry ministers. I could not share his passion for Concorde, which I saw as an extravagant diversion of public money from social needs; and found him remarkably adept at filching away for himself any opportunity for publicity. I also recognised for the first time a casuistry in debate that was harmless and amusing in a speech at the Oxford Union but intellectually dishonest and dangerous in discussions about serious politics. He would, for example, claim the validation of history for his ideas by making himself heir to the fourteenth-century Lollards or the seventeenth-century Levellers, to both of whom he would give heroic status in the pantheon of dissenters. He would count on his confident and seamless delivery and the ignorance of his audience to enable him to get away with a sleight of hand which any reputable historian would disavow. If challenged, he would gloss over the point as approximate and no more than a good-humoured flight of fancy. It was a clever performance, although at what stage a forensic device became serious self-deception it is impossible to say. But those who remember Tony Benn as an engaging television star in the early 1970s, or see him today, as a septuagenarian elder statesman, need to be reminded of the intervening years and the damage he did to one of Britain's great political parties. As Jim Callaghan had found it impossible to keep Tony Benn in line as a member of his own cabinet, the odds were heavily against his now being able to check his rolling bandwagon.

Such proved to be the case at the Brighton conference in October 1979, which was a disaster. Although the proposal on the election of the leader was lost (a very temporary remission, as it proved), resolutions on mandatory reselection and the manifesto were carried, with an instruction to bring forward detailed constitutional changes for approval in the following year. The resolution on the manifesto was particularly damaging, as it handed over to the National Executive Committee the final decision on the policies on which Labour would fight a general election and would implement thereafter. Conference also established a Commission of Inquiry on organisation and finance. Initially this seemed a sensible development but very soon the NEC minimised the role of parliamentarians on it and ensured that it had a built-in majority of the left. Apart from the leader and deputy leader, none of the nineteen MPs on the NEC sufficiently commanded the support of their own parliamentary colleagues to get elected to the shadow cabinet, and fourteen were unequivocally on the left. Amongst its trade-union members was Clive Jenkins, who had long been a wily, manipulative man of the left, and David Basnett, late of Quarry Bank and now leader of my own union, the General and Municipal Workers. For a number of years, Basnett had been identified as the voice of intelligent, modernising trade unionism, and I had lunched with him regularly when I was in government. But he had somehow failed to grow in stature while in office, and I had a row with him when he brought Tess Gill, a member of the Central Committee of the Communist Party, to brief Labour MPs on a parliamentary matter. He gave the impression of deep inner anxiety and having lost his bearings in the struggle for the soul of the Labour Party. Although appointed as a moderate, his membership of the Commission did not bring any reassurance.

Thus, with the Brighton conference over, the future looked very different from only a few months before and when the House of Commons returned from the recess, the talk was all of Jim Callaghan's failure to prevent the slide. In the tea room, a favourite place of gossip for Labour MPs, and somewhere to take the pulse of the party, there was tension. Leo Abse, a highly individual Labour MP and one of the few Europeans identified in the past with the left of the party, sat next to me and said that the situation was wholly different from the 1960s, and it was time to stop making concessions. From the influential Northern Group of Labour MPs, Derek Foster, later to be Labour's Chief Whip, said that the young pretenders (meaning Roy Hattersley, David Owen and myself) must rally round Denis Healey as the next leader. This, too, was the message of my former PPS, Ken Weetch: Callaghan must go, because he was a fixer who had failed to fix; Healey must put himself at the head of the PLP and I should tell him so. But when I spoke to Healey he was against an early change of leader, although he said he had told Callaghan to toughen up. I replied that toughening up was what I hoped to see in *him* and I would help to rally his troops if he showed more fighting spirit. He mentioned the possibility – then thought unlikely – that Michael Foot rather than Shore or Silkin would run for the leadership when the moment came, and I said that he would probably beat Foot but only by a whisker. The following week, at Denis' suggestion, Roy Hattersley, Eric Varley and I joined him for a discussion of tactics. For the first time since the election it looked as if he might now take the lead in fighting the constitutional changes, and thus strengthen his own, otherwise shaky, position.

But during the next critical year he showed no great disposition to fight. He confessed to me on one occasion that he was seriously exhausted after five years as Chancellor. But this hardly explained his frequent lecturing trips abroad, often, it seemed, to Japan, which accounted for his absences from crucial shadow cabinet meetings. Even when he was present he failed effectively to challenge Jim Callaghan on the direction events were taking or to provide the leadership for which a majority of the shadow cabinet were waiting. I assumed he took the view that acquiescence in the changes in the constitution – or at least, the absence of sustained opposition to them – was a necessary price to pay for the leadership. Shirley Williams, David Owen and I asked to see him at the end of September 1980 because of disappointment at his lack of fight, particularly on the proposals for an electoral college. His attitude – at first reluctant to find the time and dismissive of our views, then defensive about his failure – depressed us. At the end of an hour's discussion in Shirley's Pimlico flat, our worst fears were confirmed. If he won the leadership, any idea of our leaving the Labour Party would be set aside for the time being, but we found no sign that he understood the depth of the crisis the party was facing. He treated it like the routine difficulties with the left that he had lived with since he worked for Ernest Bevin more than thirty years before. For all his wit and muscular intelligence, not for the first time his fighting spirit did not match his noisy belligerence. By the time of the leadership contest in November 1980, there was no enthusiasm for him amongst many of his natural supporters, and a handful of the votes he needed were withheld from him in the ballot. There was no compensating additional support from those whom he hoped to have propitiated by his year of virtual silence. Whether Denis Healey could have ever beaten Michael Foot to become Leader of the Labour Party in 1980 we shall never know, but his failure to take risks and fight was a grave misjudgement.

The alliance that brought Shirley, David Owen and myself together to make representations to Denis Healey had been building up since the spring. Initially it had been marked by my partnership with David Owen in the shadow cabinet in resisting constitutional changes, something in which Shirley could play no part as she was out of the House of Commons. Her role was in parallel as a member of the NEC, an increasingly unpleasant and unrewarding experience. We came together in the Gang of Three in the summer of 1980, and thereafter it was close cooperation, comparing notes, talking to each other most days and meeting frequently. To my surprise, Shirley and David knew little of each other and much less than I knew of each of them. They had no social relations and did not even carry each other's telephone numbers.

Shirley was my oldest and closest friend in politics, particularly since Dick Taverne's defeat at Lincoln, but of David Owen I knew nothing until he entered parliament in 1966. He had not been amongst the talented group of Young Fabians I had recruited in my closing months with the Society, nor, he later confessed, had he even been aware of the existence of the Campaign for Democratic Socialism. But although he came to the House with no obvious experience of politics, he soon seemed as comfortable there as two other new MPs with whom he formed an early friendship, John Mackintosh, already a professor of politics, and David Marquand, who I had first met when he was a leader-writer on the *Manchester Guardian*. David Owen was welcomed into the 1963 Club as an admirer of Hugh Gaitskell and became a regular attender, always forthright in his opinions and often a fierce critic of Harold Wilson. Immersed as I was in the junior and middle ranks of government, I did not closely follow his early performance in the House or the particular intrigues of the group of young backbenchers who were becoming thoroughly fed up with the Wilson leadership. So it came as a surprise when, in the summer of 1968, he was appointed Under-Secretary of State for the Royal Navy. But I was soon impressed by his confidence at the dispatch box and, when, in August of the following year, Roy Jenkins asked me to go to the Treasury as Minister of State, I suggested David Owen as an alternative.

In the years that followed, David was increasingly drawn, as a friend and like-minded colleague, into the political grouping of which I was part. His insouciance and arrogance were attractive. He often reminded me of Tony Crosland when I first met him (they would have been of a similar age), although there was much less substance to his opinions. Crosland in his early thirties was deeply read in economics, sociology and political theory, and his ideas were richly matured and internally consistent. David had the aptitude of a doctor for making a confident diagnosis of a political problem, only to abandon it without apology in favour of another if the first diagnosis proved mistaken. This was presumably a product of his medical training, where in private the search for truth was real but in public a doctor should never admit that he was wrong.

Overall, David Owen was vigorous and bold, which made him a good companion in the political fight. But he made no secret of wishing to keep his elders and betters up to the mark. He could charm them with his approval, but show contempt for those he suspected of backsliding. Before entering parliament, he had been much impressed by *The Future of Socialism* but, like others, was disappointed by Tony Crosland's equivocal attitude to Harold Wilson and his unwillingness to provide robust, practical leadership for the Gaitskellites. From the 1970 election onwards, he was of the circle round Roy Jenkins, a supporter of our collective causes and privy to most of our private discussions. When, in 1973, I was invited to become the first Director of Fair Trading, which would have meant leaving parliament, David Owen was amongst those I consulted before refusing. He was also a member of a small group – Dick Mabon, John Harris, John Roper, David Marquand and Bob Maclennan were amongst the others – who lunched regularly in each other's homes to discuss tactics for survival in the years following the events of 1971–72. In contrast to my relations with Roy and Shirley or, of a younger generation, with David Marquand and John Roper, there was no particular warmth between us. But there was pleasure in dining with him and his intelligent and attractive American wife Debbie in London, or in seeing them both occasionally at weekends in the country. From the middle 1970s Silvia and I were invited to a regular Fourth of July party at the Old Rectory, Buttermere, which they had bought and restored as a spacious, if spartan, family home. There was a barbecue, much beer and cider, lots of noisy children and the compulsory rounders match in which David usually made the highest score and was always determined to win. He seemed on such occasions to contrive and enjoy the masculine outdoor chumminess of an American politician, surrounded in his case by the brightest and the best from publishing and television, who had exchanged Martha's Vineyard and the Adirondacks for the gentle hills of Wiltshire.

It is difficult to be sure when I perceived some slight shift in David's personal allegiances. Like me, he was disappointed when Roy failed to become Chancellor again in 1974, suggesting that even Leader of the House might be better than returning to be Home Secretary, and made it clear that he would like to become Minister of State for Defence if I turned it down. Then, in the referendum of the following year, unlike the rest of us, he played no part in the national campaign. Despite his continued forthright expression of opinions and apparent enjoyment of the company of friends, there were more occasions than hitherto when he kept his own counsel and preferred his separate ways. Alone of Roy's friends, David was unmoved by his leadership defeat and departure for Brussels. 'Roy, you're finished', he said, adding that Roy's failure had let us all down and we would now be better off without him. This distancing of himself from old allies became more pronounced when he entered the cabinet, as Foreign Secretary, in 1977. Of his contemporaries of the 1960s, John Mackintosh was soon to die and David Marquand had left parliament, and he showed no enthusiasm for preserving other political ties. Apart from Roy, Shirley had been the most consistent advocate within the Labour Party of Britain's membership of the Common Market. But on only one occasion during his period as Foreign Secretary did he initiate a discussion with

Shirley – I was also there – about how best to handle European problems, in a cabinet of which we were all members. On Rhodesia, Shirley and I were supportive if only by our silence when we doubted the progress towards a settlement which he claimed he was making. There was no reciprocal response.

It is customary for friends in cabinet to keep each other in touch with departmental developments, either out of goodwill or to ensure support, but David seemed to have no concept of such closeness. When a lobby correspondent accosted me in the Committee Corridor of the House and asked what I thought of Peter Jay as Ambassador to Washington, I treated it as a joke and was dumbfounded to be told that David Owen had already announced it. David had neither consulted his friends about the idea nor warned them that such a controversial decision was about to be made. On Rhodesia, I suggested to him that Field Marshal Lord Carver, whom I had known as Chief of the Defence Staff when I was Minister of State, would be a suitable candidate to be Resident Commissioner, should negotiations lead to an end to UDI. Lord Carver was later appointed in readiness, but there was no private word of acknowledgment from David which, in the normal courtesy of relations, I might have expected. The best explanation was that he was young, properly ambitious and weighed down by the responsibilities of office. He may also have felt the need to prove himself, on the assumption that his appointment as Foreign Secretary had been unwelcome to others of greater experience or seniority, although I cannot recall any expression of resentment, even from Roy Hattersley, whose recent time as Minister of State at the Foreign Office might have given him a prior claim to promotion.

In August 1977 I reviewed in my occasional diary my first year in cabinet and the performance of my colleagues. Of David Owen I wrote:

> He is difficult to place. He is aware of being comparatively junior and on trial. But I don't think he is sufficiently his own man and he isn't firm or mature in his judgements. Much depends on how he sees his future and the extent, direction and speed of his ambition.

A year later, considering the future of the Labour leadership after Callaghan, I noted:

> David Owen has made a great leap forward and used his opportunity with skill and flair. But after a brilliant and effective start, he now leaves many doubts in people's minds. Those who see him closely wonder whether he is not a hollow man. What does David really stand for except himself?

Despite this – and politics is a profession in which critical judgements on one's colleagues are routine – my personal relations with him remained steady, and I recognised that he would want to exercise a degree of independence to live up to and make the most of having become Foreign Secretary at the age of thirty-eight. For all of us, David included, there were few signposts to our political future after 1979.

In the shadow cabinet we worked together in increasing isolation from other members to resist constitutional changes. We were incensed by the proposal to establish a trade union-dominated electoral college to elect the Labour leader, which we believed to be wrong in principle, damaging to the electoral prospects of the party (given the unpopularity of the trade unions), and likely to produce the wrong man. Our impatience grew at the steady erosion of the will to fight the proposal amongst colleagues. Roy Hattersley, Merlyn Rees, Eric Varley, Roy Mason and John Smith shared our views but were not prepared to challenge Jim Callaghan, who was presiding over the slide, or to risk confrontation with the NEC or the trade unions. Roy Hattersley huffily registered his opposition to the changes but then drafted a 'compromise' which accepted an electoral college; John Smith would shuffle past me, avoiding my eye and rather ashamed of his feebleness. I preferred to retain the existing method of election, by Labour MPs who knew the candidates best and would have most to do with the leader day to day. It also seemed tactically the first line to defend. David moved quickly to what was my second preference, the election of the leader on the basis of 'one member, one vote' from among all the paid-up members of the Labour Party. There was a new anger in him. At the beginning he had been ready to give Jim Callaghan the benefit of the doubt as a mark of respect and because of the personal debt he owed him for appointment as Foreign Secretary. Towards the end, he was fiercely critical of Callaghan's inability to stand and fight. David felt let down, once again, by a leader, but with every justification. As they showed in party meetings, given a lead from the top, Labour MPs would have been ready to respond to an unequivocal defence of their position or to move to one member, one vote.

Further evidence of Jim Callaghan's declining authority came not in a personal defeat but in a betrayal, described by Peter Jenkins in a stinging article in *The Guardian,* as worthy of Neville Chamberlain. At a special weekend meeting of Labour's Commission of Inquiry, held at Bishop's Stortford on 14–15 June 1980, he endorsed a proposal for an electoral college in which Labour MPs would have half the votes and the trade unions a quarter. It was total capitulation on a central issue, in the knowledge that once the principle had been conceded the share of the vote could readily be changed to diminish parliamentary representation still further. On Sunday evening, after the Bishop's Stortford meeting was over, I was very surprised to receive a telephone call from Jim Callaghan at home, a rare event. He told me what had happened and put it in the best light, hoping to soften my hostility in advance of the shock waves that would strike Labour MPs. I was less angry than stunned, and listened in virtual silence.

It was the beginning of a bad week. Despite Jim's careful briefing of the press, Monday morning's *Times* headline was: 'Callaghan defeat on key party issues', a verdict widely echoed elsewhere. There was a critical leading article the following day, and the Wednesday headline was: 'Callaghan surrenders to left-wing pressure'. Jim was furious, and blamed David and me for putting the worst gloss on the weekend. A meeting of the shadow cabinet on Monday was depressed and subdued, but there was an unpleasant scene at a further meeting on Thursday when he held us responsible for Peter Jenkins' piece. I wrote to him afterwards, complaining of his unjustified personal attack. I had certainly spoken to Peter Jenkins, who was an old friend, but the words he used to describe Bishop's Stortford were, as always, his own. More to the point, I had made no contact with *The Times*, or with the *Daily Telegraph*, the *Mirror* or the *Mail*, which also carried full and critical stories. The truth was that Jim knew he had sold the pass; it was not surprising that the papers had reached the same conclusion, and that those who had defeated him were crowing about their success. The progress of all political parties is marked by the place names of their conferences, usually holiday resorts like Blackpool, Brighton and Scarborough, better known to the public for their piers and comic postcards. Bishop's Stortford is an innocuous country town, but its hapless place in Labour history is secure.

A few days before the Bishop's Stortford meeting, David, Shirley and I issued a public statement. Despite David's near neutrality on Europe in cabinet, his commitment to Britain's continued membership of the European Community was unequivocal. When John Silkin, now a member of the shadow cabinet, signed a document saying that Britain should withdraw from the Community, he was incensed and told me that he wanted to get in touch with Shirley in order to issue a rebuttal. We met, a draft was agreed and appeared in our names within two days, establishing in the public mind for the first time our identity as the Gang of Three. I was happy to sign the statement but did so conditionally. I said to Roger Liddle that I would not be prepared to leave the Labour Party on Europe alone (which seemed to be Shirley's position) or even on defence, because on both issues it had been possible to win back the party in the past. As for the party now, if we were to stand any chance of rallying it we would not succeed if Europe was seen to be our main concern. I therefore proposed that we should follow up our European initiative with a much broader and carefully considered statement of policy, and to this David and Shirley readily agreed. I did the first and second drafts, David the third and Shirley the fourth, and there were eight drafts in all. The final document of some 3,500 words represented not a compromise but a collective view and each of us would have been hard-pressed to claim any particular sentence as our own. After some discussion, we agreed that the only chance of getting it printed in full was by agreement with a single newspaper and *The Guardian*, the obvious candidate, was enthusiastic. Shirley also ensured that the *Mirror* had a preview, so that a substantial part of it would reach a wider readership. The date for publication, originally mid-July, slipped, but it appeared as an open letter to our fellow Labour Party members on 1 August 1980.

Twenty years later, our *Guardian* letter stands up remarkably both as a warning to the Labour Party on the brink of a self-induced disaster and as a manifesto for a social democratic party in the closing years of this century. We were still too corporatist on the economy, but we addressed the Labour Party plainly about the choices it was facing. We said that it would only regain electoral support if it remained a party 'firmly committed to parliamentary democracy, rejecting the class war, accepting the mixed economy and the need to manage it efficiently, and attaching importance to the ideals of freedom, equality and social justice'. The opening words of the letter said that the Labour Party was facing the gravest crisis in its history, graver even than 1931, but in a frenzy of excitement that followed, greater importance was attached to our penultimate paragraph. In this we warned that if Labour abandoned its democratic and internationalist principles, 'the argument may grow for a new democratic socialist party to establish itself as the party of conscience and reform', adding, with a clear hint of our own personal destination, that we were not prepared to abandon Britain to divisive and often cruel Tory policies because the country lacked an acceptable alternative to a Conservative government. It was a careful form of words and an unmistakable indication that the possibility of starting a new party was in our minds.

We had reached this point at different speeds by different routes. David Owen had been highly critical of Roy Jenkins' Dimbleby Lecture towards the end of the previous year, so much so that it had become a gossipy joke that Tom Bradley MP, formerly Roy's PPS, had threatened to push him off the platform at Westminster underground station and under a tube train if he did not stop his hostile mutterings. It was consistent with this that at a private conference in Birmingham he had said that there was no chance of his supporting a new party for at least another decade. But the accumulating frustration of the shadow cabinet was changing his resolve, and the moment of conversion came when he was almost shouted down for a brave speech at the special Labour Party conference, held in May, to discuss the NEC's appalling draft manifesto, *Peace, Jobs, Freedom.* Henceforth, he moved more quickly than either Shirley or I towards a new party. Shirley's position was less easy to discern but I took it to be quite like my own, facing a break with the greatest possible reluctance and much personal grief, but prepared now to recognise it as a serious possibility.

Roy had shown me an early draft of his 1979 Dimbleby Lecture after dinner at East Hendred. Perhaps because I was full of claret and sleep, perhaps because I thought that Roy was too immersed in his Brussels presidency to be saying anything of urgent relevance to British politics, I failed to recognise a forthcoming event of great importance. It was only three weeks later, on the eve of the lecture when its contents had been well leaked, that I appreciated fully the impact it would have. There was great agitation in the corridors of the House of Commons amongst many who were sympathetic to Roy's views and were desperately worried about the direction the Labour Party was taking. Phillip Whitehead was amongst those who shook their heads and wished the lecture would not happen because it would be used by the left to cast doubt on our loyalty, and would not appeal to those on the right and centre who disagreed with us on Europe. In drawing attention to the decline in public support for the two main parties, especially Labour, and making the case for electoral reform, Roy Jenkins opened the way for the realignment of what he called 'the radical centre'. Although the lecture was as much about objectives as destinations – calling for an innovative free-market economy coupled with the maintenance of public services like health and education – it was seen to point to a new political party that would break the mould of British politics.

It is difficult to say whether the Dimbleby Lecture changed minds in the Labour Party. What it certainly did was to give hope and encouragement to all those people on the centre-left – including the 'political virgins', as they came to be called – who were fed up with adversarial politics and disliked Mrs Thatcher's new government but could not identify with Labour. It opened up a new constituency for a new political party. But the importance of the Dimbleby Lecture to me was in the signal it gave that Roy was ready to return to British politics. For three years I had proceeded on the assumption that this was not the case, feeling that he had distanced himself from the practical realities of conflict and survival in the mess that political life for some of us had become.

It was not the Dimbleby Lecture but a chance lunch at Como Lario, in Chelsea, with John Horam on 22 November 1979, the day of the lecture, that did most to move forward my own perception of the future. John Horam told me, with his usual cool detachment, that the Labour Party was finished and that we should reconcile ourselves to the fact. I was neither shocked nor depressed but felt a sober responsibility to begin thinking the unthinkable and talking openly about it. I had agreed some months before to speak at the annual dinner of the Abertillery Labour Party on 30 November and I now warned Jeffrey Thomas, the local MP, whose constituency was next to Neil Kinnock's, that I would be controversial. My speech went through four drafts and, apart from Roger Liddle who helped with it, I showed it to John Horam, Bob Maclennan, Ian Wrigglesworth, Giles Radice, Bob Mitchell and Ken Weetch, a group of younger parliamentary friends who would be frank with their comments. They were content with its language and thrust and suggested few amendments. I then sent it to the Press Lobby and some thirty colleagues in the House twenty-four hours before. This was an unusual effort of promotion on my part, but if I was about to ruffle a lot of feathers I might as well do so properly. In view of his reaction to Dimbleby, I did not show it to David Owen; and Shirley and I had adopted a certain detachment in our public pronouncements, preferring not to involve each other in our different ways of putting things. Roy had asked Shirley and me to lunch at East Hendred the following day, Saturday, and he knew that I would get off the train from South Wales at Didcot, having made a speech within five miles of his own birthplace. But he had not seen the text. The message of the speech was simple. I said:

> Our party has a year – not much longer – in which to save itself. A year in which to start repairing its ramshackle organisation and to get some money in the till. A year to start winning friends amongst the men and women – almost thirty million of them – who did not vote Labour last time. A year in which to start proving that it is a credible alternative to the harsh and divisive Government of Mrs Thatcher.

But the issue went far beyond a debate about the rights and duties of MPs or the superficial slogans about accountability which had become fashionable on the left:

> The real argument is about power and policies and whether our party should remain a broad coalition of democratic socialists capable of winning an election and having a successful period in government. A party of the far left – in which *Tribune* members would be the moderates – would have little appeal to the millions of voters who reject doctrinaire and extreme solutions.

I asked on what terms and at what price was unity in the Labour Party to be bought. If the hard left wanted a fight to the finish they could have it. But if they split the party they should not suppose that the inheritance would be theirs.

Even by the convention of those times, which allowed dissenting voices, and setting aside the rhetoric, it was a strong speech, especially in giving the party a year to save itself. *The Times, The Guardian*, the *Telegraph*, the *Financial Times*, the *Mirror, Mail, Sun* and *Express* all reported it well and it ran over into the Sundays with good radio and some television coverage. I had a large postbag and, apart from the usual eccentric and irrelevant letters, they divided heavily in my favour. Some of my more nervous parliamentary colleagues preferred not to be seen with me for a few days. If they saw me approaching down the Library corridor they would slip unexpectedly into the lavatory or stoop to tie a shoelace. In the House of Commons post office they would be studiously preoccupied with sticking on stamps or counting change. But the majority were strongly supportive and much less inclined than usual to say, 'I agree with you entirely but don't think you should have said it'. I was particularly pleased to have a note from Ernest Armstrong, the much respected Labour MP for North-West Durham and a future Deputy Speaker of the House. Already into his sixties, Ernest was a man of principle, deeply rooted in the Labour movement. He agreed with me that the crunch was not far off and concluded:

> The argument in the party has continued over the years. The difference now is that whereas the so-called right – the social democrats – were always willing to work with others, to give and take and to be tolerant of different points of view, the extreme left have never given an

inch and feel able to dictate to the rest. It is their intolerance, insistence on dogma and unwillingness to compromise that harms the party.

It was a fair summary of how many felt, although Ernest was more optimistic than I
was that the party could ultimately be saved.

This was the question that Roy, Shirley and I talked over for more than an hour
before lunch on 1 December. To my surprise I found that I could soberly discuss
the prospects for a new party without being committed to one. I even went as far
as saying that a new party, launched in the right climate – Labour in terminal decline, Mrs Thatcher increasingly unpopular – might win as many as sixty seats, with
the Liberals winning a further twenty-five. I also believed that it could raise sufficient
money and survive without trade-union backing. Shirley was also relaxed about discussing the future in these terms and offered to talk to Tony King – Professor
Anthony King of Essex University – about detailed figures. Roy seemed well pleased
with the outcome, although Shirley and I both emphasised that our priority was to
save the Labour Party. I put the critical period – as in my Abertillery speech – about a
year ahead but feared a muddled and unsatisfactory outcome even then. Much, I believed, would depend on Shirley. I doubted whether she would help start a new party
unless I committed myself, but she might draw back at the last moment even then.

In January I wrote to Roy with a more careful tactical appraisal of the prospects.
After discussing the nature of a pact with Liberals less obviously committed to realignment than David Steel, and saying I believed that we could create an organisation
and probably raise the money for what I called 'a Fourth Party', I continued:

> I'm not sure whether we agree about this but I have no confidence in (and no great warmth
> towards) a party of the Centre. It would not work. The Conservative Party will always be with
> us, winning not less than ten million, often as many as thirteen million votes. A Fourth Party
> may win Tory floaters but I don't believe that it need give an ideological nod in their direc-
> tion. I see no prospect of any significant defection of active Conservatives, least of all those in
> Parliament.

I ended my letter:

> I still hope the Labour Party can be saved and I don't think we shall know just yet. If a Fourth
> Party were to be launched, I would want it to be firmly social democratic and not somewhere
> in the vague centre of the political spectrum. Meanwhile I favour a cautious and discreet ap-
> proach with wariness towards the Liberals.

The letter did not require a reply. It was intended to define my position.

Throughout 1980 I saw Roy Jenkins regularly on his visits from Brussels. I knew
that he was building a body of support for a break from amongst many of my old
friends, including Dick Taverne and David Marquand. But I was uncomfortable
about those without the ties of parliament who were already so sure of their own direction, and I rebuffed David Steel's invitation to talk things over. Roy, as always in

the past when I had a difficult choice to make, put no pressure on me. He left me to work my way through to a decision on the basis of events and my own assessment of the right course to take. He constantly made it clear that he would join with Shirley and me – and David Owen when the Gang of Three emerged – on our terms if we reached the point of launching a new party. He said, as he said separately to Shirley and David, that he would serve under the leadership of any of us if that was how matters turned out. My own assumption always was that he would become the leader – it was too early to consider when and how he would return to Westminster – and that Shirley would have a parallel role, mainly promoting the party in the country. At that stage, David Owen was not a serious candidate for either position, and I commanded more personal support than he did amongst those Labour MPs who might join us. Subsequently David claimed, in explaining their difficult relations, that Roy had committed himself in conversation to the election of the leader by the whole membership rather than the parliamentary party. It seems a minor point, and irrelevant in that Roy was eventually elected in a one-member, one-vote ballot of all members of the SDP. But whatever may have been said, I certainly did not attach the formality of a binding agreement to any of our bilateral exchanges, because Roy's patience with our slow progress was matched by his emollience. Everything was open to discussion and everything was possible once the main decision had been made. I never felt that I was bargaining with him – or with Shirley and David – about our respective future roles.

But once David had made his own decision on a break, and the Gang of Three was firmly in position after the *Guardian* open letter, this clearly became a preoccupation for him. He saw Roy as yesterday's man, a sybaritic and whiggish figure, not obviously the stuff of which new parties are made. He began to divide supporters of the new party into Jenkinsites and potential Owenites; and believing that I was irrevocably in the first camp, made strenuous and not wholly unsuccessful efforts to bring Shirley into the second. I cannot recall the Gang of Three discussing relations with the Liberals during the closing, stormy months of 1980, but I believe that David's subsequent hostility towards them was partly based on his assumption – entirely justified in this case – that they were closer to Roy than to him. He rationalised this initially by putting Roy and the Liberals nearer the centre of the political spectrum than he, declaring himself to be a radical, wished to be. But David's unease at Roy's re-emergence on to the political stage was rather like the resentment of an adolescent boy on discovering that his rejected father is dangerously attractive to his girlfriend and still a fast mover on the football field. Roy, on the other hand, was ready to accept a relationship of equality with David and hoped to re-establish something of their former mutual affection.

Silvia and I spent most of August 1980 trying to put in order our new cottage at East Woodhay, in a very beautiful part of Hampshire, a few miles from Newbury, not far from David and Debbie at Buttermere and no more than half an hour by road from Roy and Jennifer at East Hendred. But once the conference season had begun with the TUC in early September, the political momentum was regained. As this was always a frenetic time of speeches designed to win seats on the National Executive and of crazy amendments to resolutions for the party conference, it was difficult to be sure whether events were departing from normal. David Owen and I flew to Bordeaux for an Anglo-French 'Königswinter' of politicians, journalists and businessmen where the French banned all serious discussion of defence and our time was mainly spent in eating delicious meals and drinking fine wines at the expense of Giscard d'Estaing's failing government. David was teased because of complimentary references to him in the first volume of Barbara Castle's diaries that had just been published (he had been her junior minister at Health). I had entirely friendly conversations with David Basnett and Geoffrey Drain, now the head of NALGO, the local government union, but whom I had first known when he was an anti-Gaitskell member of the Hampstead Labour Party. There was an underlying sympathy for the position the Gang of Three had adopted, some apprehension about our intentions but a belief that somehow the party would muddle through, bruised, even less electable but all in one piece. It was whistling in the dark, on the assumption that if Denis Healey was elected following Jim Callaghan's impending resignation as Leader, the worst would be over.

The prior event was the party conference at Blackpool. Here everything went wrong, with votes to withdraw from the European Community and in favour of unilateral disarmament; the acceptance of most of the constitutional changes; and an extraordinary speech from Tony Benn in which he proposed a decisive extension of public ownership and control, a thirty-five-hour working week without loss of pay, withdrawal from the Common Market and abolition of the House of Lords – all to be achieved through legislation in the first month of a Labour government. The left was ecstatic and there was a smell of almost revolutionary hysteria. The General Secretary of the party, Ron Hayward – in effect, its senior civil servant – made an outrageous attack on Labour MPs and, for the first time in my experience, clenched fists were raised in salute in some parts of the hall. Tolerance had seldom been a characteristic of Labour Party conferences, but there was now also a feeling of physical menace from hard-left delegates. Unacceptable speakers were not only jeered but hissed and there was some deliberate jostling in the lobbies and corridors of the Conference Centre and the conference hotel.

In response, a Campaign for Labour Victory meeting in the Spanish Ballroom, a favourite venue for large fringe meetings at conference, was packed and passionate. There were well-placed hecklers in the audience, but here were people who felt, like us, that their Labour Party was being taken over and time and energy inexcusably diverted from providing a credible opposition to Mrs Thatcher's Government. Shirley, David and I all spoke as if we had our backs to the wall but intended to carry on fighting. We were loudly applauded, and Shirley's references, both to the silence of those who ought to be fighting with us and to the 'fascism of the left', caught the imagination of the meeting. It was all in sharp contrast to the tense and sometimes frightening mood of the conference itself. On Thursday of the week I was booed and hissed when I went to the rostrum to speak in the defence debate. I said that it was crazy to give up the nuclear weapons that had kept the peace in Europe for more than thirty years, and a government that went into an election with the defence policies conference was about to adopt would be rejected by the voters overwhelmingly. But conference was not in the mood for such realities.

Then, when the House of Commons returned and the leadership contest was joined, Denis Healey failed to be elected, beaten by ten votes in the second ballot announced on 10 November. For some, this was an unmitigated folly, but for most of the 129 Labour MPs who voted for Foot, this was the choice they preferred. At a party at the American Embassy that evening – which happened to be the eve of Ronald Reagan's defeat of Jimmy Carter for the American presidency – I came upon Ian Aitken, *The Guardian's* political editor, who remained an unreconstructed Bevanite, much as I had known him as a friend at Oxford. He was over the moon. 'It's marvellous,' he said. 'I'm delighted', then added, 'although it will be a disaster for the party'. This summed up, it seemed to me, the romanticism of the legitimate left. With Michael Foot they had won, and everything else was secondary.

For most of my friends, the election of Foot conveniently settled things. In particular, David Owen's resolve was clear, and he was admirably single-minded. In the six weeks remaining before the Christmas recess, he kept an open door to his House of Commons office, steadying those Labour MPs who were as committed to a break as he now was and encouraging those who remained undecided. I was of little assistance, shell-shocked by Michael Foot's election and struggling to decide whether all was now lost. For a brief moment it was suggested that I might stand as Deputy Leader, with not the slightest hope of winning, but on behalf of fifty or sixty colleagues who wished to cast a protest vote against Denis Healey's absence of fighting spirit. The idea was wisely and quickly dropped, but Denis, John Smith and many friends wrote, urging that I should stand for the shadow cabinet. David Owen had already announced his intention not to do so but this was attributed partly to his fear of defeat. In the end I was persuaded to stand and in turn persuaded myself that Foot, in the tradition of previous Labour leaders, would seek to propitiate the minority which I and my friends in the parliamentary party had become.

Before the result was known, I wrote to him to ease his decision about portfolios by saying that I would not expect him to reappoint me to defence, given his own unilateralist views. I was naïve, because he did not respond in the spirit of my letter. I was re-elected with much the same vote as in the previous year (Neil Kinnock scraped on in bottom place), but by telephone Michael Foot offered me, first, Northern Ireland, which would have neutered me completely in opposition; and then half of Health and Social Security, an area entirely unsuited to my experience. He seemed unable to grasp that in standing for the shadow cabinet I was making a last, rather desperate personal gesture. I wanted an excuse to believe – and to demonstrate to others – that the Labour Party was still capable of being saved, perhaps only as a leader from the legitimate left might save it. But either he did not recognise a crisis – 'I do not think it is going to happen,' he said, when asked about a new party – or saw it as a final revenge on the Gaitskellites to treat me as expendable. There is also the possibility that he simply did not think at all of the consequences of the decisions he was taking. For when, a month later, he visited me at Patshull Road with an imprecise offer of a special post dealing with regional economic development, he still seemed unaware that there was far more at stake than my own role in the shadow cabinet.

Had Michael Foot responded differently, would he have detached me from those of my friends preparing for a break? I am glad I was never tested, because had he succeeded I would have been desperately miserable throughout Labour's years of failure. I would have been even more isolated in a Foot-led shadow cabinet than David Owen and I had been under Jim Callaghan. As others kept their heads down, I would have despised them for their acquiescence and despised myself for my inability to prevent the slide. The Parliamentary Labour Party had finally turned down one member, one vote by 72 votes to 60, with over 100 absentees, and settled for an electoral college. It had plainly lost the will to fight. In the prevailing mood that continued to deepen, there would have been no purpose in my political life except to look after my constituents and collect my monthly pay cheque. I had entered parliament for more than that.

On Sunday 9 November 1980, Shirley, Silvia and I went to dinner at Narrow Street, David and Debbie Owen's Limehouse home. At the beginning of a serious evening's discussion I said, 'I am ready to declare for a new party on 2 January if you both will'. I wanted to flush out Shirley's intentions and focus David's anger on a practical timetable. But if Shirley seemed hopelessly torn on the course that made best political sense for us, so was I. As the year moved towards its end, a physical disablement descended on me to match my indecision. Shortly after Christmas, back trouble – occasional for some years, but never previously serious – struck. By New Year's Day I could barely walk and could only just roll out of bed in great pain. Incapable of action, I was free to think through the dilemma of my future.

Unlike Roy Hattersley, who was happy to say, 'My party, right or wrong', I was not attached to the Labour Party by an umbilical cord and had never liked to think of myself as 'a good party man'. But my Labour label had been entirely appropriate, because it had embraced so much of what I cared about by way of a generous, tolerant and free society marked by both responsibility and social justice. I also had a strong historical sense of the Labour Party as the focus, during the first half of the twentieth century, for all the justified grievances and aspirations of working people from the Industrial Revolution onwards. More to the point, the majority of those still active in the party, especially the party outside parliament, were decent and fair-minded people, as distressed as I was by the course of events. I had happy memories of Fabian days, the companionship of hard-fought elections, cheerful July evenings on the Terrace of the House of Commons when Silvia came to join me, the exhilaration of battles won and the loyalty and kindness of men and women who owed me nothing. How could I break with this without weeping for ever?

David Marquand, who had written me a persuasive letter in the summer, had understood these problems better than anyone, yet had urged me to make the break even if only three or four MPs were to follow. By staying, I might, he said, be able to keep the Labour Party from total self-destruction but I would not save it. The most I could achieve was 'a ten-year (or twenty-year) labour of Sisyphus, endlessly pushing the boulder up the hill only to see it roll down again'. It was a convincing image given the legitimate left's continued tolerance of the wreckers, and the lack of stomach for the fight of Hattersley and others like him. As I lay on my bed, virtually immobilised, I thought of this letter. But mainly I read Bernard Crick's recently published biography of George Orwell and reflected on the circumstances in which I had entered politics and my father's reaction at that time. Orwell – later fashionable with the Kinnock leadership, but then rather neglected – had maintained the integrity of his awkward views in defence of intellectual, cultural and political freedom at a time of dogmatic leftism. My father, who probably never read Orwell, believed with a simple intensity that men and women in politics should remain true to themselves despite ambition. To say that the scales fell from my eyes would be to make a cliché of the halting process by which I resolved the debate with myself. But eventually I decided that leaving the Labour Party was the only course open to me consistent with what my life in politics had been.

Almost at once the pain in my back began to ebb. By the time of the Limehouse Declaration it was virtually gone, and I was walking normally again.

Chapter 10

Good to be Alive

New Year 1981 promised a highly uncertain political life. I had decided that I could no longer live with myself in what the Labour Party had become. Labour's long march since the death of Hugh Gaitskell had been steadily downhill. The force and momentum of this decline was not within my capacity to reverse, but I was a social democrat believing in a party of the centre-left that could offer the country an alternative to Mrs Thatcher and her successors.

Amongst the Gang of Four, which Roy Jenkins, Shirley Williams, David Owen and I were fast becoming, in this respect I shared most with Shirley. We were, I suppose, still 1960s' Labour revisionists. I was now highly critical of the trade unions, but not ready to turn my back on them; I believed in an incomes policy, developed in a straight line from the policies of the two governments in which I had served; and I was an unrepentant egalitarian, taking for granted that only a high level of public expenditure (and therefore taxation) was consistent with achieving the social objectives about which I cared. When we came to discuss a name for our new party, my first choice was 'New Democratic Labour' or 'Labour and Social Democratic'. Since Douglas Jay's suggestion twenty years before that social change had made the name 'Labour' unattractive to a new generation of white-collar votes, the idea had grown on me. Now, however, I grasped at the prospect of continuity, perhaps as much to cushion my own transition as to bring over a proportion of the old Labour vote.

When it came to decisions on policy, Roy generally found himself close to Shirley and myself but he was much less committed to an identifiable political philosophy. Thirty years before, in *The Pursuit of Progress,* he had referred to 'more equality, more democracy and more freedom' as the key objectives. But he had moved on, not necessarily to abandon the core of his beliefs but to take a more historical view of what politics might achieve. He was a tolerant liberal, believing that the best guarantee of good government was that it should be entrusted to intelligent, wise and generous men and women who by instinct would make the right decisions.

David Owen was the enigma. His roots in the Labour Party were not as deep as Roy's, Shirley's or mine. He had been much influenced in joining by Hugh Gaitskell, but his views were consistent only in the areas of policy, like health, of which he had direct experience. Elsewhere his swings of opinion could be disconcerting. David's book, *Face the Future,* published early in 1981, was confused and almost unreadable. It was said to have been sent in draft to almost 100 individuals and amended to take account of all their diverse views. But despite such ridicule, David, much less encumbered by the past than we were, was searching for new ideas, which was no bad thing in a new party.

In the meantime, however, there were practical decisions to take around another significant date. The Labour Party's special Wembley conference of 24 January would set the seal on the constitutional changes to which we were greatly opposed. There was no doubt about the outcome, and we would be expected to respond with at least the first steps towards establishing our new party. Visitors arrived at Patshull Road to make a last-minute attempt to persuade me to stay with Labour. Michael Foot, who had dealt with me so clumsily after my election to the shadow cabinet, arrived bearing an olive branch. He sat on the red stool in our sitting room and tried to devise an acceptable portfolio for me. It was a short and formal conversation and I doubt whether he had his heart in it. Much more painful was a delegation of friends from the Manifesto Group of Labour MPs, including Ken Weetch, formerly my PPS at Transport; Giles Radice, who shared many of my parliamentary causes and who I had wanted as my junior minister; my neighbour, Phillip Whitehead; and George Robertson, a new and young MP who had quickly shown his maturity. All would have been marvellous recruits to our new party, but I knew that none would join. They brought a message of affection, asking me to stay with them and lead their part of the Labour Party. I responded only with uncontrolled anger and when they rose to leave, Silvia found Giles Radice and I in the hallway, squaring up to each other as if to start a fight. They were the unfortunate victims of my continuing distress. My new life had not yet begun and I did not want my old life to keep summoning me back to reopen the pain of the decision I had made. George Robertson later wrote me a letter of such warmth that I never felt we had really parted company, and my relationship with Ken Weetch and Phillip Whitehead was also restored. Giles Radice was a different case; whether because of his guilt at not joining us or my disappointment in him, there was no reconciliation for fifteen years. But although their mission had failed, they were four amongst a handful of Labour MPs who I always declined to campaign against in their constituencies. Sentiment and personal loyalty continued to have its place.

Throughout January we prepared ourselves for our response to the Wembley conference and the steps we would then take towards the launch of our new party. We were not always entirely at ease with each other. We would meet once or twice a week in each other's homes, and on Sunday 18 January planned to do so at East Hendred. But when *The Observer* carried a photograph of Roy waiting on his lawn, having apparently summoned his junior partners, Shirley was incensed, as she was not ready for such public exposure. Only after the most persistent coaxing did she agree to a meeting, provided that it was transferred to London; and, having parked her car, she crossed Patshull Road to our house with her face covered by a newspaper, rather like a criminal entering court. Silvia liked the meetings at Patshull Road. But on this occasion, with Shirley at her most difficult, eight people present (Matthew Oakeshott, John Lyttle, Alec McGivan and Roger Liddle had joined us as spear-carriers) and a substantial press corps to be kept happy, she was mildly fed up. 'I've had enough', she said, and did not protest when our next meeting was moved to David Owen's home in Docklands. Thus, to her later regret, what might have been the Kentish Town Communiqué became the Limehouse Declaration.

It was formally called 'The Declaration for Social Democracy', and a first draft had been agreed at Patshull Road once Shirley had subsided from her rage. When we met on the morning of the following Sunday, the day after the Wembley conference, we each brought our own amendments and added opening sentences which referred to Wembley and the dominance of the trade unions in the election of the Labour leader to which the conference had agreed. We were all anxious to reach agreement, buoyed up by the excitement of the irrevocable step we were about to take. In about 500 words we declared our intention to: 'rally all those who are committed to the values, principles and policies of social democracy', and said that the 'realignment of British politics must now be faced'. We proposed to set up a Council for Social Democracy as a halfway house to a new party, and appealed beyond the Labour Party to those outside politics who also wanted change.

Once the drafting was done, Debbie Owen went off to have it typed, and the press were summoned for four o'clock, as late as we could safely leave it for newspaper and television deadlines. Roy, as usual, was in a suit appropriate to such an occasion, and David changed into one. Shirley was also concerned about her appearance and Matthew Oakeshott was dispatched to her Pimlico flat, five miles across London, to find a change of clothing. I alone decided to stay with my Marks and Spencer pullover and tie-less shirt, my usual weekend wear. The photographs taken on the Narrow Street bridge have us all looking pleased but rather self-conscious against a darkening January sky.

We knew that eight or nine other MPs would immediately join us and believed that we would soon get 100 names from amongst the great and the good to endorse our Council for Social Democracy. But otherwise we were in the dark about the response we would provoke, expecting to build steadily over a period of months to the launch of a new party. But the publicity given to the Limehouse Declaration brought a snowstorm of letters, which became an avalanche when the names of the first signatories to our Declaration for Social Democracy appeared in *The Guardian* on 5 February. I had letters from old school friends, former civil servants and, more predictably, men and women who had supported the Campaign for Democratic Socialism twenty years before. Instead of having to recruit, like Garibaldi, a thousand political irregulars with whom to start our bold campaign, we found that we had placed ourselves in the leadership of an army already formed and waiting. These new soldiers of social democracy even sent money with which to pay for rations, equipment and logistics. It was an altogether exhilarating experience which removed any doubts we might have had about timing or intention. The momentum was irresistible and we decided to bring forward the launch to 26 March.

A year earlier I had been telling Roy – optimistically – that I could envisage a new party winning sixty seats at its first general election. Now we began talking seriously amongst ourselves of forming the next government or, in more sober moments, of holding the balance of power.

In the period between Limehouse and the launch, the Gang of Four worked well together, given not only the immense pressure now upon us but a prospect which naturally fertilised ambitions. On 5 February there was one disturbing occasion. We met at Shirley's flat to settle on a provisional division of labour between us. So far we were agreed that the collective leadership would remain and we would each in turn chair the Steering Committee. We would also decide between ourselves which of us would represent the Gang of Four on major radio and television programmes. Roy and I arrived early and when Shirley joined us, accompanied by David, they jointly proposed that Shirley would look after press and public relations, David would be parliamentary leader, I would be in charge of organisation and Roy would raise the money. I could have jibed at the parliamentary arrangements, knowing that in an election amongst our small group of Social Democrat MPs I could count on a majority over David. But I was more than happy to build the party in the country, given that that was where our immediate future lay, and that, in public perception, I would be the fourth among equals in the Gang of Four. I had been intercepted in the lobby by Elinor Goodman, then representing the *Financial Times*, who had been irritatingly incredulous about how we could create a new party from scratch. I had total faith that it could be done, and so could hardly decline the opportunity with which Shirley presented me. With Roy it was quite a different matter, as it was preposterous to suggest that his major role in our new party should be in finding ways of paying for it. Roy was taken aback by the idea and obviously hurt, and I said immediately that it was nonsense. In the end we settled for Roy being in overall charge of policy, although Shirley and David insisted that each of us should carry responsibilities for specific areas, mine being for industry.

Both Shirley and David were anxious to diminish Roy's role, believing that his age and image did not suit a new, young party and that his four-year absence in Brussels had rendered him out of touch. For his part, Roy did not much enjoy the collective leadership. At dinner with Jack Diamond and me, Jack tempted him with the idea of a single leader being chosen soon, and of his taking the chair for the launch. I said neither would be acceptable. The innovation of the Gang of Four was proving popular in the country, even if it could not last forever; and to take the chair would be seen to establish a seniority that would be unwelcome to Shirley and David and, for that matter, at this stage, to me. I wrote in my diary on 14 March: 'All three of them have a sharp eye for the future. I see my role as keeping them together and preventing any one of them from jumping the gun. We will be a new party, breaking new ground. Why shouldn't we show that collective leadership can work?'

In our discussion on the day of the Limehouse Declaration, we had seen the German SPD as a model for our own new party. The SPD had both a parliamentary leader, Helmut Schmidt, and a leader of the party in the country, Willy Brandt. We saw attractions in a similar division of power and source of creative tension. A president in addition to a parliamentary leader would be free to travel the country, raising morale and attracting new voters. Neither Roy nor Shirley was currently an MP, but by-elections should soon return them to Westminster. My view was that Roy would then become Leader and Shirley President. Shirley had immense popular appeal, but it remained to be seen whether she was credible as Prime Minister. As for Roy, although he had yet to prove himself in the new political environment, his personal standing was beyond question and, since his Dimbleby Lecture, he had a great appeal across party to those without fixed allegiance. The two of them together could be an irresistible combination.

The press conference that marked the launch of the party on 26 March was a brilliant success, planned and stage-managed with great energy and notable entrepreneurial skills by Mike Thomas, the MP for Newcastle East. Silvia had no great difficulty in reminding me to put on my best suit, but she also persuaded me to visit her fashionable hairdresser, John Frieda, for the most expensive haircut of my lifetime. The four of us sat alongside each other on the platform at the Connaught Rooms, off Kingsway, in central London, each to make a short, personal statement and to answer questions on an allocation previously agreed between us. Apart from the largest contingent of UK press, radio and television I had ever seen, there were reporters and camera crews from most of Western Europe, the United States, the Commonwealth and the rest of the world, some 500 people in all. There was to be no comparable interest in British politics until Mrs Thatcher's dethronement as Prime Minister almost ten years later. A press statement announced that our membership – uniquely for a British political party – would be registered nationally on a computer; our advertising had been placed with Abbot, Mead & Vickers, a top-flight London agency; and our blue-and-red logo had been designed by Dick Negus of Negus & Negus (although it did not announce that Silvia had made a contribution by convincing him that a thick red line below the letters would add weight to them). At this stage we had fourteen MPs and eighteen peers as our parliamentary group.

The statements we made were unexceptional, but I included one sentence in mine that may have struck a discordant note in the liberal internationalism which we chorused. Our new party, I said, 'will be a patriotic party'. I was clear that patriotism – uneasy although we might be with the word – was an essential component in the image that any party of the centre-left had to project to middle England.

What was more widely noticed that morning at the Connaught Rooms was my reply to a question from Bonnie Angelo, head of *Time* magazine's London Bureau, about how many parliamentary seats the SDP would fight. 'About half, at least 300', I said without hesitation. Had I been asked before Limehouse I would have talked cautiously of sixty; and David Steel certainly thought that Liberal candidates would have to stand down for the SDP in far fewer than half of the seats they had contested in 1979. But the immense enthusiasm we had aroused and the skeleton of a nation-wide organisation for which there was already a blueprint, made me confident in my announcement.

My reply was made on the spur of the moment, but it did not occur to me that exception would be taken to it by anyone in our own ranks. I was mistaken. Although he made no immediate complaint, David Owen soon took his cue from Mike Thomas and argued that far from being bold in my suggestion that we would fight half the seats, I had made a serious error by giving the other half away to the Liberals. In his view, the threat to fight them all would have been a measure of the SDP's independence and the dominance we proposed to achieve. We would then be able to negotiate an electoral arrangement from strength. Mike Thomas also said that to fight the Liberals in a by-election (and, it was assumed, to trounce them) would be another way of asserting who was top dog.

In one of the more tendentious passages – and there are several – in his book *Time to Declare*, published ten years later, David Owen argued that my reply to Bonnie Angelo exceeded what had been agreed beforehand and had far-reaching implications. It assumed parity with the Liberals and undermined the SDP's negotiating position. These arguments were new, but had I heard them before the launch I would have dismissed them as absurd. The Gang of Four had already decided to cooperate with the Liberals and to consider an electoral arrangement. At least as important, we were out to give the voters what many of them craved for – an end to needless feuding and narrow party politics. Our prospects would have been wrecked from the start if we had declared war on our natural allies. Nor would such an obvious and important question – 'How many seats will you fight?' – have gone away had I given a bland and evasive reply. David Owen had been present in December 1980 when Tony King and

Ivor Crewe of Essex University had presented a paper on the electoral prospects for a new party to a small group of us in Shirley Williams' flat. One point had stood out clearly: that more voters than ever before had become detached from their loyalties to the two main parties, but a new party would only succeed through an electoral alliance with the Liberals because there was simply not enough room on the centre ground for two parties in competition, given the electoral system. The challenge to a new party was to establish itself alongside the Liberals in an equal partnership. Each party would have a distinct identity and might develop a different electoral appeal, but an alliance was inescapable. To me the logic of this – and the first step – was to acknowledge that each party would fight half the seats.

In an article in the *Financial Times* in February – between Limehouse and the launch – Malcolm Rutherford had detected some difference between Roy Jenkins and David Steel, for whom an alliance of the two parties already featured large, and David Owen and myself who were primarily concerned with establishing a new party. This was quite right. In the negotiations over the allocation of seats which began later in 1981, I came to be seen as a hard man by the Liberals and upset some social democrats by the way in which I fought the SDP's corner. But to have had a row on the day of our launch and to have claimed more than half the seats, threatening to fight Liberal candidates or turf them out, would have been crazy.

Once the London launch was over, we all departed to carry the message to press conferences at a dozen different centres round the country. Together with Silvia, Dick Taverne, Oliver Walston – a close friend since we had worked together for George Brown twenty years before – and Max Hastings of the *Evening Standard*, I took off in a rather tired HS 125 jet for Norwich, Leeds and Newcastle. The reception we received was less dramatic than in London, the provinces seeming more sceptical about it all. But the reports from our accompanying journalists (we had each been allowed one) helped to ensure that in the national newspapers alone we had over 500 column inches of exposure the following day. Given photographs in every paper, with a cartoon soon to follow, there could never have been such a wonderful send-off. It was not surprising that within ten days we could claim 43,566 paid-up members and more than half a million pounds in the bank.

On the Monday after the launch I returned to the House of Commons, knowing that I must face it without delay. I took my coffee to the table in the tea room frequented by North-East Labour MPs, and there was only a momentary pause before the conversation resumed. No-one left and Ernest Armstrong came to sit beside me. They did not approve of what I had done, but they understood and had no intention of erasing loyalties from the years we had worked together. Other colleagues, of all parties, looked at me unsure whether I was a hero or a fool, but somehow envious of my part in the political drama that, for the moment, was being played mainly outside parliament. Only Roy Hattersley seemed confident in the role he had chosen for himself as spokesman for the my-party-right-or-wrong loyalists, claiming a firmness of purpose he had seldom shown at critical moments in the preceding months. Infuriated by him although I often was, I rather liked Hattersley in all his Arnold Bennett pomposity because his behaviour was so patent and he could laugh at himself. But David Owen could not stand him and, as if he remembered some passing slight or feared revealing a secret, declined any confrontation with him on radio or television.

Quite soon, however, there was pressure on all of us to resign our seats and fight by-elections. We argued that there was no constitutional obligation to do so, as MPs were elected individually and were not delegates chosen from party lists. We also claimed, with some justification, that whatever our party label, the views we held as social democrats were no different from the ones we had personally expressed in the course of a general election two years earlier. But whatever our legitimacy, most of us felt awkward about our status and, although we thought we could successfully explain ourselves, our supporters were less confident in doing so.

At an early stage, David Owen said that we should all resign and fight by-elections. This was an attractively defiant solution, especially to those like David with a constituency they were expected to hold as a social democrat; and in the mood of euphoria, I was momentarily tempted. But the practical case against doing so was overwhelming. There was not the remotest chance of staging a dramatic mini-general election with fourteen by-elections on the same day. Once we had all resigned our seats it would be for the Labour Party to choose the date and move the writ for each of the by-elections (and the Government for the by-election of our one former Tory MP). We might have to wait three or four months, with our new party's organising resources stretched to the limit and our MPs, now candidates, without a parliamentary salary. We would be picked off one by one, probably starting with those MPs most vulnerable to defeat. I doubted whether even half of us would survive, and the morale of the party would be severely damaged.

With hindsight, and given Roy Jenkins' remarkable result in the Warrington by-election in July, I may have underestimated the mood of the voters. But it was one thing to put all the SDP's resources behind Roy, a star candidate in a by-election not of our own making (the vacancy occurred through the resignation of the sitting Labour MP), quite another to have handed over the fate of fourteen MPs to their political opponents.

When I discussed with Roy early in the previous year what I then called a Fourth Party, I was doubtful whether it would attract many recruits from amongst Tory MPs. Whatever their disaffection, their party was in power and the prospect of becoming a minister was an adhesive for the ambitious. My best hope was that a lead might be given by Sir Ian Gilmour, who was the most loosely attached of Mrs Thatcher's cabi-

Peter Shore, a prefect when I was in the fourth form at Quarry Bank High School, comforts me at a Labour Party conference. We disagreed on much, especially Europe, but never had a personal falling-out.

Casualties of Labour's Common Market split. George Thomson (left) left Parliament to become one of Britain's European Commissioners; Dick Taverne (right) lost his Lincoln seat, victim of an intolerant constituency party.

Limehouse: the Gang of Four's Declaration is published. Perhaps I should have worn a jacket.

'What do you mean, can't we slow down a bit? We haven't even started the motor yet!'
How *The Guardian* cartoonist Gibbard saw the genesis of the SDP.

The SDP is launched. Silvia insisted that I had a proper (and expensive) haircut.

PRIVATE & CONFIDENTIAL   SOCIAL DEMOCRATS

ON MONDAY, 30th March, 1981, The House will meet at 2.30 p.m.
        Questions: Wales (T.E.), House of Commons Commission, Arts (J.R)
        There will be a debate on AN OPPOSITION MOTION ON
        UNEMPLOYMENT IN THE MIDLANDS (T.E.)
        Afterwards: Remaining stages of the Parliamentary Commissioner
        (Consular Complaints) Bill (E.L.)

ON TUESDAY, 31st March, 1981, The House will meet at 2.30 p.m.
        Questions: Social Services (M.T.)
        Ten Minute Rule Bill: Town and Country Planning - Wigley
        REMAINING STAGES OF THE FORESTRY BILL (R.A.R.M.) and of the
        CRIMINAL ATTEMPTS BILL (E.L.)
        DIVISIONS WILL TAKE PLACE AND YOUR ATTENDANCE IS NECESSARY FROM 5 p.m.
        Afterwards motions relating to the NATIONAL HEALTH SERVICE (DENTAL AND
        OPTICAL CHARGES AND REMISSION OF CHARGES) REGULATIONS. (M.T.)
        A DIVISION WILL TAKE PLACE AND YOUR ATTENDANCE IS NECESSARY

ON WEDNESDAY, 1st April, 1981 The House will meet at 2.30 p.m.
        Questions: Environment (J.C)
        Ten Minute Rule Bill: Road Traffic Offences - Neale.
        REMAINING STAGES OF THE BRITISH TELECOMMUNICATIONS BILL (I.W.)
        DIVISIONS WILL TAKE PLACE AND YOUR ATTENDANCE IS ESSENTIAL FROM 5 P.M.
        AND UNTIL THE BUSINESS IS COMPLETED.

ON THURSDAY, 2nd April, 1981, The House will meet at 2.30 p.m.
        Questions: Home Office (E.L.)
        REMAINING STAGES OF THE ENERGY CONSERVATION BILL (LORDS) (T.E.)
        MOTION ON E.E.C. DOCUMENT ON RESEARCH AND DEVELOPMENT IN BIOMOLECULAR
        ENGINEERING
        MOTION ON QUEEN'S UNIVERSITY OF BELFAST (NORTHERN IRELAND) ORDER (N.S.)
        At 7 O'clock Opposed Private Business.

ON FRIDAY, 3rd April, 1981, The House will meet at 9.30 a.m.
        Private Members' Motions: Industry and the School Curriculum - Neale.

ON MONDAY, 6th April, 1981, The House will meet at 2.30 p.m.
        Questions: Industry (I.W.)
        REMAINING STAGES OF THE INSURANCE COMPANIES BILL (M.T.)

The first whip of the SDP, already professional in its conduct of parliamentary business.

The Königswinter Compact, agreed with David Steel in the margins of the 1981 conference, and written out hastily by Richard Holme. Shirley Williams and I were almost disowned for negotiating it.

Campaigning for Roy Jenkins with Shirley Williams in Warrington. The loudspeaker became my trademark at by-elections.

January 1982: David
Steel and I admit that
negotiations over
parliamentary seats have
reached a crisis. John
Cartwright is between us.

Shirley Williams, with whom
I have shared many political
causes for half a century.
Ours, someone said, was
like a sibling relationship.

Anything to win attention in the 1984 Euro-elections. I was in the centre of Manchester, in support of Alliance candidates.

On the eve of the 1987 election, when I fought Milton Keynes. No return to Westminster, as it turned out.

In his East Hendred garden – Roy Jenkins, my elder brother in politics, as I often felt him to be.

With John Roper, a staunch ally at all times, and David Marquand, forever rich in ideas, outside Willie and Celia Goodhart's house on Boar's Hill, Oxford.

Introduced into the House of Lords, between Roy Jenkins and Lord Croham, who, as Sir Douglas Allen, was a civil servant I saw much of during my eleven years in government.

net ministers and a friend of Roy's. It seemed to me that unless at least a handful of Tory MPs joined us we would lack credibility as a new political force rather than a splinter from the Labour Party.

Throughout 1981 there were tentative approaches from a number of Tory back-benchers. John Wells made a half-offer to resign his seat at Maidstone so that Roy could fight an early by-election and thus return to the House of Commons. Stephen Dorrell, MP for Loughborough (and a future cabinet minister), asked to discuss his position, and Robert Jackson, then a Euro MP, lunched me at the Garrick Club and dined me at All Souls while wrestling with his conscience, finally deciding that his place was still on the Conservative benches. But the most persistent on-and-off enquiries came from Hugh Dykes, the MP for Harrow East, speaking for a group of four or five other MPs who were waiting in the wings. Dykes was a strongly committed European, and he tel-ephoned me frequently and sent messages through John Roper following discussions in the course of a conference abroad. But all these contacts came to nothing (although Hugh Dykes eventually joined the Liberal Democrats after 1997) and ceased altogether when the Falklands War redeemed the fortunes of the government and halted the SDP bandwagon.

Despite the exhilaration of the launch and the excitement of building a new party, all of which made the first few months totally absorbing, there were some sad farewells and disappointments. In Stockton, Michael Fitzgerald, who had done so much to get me elected twenty years before, came with me into the SDP and played an active part on Teesside. Virtually all my closer friends in the local party did the same. But others were uncomprehending, and Harold Hicks, an official of the Building Trade Workers, was in tears as he said 'Goodbye.' I was also removed from membership of the Fabian Society, together with other members who joined the SDP, on the grounds that we were now disqualified through the Society's affiliation to the Labour Party. This was strictly true but the decision, made by a narrow majority, seemed an attempt to erase all the years when, as Assistant and then General Secretary, I had been a full-time Fabian. This sense of a Stalinist rewriting of history – as if our names and faces had been ex-punged from all records – was strengthened when the Society celebrated its 100th anniversary in 1984 and neither I nor Shirley, two out of fewer than a dozen General Secretaries, was invited to attend.

Our three children, Rachel, Lucy and Juliet, decided collectively – as, since child-hood, they had decided so many things in relation to their parents – that they could not support the SDP. With the youngest, Juliet, just coming up to twenty, they were quite able to make their own political choices; and they were not convinced that the SDP would prove radical enough on social issues. Juliet attended the launch of the party and accompanied me when I canvassed for Roy in Warrington and Shirley in Crosby, and visited SDP conferences when they were within easy reach of her home in Manchester. All three were delighted when Roy, of whom they were very fond, won Hillhead. But when the general election came, they agreed that they could not actively campaign for me in Stockton, although Lucy was sent as an emissary to keep me company and say that they loved me still. In such a way are compromises reached in all families. I was luckier than many parents might have been; and in the wholly committed and actively partisan support of Silvia, I had none of the tensions – and indeed the falling-out of spouses – experienced by some of my colleagues.

By-elections were occasions when our energy burst out with glorious and trium-phant vigour, and it was good to be alive. Our first by-election at Warrington started slowly and with no great expectations, when Shirley declined the nomination for what seemed a safe Labour seat and Roy stepped reluctantly into the breach. A week into the campaign John Roper, who was the MP assigned as the on-the-spot over-seer of the by-election, telephoned me to say it was too quiet and had I any ideas about how it might be brought to life? I said that I would do what I could if he found me a portable loudspeaker. I had used one occasionally in Stockton and found it in-valuable for attracting a crowd on a street corner and generally enlivening events. Now I discovered a new technique as a one-man Greek chorus commenting on the passing scene and treating politics as entertainment. Walking the streets of Warrington accompanying the candidate, I talked irreverently about anything that took my fancy. 'And now Roy Jenkins is speaking to a lady in a bright green dress – and very fetching it is – just outside Harrison's the greengrocers, where they have some excellent cauliflowers on sale for only 41p', I would say. Or, riding on top of a landrover, I would interrupt a simple political message with a greeting to a pedestrian and an occasional 'Hello, dog' to the animal he was walking. It was so much nonsense, but it drew attention to our campaign and gave it a lighter touch than those of our opponents. I would also interview Roy on the street, much as a BBC interviewer might have done, which always attracted attention; and when Shirley came up to add her support, we did a successful double act. Henceforth, my loudspeaker became a feature of by-elections, although it needed a responsive candidate and an atmosphere of infectious excitement to be used to best effect.

SDP supporters eventually poured into Warrington in a way that I had never seen Labour activists rally in a by-election, and the presence of both Jo Grimond, rather diffidently accompanying Roy round the shopping centre, and David Steel, attract-ing attention at the local funfair, raised morale still further. We never expected to win, but by the last Saturday of the campaign the feeling was of a festival. Losing on the following Thursday was no anti-climax when Roy captured a spectacular forty-two per cent of the vote.

We carried this carnival spirit into all the by-elections we fought, but most notably to Crosby in November 1981 and Hillhead in March 1982, simply because Shirley

Williams and Roy Jenkins – fighting this time with the expectation of winning – were candidates with a large personal following and capable of instant recognition. I had known Crosby since childhood as a sleepy and comfortably-off outer suburb of Liverpool, although it hardly admitted to such a relationship. The constituency contained some of Lancashire's bleak, flat-as-a-pancake potato fields, but even these glowed like the Tuscan hills when we campaigned across them to music from the film *Chariots of Fire,* which had become our defining signature tune.

Shirley had initially been almost as reluctant to fight Crosby as Warrington and, with a Tory majority of 19,272, it certainly looked a bridge too far. In the previous summer I had discussed with her the prospect of a by-election in the London constituency of Bermondsey where the sitting MP, Bob Mellish, was expected to resign, but she still clung to the idea of returning to her former seat at Hertford and Stevenage. When a by-election was declared at Croydon North-West, she expressed an interest but declined to push her claim – I agreed with her about that – when the incumbent Liberal candidate refused to budge. Now, faced with Crosby, she hesitated again even though David Steel promised to square the local Liberals. Although David Owen and I tried to persuade her to fight, she began her keynote speech to our Bradford conference with no more than a weary half-promise that she would do so and, as the speech progressed, it looked dangerously as if she would not. I was sitting next to her on the platform and, appalled that the moment might pass, I printed in block letters on a scrap of paper: 'Say, "so I am willing to fight Crosby"', and propped it against a glass of water in her line of vision. She glanced down, and a moment later the necessary words were spoken to tumultuous applause. The irony on this occasion is that Shirley was unfairly blamed, not for dithering but for jumping the gun before the arrangements for a smooth transfer of the seat from the Liberals had been completed.

Once she had made her decision, she was a superb candidate with all her energy, intelligence and charm helping her around awkward questions, even if this meant making SDP policy as she went along. Meetings were packed and over 1,500 Social Democrats and Liberals turned up to man telephones, fill envelopes, put up posters, deliver literature and canvass. From our headquarters in the Corona ballroom in the middle of Great Crosby, I went out to buy fish and chips and a bottle of red wine to sustain the party workers. 'Claret and chips for lunch'. I announced, and *Claret and Chips* became the title of one of several books rushed out to chronicle our phenomenal progress. When Shirley won a majority of 5,289, the SDP's success carried over into the opinion polls. The Gallup poll for December 1981 recorded that fifty-one per cent of the electorate would vote for the SDP or the Liberals at an early general election; and in the fourth quarter of 1981 as a whole, an average of all polls still gave us a massive 42.1 per cent. It was far, far better than we had ever dreamt.

Glasgow Hillhead was a different kind of constituency, and Roy Jenkins a different kind of candidate, statesmanlike where Shirley Williams was ebullient, deliberate where Shirley lived by her wits. The by-election also had one critical moment when the polls showed that all might be lost. Indeed, the dangers of an anglicised Welshman fighting a Scottish seat, given the fluid state of Scottish politics and the potential strengh of the Nationalists, were very real. For once I had no view of my own about whether it was a gamble worth taking, especially as anything short of winning would now be regarded as a major setback for the SDP. I canvassed, attended coffee mornings and did a certain amount of work with my portable loudspeaker. But the great event was the coming together of the Gang of Four a week before polling day to address a meeting packed to the doors and overflowing in a local school and then a crowd, put at 1,000, waiting outside. My two abiding memories are of an elderly couple, warmly dressed against a frosty wind, sitting patiently on a bench outside the school, waiting for the speeches to begin; and of Donald Dewar, the Labour MP for Garscadden (who would have been a very welcome recruit to our ranks) reconnoitring the meeting and marvelling at its size and vibrance. Once again, for a moment, we were conquering all.

The Alliance fought thirteen by-elections beween the launch of the SDP and the general election of 1983, and I spoke at all of them. But my greatest pleasure was in travelling the country helping to establish new branches – or area parties, as we called them – and addressing their inaugural gatherings. One of our most unexpected areas of recruitment was the armed services, who had felt dispossessed of any alternative to the Conservatives, given Labour's habitual equivocation on defence. I took the train to Salisbury, in the heart of Southern England's military belt. Two officers were in my compartment, and when they left the train the colonel said, 'Good luck for your meeting, my wife will be there.' At the meeting itself, a retired Wing Commander was selling tickets, and when I visited Salisbury again a year or so later I found that the colonel had himself now retired and become an SDP councillor. As late as 1992, when I addressed an outdoor meeting in the market place in Salisbury, the leader of the team of helpers (now Liberal Democrats) introduced himself as having met me when he was in command of his regiment on my ministerial visit to Hong Kong in 1975. In a number of these constituencies in Hampshire and Wiltshire there had been a good Liberal vote in 1979, but the new SDP recruits helped to turn them into marginal seats and played their part in the remarkable advance in local government that eventually followed.

At the end of 1981 I wrote a long assessment of the year in my diary. Like so many of my entries, it rejoiced in our success but documented some of the tensions within the Gang of Four. We had worked well together and were more than our separate parts. We had brought something new to politics, and the novelty of the quadripartite leadership had not yet worn off. This could not, however, last forever and we were agreed that we should choose a single leader by the summer of 1982, and also elect a president. My view had strengthened that Roy and Shirley respectively were the right candidates for these roles. Shirley had not settled back into the House of Commons very confidently, having chosen to call it a 'boozy men's club' on the day of her introduction, and then made a rather superficial re-entry speech. But she was marvellous as a campaigner and much loved in the country where she drew the largest audiences.

In the summer of 1981, at the Aspen Institute in Colorado, I had had a conversation with her in the unlikely venue of the swimming pool, Shirley almost up to her neck in water and me crouching at the water's edge. She had then been firm in her support for Roy as leader, and not intending to press her own claim. Now I had a feeling that her loyalty was slipping under pressure from David who, in turn, Roy was finding particularly tiresome. 'I don't look forward to lunches where David behaves like an arched cat', he told me. David was not popular with SDP MPs but he was tolerated as leader because he was tough, worked hard and did a good job in the House. Despite all this, my diary recorded with delight and optimism:

> We are wonderfully on time, running to keep up with ourselves … Next year we shall be fully armed, not too soon for a general election only eighteen months away but in time enough given the state of the Tory Government and the Labour Party. That is our great good fortune.

We had been photographed together by Lord Snowdon for the *Sunday Times*, by David Bailey for *Vogue*, and by Norman Parkinson for the National Portrait Gallery. We were already part of history.

But if burgeoning SDP membership and successful by-elections were the warp in the fabric of our lives, relations with the Liberals were the weft. They were not the sole cause of stress within the Gang of Four, but they often provided the focus for our differences. And despite the anger I had provoked in David Owen at the launch by setting our sights on fighting only half the parliamentary seats, the implementation of this division of seats from the launch until well into 1982 made me the most unpopular SDP person with many Liberals.

Nine days after the launch, Shirley and I departed for the 1981 Anglo-German conference at Königswinter. There was embarrassment and confusion amongst our German social democratic friends who were acutely conscious that our new party was modelled on theirs, while they had less and less in common with Labour, now unilateral and anti-Europe. At the state reception, the German Chancellor, Helmut Schmidt, was particularly warm towards Shirley and me and, in welcoming the guests, pointedly omitted the name of his old sparring partner Denis Healey.

But the all-party nature of Königswinter and the presence of journalists, academics and businessmen, as well as politicians, had long meant that informal, social contacts in the margins of the conference were as useful within the two national delegations as between them. Now the serious business within the British delegation was between

David Steel and Shirley and myself. At his suggestion we lunched together on the second day of the conference and were joined by Richard Holme, who was David Steel's right-hand man, and David Marquand, who was a key figure in our new party. Then after lunch, following a Königswinter custom, we climbed a neighbouring slope of the wooded Drachenfels mountains which flanked the Rhine on its eastern side. It was clear that David Steel had foreseen the opportunity for a serious discussion with us. With a typical sense of occasion, he had even tried to hire a motor launch to ensure publicity for the event.

From these early days, through the life of the Alliance, David Steel was often accused by Social Democrats of 'bouncing' them into awkward decisions that put them at a disadvantage. What Social Democrats assumed to be private meetings became well-publicised events in which the Liberal Leader was cast as taking the initiative and having the ideas, because over the years Liberals had remained in the public eye only by allowing the press access to anything they were willing to report. The Liberal Leader had also remained ahead of his party in this way, sometimes using publicity to present them with a *fait accompli* on a matter in which he saw no hope of otherwise persuading them. 'Open covenants, openly arrived at', in the words of Woodrow Wilson, might have been the ideological justification for such behaviour in relation to the SDP. In fact, it was a habit of a lifetime, seen as no less appropriate in the new circumstances in which Liberals found themselves.

But there was another factor. David Steel had thought hard about realignment. He no longer believed that the Liberal Party alone could beat the system, and he was ready for our new party by the time of Limehouse and entirely clear that an alliance was the only way forward. Free from the massive task of building the SDP, he could concentrate on the nature of the partnership between the two parties. Time and time again he was thinking ahead of the collective mind of the SDP, irritating even those who hoped to move in his direction, thus giving comfort to those who did not. But on this occasion at Königswinter there was no such inhibition in Shirley's mind or mine. We were full of our new party, eager to chart its future and not averse to the great interest our discussions aroused amongst the journalists present. If we were making history, we should do it boldly.

Our discussions covered familiar and obvious ground, and agreement presented few problems. There should be a common statement of principles, and this should be formally endorsed by our autumn conferences. Subsequently, there should be two joint commissions to develop policy, one on industry and the other on electoral and constitutional reform. Finally, there should be what we cautiously described as 'an exchange of information about our respective priorities', with a view to dispelling misunderstanding and helping negotiations over the division of seats. The preamble said: 'Believing that it is desirable that we should fight the next election in alliance, as distinct parties but together offering the nation a government of partnership, we therefore agree, subject to the agreement of colleagues ...', and the three headings followed. At my rather flippant suggestion, reflecting peace-making during the Thirty Years' War, our agreement was described as 'The Königswinter Compact'. It was written out by Richard Holme on a lined sheet of greenish paper that looked as if it had been torn from an office ledger. It was dated 5 April 1981, and my initials and Shirley's were inscribed on one side of the heading and David Steel's and Richard Holme's on the other.

Shirley and I returned to London well pleased. Our agreement seemed totally consistent with what had been said at the press conference at the time of the launch. It was also carefully subject to the endorsement of our colleagues. It referred both to 'distinct parties' and to 'partnership', which was the acceptable language of our burgeoning relationship with the Liberals. Above all, if David Steel was able to carry his party in its support, he would now have a free hand in dealing with the SDP, which would be greatly to our advantage.

But the mood in the SDP was not universally welcoming. At our regular Gang of Four lunch the atmosphere was cool, with David Owen disapproving of our Königswinter activities, for which he thought we had no mandate; and a special meeting was called for the following day, bringing together twenty of the key people in the new party. There was unanimous agreement both that the SDP should maintain its identity and that an electoral alliance with the Liberals was required. But there were substantial disagreements on timetable and tactics. Ian Wrigglesworth was strongly against any early deal with the Liberals who, he said, were perceived by the public as representing failure, a view endorsed by Mike Thomas, amongst others. David Marquand and John Roper felt, in varying degrees, that there should be no impediment to working together with the Liberals and helping David Steel establish authority over his difficult party. Thus the lines were drawn which were to persist up to the decisive vote on merger over six years later. Ian Wrigglesworth played a constructive role with the Liberals at all times, and went on to be the first President of the Liberal Democrats. But the passage of time did not greatly change the views of the hard-core opponents of closer relations with the Liberals, and their position was immensely strengthened as David Owen's antagonism became more clearly articulated.

However, in the weeks that followed the post-Königswinter discussions, I felt no alarm at David Owen's position on the Liberals. I welcomed *A Fresh Start for Britain*, the joint 'Statement of Principles for the Alliance' that emerged in June as the first by-product of the Königswinter Compact, and at least David Owen did not dispute the need for it. He agreed in due course to serve on the Commission on the Constitution, which he saw as an integral part of cooperation between the two parties in parliament under his leadership. I did not share his irritation when

Roy and Shirley appeared together with David Steel and Jo Grimond at the Liberal assembly at Llandudno in September, but if the choice was between a rapid coming together of the two parties or a more cautious approach, I preferred the latter. For the time being we were creating the essential organisation on the ground without which the SDP would appear highly centralised, all chiefs and few Indians. In any case, many members of the SDP had belonged to no political party in the past – they were the political virgins – and had fresh ideas to contribute, as well as much to learn. It was not acceptable, as David Steel seemed to imply, that the SDP should mainly bring to the Alliance the experience and reputation of four senior politicians who had served in cabinet. Our new party needed the whole apparatus of policy-making and campaigning, including the ability to select and then elect its own MPs and local councillors. It was for our members in the constituencies – 'bottom-up', in the current jargon – to determine the pace at which we and the Liberals would come closer together. This in turn would depend on how well they could cooperate and how much they had in common on policy. Discussion of merger was entirely premature this side of an election. It would come only as a result of a natural convergence at the grassroots.

But an agreement on the allocation of parliamentary seats, to implement the third element in the Königswinter Compact, was urgent. Given my overall responsibility for organisation, this was my responsibility, with David Steel himself leading for the Liberals. The task that faced us was forbidding, infinitely more so than when Ramsay MacDonald and Herbe```rt Gladstone had negotiated an agreement between the Liberals and the infant Labour Party in 1903. Clear differences of opinion had already emerged in the SDP about our closeness to the Liberals and acceptable terms for the division of seats, which the composition of my negotiating team was bound to reflect. But amongst Liberals Cyril Smith had not been alone in wanting to 'strangle the SDP at birth'. Michael Meadowcroft, a leader of the Liberals in Yorkshire, and Tony Greaves, of the Association of Liberal Councillors, started from the proposition that, at best, the SDP should be allowed to fight 100 seats. The new party was, after all, a very uncertain quantity and its leaders, they believed, could be dismissed as 'old Labour' and heavily corporatist, having no claim to put up candidates where Liberals had long worked tirelessly to establish themselves.

My first suggestion was a simple one: that each party would fight the seats it now held but, after that, seats would be allocated in tranches of twenty-five, with the Liberals choosing the first twenty-five they preferred, the SDP the second, and so on until all 623 seats in England, Scotland and Wales had been allocated. The process of dividing the seats would thus be hardly more than an afternoon's work. But the Liberals rejected my proposal out of hand because Liberal candidates had already been adopted in 200 seats, including in most of the eighty-one in which they had been second in the 1979 election. This gave them the powerful advantage of part possession, which was strengthened by a considerable degree of local autonomy. But we could not leave the division to chance and local agreements, and it was inconceivable that individual negotiations should begin in many hundreds of constituencies without clear guidance from the centre about how they should be conducted and the outcome the leadership was seeking. But it proved extremely difficult to reach agreement with David Steel, even on this.

Between July and October 1981 my team and David Steel's, which included his parliamentary colleagues Alan Beith and David Penhaligon, met frequently. Successive drafts of the guidelines were scrutinised and interpreted with an intensity and precision more appropriate to the Dead Sea Scrolls. The day after one particularly fraught meeting, held in a conference room at Dean's Yard within the precincts of the Palace of Westminster, David Steel wrote me a long and furious letter from his home at Ettrick Bridge. It had been the worst meeting between the two parties he had ever encountered, he said, depressing and negative. The collective leadership of the SDP was unable to exercise authority (precisely the same complaint that we were making of him) and Mike Thomas, a member of my team, was 'insufferable'. On the substance, he added:

> I have told you consistently that I am quite happy to accept your 300 seats as a target but not as a principle. It makes no sense to elbow aside a working Liberal organisation simply to reach a notional parity if there is nothing to put in its place. I think it is only to be expected that Liberals will have slightly more seats than the SDP simply because of our superior organisation.

He ended by regretting that 'the trust and goodwill and, indeed, friendly optimism which was so apparent between our two parties at Warrington and Llandudno, was markedly absent from Dean's Yard'.

It was the first major crisis in the negotiations and revealed the gap between us. An important difference of conception underlaid it. The SDP was bargaining hard but had every intention of reaching an agreement which would be honoured. The Liberals found this process unfamiliar and hoped for a more informal outcome from which some departure would be permitted. In the event, agreed guidelines were signed and published on 21 October 1981. 'It is the objective of the two parties to fight the next general election in Alliance', they began, in a useful reaffirmation of our previously declared position. The aim would be 'rough parity in the total number of seats each party fights'. These would include 'preferred and less promising seats' (a euphemism for winnable and hopeless ones). The advantage of the scheme was that it satisfied the wish of the Liberal leadership to involve local activists. The disadvantage was that it would take very many hours over several months to implement, and would give infinite scope for delay and misunderstanding.

However, in accepting it in good faith I did not anticipate any unusual difficulties, and the SDP prepared with great thoroughness for the negotiations ahead. Each constituency was analysed in detail to show the possibility of its being won, the effect of forthcoming boundary changes and the relative claims of the SDP or Liberals to fight it on the basis of local strength and preferences. We hired Sarah Horack, a statistician who had worked for Gallup, and 'trading rules' were drawn up to indicate how a deal might be reached and the minimum acceptable outcome from the SDP's point of view. We aimed to get the best agreement, irrespective of personal interests, although with the advice of our members on the ground.

The process did not go smoothly. The Liberals were sometimes leaderless and seldom adopted a common view. Each of them was heavily committed to an individual constituency and had little conception of a bargain by which they abandoned one seat to the SDP in return for another. We looked for a fair division of seats and not an unfair advantage, but 'fairness' had another side to it, of which Liberals were very conscious. One Sunday morning I had an anguished call from Gloucestershire. 'My husband said I shouldn't telephone you but Harry's at his wits' end. He's lost his future.' I was nonplussed, but coaxed my caller into an explanation. In tears, she said that her husband had given up his job and moved his family to the constituency to fight the seat. Now it was to be fought by the SDP, and the bottom had fallen out of his life. This was one of several telephone calls from Liberal wives – there was one from a Liberal husband – pleading that their spouses be allowed to fight seats that were about to be taken from them by the SDP. It was an entirely human response to the exigencies of the political process.

What I had not allowed for was the inability of Liberal negotiating teams to reach an agreement and stick to it. I had driven to Chesterfield on Sunday 13 December 1981 (it was the day General Jaruzelski seized power in Poland, and I listened to the depressing news on my car radio), accompanied by David Marquand. We were to reach agreement with the Liberals on the twenty seats in Derbyshire and Nottinghamshire which, for the most part, was a wasteland for the Alliance. We made progress through the day and finally came to allocate Amber Valley and Erewash, two neighbouring seats of little merit, but both with a handful of Liberal and Social Democratic activists. I persuaded my colleagues to let the Liberals choose, although we had a preference of our own. They chose Amber Valley, our preference, but that was the end of the matter. We had reached agreement and shook hands on it.

But within a week I received a telephone call from Viv Bingham, a senior figure in his party, who had been the leader of the Liberal team in Chesterfield. They had changed their minds, he said, because a displaced Liberal candidate now wished to transfer his interest to Erewash, which had been given to the SDP. We must meet again and find a different solution. I was upset and impatient. We were weeks behind our agreed timetable for negotiations, and the allocation of seats in Derbyshire and Nottinghamshire had been acknowledged as fair to both parties, with the Liberals given the final say. Now they wanted to unwind it all. If this experience was to be repeated across the country, we would never settle the allocation before the general election, and every delay meant less time for campaigning.

I checked with my negotiating team about their initial experience, and their reports were unanimous. Everything was slow going because the Liberals were unorganised, badly informed about the quality of individual seats and, it seemed, quite without instructions from the Liberal leadership about how to proceed and the object of the negotations. Clearly, David Steel had baulked at explaining our agreement on a fair division of seats between the parties and the need to make concessions in seats where Liberals had already been adopted. It seemed yet another example of Steel reaching agreements in principle and then washing his hands of the hard, time-consuming and unpopular task of implementation. But if I was wrong, here was a specific case in which he should intervene. I telephoned him and explained the position. He listened carefully, but expressed the hope that it could still be resolved locally and asked me to talk again to Viv Bingham. I did so, but made no progress. I then wrote to David Steel on 23 December, restating the problem and adding:

> The question of principle is important. Both sides should do their homework in advance and decide on negotiating priorities – otherwise the whole process will continue for ever and ever. So stalemate for *all* negotiations while this is settled, because I can't just let my people spend time negotiating and then discover that the views of a single PPC [prospective parliamentary candidate] *after the event* can throw everything back into the melting pot.

He replied on 29 December, defending the need for the Liberals to proceed *ad referendum* their constituency associations and, in respect of Derbyshire, saying only:

> I trust you and Viv will be able to resolve it satisfactorily after the hiccups.

This was a wholly inadequate response, and David Steel could not be allowed to get away with it. I wrote again on 31 December, coupling the Derbyshire problem with trouble in Greenock, where local Liberals were denying the seat to Dick Mabon, the sitting SDP MP.

> We are getting into an impasse. In both cases your people are clearly at fault. You have made this plain to me in private, but have not used your authority in public. Frankly, this is bound to undermine confidence. The overall negotiations cannot proceed further in such an atmosphere.

As I waited in the hope that David would appreciate the urgency of the matter, I reflected on the gloomy alternative prospect. If nothing were done, a series of protracted meetings would be required to bring every negotiation to a conclusion. Already my negotiators were leaving clusters of difficult seats to be settled through my personal intervention, and progress in reallocating winnable former Liberal seats to the SDP appeared to be nil. I now saw the negotiations stretching on and on, causing increasing strain between the parties and inhibiting preparations for the general election. There would then be a major confrontation at precisely the moment when the unity in the Alliance should be cemented, and those in the SDP hostile to a closer relationship would say, 'I told you so'. I decided that a public airing of the matter, if it had to come, was better now than later and I would tell the story to Adam Raphael of *The Observer*, who was personally well disposed towards the SDP and the Alliance and who would couch his report in understanding terms. But Adam Raphael was away skiing, and I spoke instead to Anthony Howard, the Deputy Editor. I have no complaint about how he treated the story, but its prominence on the front page of *The Observer* on 3 January was much more than I had expected.

The conventional wisdom is that I made an error. At its most extreme, this attributes a dip in the fortunes of the Alliance in the first quarter of 1982 entirely to my doing. Roy Jenkins was moving into position to fight his second by-election, and when on Sunday morning the telephone rang early, his first words were ominous: 'You have just lost me Hillhead'. It was an untypically harsh reprimand and he was angry. Later in the week he and David Owen came to lunch (Shirley was abroad) to discuss the situation – the press insisted on knowing the menu, and Silvia said marmite sandwiches, which was happily wide of the mark – and he showed greater understanding of what I had done. But his disquiet remained, although my negotiating team were unanimous in their support, including David Marquand, who was close to the Liberals and well-trusted by them and who had accompanied me to Chesterfield.

David Steel put on his disapproving son-of-the-manse face and pretended that the row had come as a surprise, but after another healing lunch – this time at Como Lario – there was a welcome change in his mood. He appointed 'firemen' from amongst his negotiating team and David Penhaligon, amongst others, played a very useful role in putting out local 'blazes' and obliging Liberal associations to recognise the guidelines. The Liberals finally identified their 'golden seats' (those they most hoped to win) and agreed that the SDP should have a major share of 'silver seats' if their right to the golden ones was acknowledged. By the middle of March 1982, David Steel and I were able to announce that the allocation of two-thirds of the seats in Great Britain had been completed, which was only a slight gloss on the figures; and by the end of April we were jointly telling local negotiators to complete their discussions without delay and threatening ones that failed to do so with arbitration, an unheard-of intervention from the centre in Liberal terms. Increasingly, the argument ceased to be between myself and David Steel, and became between each of us and local activists in our separate parties. Social Democrats who complained about the allocation of Trafford, Harrow, Conwy and Rugby to the Liberals were matched by Liberals who complained about the allocation of Hastings, Harlow, Saffron Walden and York to the SDP.

In the final stages, in the autumn of the year, David Steel threw his full weight behind the solution of difficult problems and was entirely fair in seeking a satisfactory outcome for both parties. When the election came, he refused to campaign in any seat where Liberals had failed to reach and respect an agreement with the SDP, most notably in what then looked like the winnable seat of Liverpool Broadgreen. Whatever the problems I had with him, he was much criticised by some Liberal activists who felt that he had conceded far too much to me. At the election, the SDP fought 311 seats and the Liberals 322, almost the parity I had been seeking. We did much less well in winning, but nor did the Liberals succeed in those 'golden seats' like Richmond, Cheltenham and Chelmsford that we readily left to them. Had the Alliance really broken through with over 100 seats, the SDP and the Liberals would have won roughly equal numbers.

The deal on parliamentary seats reached between the SDP and the Liberal Party was a remarkable achievement, certainly without precedent and unlikely to be repeated. The allocation of seats that took place between us in the next parliament was unnecessarily prolonged and in some ways more stressful. But in 1981–82 we were on entirely new ground, making up the rules as we went along. The Liberal Party was well entrenched in many parts of the country, and it was natural that they should resent giving up constituencies in which they had worked for years and which now seemed within their grasp to win. The SDP was insisting on its separate identity, often emphasising how different it was from the Liberal Party; and some of its members in their Labour days had been bitter opponents of the Liberals at local level. My action in making public my row with David Steel was profoundly disturbing to those who supported the SDP expecting that its politics would always be sweetness and light. But what I did – variously attributed to vanity or a rush of blood to the head – was entirely consistent with my belief that an equal partnership between our two parties was the key to the strength of the Alliance, and an equal partnership meant an equal share of parliamentary seats to fight. It would have been deeply damaging to the morale of SDP activists if the Liberals had fought all the best seats and the SDP was left with the rubbish. The resentment would have made more difficult, not less, the natural convergence between the two parties that I anticipated.

My only regret is that the row provided fresh arguments for those who believed the Liberals were impossible to work with and should be elbowed aside. David Owen accepted the practical need to work with them but believed that it should be at arms' length and competitively; later, in his memoirs, saying more starkly that he: 'always thought that a trial of strength with the Liberals was inevitable'. By contrast, he attributed to Roy Jenkins the belief that the SDP 'was merely a transit vehicle' to merger with the Liberals. I believed that such polarisation served no purpose and grossly misrepresented the position of many of those in the party whom David Owen foolishly came to regard as his enemies. With a somewhat patronising benediction, he half exonerates Shirley Williams and myself from the blame he attaches to Roy Jenkins, attributing any later fall from grace to our selection to fight seats in the 1987 general election by joint meetings of Social Democrats and Liberals.

David Owen was right that our members were men and women who had been free to join the Liberals but had not chosen to. He was right also that there were many advantages in the House of Commons and in dealings with the radio and television authorities in emphasising our separateness. But to resist a closer union on principle was increasingly, especially after 1983, to deny the instinct of many of our members, to distract us from the real political task of winning votes and to divide the leadership of the party.

For the most part over the years, the Liberals had not featured in any serious political calculations. The familiar surge in Liberal support at by-elections had added excitement to the scene, but seldom anything more. Torrington, which had returned Mark Bonham Carter in 1958, and Orpington, which was a famous victory for Eric Lubbock in 1962, were place-names to be conjured with. But they signified temporary Liberal uprisings rather than milestones on Jo Grimond's march towards the sound of gunfire. The fate of Liberal leaders in the House of Commons was cruel. If, in a major debate, Jo Grimond was fortunate enough to be called soon after the Leader of the Opposition, he would speak to a noisy House as it emptied of all except a couple of dozen Members on either side. Even his most thoughtful contributions to debates seemed an interval before the real business resumed. After his speech he would hurry, slightly hunched, from the Members' Lobby, down the corridor towards the library. There were few of the nods and friendly greetings which usually followed a major speech. The Liberal Party was outnumbered by a hundred to one in the House, and neither Labour not the Conservatives wished to acknowledge that its ideas were worth considering.

In general, Liberals in the House of Commons survived in isolation, barely acknowledged as being there as of right and resented when they won a by-election. A few weeks after Cyril Smith took Rochdale for the Liberals in 1972, I met him and exchanged a few words on York station where we were both changing trains. He said that I was the first Labour Member who had spoken to him since his election. Individual Liberal MPs – Russell Johnston, Emlyn Hooson, John Pardoe – made useful contributions to debate, but in hard, political terms they seemed an irrelevance. At local level, Town Hall bosses, Labour and Conservative, looked askance at the pavement politics of the Liberals who promised the voters the earth, secure in the knowledge that political control would elude them and they would never be required to deliver. For those – like me – who had fought unilateral disarmament in the Labour Party for years, the erratic progress of the Liberals on defence was particularly disturbing.

All these factors were within my experience, and I felt that many Liberals had developed a ghetto mentality which restricted their vision. But this was not true of David Steel and, as I came to know them better, of old troupers like Nancy Seear, apparatchiks like Richard Holme and media-men like Alan Watson. As for grassroots Liberals, they worked harder and with sharper focus than many of their opposite numbers in the Labour Party and had brought their by-election campaigning to perfection. We would continue to have our complaints about the Liberals, but the fault was not only on one side and we should learn to live with the foibles of our partners rather than hold them at a distance on every occasion. In challenging the two-party system we were besieging Jericho. The Liberals, with years of political engineering behind them, believed in patiently undermining the foundations of the citadel. The SDP, confident in its own irresistible progress, expected the blast of its trumpets to win the day. But what mattered was that the walls should come tumbling down, and they were far more vulnerable to our joint endeavours than to either party alone.

Within a week of the Hillhead by-election and as the allocation of parliamentary seats moved through its calmest phase, we were confronted by the Falklands War. This again demonstrated that David Owen's view of the SDP as irrevocably divided from the earliest times between Jenkinsites and Owenites did not stand up to scrutiny. Very early on the morning of 3 April 1982, with the House of Commons poised to hold an emergency debate later in the day, David telephoned me at home. I was still in bed and half asleep, and Silvia passed me the telephone. 'What am I going to say if Thatcher declares her intention to repossess the Falklands?' he asked. 'What do you have in mind?' was my first response. 'Well, I don't rule out a naval task force, but it's a high risk. I'm inclined to oppose the Government.' This time I was clear. 'No, you can't do that. We have to support military action. There is no other way.' In my own Foreign Office days, fifteen years earlier, the Falklands were seen to be vulnerable and I supported a peaceful transfer of sovereignty to Argentina. But this moment had unhappily passed and as the islands had been seized in defiance of international law, Britain had to recover them. I spoke strongly to David to this effect, adding that quite apart from the question of principle and legitimacy, the SDP would lose heavily with the voters if we equivocated and failed to support the Government. By the time we met at the House shortly before the debate, this had also become his view, and together we argued the case against those SDP MPs who wanted any military action to be opposed.

Throughout the weeks that followed, I supported David Owen on every occasion while Roy remained detached and Shirley uneasy about our stance. In view of my defence experience, David asked me whether I wished to play a larger part in the parliamentary exchanges, but he was very effective and had my full support. The Falklands War made his reputation in the House of Commons and as a serious candidate against Roy for the leadership of the SDP, but opinions were not divided on Jenkinsite-Owenite lines.

The contest for the leadership began in May 1982. Quite apart from my affection for him, I had no doubt that on all-round performance and potential – we were, after all, thinking of a future Prime Minister – Roy was much the better choice, and I put it to David Owen, although without much hope, that he should let Roy be nominated without a contest. But Shirley, although not in David's camp, sometimes hunted with him and, despite her promise to me at Aspen in the previous summer, she now nominated him for the leadership. I did not realise at the time how strongly she resented what she saw as the habit of some of Roy's friends (not me) of unfairly rubbishing her for what was seen as her indecision, bad time-keeping and general untidiness of behaviour. This seemed to me to be the principal reason for her switch, although she may have reached an accommodation with David by which her support for him would ensure his promise not to seek the presidency.

During a decorous campaign Roy and David set out their alternative views on relations with the Liberals, but not in a way to which the other could easily take exception. It was a choice between the statesman and the young radical and although, to my relief, the statesman won, it was by the comparatively narrow margin of 26,256 votes to 20,864.

The election of the leader marked a watershed in the development of the SDP. Two months later Shirley easily beat me and a third candidate in an entirely relaxed contest for the presidency which, as a gesture, I entered because I did not think that Shirley, for all her public virtues, would take a sufficient grip on the party organisation. The collective leadership was ended, but the more the Gang of Four could keep together, the greater the momentum the SDP would retain; and in so far as there were differences between us it was far better that they be resolved in private. The party was now run professionally by a Chief Executive. My initial preference had been for David Young, my excellent former Private Secretary at Defence, because I believed a former civil servant would best keep the Gang of Four in order. But David Owen and I then agreed on Bernard Doyle, a businessman, and persuaded Roy and Shirley to acquiesce reluctantly in this choice.

At weekends I spent time interviewing members who wanted to be added to our list of prospective parliamentary candidates. We arranged training courses, and I particularly enjoyed those specifically aimed at helping women to get selected. We did not insist on a quota of all-women shortlists which would have denied to local parties the right to choose, and ruled out some excellent candidates in waiting. But we required two women (and two men) on every shortlist, and so gave women the chance to overcome the first – and, traditionally, the most difficult – hurdle to selection. With forty-three women candidates in 1983 we had more than any other party, and the figure rose to sixty in 1987.

Our potential women candidates had ability in abundance but lacked confidence. They saw male candidates as effortlessly facing election conferences and treating rejection as calmly as missing a bus. 'Men have no inhibitions about putting themselves forward and don't suffer when they lose', was how they saw it. Now they seemed to draw strength when I told them that the process of selection could be as cruel to men as they feared they might find it. 'You'll recover if you have resilience', was my message. Our women candidates were mostly highly educated professional people, often with careers of their own. But they found being a candidate expensive, especially if they were adopted for a constituency far from home. The party had raised, mainly from membership subscriptions, sufficient to finance a core of headquarters activities. Our local parties, especially the larger ones, had discovered ways of raising enough money to keep afloat. But there was no money to pay for the travel costs of candidates or their postage or telephone bills, or the cost of staying overnight.

I began to experience some of the costs of SDP activities myself. As Member of Parliament for Stockton, my legitimate constituency expenses were all covered, and until the election of Roy as Leader, an allowance for leadership expenses had been equally divided between the four of us. Now none of it was available to me, and I quickly found myself spending substantial sums out of my own pocket or, more dangerously, next year's income tax. When the reckoning finally caught up with me, I decided that the SDP must have cost me several thousand pounds a year, falling particularly heavily after I had lost my seat. Being a Social Democrat did not come cheap.

Nor, in the second half of 1982, did it come so easy. In a speech to SDP activists in Camden in the early summer, I said that the revival of Conservative fortunes as a result of the Falklands War had lost us at least 5–10 per cent of our vote. This falling back in our support was reflected in the results of all the by-elections we fought after Hillhead. At Beaconsfield, the Liberal candidate, Paul Tyler, pushed the young Labour pretender Tony Blair into third place; and at Peckham, the young Conservative candidate John Redwood suffered the same fate at the hands of Dick Taverne. In both cases the Alliance substantially increased its share of the vote, but we were not even close to winning any of the six by-elections between May and the end of the year. Much to my irritation, at Mitcham and Morden my Oxford friend and contemporary Bruce Douglas-Mann, who was a leading figure in the housing charity Shelter, insisted in resigning his seat when he joined the SDP, but he too lost while the Conservative vote remained steady. My loudspeaker made no impact in a sluggish campaign in the suburbs of south London.

It was important to regain momentum and begin preparations for the general election but, unfortunately, the election of a single leader did not bear fruit in a new surge of energy. Roy Jenkins found difficulty in adjusting to a House of Commons very different from the one he had known before his departure to Brussels, and to a different role and status within it. For most of a dozen years he had spoken from the dispatch box to an increasingly respectful House. I had always found the dispatch box – there are two of them on either side of the clerks' table that separates government and opposition across the Chamber – a symbol of authority, conferring this on me when I stood there. It was also a convenient desk on which to lay notes and lean an elbow, a reassuring object to grip during a difficult speech, and a protective barrier between me and my opponents when under attack. But the SDP front bench, like that of the Liberals, was below the gangway and quite without the reassurance of a dispatch box. Initially I had felt exposed, naked even, when speaking there, and Roy found it no easier.

The House was also a rowdier, less disciplined place than when he had left it. Speaker Thomas' Welsh lilt, his obvious enjoyment of his role and his sonorous call, 'Order! Order!' were making him a household name, as the proceedings of parliament were now broadcast. But the good humour with which he sometimes turned away wrath in a noisy Chamber could be a smokescreen for allowing disruptive Members, like Dennis Skinner, too much freedom. As a result, George Thomas presided over a decline in parliamentary behaviour. Outside the Chamber I found him as apparently friendly as ever and studiously correct in his dealings with the SDP. But in the chair he did not always offer us the protection to which a minority party was entitled when subject to disruptive heckling.

The difficulties Roy Jenkins had in the House of Commons were matched by some hesitation in getting preparations for the general election under way. He was tired after an immensely busy year which had included fighting two by-elections; and no doubt the illness that was later to trouble him was already casting its shadow. He also found it difficult to handle David Owen, to whose abilities he gave generous recognition but whose black moods made working together unrelaxed. Before the House rose for the summer recess, Roy said that he would set up a campaign committee which he would normally chair but which I would chair in his absence. This was entirely compatible with my experience of campaigning, but David wanted to be the alternative chairman himself. Roy found this wearisome but, instead of either insisting on my role or conceding to David's wishes, he postponed a decision.

With Roy insufficiently driving the party forward and David resenting his defeat for the leadership and deep into a prolonged sulk, we were dangerously becalmed. Until now I had taken for granted that Roy would become the leader of the Alliance, with David Steel as his deputy. But while still arguing with others that Roy would come into his own when the election began, I admitted to myself that I could not rule out a switch to make David Steel effectively the Alliance candidate for Prime Minister if Roy proved unable to find his feet.

Roy was depressed by David Owen's black mood, but I was not too much surprised. At the end of 1981 I had written in my diary of him:

> He has had a good run. His sharp style has made an impact. He has been pretty effective as our parliamentary leader. But what happens if he loses one of the top jobs to Roy and the other to Shirley? David is proud and ambitious and not very tolerant. He won't take kindly to it.

My working relations with him remained good, although I found his political judgement sometimes impaired by convoluted thought processes that owed much to his character and ambition. At the Newcastle conference of the SDP in January 1983, the platform, on whose behalf David was to reply, came under pressure on the question of a nuclear freeze and the siting of cruise missiles in the United Kingdom. Previously there had been no doubt whatever about the SDP's robust attitude on defence, but now a handful of unilaterists were joined by a larger group led by Sir Peter Swinnerton-Dyer, a distinguished Cambridge mathematician and Master of St Catherine's College. To my great surprise, David Owen proposed to accept an amendment from Swinnerton-Dyer, largely because he believed it could not be defeated. But to me and to John Roper, who had helped to hold the line on 'Yes to Cruise, no to Trident' when I was Labour Party defence spokesman, this would be a dangerous shift of policy. It was only after intensive lobbying that David was persuaded that Swinnerton-Dyer should be opposed; and in the event, far from defeat, the platform won the votes with handsome majorities. I was then amazed to be telephoned by Geoffrey Smith of *The Times*, who opened the conversation by saying: 'I hear you supported David Owen in holding the line ...' Geoffrey Smith took on board my astonished response and printed a revised and accurate story. David Owen was at his blackest. But I was not going to let him get away with it; he was about to be given credit for firmness of purpose (in contrast, it was implied, to Roy and Shirley) when he had notably lacked it.

The relevance of this, otherwise small, episode was twofold. First, it confirmed that although David could fight hard and courageously, he found defeat humiliating (as he had done over the leadership) and would look for a way out of a contest he believed he could not win. Second, it was a strange precedent for his behaviour three years later, when he was to disown the report of the Joint Alliance Commission on Defence and Disarmament – and me, as one of its authors – as soft on nuclear weapons. It was a reversal of roles that owed more to David Owen's ambitions and pride than to consistency.

But I was now turning my attention back to Stockton and considering in what circumstances I might hold my seat. Six of my most middle-class wards had been joined to the bulk of Ian Wrigglesworth's former Thornaby constituency to create Stockton South, matched by Stockton North, which comprised most of my old constituency with some rural additions. In Stockton South, one in five heads of household were in the professional and managerial class (good SDP material); in Stockton North it was nearer one in ten. In Stockton South, seventy per cent of houses were owner-occupied (again, good for the SDP); in Stockton North, it was less than fifty per cent. These social characteristics made Stockton South much the more winnable constituency, and Ian Wrigglesworth generously offered to surrender to me his prior claim to fight it. But I decided that if Stockton South was to be won, Ian had a marginally better chance and, in any case, my roots were in Stockton North, which I had now served for over twenty years, longer than any other MP. On 7 December 1982 I accepted nomination and began to plan my campaign. The popular view was that the two great council housing estates of Roseworth and Hardwick, together with the deep-rooted Labour loyalties of the North-East, would defeat me. But I believed that I might win up to half of the former Labour vote and perhaps a quarter of the Tory vote, which would see me through to victory.

But the New Year 1983 did not start well. Ian Wrigglesworth and I soon received news of a BBC North television programme on 'The Defectors' which was to feature a specially commissioned MORI poll which drew unfavourable comparisons with a similar poll conducted after the launch of the SDP in 1981. It was said that whereas in 1981, 39 per cent of Stockton voters would have supported me, this had now fallen to 16 per cent. The more I heard about the programme, the more worried I became. The principal commentator was *The Observer's* Northern correspondent, who was well known as a Labour supporter, and the programme's tame academic was a Labour Party member from Sheffield University. There was also a subtle difference in the questions. In 1981 my constituents had been asked, 'If there were a general election tomorrow and your Member of Parliament stood as a Social Democrat, how would you vote?' But the question now was simply, 'How would you vote if there was a general election tomorrow?' It seemed to me that the decoupling of the question from a reference to 'your Member of Parliament' (identifiably me) would minimise any element of a personal vote; and the dropping of 'Social Democrat' would reduce the chances of a positive response. The BBC claimed that the comparison was valid, and Robert Worcester of MORI wrote me a stuffy 'Dear Sir' letter which threatened 'further action' when Ian Wrigglesworth and I dared to suggest that the programme might be biased because he was currently advising the Labour Party. But the damage was done.

The Darlington by-election on 24 March 1983 was a much bigger blow, in this case both to my own hopes and to the expectations of the SDP and the Alliance as a whole. In the seat negotiations with the Liberals, I had been successful in getting

Darlington allocated to the SDP. The town had adjusted remarkably to the closure of the railway workshops, and unemployment was low by the standards of County Durham. With over two-thirds of homes in owner-occupation, it seemed as good a territory for the SDP as any in the rather unpromising North-East. Darlington was twelve miles from Stockton, at the other end of the first passenger railway in the world, opened in 1825. Although the Liberals had won only ten per cent of the vote in 1979, and it was the archetypal 'squeeze' seat difficult for a third party, with a good candidate we might achieve a good result.

Late in 1982 I had learnt that the initial selection process had produced a poor short list for the general election. I then telephoned the local SDP chairman, saying that I had in mind to stop the selection until better candidates could be found. But he reassured me. 'The list isn't inspiring but we'll choose a popular sports presenter from Tyne-Tees television.' That was fair enough, and I did not press my objection further, as I was anxious that our general election candidates should now all be in place. What I had not allowed for was a sudden by-election. Under the SDP's constitution we were permitted to replace an existing candidate with another, more suitable, one, given the intense pressure of by-elections and our wish to get able men and women elected to the House. But many of our best people had already been selected elsewhere, and I received no eager telephone calls from those still seeking seats. In any case, only a star candidate would have been acceptable as a replacement for a local television personality. So our existing candidate for the by-election remained in place, and this turned out to be a disaster. We went into it as favourites and came out a poor third.

A month before polling day in Darlington, Simon Hughes won the Bermondsey by-election for the Liberals. I spoke at his adoption meeting, and his forty-minute speech was much the longest I had ever experienced on such an occasion. But he was an excellent candidate, and the council flats and houses, which were eighty per cent of the constituency, were soon decked out with a display of yellow Alliance posters. The Labour Party was badly split, in what was formerly the south London docklands, by the choice of left-wing candidate Peter Tatchell, whose overt homosexuality also made him the target of abuse in a universally hostile press. It was a stunning victory for Simon Hughes in an inner-city area where Labour had reigned supreme for generations. It should have set the Alliance band-wagon rolling again.

It did not do so because shortly after the media by-election circus had abandoned Bermondsey for Darlington, our candidate came unstuck. He won instant recognition on the council estates, and his folksy manner had a strong appeal to Labour voters, especially women. But when press conferences, platform speeches and a debate with the other candidates replaced a friendly wave and a handshake as the currency of electioneering, he showed little knowledge of politics and limited aptitude for learning. He was sent to London for intensive training and given full-time research assistance and a speech-writer. Every morning he was driven to headquarters from his home so that he could read the daily papers. But he remained a lightweight, with neither ideas nor passion. As a candidate in a general election he might have got away with it, but in a high-exposure by-election there was no chance of making him a silent candidate who refused to answer questions or to appear with the other candidates. Even out canvassing, his shortcomings would have been quickly rumbled by the press corps who, after Bermondsey, were anxious to be fair towards Darlington's Labour candidate, who was respectable, serious and a native of the town. Nor would a diplomatic illness have escaped detection. We were stuck with our candidate and, as the days passed, the by-election slipped through our fingers. On a record turn-out of eighty per cent the SDP came in third, with only a quarter of the votes cast.

Optimistic canvassing returns and an ineffective response to Labour's resurgence played their part, but our failure was widely attributed to the shortcomings of our candidate and, had the by-election come earlier in the Parliament, it might have been forgotten as ill-luck. But the SDP and the Alliance needed to regain momentum, and success at Bermondsey should have been followed by a breakthrough in the North. I was more sensitive than others to the outcome because I had been closely involved in the campaign, which would have a spin-off effect in Stockton. It is impossible to say that with an outstanding candidate we would have won, but had we done so it would have been a marvellous springboard for the general election. We might have closed the narrow gap between the votes polled for the Alliance and those polled for the Labour Party, leaving us morally in second place behind Mrs Thatcher and the Conservatives. I might even have won Stockton.

I had a good local SDP which worked hard, but only a handful of members had experience of the messiness of politics, or the confidence to stand on their own. In the May 1983 local elections that heralded the general election, we fought too few seats, and none of them with much panache. The Labour Party, meanwhile, had worked out its tactics and realised where I was vulnerable. My supporters would be harrassed through the columns of the local newspaper and made uncomfortable on the doorstep. The trade unions – mostly moderate and respected in Stockton – would express their disapproval of me, and some black propaganda and less than white lies would feed anxieties.

A major employer in Stockton was Hills, who had built Mosquito aircraft during the war but were now in the more prosaic business of manufacturing wooden doors, mainly for houses. It was a well-run firm which I had helped on several occasions in their dealings with Whitehall departments and, in turn, they kept me in touch with their development plans. They had installed a new, highly automated production line and invited me to perform the opening. But three days before the event the *Evening Gazette* printed a story that the trade unions would call out all their members unless my invitation was cancelled, thus turning a celebration into a confrontation. My own position was clear. I had been invited in good faith as the local MP to a non-political occasion. I had a constituency duty and I had no intention of being sidelined because I was now a Social Democrat. All I could do was to stay cool (even if I didn't feel that way) when the storm broke, and show that I could not be so easily put down.

I turned up at 11.30 on the day and found the chairman and directors tense and awkward. They were apprehensive of what might happen, despite the note of friendly insouciance I affected. Then the time came for us to walk from the administrative block into the main workshop. As we did so, employees appeared at doors and windows and the workshop was crowded with others. Many of the employees were women, but men who were trade union branch secretaries showed no sign of hostility. There was no protest, no-one walked out, everyone was eager to demonstrate their part in the new production process and the whole occasion passed off entirely without incident. The story had been invented by a few individuals and swallowed by the *Evening Gazette* because it made news.

Once the election was declared, Stockton became my base. I agreed to make a number of sorties in support of SDP and Liberal candidates into other constituencies in the North-East, including neighbouring Sedgefield, whose new Labour candidate was a fugitive from the Beaconsfield by-election, Tony Blair. But unlike my Labour Party days, when I had no responsibilities whatsoever for election matters nationally, now I kept in frequent touch with headquarters in Cowley Street, Westminster, talked to those responsible for press, radio and television, and attended weekly strategy meetings.

So it was no surprise when David Steel telephoned me at the Swallow Hotel, Stockton, to confirm that the Alliance campaign committee fixed for Sunday 29 May was to be switched from London to his home at Ettrick Bridge in the Scottish Borders. With ten days to go until polling day, the Alliance campaign had not caught fire, and a well-publicised meeting at Ettrick Bridge would do no harm. I was surprised, however, at Steel's suggestion that he should change places with Roy Jenkins to become effectively leader of the Alliance, and his news that Roy had tentatively agreed. Despite my earlier hopes, the campaign had not brought the best out of Roy, but I was very doubtful whether changing horses now would result in a surge of support rather than ridicule. Steel seemed content to hear my arguments and that I would go along reluctantly with his proposal only if Roy was convinced it was right. I then telephoned Jennifer Jenkins – Roy was inaccessible on the road – who very sharply said: 'Don't believe Steel for a moment. Roy has not agreed. It would be madness to make a change.' That put quite another complexion on the matter. Steel had told at best a half-truth, but the idea was now dead. This assumption was confirmed by no further message from Steel and no urgent call from Shirley Williams, which I would have expected had there been an issue to resolve. It was a passing episode, or so it seemed.

On Sunday morning, 29 May, I left Stockton early, drove past Consett, whose blazing steel furnaces had once made it a landmark in the night sky, across Hadrian's Wall to Selkirk and then Ettrick Bridge. The A68 is a switchback road where it crosses the wild and beautiful uplands of Northumbria north of the Wall, and heavy mist lingered dangerously in its hollows. But I arrived at David Steel's home on time, while those who had planned to travel by helicopter found their journey disrupted by fog. We eventually sat round the dining-room table and began reviewing what seemed a mismatch between good and friendly crowds around the country – Roy and David Steel both seemed happy with their reception – and the polls, which continued to give us no more than 18–21 per cent.

John Pardoe then suddenly embarked, in his uncompromising way, on the case for changing the balance of the leadership precisely as Steel had suggested earlier in the week; and Steel produced what I could only call an abdication statement for Roy, which handed over the further leadership of the campaign to him. Roy looked bruised and embarrassed, but I said it was quite wrong that the matter had been raised at all, attacked Pardoe for his clumsiness and ruled out any change as simply impractical. I was angry, but my conversation with Steel earlier in the week had at least prepared me. Shirley had had no such advantage. She was taken aback, but totally firm in supporting what I had said. After a brisk exchange, we slipped back into discussion of television presentation. I assumed that the interruption had served its purpose in enabling Steel to tell those of his supporters critical of Roy's performance that he had made their case. But Pardoe resurrected the matter and it looked as if we were to have a re-run of our previous discussion. Now I was outraged. It was quite disgraceful, I said, to be returning to an issue that had been settled half an hour ago. 'The Alliance is based on trust and there will be no trust left if this behaviour continues.' Shirley was again outspoken, and we had the unequivocal support of Jack Diamond, with several of the Liberals present at least emollient. In the end, Steel and Pardoe gave up, and Steel and Roy eventually gave a successful press conference which made the Ettrick Bridge summit a good lead story for the following day, with not a breath about the Liberal coup that had failed.

After lunch I drove Shirley and David Owen to Edinburgh to catch a plane. David had remained mostly silent in the exchanges with Steel and Pardoe, distancing himself from Roy, as he frequently did, and justifying this by saying that the arrangements for dual leadership with Roy as Prime Minister-designate had been made by Roy and Steel and were for them, and them alone, to change. This was to dissemble, because he had enjoyed Roy's discomfiture in the face of criticism and as the victim of Liberal sharp practice, evidence of his own belief that the Liberals were thoroughly unreliable. He volunteered one concession, and it was to Steel. As we discussed the events of the day, and Steel's provocative performance, David Owen suddenly said: 'I didn't know he had it in him!' I glanced at David in the passenger seat beside me and caught a half-smile of genuine admiration, perhaps his first and last for David Steel in the six years of Alliance.

Back in Stockton, I reviewed my own campaign. My constituents were friendly and often warm. They waved vigorously to me from their houses and honked the horns of their cars in recognition. Women in particular were very ready to listen to the SDP case and to volunteer their support. But there was not, I admitted to myself, great excitement. My usual meetings, two a night to cover all districts, were much better attended than in 1979, but they were not big. Twenty on a bleak housing estate was better than half a dozen; and fifty in middle-class Norton was good. But audiences listened respectfully, and the bubbling enthusiasm of by-elections was quite lacking. It was also chastening to discover what ought to have been obvious to me: that changes in the electorate over the years meant that many voters knew little of my personal record and were not easily convinced that a former Labour MP – for whom they would *not* have voted – had developed into a Social Democrat with acceptable views.

Four days before polling day I noted in my diary that Mrs Thatcher was on course for a spectacular landslide victory, and feared that the Stockton Tories, very unsettled two years earlier, would now remain firm, not yielding me the votes I needed. After all, this was their best chance to recapture the seat since Harold Macmillan had lost it in 1945. I could still win, but I might find myself in third place.

The following day I had what I regarded as decisive news. An opinion poll, this time for Tyne-Tees television, put me convincingly behind both Labour, now set to win, and the Tories, who might almost hold their 1979 vote. I had no resources to throw into a last-minute blitz and the national opinion polls, although fast improving, would not carry me through. I telephoned Jack Diamond in London and asked him to arrange for all my belongings to be cleared from my House of Commons rooms as I had no intention of returning there if I had lost, as I had seen other dejected colleagues do over the years. That evening, when I spoke at a meeting on the Roseworth estate, I forced out my words with an intensity that subdued the audience into sharing my unspoken presentiment of defeat. After a good night's sleep, I continued to campaign as I had planned, doing what I could to keep up the morale of my supporters. But I knew that my time was running out.

Shortly after midnight, in the early hours of Friday 10 June 1983, I ceased to be Stockton's MP after twenty-one years. About a third of my previous Labour vote stayed with me, but I attracted less than a tenth of the Tory vote. With 29.6 per cent of the votes cast, I was only a few thousand behind the winner, but in third place nevertheless. As Silvia and I waited for the result to be declared from the Town Hall in the High Street at the end of my eighth Stockton campaign, we listened to the radio. It looked as if few SDP MPs would survive. The Labour Party was facing a disaster it had brought on itself, but the SDP and the Alliance, once so buoyant and hopeful, would find it harder to bear their own disappointment.

Chapter 11

Losing and Winning

We were back in London by the Friday evening, but left the following day to spend the rest of the weekend at our cottage in East Woodhay. I began to feel a strange relief about Stockton. Freed from the need to catch a Friday train from King's Cross and sometimes the sleeper, the memory of such journeys became disagreeable. As for Stockton itself, for over two years I had been living on borrowed time, while facing some unpleasantness. Now that two-thirds of the voters had turned against me, it seemed good riddance; let them manage on their own. But the break was not as clean-cut as that. Rejection does not raise the spirits: it dents confidence. I now understood how Harold Macmillan felt when he wept after his Stockton defeat in 1945. Once the formalities of my farewell party were over, I did not return there until the 1990s when I experienced the slightly awkward residual affection for an affair happy in its time but long over.

More surprising and less qualified was my detachment from the House of Commons. When the time came for the Opening of Parliament and the Queen's Speech, I had no wish to be there. I listened to 'Today in Parliament' and followed the debates, but when the light beneath Big Ben signalled a late sitting, I did not grieve for my absence, even though my evenings often seemed empty. I could not avoid visits to the Commons for political business but I preferred to exercise none of the privileges of access available to a former Member and on one occasion declined to walk down the library corridor with Roy on the grounds that it was the intimate heart of parliament. When I returned to Westminster almost ten years later to sit in the Lords, most of these inhibitions fell away but unlike many former Members I still do not use the MPs' dining room.

In perspective, the election result was far from a disaster for the SDP. The six SDP MPs were part of a larger Alliance group of twenty-three, not equalled in size for a third party since the 1930s. Our joint share of the vote was 25.4 per cent, against the previous high-water mark for the post-war Liberals of 19.3 per cent in 1974, and this represented approaching two million more voters. Labour, whose decline had been our opportunity, had won only 2.2 per cent more of the vote and was in turmoil. The Alliance had come first or second in 332 parliamentary seats, with Labour coming first or second in 341. It was a remarkable achievement.

But that is not how it felt. The unfairness of the result, comparing our share of the vote with seats won, was plain and the case for proportional representation was demonstrated as never before. But as long as the first-past-the-post system endured, we would be judged by its rules and twenty-three MPs (Labour had 209) was just too few. Fourteen years later, in the general election of 1997, the Liberal Democrats would win only 16.8 per cent of the vote, but forty-six MPs ensured a much bigger splash both with the public and in the day-to-day business of parliament.

We were also victim to comparisons with the drama and size of earlier SDP triumphs, the victories at Crosby and Hillhead and opinion polls that showed us with the support of over half the country at the end of 1981. Even those of us who were strong supporters of the Alliance took little comfort from the election of six more Liberals than in 1979, while the SDP had been decimated.

That was the mood when Silvia and I sat in our East Woodhay garden on the Sunday afternoon and Roy came over from East Hendred. But the immediate issue was whether he should resign as Leader in the knowledge that David Owen would then succeed him. David had already been on the telephone to Roy saying he should go without delay and Roy said that 'when' was now the only question. He may have hoped I would challenge this assumption but I reluctantly agreed, saying it would be better to resign at once than carry on with David snapping at his heels. Had Roy been able to continue through our forthcoming annual conference he might have been able to set the agenda for the next few years, especially on cooperation with the Liberals, but that did not seem to be a possibility.

The following day, David, Shirley, Jack Diamond, John Roper and I joined Roy at East Hendred. Roy indicated his intention to resign, which came as a shock to Shirley and Jack, who argued vigorously against it. David grudgingly conceded a delay of six or seven weeks but said that the principle of resignation was not negotiable. That effectively decided the matter and Roy's resignation followed within hours.

A core of Roy's closest supporters who had seen him as their undisputed leader since the days of Dimbleby were surprised and disapproving. They believed that his stature would enable him to defeat any challenge from David Owen when the post-election spasm of disappointment had passed, and the need to work closely with the Liberals had been positively reassessed. I thought then, and think now, that they were wrong and Roy would have lost in any contest by a margin possibly as large as two to one. His personal standing had not diminished, but he had failed to sparkle as a campaigning leader and in the House of Commons, and there was a long haul ahead through another Thatcher Parliament. SDP members would have voted for change.

That Sunday's work effectively ended the Gang of Four. Shirley remained President with an active role from which she could not be removed by David. Roy's views continued to carry weight, particularly in the country, and despite two years of debilitating ill-ness, he restored his parliamentary reputation to become Backbencher of the Year.

I also managed, after a while, to find a tolerable working relationship with David that brought us closer together for a couple of years. But the four of us did not meet over lunch in a way which was routine until just before Christmas 1983. The SDP was now David's own show, and he had no intention of letting the spotlight shine elsewhere. 'Stiff and unyielding, very much Dr Death, with suspicion his main char-acteristic', is how I described him in my diary. Determined to be the undisputed leader of the party, he quickly built his personal team of loyalists. He was not in a po-sition to give himself an entrenched majority on elected committees, but a nucleus of friends ensured that his views and wishes were never in doubt.

He was determined to define early in his leadership a position different from Roy's or, for that matter, from Shirley's and mine. He was helped in this by premature talk of a merger with the Liberals by some of those who had been closest to Roy. In my view, it was too early to advocate merger; better to allow natural convergence to continue and then assess the overall position of the Alliance halfway through the new parliament. Attitudes towards the Liberals (and their attitudes toward the SDP) were uneven over the country, with a marked absence of goodwill in many of the old in-dustrial areas of the North. In any case, given that our party would certainly give the new leader the benefit of the doubt, there was no point in going into head-on colli-sion with David, who would personalise the argument as between Owenites and Jenkinsites. I was proved right about this. The advocacy of early merger gave David Owen an excuse to harden his position against it, and to establish this as the settled policy of the party until the next election.

He was careful not to close the door on merger but always with a form of words that was ambiguous. 'After the general election,' he said in the course of a radio discus-sion, 'the issue of merger or of a closer relationship between the two parties will come back on the agenda, and rightly so'. This view was reiterated in a defining motion put down in the name of Christopher Brocklebank-Fowler for the party's 1983 Salford conference, which was drafted to David's dictation. This motion called upon the SDP 'to deepen and strengthen the arrangement for working together between the par-ties'. On the face of it, here was a call for growing cooperation with the Liberals, but in practice the dominant theme was the preservation of the SDP's separate identity by reference to the party's constitution and to seat allocation. It meant no joint mem-bership of the two parties and no joint selection of candidates; the Liberals were to be held at arm's length. It was impossible to see how on this basis relations were to be deeper and stronger.

Meanwhile, I had to sort out my own role and, more particularly, how I was to make ends meet. In the run-up to the election, fighting to hold Stockton, the problems of earning a living if I lost my seat had never crossed my mind. I had not applied for a job for thirty years and hardly knew where to begin. Even though the children were leaving home, I needed something at least close to a parliamentary salary and I had always earned more. But for the moment I had my redundancy pay which would keep me going until new sources of income were in place.

It was not to be as easy as that. There was a move to make me Chief Executive of the party (Bernard Doyle having resigned) and I might have agreed had David not exercised his veto, wanting no such cuckoo in his nest. The appointment went instead to Dick Newby, who was an impeccable civil servant for the party for four years, efficiently organising its business, staying above internal controversies and courageously standing up to David Owen when he overstepped the mark. However, as I slowly discovered, it was assumed in the wider world that I remained in full-time politics, paid by the party, and would return to the Commons at an early by-election. This ruled out consideration for major jobs (a Chatham House vacancy occurred about this time), while part-time opportunities emerged only to fade away. I was offered, so I understood, the chairmanship of a shirt manufacturing subsidiary of the textiles group Vantona-Viyella. This was attractive, as it would give me experience of industry and take me regularly to Lancashire, close to Juliet at Manchester University. Then, after two months in which I had come to take the appointment for granted, the reorganisation of the company removed the post I expected to fill. I was disappointed and puzzled, because in the public sector no-one was offered a job unless the vacancy existed and they had already been identified as the best candidate available. Comparing notes years later with Sir Robert Andrew, who, since my Defence department days, had been Permanent Secretary of the Northern Ireland Office, I found his experience of seeking jobs on retirement to be precisely the same. Offers in the private sector were often tentative and expected to provoke a good deal of self-advocacy from an interested candidate. By the end of the year, as my redundancy money ran out, I was alarmed that my precarious income was coming from a firm in Stockton that made lifts and wanted help in reaching a wider market in the construction industry; Mercke, Sharp and Dohme, the American pharmaceuticals giant that sought strategic political advice; and a column in *The Guardian*, reviews for *The Listener* and other assorted bits of journalism. Margaret Wallington, my secretary for twenty years, was working for me for nothing.

I tell this story to redress the balance against those who believe that politicians who lose their seats fall into lucrative employment. Some certainly do, but they are mainly Conservatives for whom a City casualty service seems to exist. Many of my SDP colleagues who involuntarily left the House in 1983 had a hard time. Gradually I built up an adequate portfolio of activities, taking seminars at University College, London; reporting to Guinness Peat, the bankers, from conferences abroad arranged by the World Economic Forum (which sponsors the annual assembly of the great and the good at Davos); lecturing to business schools and foreign students; designing and editing a guide to parliament for business; and making two trips a year to the United States to lecture at colleges and universities. Friends were helpful in devising opportunities for me, Jeffrey Jowell, Alastair Morton and David Sainsbury prominent amongst them. I was never badly off but my overdraft grew, especially as SDP activities, including a full programme on the rubber-chicken speaking circuit, only rarely resulted in all expenses paid.

Having completed her Oxford doctorate in social anthropology, Silvia was contributing again to the family coffers by the autumn of 1984. She began teaching at London semesters of American universities and then joined the University of Maryland's academic programme for American servicemen at bases in Britain. This took her on long drives to Greenham Common – crossing the Greenham women's picket line – Alconbury and Lakenheath, often returning after midnight. This was not, I thought, an ideal way of life for a woman in her mid-fifties who had better things to do, but it helped to pay the bills. She was committed to the SDP and to my part in it. A lonely night drive on the M4, A1 or M11 was just one more contribution amongst many of a politician's wife to his survival.

For the time being survival meant involvement in a somewhat unstructured variety of activities. As Vice-President of the SDP, formally third in the hierarchy, there was no corner of the kingdom I failed to reach to speak at annual dinners, fund-raising occasions and public meetings. I enjoyed this peripatetic role, carrying the message and raising the morale of the troops. As I travelled, I found once again both excitement and deep pleasure in the physical characteristics of the countryside and of urban landscapes – the curve of the hills, a copse of trees, the texture of buildings, the pattern of streets. Back in London I was Chairman of the Finance Committee, agreeing priorities for spending and keeping a tight control on where the money went. Fund-raising from amongst the larger personal donors became the responsibility of a group under David Sainsbury, but I was aware of the danger of becoming dependent on a handful of individuals. In practice, membership subscriptions always provided at least half the party's regular income and the pioneering use of direct mailing techniques brought in hundreds of thousands of pounds in relatively modest donations.

From the beginning, we had been determined to escape the incestuous financial relationship of the Labour Party and the trade unions, and the close ties of the Conservatives with business and the obligations these carried. But this did not mean the rejection of corporate donations altogether or even, as time went by, some soliciting of them. What I found noticeable was a preference for making donations to the Alliance rather than to one party. This was also the choice of some individuals who even took their preference further. Sir Terence Conran, designer and entrepreneur, wrote in reply to a letter about money: 'If it was not an Alliance but a true merger between the SDP and the Liberal Party then it would certainly have my support, and I believe a great many other people's as well', and he sent no cheque. This was not, however, a message that we were ready to heed.

On the contrary, for we were soon on another long series of negotiations about parliamentary seats; in this case not only with the Liberals but with our own local parties. My preference would have been to leave the ownership of seats where it had been for the 1983 election, allowing local swaps by mutual agreement. But the Liberals wanted to reclaim seats in which they were historically strong and SDP candidates had put up a poor performance; and in some cases, good working relations between the two parties had made SDP supporters indifferent to which party was to lead. David Owen was quick to conclude that there was a grave danger of merger gaining momentum at the grassroots and blunting the identity of the separate party he was so anxious to preserve. The threat, as he saw it, came principally from what was clumsily called 'joint *closed* selection' – a seat allocated to either the SDP or the Liberals but with members of both parties choosing the candidate – or even worse 'joint *open* selection', where members voted together to choose between competing candidates from both parties. Guided by David, the Salford conference agreed that joint selection of any kind should take place only in 'exceptional circumstances' and by 1984 the Liberals had acquiesced in an agreement which embodied this principle. In deference to them there was an emphasis on local negotiations, a conscious break with the approach of two years earlier. Despite this, a formal written agreement to proceed to the selection of a candidate required the approval of a joint working party led by Shirley Williams, President of the SDP, and Geoff Tordoff, President of the Liberals; and, more particularly, any joint selections could only go ahead with the approval of the National Committee of the SDP, its governing body.

For almost eighteen months, this tedious process absorbed a vast amount of time, the destination of individual seats being endlessly argued about, then voted upon. To a lesser or greater degree we all felt bound by the Salford decision, and David Owen often preferred no decision at all to one that might give the Liberals an advantage or blunt the SDP's profile. By October 1984, Wales had been settled, under the leadership of the former MP for Wrexham and my PPS from Defence days, Tom Ellis, who had ignored the guidelines and infuriated David Owen by agreeing eight joint selections. 'Wales is a nation', David was told, and outsiders should not interfere. Similarly an agreement was reached in Scotland on the basis of no change in the seats contested by the SDP and the Liberals in 1983. But in England the position was very different, with barely over half the seats settled and as many as 140 with serious problems about allocation.

I had hitherto managed to avoid day-to-day involvement in the selection process.

The overseeing of the Williams–Tordoff agreement had fallen to Mike Thomas, one of David Owen's closest circle. But the National Committee became dismayed at the lack of progress and proved sympathetic to a suggestion from Roger Liddle that a new approach was required. David was reluctantly convinced of this and asked me to persuade the Liberal leadership to put more pressure on their local parties and then to accelerate the whole process. David Steel and his senior colleagues had been much criticised for infringing local autonomy and allowing the SDP to get a better deal than it deserved last time round. But led by David Penhaligon, by temperament at least as much a local activist as MP for Truro – and my opposite number at the time of the Lib-Lab pact – they now agreed to risk the wrath of their rank and file.

For several months we worked successfully and local problems were solved, often needing more courage on the Liberals' part than awkward confrontation on ours. But by the early summer of 1985 I had had enough. The whole process needed to be wound up if candidates for the general election were to be in place in key targeted seats. If this meant joint closed or joint open selection, so be it. I went to see David Owen and said that I would produce a final indivisible package of proposals agreed with the Liberals which would contain twenty joint open selections and which would stand or fall as a whole. If it was agreed, my work was over, but if it was rejected I would resign from my task. He put on his look of blackest disapproval, knowing I had put a gun to his head. But he also knew that my resignation would not lead to a better deal, and a failure to end the long negotiations would be damaging to the SDP. Two weeks later, at its July meeting, the National Committee accepted my recommendation. Both parties were now free, quite often together, to choose candidates where for many months they had faced frustrating delay.

David Owen ungraciously attributed my decision to put forward a final package to my wish to be selected for Milton Keynes, where joint open selection was an unbending Liberal preference. But at that stage I was still far from certain where I wanted to stand, or that the Liberals would have me, given my track record over previous negotiations. I had faithfully supported the policy agreed at Salford, but we had achieved all we could reasonably expect, often with our own members wanting a more accommodating attitude to the Liberals than they were allowed to adopt. In the interest of both parties it was time to draw a line.

Despite these disagreements over how best to choose parliamentary candidates, David and I were now into the most constructive and harmonious period of working together we were to enjoy in that Parliament. In his early days as Leader, he had tried to reduce Shirley's effectiveness as an independent presidential voice, out-manoeuvring her at the Salford Conference. The result had been to detach her from any residual personal loyalty dating from her nomination of him in 1982. But her insistence that he should broaden the basis of his advice led, from the beginning of 1985, to regular meetings of an informal coordinating committee, of which she and I were members, together with Ian Wrigglesworth, Mike Thomas and John Cartwright. It was a form of inner cabinet, much concerned with practical questions of running the party. In parallel, a new Parliamentary Advisory Committee brought Anthony Lester, John Harris, Anne Sofer and Polly Toynbee, amongst others, into the regular discussion of parliamentary tactics at the weekly meeting of SDP MPs. In my diary I wrote, 'David has become much surer in his political touch ... For the first year he led the party rather unheedingly; now he listens and recognises the extent of his dependency'. It was a somewhat premature judgement.

He was certainly not more tolerant of public dissent. He treated it as an immediate and unacceptable challenge to his authority. On policy, as on so many other things, he saw 1983 as a watershed. He believed that before the election the SDP had promised, in Ralf Dahrendorf's phrase, 'a better yesterday'. Now, under his leadership, all that had passed. His guru was the American political philosopher, John Rawls, whose complex theory of justice supported the idea of equality of rights and liberties between citizens but not the social and economic equality in which the centre-left had always believed. The practical result was that, in the view of many of his members, David was pushing the SDP towards the sub-Thatcherite right. SDP members were more sympathetic than he was towards the human and social consequences of the prolonged miners' strike of 1984–85; and they greatly welcomed the proposals for merging tax and benefits (largely the brainchild of Dick Taverne) as a solution to the problem of sixteen million people in Britain living on or below the poverty line. While David Owen made a virtue of radicalism itself, most Social Democrats preferred a party of conscience and reform, challenging Margaret Thatcher.

Under the title *My Party – Wet or Dry?* I decided to examine some of these dilemmas in a lecture to the Tawney Society, which had been set up by Michael Young as the SDP equivalent of the Fabians. I referred to the open letter that David, Shirley and I had published in *The Guardian* in August 1980 that marked the emergence of the Gang of Three; and my own form of words about a new party 'taking over many of the traditional values and voters of the Labour Party'. I said that this was not inconsistent with a market economy provided we remembered our commitment at Limehouse to 'an open, classless and more equal society.' I conceded that David Owen's antithesis of 'tough and tender' brilliantly encapsulated our approach provided we did not allow 'tough' to elbow 'tender' out of the way.

This was not a personal attack on David, not least because such an approach would have been counter-productive in our deferential party. It was a legitimate contribution to the debate on the party's future direction which rang true with many of our members. But David did not see it like that. He made no comment to me, least of all to discuss the substance of what I had said. But when the theme of my lecture, and some of its key phrases, were incorporated into a resolution moved at our Torquay conference in September 1985 by Ben Stoneham, he took great care – as usual, through the speeches of his close circle – to ensure it was emasculated. That was how he preferred it: the short, sharp shock of dismissal rather than the search for understanding.

It was a dominance that Roy, Shirley and I had no alternative but to accept. David was outstanding in the House of Commons, impressive on television and commanding in the councils of the party. It was a bravura performance and did much for the reputation and morale of the SDP. But he was often short-tempered and his body language seemed to reflect the burden he carried. I took him to lunch at Como Lario on his forty-eighth birthday. It was a moment of calm between us, following a stormy period. I talked about what might lie beyond the next election and that there could be an important role for him if he was able to face up to merger. 'I am very tired', he wearily replied, 'and could not go through another parliament in this way'. His attitude to merger at the moment of decision must have been partly affected by his exhaustion and the forbidding possibility of leading a merged party – much less manageable than the SDP – if he chose to carry on.

Nothing better illustrates the tides, currents, eddies and storms of life with David Owen than the messy episode of the Alliance Commission on Defence and Disarmament. The Commission was set up in July 1984, with the task of making recommendations to the annual conferences of the two parties in the autumn of 1986. *A Fresh Start for Britain*, the first joint statement of the two parties, agreed three years earlier, had referred to 'the proper defence of Britain through membership of NATO' but whereas the SDP was robustly committed to the retention of nuclear weapons, there was a strong unilateral tendency amongst the Liberals. Current arguments about the deployment of nuclear-armed cruise missiles in Western Europe and the replacement of Britain's ageing nuclear-armed Polaris submarines had brought defence back on to the political agenda. It was vital that the Alliance should speak with a single voice in the election that was likely to come in 1987, which was the obvious motive behind establishing the Commission.

In fact, the three leading Liberal members, Laura Grimond, Christopher Mayhew and Richard Holme, were not on the unilateral wing of their party. Of the other two, one was a maverick who David Steel claimed to have picked out of a hat, and the other a new Liberal MP called Paddy Ashdown who rushed in late, left early, expressed vigorous opinions but was open to persuasion. The SDP team included Elizabeth Young and Edwina Moreton; two well-informed commentators on defence; John Roper, my former parliamentary colleague and ally on the front bench during my short time as Labour's Shadow Defence Secretary; and John Cartwright, now David Owen's Chief Whip in the Commons. When David asked me to serve as the senior SDP member I took it for granted that he wanted an agreed report, knowing that I would not sign unless the policy was consistent with all I had stood for in the quarter century since I had rallied opinion in support of Gaitskell's 'fight and fight and fight again'. If anything, I had been more hawkish on defence than he had been. It seemed natural, given the sensible overall composition of the Commission, that he should leave me to settle for a credible policy.

As the Commission wound its leisurely way through the intricacies of defence policy under its independent chairman, John Edmonds, a former senior diplomat, David and I exchanged a passing word about progress but no significant discussion of any anxiety on his part took place. The Commission's task was to report to both leaders when our work was completed. If David had a special message to convey he could always talk to me or, for that matter, John Cartwright whom he saw daily in the House of Commons. But there was no whisper that he was not prepared to wait for publication, and then consider the report in conjunction with David Steel.

Then, without warning, there was a thunderclap. David Owen used a speech at the SDP's 1986 spring conference at Southport to reject in advance key proposals in the draft we were preparing that dealt with the future of Britain's nuclear deterrent. In a last-minute addition to his speech David said that he had not yet seen the document – which was a strange prelude to disowning it – but declared in an unequivocal passage:

> I must tell you bluntly that I believe we should remain a nuclear weapon state … I certainly do not believe that I would carry any conviction whatever in the next election were I to answer on your behalf, on the question of the replacement of Polaris, that would depend on the circumstances of the time. That would deserve a belly laugh from the British electorate.

I got wind of this change in his speech only shortly before it was to be delivered. In the lift in the hotel where we were staying, I met John Cartwright, just arriving back from a visit to the United States. I told him what I had heard and asked whether he was still content with the Commission's draft report. 'Absolutely', was his reply and he was dismissive of any suggestion that David should or would upset it.

The draft said that no decision could be properly made 'on whether, and if so, how' strategic nuclear weapons should be retained beyond the life of the Royal Navy's Polaris submarines except in the light of certain criteria. In effect, this meant postponing for the moment a verdict on whether to proceed with the Trident replacement programme of the Thatcher Government. This was an entirely tenable position for a party in opposition, reached on merit and not in deference to Liberal views. It chimed well with the mood of informed opinion, given new arms control initiatives from Mr Gorbachev in Moscow, and the fact that the life of Polaris could be prolonged until the end of the century.

The cause of David Owen's extraordinary behaviour then emerged. It was a story in *The Scotsman* newspaper (which few of us assembled at Southport were likely to read) of an interview with David Steel in which he had said that the draft report of the Commission did not commit the Liberals to replacing Polaris. This was strictly accurate, but the twist – the reference to the Liberals – was misleading. The offence was also heightened by a headline, 'Owen's nuclear hopes dashed', which clearly marked down David Owen as the loser.

The story should have provoked no more from David Owen than a wry smile and a sharp word on the telephone for David Steel. The message could have been passed to the press that he would reserve his own verdict on the Commission's report until it had been completed. But the suggestion that on defence policy, where historic differences between the SDP and the Liberals were at their greatest, he was now the loser, was too much to stomach. *The Scotsman* story made David very angry indeed. Between its Friday publication and his speech on the morning of Saturday 17 May there was time to discuss with me and others an appropriate form of words if an oblique reference to David Steel's indiscretion seemed appropriate. But that was not David Owen's way. The revised part of his speech was made without consultation; it was a rebuke to David Steel and a direct challenge to the Commission. It rejected any compromise and pre-empted further policy-making on the matter by the SDP.

In this mood David was not open to reason. The best hope was that he would cool down and reconsider. But all his insecurities seemed to have been aroused, to be cloaked by the macho image he so often chose. He took every opportunity to raise the temperature, to imply that agreement with the Liberals on defence might not matter after all and to draw a line between himself and me, Shirley and Roy. In a magazine interview thirteen years later he construed our differences by saying, 'They tried to get me to support unilateralism', a rendering of our views that was laughably at odds with all we had ever stood for on this issue. He also claimed, in letters to members who had been upset by his conduct, that the Commission's report was being systematically and deliberately leaked by Liberals other than Steel. But he never said this to us and there was no evidence of it.

Had I chosen a private shouting match with David it might have cleared the air. Instead, I tried to persuade him to draw back while maintaining my support for the Commission's report in press and radio comments and in an article for *The Times*. On 4 June I wrote him a damage-limitation letter which suggested a form of words he might use when the report was published. He could agree that a final decision about strategic nuclear weapons would be made by the Alliance, in the event of government, in two or three years' time. He could agree also with the criteria set out by the Commission, which in any case were very much his own. But he could say plainly that whereas the Commission remained agnostic about a successor to Polaris, he believed that Britain should remain a nuclear weapons state. This would have involved no retreat on his part, but bridge-building would be apparent. In addition, I suggested a working party of experts to answer the 'if so, how?' part of the offending Commission phrase.

But David was not prepared to listen. The following day, in a speech in Bonn, he hardened his line and removed any doubt about his intentions. Then, on 9 June, he replied to my letter with a 2,000 word letter of his own. His message was that he 'could not live with' (a favourite phrase of his) the Commission's conclusion on strategic nuclear weapons and that my reconciling form of words was unacceptable. In any case, the gap between the SDP and even the most sensible Liberals was too great to bridge. The best hope was that they might come round to the SDP's policy as the election approached. As for myself, I had changed my views without even telling him and he was – his words – 'very sad'. It was a careful and well-organised letter with much about his preferred option of vertically launched cruise missiles on submarines as a replacement for Polaris and an alternative to Trident. But nothing it said justified the damaging public issue that he had opened up – damaging to the SDP because of our internal disagreement (the Gang of Four divided three to one against him) and damaging to the Alliance.

A week or two later John Roper and I – John having also robustly justified his signature of the Commission's report – were arraigned before the Parliamentary Advisory Committee. The charge was that we – and Shirley, as President, in her absence – had deviated from party policy and, in so doing, put ourselves at odds with the Leader. For a moment I knew how prisoners must have felt when brought before the Star Chamber at its most arbitrary and oppressive under the early Stuart kings. David Owen declared himself to be the independent chairman although he had encouraged and briefed our tormentors, who denounced what they claimed was our apostasy. However, I judged that most of those who stayed silent were on our side and others were clearly very uncomfortable at this show trial.

The meeting was intended to confirm David's authority – which was never in doubt – and relegate to history the controversial part of the Commission's report. But at an unrelated National Committee meeting shortly afterwards an unprecedented and hostile cross-examination of me as Chairman of the Finance Committee was staged. It was carefully orchestrated by David's inner circle – led by Sue Slipman and Colin Phipps – with David leaving the room at the relevant moment so as not to be witness to the anticipated spectacle. In his attitude to me – and to others who had crossed him on this issue – David believed not only in rebuke but in punishment. It was in that spirit that he ensured by his casting vote that I did not open the debate on defence at our autumn conference at Harrogate, Charles Kennedy taking my place while speaking much as I would have done.

The Commission report was published on 11 June to widespread approval. It was, said *The Guardian,* 'a thoroughly intelligent and workmanlike document', and its policy on Britain's nuclear weapons 'was as prudent and positive as could have been contrived'. The verdict of the *Financial Times* was that we had put forward a position that was 'defensible and sustainable well beyond the next election'. The *Financial Times* also said that the quarrel David Owen had provoked which had dominated newspaper headlines was 'regrettable' because it overstated the differences between the SDP and the Liberals and distracted attention from the wide range of other sensible and interesting proposals put forward by the Commission.

Why did he do it? In *Time to Declare,* published in 1991, he gives his own convoluted account of the episode, justifying his rejection of the report because 'Bill had deliberately decided to go his own way'. He believed, or so he implies, that when serving as a member of an independent Commission, I should have been a surrogate for him, refusing to reach any compromise on the sensitive issue of the Polaris replacement. Beyond that he appears to have detected a conspiracy, also involving Roy and Shirley, once again targeted at getting closer to the Liberals. But all I did was to make up my mind on the merits of the issue, and there was no conspiracy or anything like one. The whole damaging affair sprang from David's over-reaction to David Steel's *Scotsman* remarks and his anger at the Commission for reaching an agreement on nuclear defence when he wanted to maintain a clear distinction between the SDP and the Liberals, except in so far as he might later browbeat David Steel into his way of thinking.

There was, however, a difference in perception behind this. David, although unelected, was the undisputed leader of the party, but he did not own it as his personal fiefdom. Roy, Shirley and I had been equal with him in creating it and we continued to have a major interest in its survival and success. There were also over 60,000 members whose claims were embodied in 'one member, one vote'. Their underlying disposition was for persuasion and consensus, not for conviction politics taken to the extremes of Mrs Thatcher. But that was not how David saw it. To him, leadership meant having his own way and the more he felt challenged – or, worse still, in danger of losing or being humiliated – the more he asserted his sovereign rights. The SDP must be a party made in his own image, following wherever he chose to lead.

As the immediate crisis passed and the anger drained away, some of the personal wounds began to heal, although the accumulation of scar tissue was becoming serious. But the real damage of the defence confrontation was not to be measured until the Liberals' Eastbourne assembly in September, where a vote in favour of the Commission's report was overshadowed by a vote against any European cooperation on nuclear weapons. I went to Eastbourne to take part in a long, pre-assembly talk-in (as such boring discussions were called) on the Commission's report. It was clear that the shadow of David Owen fell across the proceedings and it was difficult to persuade delegates – as it was difficult for most of the press to accept – that David's behaviour had been deplored by many members of the SDP who were satisfied with the Commission's proposals. The main debate was scrappy, with platform speakers nervous to confront the issue in unequivocal language, and I was very surprised to find David Steel (unlike Gaitskell in 1960) not bringing his persuasive powers to the debate at all. I was no judge of the mood of a Liberal assembly but the outcome seemed predictable. The muddled anti-nuclear vote was not only on the apparent merits of the issue; it was two defiant fingers up to David Owen.

The harm to the Alliance was great. The Alliance, a partnership of two parties working together, was seen by the public to be seriously divided if not positively at war. In the first quarter of 1986, before David Owen had rubbished the Commission's report, support in the opinion polls had been running at 31.3 per cent; in the fourth quarter of the year, with the party conferences over, it was down to 20.6 per cent.

On 16 December 1986 Shirley and I had lunch with Alan Watson, who remained close to the Liberal leadership and was one of the wisest heads in the Alliance. He said that the defence dispute had been very damaging to David Steel, whose morale was low. He had been bullied mercilessly by David Owen but the real blow had been the vote at the Liberal assembly. Shirley said morale was also low in the SDP and that when the election came the Alliance share of the vote could be smaller than in 1983. On the assumption that the Alliance might not hold the balance in a hung parliament, we agreed that merger would then be urgent, although David Steel no longer had the will to lead a new party and David Owen had ruled himself out.

One of the other persistent problems of David Owen's leadership had been his refusal to describe the purpose of the SDP – or the Alliance – as 'fighting to win'. He jibbed at the claim, believing it might invoke the ridicule he could not bear. But the shorthand phrase was part of the day-to-day currency of politics, and its absence blunted the Alliance's sense of ambition. I suggested to him that for the sake of our candidates, all of whom would feel they were fighting to win, he might make the addition of 'in every constituency', which was slightly non-committal about the overall prospect. But that also was too much for him. We went into the election with the uneasy objective of hoping to hold the balance of power, although with no indication whether we would prefer to sustain a Labour or a Conservative government.

By the beginning of 1987, the current Parliament had run for three and a half years, the average for the post-war period. The prospect of a general election following the local elections in May concentrated the mind and put the emphasis on unity both within the SDP and the Alliance. I had one more dispute with David Owen, who wanted to appoint me transport spokesman in the team that was to be paraded at a relaunch of the Alliance at a rally at London's Barbican Centre in January 1987. But I had no wish to shadow the office I had filled in cabinet eight years earlier, so I settled for energy.

But I was now turning to my own bid to return to the House of Commons, there having been no suitable by-elections. The two seats that had interested me were Oxford West and Milton Keynes, both of which might fall to the Alliance if we increased our share of the national poll. Oxford was the better seat, with a greater prospect of squeezing the Labour vote, but the party wanted to select earlier than I was ready. So I went instead to Milton Keynes, less than an hour up the M1 from home, easy to reach by road or rail. From early 1986 I travelled there at least two or three times a week.

The idea of a new town at Bletchley – as it was then described – had crossed my desk at the DEA twenty years before. I had since followed its rapid progress as the last great experiment in social planning inspired by the Garden City movement of the first half of the century, and the New Towns legislation of the Attlee Government. It was a scheme that had brought together outstanding town planners and architects under an imaginative development corporation that gave the lie to those who saw only red tape, mediocrity and Big Brother in projects of this kind.

Its life-sized black-and-white concrete cows, a sculpture given to the city by the artist Liz Leyh, were often made fun of as a token of the artificiality of a project to provide homes and work for a quarter of a million people on flat land in the north of Buckinghamshire. In fact, it was a joke that the planners had played on themselves. Milton Keynes was not all a success. There were leaking roofs amongst the houses, too few amenities for young people and a long walk from the new railway station to the city centre. But the city was green and spacious and without destroying their character had successfully incorporated existing settlements like Bletchley, an old railway junction (where I had changed trains for Oxford on my first, 1947, visit) and Stony Stratford, once a coaching stop. There was a fine, uncluttered shopping mall which deserved in due course to become a listed building, with housing mainly in small, distinctive neighbourhoods. I liked Milton Keynes, and there was no hardship in the eighteen months I spent becoming familiar with it and introducing myself to its inhabitants. The constituency also included some attractive country towns and villages, from Woburn Sands in the south to Olney on the boundary with Bedfordshire, and it gave me pleasure to think that I might represent it in parliament.

Many of those I met in local campaigning groups, in offices and workshops – for there was nothing that qualified as a factory – and in public or private meetings took for granted that I would become their MP. I had 'chosen' Milton Keynes, as they put it, which they took to be an assertion of my confidence. They talked of contacts we would have after the election and of coming to Westminster to see me. At a packed meeting with the sitting Conservative MP and the Labour candidate, the platform and much of the audience rose to their feet when I entered the hall, as if greeting a celebrity. It was a heady experience, being a prospective parliamentary candidate with such goodwill and obvious expectations of me.

I also had an excellent local party or, more to the point, excellent Alliance support drawn from both parties. The Liberals had initially been wary of me, hoping to select one of their own. They were well established in campaigning and held almost a third of the seats on the council. They were doubtful whether I would give adequate time to the constituency or show much taste for doorstep canvassing and other routine chores. As for policy, a strong CND element regarded me as essentially old Labour. In advance of letting my name go forward for selection I invited a delegation to Patshull Road for a cold supper prepared by Silvia and to talk things over. I did not want to fight the seat without their active support and cooperation. But they proved open-minded, and after my selection their involvement was never in doubt. A Liberal who was a graphic designer helped me to produce the best literature I ever had in any election. Other Liberals were responsible for a first-class vote-winning organisation in Newport Pagnell. Most of my SDP colleagues had less direct political experience, but some of the shrewdest advice I received came from a pop record producer who was a keen psephologist; while a former borough treasurer brought business acumen and dug deep into his own pocket to make a significant financial contribution to the campaign. Together, Liberals and Social Democrats made a powerful single team, especially when supplemented by staff from Cowley Street and friends who came to help, many more than I had ever known in Stockton. The election was announced on 10 May, with polling on 11 June, and I soon moved to Milton Keynes for the duration.

Learning from last time, when my wider responsibilities had led me to neglect Stockton (not that the outcome would have been different), I decided to make very few visits outside my constituency and limited them to helping Celia Goodhart in nearby Kettering and Shirley in Cambridge, where our main joint activity was to be seen cycling around the city. David Owen largely excluded me from the central campaign, or 'campaigns', because there were three, supposedly parallel, campaigns: SDP, Liberal and Alliance. I did an 'Ask the Alliance' question-and-answer session which was a worthy but dull format for what was meant to be a major public meeting; and some three-party television. I also came up to London for Sunday evening meetings of the Alliance Campaign Committee, but these were rather fruitless occasions as the two Davids made separate decisions with their own inner circle which they then met to reconcile (or not, as it sometimes seemed). As the election moved on and the Alliance standing in the polls remained stubbornly at about twenty-one per cent, we unanimously agreed that our campaign lacked drive and inspiration and often seemed remote from the real issues close to the voters.

Rosie Barnes, whose victory at Greenwich in February had been an unexpected bonus (led by the SDP's National Organiser, Alec McGivan, the by-election was a brilliant example of what the two parties could achieve together) was put on television in a party election broadcast, together with a pet rabbit. Her well-meaning chatter about the family could have been a commercial for shampoo or sliced bread and lacked any impact. By contrast, the Labour Party, while also filming in soft focus and with Brahms providing the music score, produced a weepie that was marvellously strong, about the life and hopes of Neil Kinnock as he and Glenys walked hand-in-hand across a sunny headland. It was a film worthy of Leni Riefenstahl at her most dangerously persuasive, and, I hate to say, it moved me then and moves me now.

On another televised occasion, David Owen and David Steel discussed constitutional reform on what appeared to be a small jet aircraft, high above the clouds, at a time when jobs, health and education were the down-to-earth issues most in the minds of voters. The meetings of the Campaign Committee, in the gloomy half-light of a room in the Royal Horseguards Hotel, could only remark on the failure of the campaign to gain momentum; pleas to give it vigour and direction fell on deaf ears, perhaps because the two Davids did not know how.

In the early days of my own campaign, the response from the voters was promising. Olney was normally a safe Tory country town, but when canvassing in its open market on a Saturday morning I found support being volunteered, with virtually no-one avoiding at least a greeting. But within a fortnight the mood had changed. Where there had been warmth there was now neutrality, almost an uneasiness to engage in conversation; and a 'Rodgers' poster put up in my support had been taken down. This had nothing to do with local circumstances, but a sudden surge of belief that Labour nationally was doing much better than expected. Tory voters who had previously felt that they could safely vote for the Alliance had become scared that they might let Labour in; Labour voters had their old loyalties aroused by the improving prospect of their party. Against this, we appeared to have nothing new to offer.

On the Saturday before polling day I toured the constituency, sometimes in pouring rain, on the back of an open truck. Silvia was with me, together with a party of eager supporters, and stirring trumpet music by Purcell echoed from my loudspeaker system when I was not addressing the crowds, such as they were. I was also accompanied by a young woman from the *Daily Telegraph* and her report appeared in the paper the following Tuesday. It was a fair account of the occasion and she quoted me as saying 'We would win this seat if it were a by-election'. This was a precise measure of my despair. Locally, we had a brilliant campaign, but we could not isolate ourselves from larger events. The two Davids' double act had failed and we would be amongst the many losers.

Against the trend which saw the Alliance vote fall by 2.8 per cent in the United Kingdom, I had a swing of one per cent in my favour, winning 5,000 more votes for the SDP and the Alliance than in 1983. But there was not much joy in this, as I was a long way behind Bill Benyon, the sitting Tory Member. In the early hours of the Friday morning, I drove back to London and to the BBC Television Centre at Wood

Lane. At 4.00 A.M. Alan Watson and I appeared together, and when Robin Day asked the obvious question I said, without hesitation, that merger was now the only course, a view Alan endorsed. I added that there was no point in postponing a decision which should be made by our two parties without delay. This statement involved no direct criticism of David Owen and David Steel, because it was plainly the case that a two-headed Alliance did not work and to continue this way year after year was a formula for extinction. David Owen later complained that David Steel tried to bounce him by making an early public call for merger, a strange judgement on a man who, according to *Spitting Image*, was always in David Owen's pocket. But David Steel's views were well known and his timing entirely appropriate given that Roy, Shirley and I all-believed in merger. With Mrs Thatcher securely back in Downing Street, the future of the Alliance was for the moment the biggest and most urgent political question.

David Owen did not bother to discuss the future with the three of us, even to ensure that there should be an orderly process of decision-making. Apart from a brief word at a meeting on the Monday after polling day, I heard nothing from him. So on 23 June I decided to write. I said it would suit neither his temperament nor talent to lead a group of only five MPs through another parliament. The real challenge was to accept union – merger – with the Liberals and make the new party as far as possible in the image of the SDP. I continued:

> To accept union would be to show you were magnanimous and capable of recognising political realities; to help make the new party would be to express confidence in the fundamental strength of the SDP as you helped to form it; and to offer yourself for leadership would be in keeping with the courage you have shown in politics and your belief in the democratic process.

I said that he might fail to win the leadership and conceded that he found losing more painful and humiliating than most people. I recognised that leading a party of which former Liberals might be more than half would be difficult, demanding all his political and diplomatic skills. But his choice was to be creative or destructive and the latter meant a solitary future, going nowhere.

David Owen never referred to my letter. Perhaps he thought it was part of a subtle plot to embarrass him, although it was written without consultation and I did not show Shirley a copy until some weeks later. But the letter was naive – I shudder a little at the memory of it – for he had already made up his mind to fight merger with a disingenuous proposal for a closer relationship with the Liberals – an echo of the Salford resolution of four years earlier – and, if he lost, to lead a rump of members into what he would call the continuing SDP. In the event, through the coming months David and I met only in committees, exchanging words on the terms of the merger ballot and its consequences. It was the end of a journey together that had begun in Labour's shadow cabinet of 1979. The meetings we were now obliged to attend were as difficult as those of eight years ago, but we were on different sides.

David said that he hoped for 'an amicable divorce' from his old political friends, but the arguments over the division of property – the membership of the SDP – were bitter. In turn, members were puzzled and distressed by the conflicting messages they were receiving from the Gang of Four, SDP MPs and the National Committee of the party. Since Limehouse and the launch, differences between David and Roy, Shirley and myself had been concealed, through acquiescence in David's leadership and a common wish to win. Now they were visible for all to see.

My postbag was heavy. Typical was a letter that said:

> I feel ashamed. If those at the centre are incapable of demonstrating that consensus can be a reality, we deserve the scourge of extremism. Internal warfare, fratricide, where is the party of partnership?

Letters came equally from those who wanted merger and those who did not; and of those who wanted merger most wanted to keep David Owen, and of those who did not, most wanted to keep Roy, Shirley and me.

On the face of it, if a ballot on merger was quickly held, there was no reason for any such break-up. The idea of a members' ballot on major issues was built into the party's constitution and had been used to confirm acceptance of the constitution itself. The assumption – the only conceivable assumption from a one-member, one-vote ballot – was that the outcome would be accepted by both winners and losers. But David Owen had no intention of accepting the verdict of members if it went against him, or of leaving the field with good grace if he felt unable to play any further part. For him, it was heads I win, tails you lose.

This left David with a tactical advantage. He had a simple goal – to carry on re-gardless with troops who would follow wherever he chose to lead. For those of us who preferred merger, there was the need to win the ballot, to negotiate an accept-able deal with the Liberals, to have it endorsed by a party conference and to ensure that as many members as possible stayed on board during this process.

At this early stage, not surprisingly given his dominance as parliamentary leader, David had the remaining four SDP MPs on his side. With one of them, Bob Maclennan, I had shared campaigns and good causes for twenty years and I was outraged to see him now devising a wording for a ballot paper that would given the Owenites an unfair advantage by claiming that merger would involve 'the abo-lition of the SDP'. I accused Bob of trying to manipulate the ballot in order to prejudice the outcome and he in turn threatened legal action if I repeated any such statement. Given the stress and exhaustion, those who behaved badly deserve to be forgiven except, I regret to say, David himself, who was the catalyst of most of our troubles.

Once the options to be put in the ballot had been agreed, I became Chairman of the 'Yes to Unity' campaign that was launched at the beginning of July. Option Two on the ballot paper proposed 'a merger of the SDP and the Liberal Party into one party'. This was straightforward. Option One – the Owenite preference – referred to 'a closer constitutional framework for the Alliance', which had the apparent attraction of a halfway house, offering something for everyone, even the prospect of merger at some future date. Option One was also endorsed by eighteen members of the National Committee against the thirteen who preferred Option Two. In effect, the ballot appeared to be heavily weighted in David Owen's favour, especially if there was a modest turn-out of voters.

However, my own best estimate, given my knowledge of the mood of members throughout the country, was that our 'Yes' campaign would win by about three to two, and this is what we did on a poll of over seventy-seven per cent. It was a decisive margin, and within the minority there were clearly many members who would nevertheless accept the decision and play a part in the merged party. The SDP had some 60,000 paid-up members and I believed that perhaps 50,000 might be carried over. It all depended on how quickly we could conclude the business of merger and sideline David Owen if he persisted in being troublesome, because a prolonged transition would send many potential members of the merged party weary away. It would also push our wider voter appeal far below the 22.6 per cent we had achieved on 11 June. But the transition lasted a full six months and a great deal of further damage was done.

In my thoughts about merger immediately prior to the election, it had never occurred to me that David Owen would fight on after a ballot to try to wreck the outcome and to carry over a rump of SDP membership into a party of his own. Nor did the 'Yes to Unity' campaign give much thought to what precise steps he would take if he lost, given his intention not to retire from the scene. It was assumed that David would soon resign and that a leaderless party would be held together by Shirley as President with Charles Kennedy, who had broken with David Owen to vote for merger, eventually becoming leader by default. Then, given both my previous experience of negotiations over seats and my unequivocal position on merger, negotiations with the Liberals would be led by me. Otherwise, in so far as we discussed the future, we believed it would be a matter of living from day to day until merger was complete.

The result of the ballot was declared on 6 August, but two days earlier, with the 'Yes to Unity' campaign effectively over, Silvia and I had flown to the Aegean to spend a fortnight with Willie and Celia Goodhart at their house on the island of Andros. It was to be a bizarre holiday. With all the key players dispersing to distant parts, a lull in political activity might have been expected. There was no telephone at the Goodharts' house so Celia, usually accompanied by Silvia, would use a public telephone in a bar in the village to keep in touch with London. First came the good news of the ballot, followed by the sudden resignation of David Owen. Then, sitting on the beach, we played a frivolous holiday game of speculating as to which of the high-flying aircraft was carrying Charles Kennedy home from his Turkish holiday in order to don the mantle of leadership. Finally, a few days later, Celia and Silvia came back from the village wide-eyed and bubbling with amazement, to announce that Bob Maclennan, opponent of merger and fierce custodian of David Owen's interest in the ballot, had suddenly announced that he now accepted the verdict, was prepared to fill the leadership vacuum and would lead the negotiations with the Liberals to merger provided the terms were right. By the time we returned to London, Bob's new role had been confirmed in discussion with Shirley at, of all places, Cape Cod, Massachusetts; and, soon after, the Owenites decided not to contest the leadership as they were strictly entitled to. We were entering a strange period, with two parties living within a single shell, operating separately, competing bitterly with each other, but meeting within a formal framework of committees that stood no chance of reconciling differences.

My diary for 22 September records:

> Yesterday we had quite the nastiest meeting of the National Committee. After careful consideration the previous evening it didn't seem likely there would be trouble. Dick Taverne was able to say 'I assume it will be a short meeting' (although he often says that). The meeting started very promptly. The Owenites were notably absent and we wondered whether they had decided to stay away. Then they all trooped in. As many as could wrapped themselves round the extra wing of the table with David at the end, looking directly at me. At first they behaved well. Everything was put in the friendliest spirit.

The row, my diary reminds me, began when we reached a report from the Electoral Reform Society on a dispute between the Owenites and 'Yes to Unity' in the ballot of two months before. As usual, David at first stood aside, letting his team make the well-rehearsed running, the object of which was to obtain a full list of SDP members.

> Shirley was very firm. We must have advice on the legal and constitutional aspects; no-one needed the list now. And Dick Taverne challenged them to say they wanted the list to set up their own new party, which produced total silence on their part. David, with hypocritical silkiness, said that all he was asking for was a political decision on making the list available; legal advice could follow. I said that as he knew, the cabinet was always free to ignore the advice of the Law Officers but I could remember no instance of cabinet making such 'a political decision' without having the legal advice first.

In the end, Shirley, as President in the chair, simply said that she would allow no vote on membership lists without first taking advice, and challenged Mike Thomas – who was leading the Owenite pack – to move her out of the chair if he would not accept her ruling. He did, and it was 14:13 to unseat her until she used her vote to make it 14:14 and then, as she was entitled to, used it again as a casting vote to reach a decision by 14:15. The Owenites were furious. It was a well-planned coup which had just failed. When I was later asked by *The Guardian* about these events, I said: 'It was the ugliest meeting I had ever been to. We had two hours of the most vicious mistrust.' I may have exaggerated but that is how it felt. It was an unpleasant occasion: I can think of nothing worse during the life of the SDP, not even during the row on defence and disarmament.

Shirley's position was difficult. She was President of the whole, divided party and, as ever, she was anxious to reconcile rather than take a hard line. But given the outcome of the ballot, it was her duty to guide the party to merger as smoothly as possible. She was incensed by what she saw as the outrageous behaviour of the Owenites and showed great toughness in seeing the whole process through to a conclusion. It was not her fault that it took so long.

Bob Maclennan's determination to lead the negotiations with the Liberals left no obvious role for me. He tried to persuade me to join him but I was out of sympathy with both an outsized team of negotiators on either side (I would have chosen three or four) and an over-insistence on 'if the terms are right' as the condition for merger. Clearly there had to be agreement. I shared the view – common to the SDP and the Liberal leadership – that the existing SDP constitution was a good model for the merged party. But I would have set a much faster pace and struck a more confident note from the beginning. The delay and uncertainty meant a crucial erosion of support, to David Owen's advantage. Most of the SDP's financial backers also took their leave. With some, like Sir James Spooner, Chairman of Morgan Crucible and other companies (an outstanding businessman typical of the best attracted to the SDP), I tried to explain the ballot and the prospect of a merged party beyond it. But these democratic procedures were outside the experience of most of them and they could not grasp why a discreet separation could not be arranged without a public row. They often took a simple view of the leader's prerogative, believing that the proper choice was to follow him or to resign, not to argue and fight.

Both Sir Leslie Murphy and David Sainsbury, the trustees of the SDP, were firmly in the Owen camp. This came as no great surprise. Fifteen months earlier, at the height of the row on defence and disarmament, Leslie Murphy, civil servant (once Hugh Gaitskell's private secretary) turned City banker, had taken me to lunch at the Oriental Club to give me a thorough wigging for daring to disagree with David. Now he was positively acerbic when I asked for his comments on a story in *The Times* that the Owenites were trying to divert membership income into David Owen's new party. David Sainsbury was quite different. He was clearly distressed by the whole course of events and although loyal to David Owen, was anxious to stop provocative behaviour on either side. My own relations with him remained friendly and when, three years later, Silvia and I were invited to dine and dance at the Natural History Museum to celebrate his fiftieth birthday, we found ourselves tactfully seated on one side of a tyrannosaurus rex while David Owen and his friends were hidden from our view on the other. An additional pleasure in the occasion was that it fell by chance two days after the Eastbourne by-election, which the Liberal Democrats had won. This produced a steady stream of guests to our table bringing congratulations. A few months earlier, David Owen's continuing SDP had been wound-up when his candidate in the Bootle by-election had come seventh behind Lord David Sutch's Monster Raving Loony Party.

The autumn of 1987 was not only a turning point for the Gang of Four and the party we had created, it was also a turning point for me. My main source of income had gone in the weeks following the election and I was now running badly into debt. Either I must give my time to building up consultancies or look for a 'real job', full-time and outside politics. That might also be difficult, given that I was now fifty-eight, but it would give me the security that I had never really enjoyed and an additional pension which I needed to supplement the modest conse-quences of my twenty-one years in parliament.

There was one further possibility to take into account. In the run-up to the election, Shirley had raised with me the likelihood that it would be our last as can-didates and asked me what my attitude was to becoming a life peer. We agreed that, disapproving although we were about an unreformed House of Lords, it was a pos-sible destination. We would have a parliamentary role, if a more subdued one than we had previously enjoyed; and, as former cabinet ministers, reversion to the Lords was a convention on which we should be entitled to draw. It was not an option which either of us had in mind to exercise yet – we both had to earn a living, which attendance fees at the Lords certainly did not provide – but the time might come. However, when I made clear my intention to withdraw from active politics – once the merger went through, a new generation would be at the centre of things – Bob Maclennan asked whether he might put my name forward for the New Year's honours. It was, he said, the strong wish of my friends that he should do this, although the chances of Mrs Thatcher agreeing were very slim. On that basis, not wanting to say 'No' to Bob but not wanting to go to the Lords yet either, I agreed. In turn, Mrs Thatcher was swift in her anticipated reply.

It was John Roper, alert to my interests as ever, who drew my attention to an advertisement for a new Director-General placed by the Royal Institute of British Architects. I was fascinated by architecture, although totally ignorant of its techni-calities. It would be a leap in the dark, but here was a job requiring administrative skills that would give me new opportunities. I wrote to the President of the RIBA,

Rod Hackney, to discover whether I would be an acceptable candidate, and the answer was 'Yes'. I had not applied competitively for a job for almost thirty years but after two interviews I was appointed. I decided to make the break without delay and on 1 December 1987 I walked through the doors of 66 Portland Place. When the SDP put its seal on merger at a special conference at Sheffield two months later, I sat silent at the back of the hall. The caravan would move on but I had pitched my tent. Politics would no longer be virtually my whole life, as for so long it had been.

Within a year of these events, Patricia Lee Sykes, a young American academic who had spent much time observing the SDP, including time with me in Milton Keynes, published an extended obituary of the party under the title *Losing from the Inside*. It was ironic, she said, that we who had abandoned the Labour Party to escape internal wrangling and bitter conflict had eventually fallen victim to it in the SDP. This verdict was a painful twist of the knife, justified in so far as it focused on personal, not ideological, differences which were always relatively minor, although Danny Finkelstein, an engaging young disciple of David Owen's who later became the Conservative Party's Head of Policy, had tried to give a distinctive conceptual framework to 'Owenism'. None of the Gang of Four was ready to acquiesce uncritically in the leadership of another; and the tension between Roy and David Owen, and the eventual alienation of David from all of us was an inescapable theme played as background to most of our endeavours. What Sykes calls 'elite competition' is endemic at the top of every profession, and politicians are less guarded in their competition than many (while more frequently denying it).

But failure did not owe much to our vanities and squabbles, which did little to inhibit the early success of the party and only broke out into serious public conflict after the 1987 election, over merger. Roy as Leader was ready to listen and open to argument and was a far more consensual politician than David, but the nature of our relationship with the Liberals was a matter of judgement, not principle, and it was legitimate to hold differing views. We made few critical errors. I have often reflected on my decision to go public in my dispute with David Steel about the distribution of parliamentary seats early in 1982. But if I was wrong the poll evidence nevertheless suggests that the SDP was already slipping off its peak performance, and it was the Falklands War shortly afterwards that rehabilitated Margaret Thatcher, to our loss. Similarly, our collapse at the Darlington by-election of 1983 severely affected our fortunes in the general election that followed. But if the tide had been flowing strongly for the SDP and the Alliance, Darlington should have been no more than a sandcastle of failure to be washed away. We all made mistakes, but none of them were disasters.

There were achievements. As Ivor Crewe and Anthony King concede in their ultimately dismissive history of the SDP, the SDP in partnership with the Liberals mounted by far the most serious challenge to the two-party system for more than sixty years. It established a democratic constitution, a large, paid-up national membership, branches throughout the country, a viable financial base and a professional headquarters, all in the space of two years. It was also ahead of other parties in developing targeted, direct mailing to voters, in keeping accurate central records (the Conservatives held no central records of membership until 1999) and in using computers for every conceivable purpose. Above all, it built an effective campaigning organisation. In many areas where the SDP led in those years, other parties have since followed.

Then there is the very existence of the Liberal Democrats, who are the product of our chequered merger of 1988. Just over ten years later there are forty-six Liberal Democrat MPs, ten members of the European Parliament and members of the Scottish Parliament (where they are part of the governing coalition) and the Welsh Assembly. There have been around 5,000 Liberal Democrat local councillors, and many towns and counties have elected Liberal Democrat administrations, including Liverpool, my birthplace and long-lost love, and Sheffield. Liberal Democrats have played a major role in the great constitutional changes of the 1997 Parliament and are now an integral part of the political geography of Britain (even though recently described by David Owen as coming from 'a very noble tradition of anarchism'). Only the absence of proportional representation for Westminster continues to deny proper recognition to the views of five million voters – and many more potential voters in constituencies where voting Liberal Democrat is still seen as a wasted vote. It is pointless to conjecture what proportion of this success is attributable to each of the predecessor parties, but the Liberal Democrats are a progeny to which we of the SDP helped to give birth.

The fact remains that the SDP did not break the mould in the way or to the extent which the Gang of Four planned. My favourite adage was that the Labour Party was in terminal decline, with occasional periods of remission. I hoped that the SDP, as a non-ideological party of the centre-left, would replace Labour in the two-party system until such a time as fair voting made a multi-party system possible. That did not happen. I underestimated the extent to which loyalty and sentiment, institutional ties, inertia and luck would hold Labour together until such a time as, at the nadir of its fortunes and facing death, it would eventually rally.

Denis Healey has said, in sentiments echoed by Roy Hattersley, that the SDP's 'most important effect was to delay the Labour Party's recovery by nearly ten years and to guarantee Mrs Thatcher two more terms in office'. That begs the question of what was the worst option in 1983 and 1987, Mrs Thatcher or the Labour Party, still unreformed. But in any case the arithmetic does not sustain the Healey–Hattersley view. It is inconceivable that in 1983 the absence of the SDP vote would have bridged the fifteen per cent gap between Labour and the Tories. Some SDP voters might have drifted back to Labour but the majority would have voted Liberal (with the Liberals contesting all seats) and others Conservative. The anti-Thatcher vote would still have been split. In 1987, the gap between Labour and the Conservatives remained over ten per cent, and there is no evidence of a greater disposition on the part of voters to turn to Labour if SDP candidates had not been on the ballot paper. It is flattering to believe that the SDP kept Labour out of power but in many eyes (including my own) Labour simply remained unfit to govern.

Denis Healey's alternative argument is that the SDP 'did grievous damage to those who shared its views in the party it deserted' by shifting the balance further to the left and making them suspect as possible defectors. But Healey was elected Labour's Deputy Leader over Tony Benn – if only by a hair's breadth – despite our absence. He was then prepared to go along with a manifesto in 1983 that was, in Gerald Kaufman's memorable phrase, 'the longest suicide note in history', however much he detested it. Hattersley succeeded him but it was Neil Kinnock, the prodigal who discarded his soft-left inclinations, who bravely took on Derek Hatton and the Militant Tendency and then initiated the fundamental review of policy that eventually made Labour an electable party again by shifting it on to SDP territory.

The sheer experience of humiliating defeat in 1983 and, despite a good campaign, 1987, forced Labour to recognise how power had slipped away from them. Margaret Thatcher's success and then John Major's in 1992 confirmed that parts of Thatcherism – trade union reform, council house sales and privatisation – had caught the public mood and could not be reversed. But the SDP had shown that there was scope for a party of the centre-left that appealed across class, endorsing the market economy but strong on public services. The SDP may not have been a conscious model for New Labour; it would be strenuously disowned as such by most of those in Labour's senior ranks at the time of the 1981 break. The SDP was nevertheless seen to be an example of what Labour might recover to become by some influential voices who remained in the Labour Party; and they were joined in the 1990s by a younger generation, more open in their recognition of what the SDP had tried to do, and much less partisan about party affiliations. Many Labour MPs elected for the first time in 1997 had been at school or university in the heyday of the SDP; and amongst advisers and policymakers, others had been members or close observers of it. Amongst my colleagues in the House of Lords sent to the Labour benches by Tony Blair, several greet me warmly as former members of the SDP. Nevertheless, Labour's loss may be in a generation of able men and women who turned to the SDP rather than Labour in the early 1980s, and who might now have been available as talent for senior offices in Tony Blair's Government.

Chapter 12
Goodbye to All That?

In my early Fabian days I met Leonard Woolf, author, founder of the Hogarth Press and, until her suicide, husband to Virginia. Dressed always, it seemed, in a heavy, pepper-and-salt suit, he still lived in the world of the League of Nations, although we were well into the Cold War. I dismissed him as a doddering old survivor of Bloomsbury with nothing left to say. Then, a few years later at the age of eighty, he published the first of five remarkable volumes of autobiography. One was an enthralling evocation of his life in the Colonial Service in Ceylon; another, which he called *Downhill All the Way*, covered the inter-war period, with the rise of Hitler and Virginia's developing illness. 'Twilight' he said, 'was in one's private as well as in public life'.

Nothing as remotely dramatic or searing had happened to me when I contemplated the future from my new office at the Royal Institute of British Architects. The Cold War which had helped to provoke my impatience with Leonard Woolf was moving towards its end; and my private life continued to give me the comfort and stimulus of a close family, affectionate relationships and many friends. But for almost forty years I had lived near the centre of political affairs, witnessing them at close quarters even when not a participant. Now I had turned away, not into retirement – which I could not afford and had too much energy to contemplate – but into an apparent cul-de-sac.

For four years I played no part in politics except discreetly as the Chairman of the panel that dealt with membership disputes amongst Liberal Democrats and in fleeting visits to by-elections; and for a further two years in the House of Lords I contributed little to debates. I took the view that I was essentially a public servant, but in any case the Director-General's job was demanding and full-time. For four days a week, I could expect to do a nine-hour day and to take work home.

On the fifth, Friday, I would recover by travelling out of London to visit architectural practices in towns and villages from Cornwall to Northumbria, contriving to pass through some of the loveliest parts of Britain. I explored Dartmoor, travelled north up the Wye Valley and beyond to the strange land of the Stiperstones of Shropshire and then on to the Forest of Bowland and eventually the border country near Hadrian's Wall. Many of the smaller practices were in the remoter parts of the country and they particularly welcomed a visit – almost always the first visit ever – from the Director-General. Like members of most professions, they were often resentful of the dominance and advantages of those who worked in London. In the late 1980s most practices had no shortage of commissions and were enlarging their premises and taking on new people. But as the Lawson boom collapsed and the construction industry experienced its worst recession since the war, mortgage debts went unpaid and staff were cut by two-thirds to enable practices to survive. The average remuneration of architects was always low by the standards of doctors, lawyers, and even the surveyors who were often seen to be their main rivals. The recession forced many of them out of business altogether.

At the top of the profession there were three highly successful architects who had shared an exhibition at the Royal Academy a few years earlier. The well-known political sympathies of Richard Rogers had led the SDP to treat him almost as a member, and his son had been active in the party. I visited him at the River Café in Hammersmith, which was more of an elegant works canteen than the chic rendezvous for famous faces it was later to become. He was welcoming, relaxed and warm. The similarity of our names was sometimes to lead to misunderstandings. On one occasion, I came out of a meeting to be greeted by a Canadian television crew. 'Mr Rodgers?' I was asked and when I replied 'Yes', they requested an immediate interview as they had to catch an afternoon plane to Toronto. Questions on urban regeneration, the growth of post-modernism and public attitudes to architecture went smoothly until I was asked about the attitude of the Prince of Wales to the Lloyd's building. 'Has he told you what he thinks?' It was a question to which I could honestly answer 'No', but at that moment I realised the obvious and that my interviewer thought I was Richard Rogers. I told her the truth and she was horrified. It had been a good interview and she had no hope of finding the real Rogers to do another. She looked at me for help. 'You can take a chance', I said, 'I'll not talk to anyone'. For a moment she struggled with her conscience, and then smiled with relief. As far as I know, a few days later my unwitting impersonation was seen by Canadian television viewers. Ten years ago, Richard Rogers was much less visible than he has since become, but our confusion of identity continues in the House of Lords, where he regularly gets my mail and I get his.

Norman Foster and James Stirling were the other two acknowledged leaders of the profession. Where I found Richard Rogers outgoing and stylish (later, an Armani jacket and trainers in the Lords caused some tut-tutting amongst the hereditaries), Norman Foster was cool and dressed like a businessman. James Stirling had an altogether different demeanour. He was square and tough with a hint of the wartime paratrooper he had been. He had a mischievous sense of humour, although I thought him irascible when we first met. I discovered to my great surprise that we had overlapped for a couple of years at Quarry Bank High School in Liverpool, although he was not inclined to reminisce about those times. One of his major buildings had impressed me in Milton Keynes and I made a point of visiting his remarkable competition-winning

Staatsgalerie in Stuttgart. James Stirling died during a routine operation in 1992, better known and more respected abroad than in the United Kingdom.

In the second half of the twentieth century in Britain we have not prized our architects. In recent years we have done something to remedy this, with Richard Rogers and Norman Foster brought into the House of Lords, Sir Denys Lasdun made a Companion of Honour, and knighthoods for Sir Michael Hopkins and Sir Colin Stansfield-Smith, Hampshire's outstanding county architect, amongst others. But in the public debate about architecture, the profession has been on the defensive, thanks largely to the Prince of Wales.

I was reading papers in my office at the RIBA on my first day in my new job when the telephone rang. It was Peter Snow from *Newsnight* asking me to appear on his programme. The Prince of Wales was to make a speech at the Mansion House in which he would attack architects and others for doing more damage to the City of London than the Luftwaffe in the blitz. Would I be prepared to do a rebuttal? There was no confusion of identities with Richard, because Prince Charles' intervention went beyond architectural tastes into constitutional issues. But with the greatest reluctance I said 'No'. I knew this was an area of acute controversy for architects and I wanted to be sure of how most effectively to give my support before venturing into it. The shock waves from Prince Charles' interest in architecture had been rolling over the profession for three years and the controversy was to be the mood music to much of my six years at the RIBA.

The first royal intervention had come at the 150th anniversary banquet of the Institute at Hampton Court in May 1984. It was a time to celebrate and to award the prestigious Royal Gold Medal to Charles Correa, the distinguished Indian architect. The Prince of Wales was the guest of honour and, like any guest on such an occasion, was expected to offer congratulations and spread goodwill. Instead he attacked the design of 'another giant glass stump' in the City of London (by one of the great architects of the twentieth century, Mies van der Rohe) and a proposal currently under discussion for an extension to the National Gallery in Trafalgar Square. 'It looks,' he said of this, 'as if we may be presented with a kind of vast municipal fire station … what is proposed is like a monstrous carbuncle on the face of a much-loved and elegant friend'. His hosts at the banquet were deeply shaken, and it was an outrageous speech to make at a celebration. The respected and innovative architectural practice responsible for the National Gallery design – its partners, Peter Ahrends, Richard Burton and Paul Koralak were friends and neighbours of ours in Kentish Town – lost business and nearly folded; and other outstanding architects of 'modern' buildings suffered a similar fate. Clients eager to please the Prince of Wales – in the hope that he might then perform their opening ceremony – looked for architects who would design buildings acceptable to him.

Apart from his inappropriate choice of time and place, it was quite wrong for the Prince of Wales to attack individual architects. He had an obligation to recognise that a royal voice carried an influence far beyond the merits of its message. It was not sufficient for him to claim in justification that he was only contributing to legitimate public debate, appealing over the heads of the profession to 'the feelings and wishes of the mass of ordinary people in this country'.

As a result of these events, I found the profession cowed, bewildered and divided. Few architects welcomed the Prince's mocking remarks – 'magnificent effrontery', Ben Pimlott, biographer of Queen Elizabeth II, was to call them – because they were seen to diminish the profession as a whole. Catching at straws, they drew some comfort from the wider debate about architecture that the Prince had provoked with more serious newspaper coverage than ever before from well-informed journalists like Jonathan Glancy in *The Independent* and Hugh Pearman in the *Sunday Times*. But they did not know how to mount their own reply.

Peter Ahrends denounced the Prince's remarks as 'offensive, reactionary and ill-considered', and Michael Manser, who as President of the RIBA had been obliged to preside over the unhappy banquet, disputed the Prince's claim that new buildings could not live in harmony with old. But many architects were afraid to put their heads above the parapet or, like Norman Foster, prefaced a bland explanation of the role of the architect with congratulations to the Prince on rallying the nation. Norman Foster was right to criticise the quality of much post-war development, with hack architects in tow to greedy developers. I had experience of this when Stockton High Street was vandalised by redevelopment, and the profession would gather strength by admitting its mistakes. But after his 1984 speech, the Prince's arguments should have been tackled head-on, although the inhibitions from which architects suffered were characteristic of other groups upon whom the Prince of Wales has since turned his unpredictable wrath. Royalty has an uneven advantage in public controversy. That is why the heir to the throne should show restraint in his outbursts and not make others the victims of his frustration.

I first met Prince Charles in the early 1970s. He had completed his year at Cambridge and service in the Royal Navy and it now appeared that he was being launched into a world close to his future constitutional role. At least, that seemed to be the explanation for the dinner for a handful of Labour MPs to which Silvia and I were invited. I thought he was a decent young man who took his duties seriously but without enough to fill his life. More than twenty years later, at the RIBA, I found him very little changed. He had an entirely genuine concern about the social problems of inner cities, and when he presented the annual *Times*/RIBA community enterprise awards he was assiduous at inspecting projects and making conversation with participants. His interest in community architecture had brought him into contact with Rod Hackney who, at Black Road, Macclesfield, had involved house-owners and tenants in the rehabilitation of sub-standard Victorian property. In turn, because of his public association with the Prince of Wales, Hackney, a street-fighter amongst architects, had been elected in 1986 as the new President of the RIBA in the hope that he might have been able to restrain the Prince and teach him to be fairer to the profession. It did not work out that way, but community architects – who were not regarded as serious architects by some of their colleagues – always gave Prince Charles the benefit of the doubt.

If I had responded positively to Peter Snow's *Newsnight* invitation, it would have immediately put me into conflict with Rod Hackney who wanted no stand-up row with the Prince. But I strongly urged on him that the Institute could not continue to run away from the issue of the Prince's views and that its governing council should debate them. He agreed only when I had drafted a motion that was acceptable, prefaced by a welcome for the Prince's interest in the built environment, and expressing a shared concern about both urban and rural problems. But the key sentences addressed to Prince Charles in the name of the RIBA Council hoped that he would 'accept that the errors of the past were due as much to politicians, planners and developers, among others, as to architects', and encouraged him 'to acknowledge that there is room for the best in all styles and periods of architecture in creating a high quality of life'. There was an admission here which I thought important, that there was quite a lot of dross amongst the gold, silver and bronze of post-war architecture. But in turn the motion invited Prince Charles to admit that there was a place for modern and high-tech buildings as well as the classical pastiche and vernacular so close to his heart.

The RIBA could not have coped with a more confrontational motion and it enabled a past President, Gordon Graham, to say more precisely what the profession was thinking. 'Be careful not to abuse your privilege', he said during the debate. 'We admire your capacity to create amusing catch phrases but … this profession longs for the debate to move on from the propaganda phase to a more profound discussion.' Gradually it did. When Prince Charles turned his BBC television programme *A Vision of Britain* into a book and then an exhibition at the Victoria and Albert Museum there was much with which both the public and the profession could agree. Most of his ten principles for architecture – scale, materials, the role of artists working with architects – were unexceptional and many of the targets of his disapproval – the Bull Ring of Birmingham, the Tricorn Centre in Portsmouth – were widely shared. He even admitted that the prospect of St Paul's had been compromised as long ago as the 1920s (although not that St Paul's had itself been a controversial modern building when it was constructed).

Nevertheless, a gap remained – and remains – between the Prince of Wales and the architects, and I am unequivocally on the side of the profession. Only when in the autumn of 1990 I visited Germany – home to the Modern Movement in the years of the Weimar Republic – to lecture on *A Vision of Britain* did I fully realise how profoundly nostalgic and dangerous were the Prince's views. We should recognise environmental disasters and learn from them; and we can agree on conserving the best of the past. But re-recreating medieval streets (which would have been running with sewage) or preserving the often bleak commercial buildings of Victorian England (entirely suitable for clerks on high stools, hopeless for information technology) is a romantic illusion. Even Poundbury, the Prince's very own 1990s village on the outskirts of Dorchester, looks like a film set, not a place in which to live and work. It would hardly have pleased Thomas Hardy, professional architect as well as author, who made Dorchester the Casterbridge of his Wessex novels. In architecture no more than in literature, music or the visual arts can we make the future by reinventing the past. As for new and old buildings living harmoniously together, Siena, which Silvia and I have visited so often, is a spectacularly beautiful city whose grand buildings were erected over centuries and represent many styles. I only regret that my own Oxford college, Magdalen, whose New Buildings dating from 1733 fit comfortably with the fifteenth century gothic of most of the college, chose an eclectic pastiche for additions to the college in the 1990s.

For the last twenty years Britain has suffered from a surfeit of what is loosely called post-modernism. At its most familiar this means banded brickwork; classical, triangular pediments; pitched roofs; and the use of decorative colour for pipework. Within a generation much of this will look as dowdy as many of the low-grade concrete and steel buildings of the 1960s. I much prefer the clean, white lines of Highpoint, a block of flats standing a few hundred yards from my home which was designed and built in the 1930s by architects of the Modern Movement. Another architect of that time, Wells Coates, summed it all up brilliantly. 'The past,' he said, 'is not always behind us, but more often in front, blocking the way'.

Between my first day at the RIBA and my last, the Prince of Wales made no further seriously provocative speech prompting an invitation from Peter Snow. In any case, as a layman, I saw my task as giving the profession the confidence to make its own response rather than becoming personally involved in the complex style wars that divided architects amongst themselves as well as from the Prince of Wales. Architects are highly individual and creative and not natural committee-men and -women. In my early days I was frequently taken aside almost as a good man fallen amongst thieves and asked in a mischievous whisper how I found them. My reply was that dealing with the Militant Tendency in the Labour Party had been an ideal preparation. This was quite unfair and not to be taken seriously, because most architects were engaging, clever and entirely reasonable. One past president was difficult because I had been appointed by his deadly rival, Rod Hackney, and as a Thatcherite he could not approve of any Liberal Democrat; another aspiring president had a bitter enmity born out of personal disappointment and his Communist past. But politics seldom intruded, perhaps because much of the profession was somewhere on the centre-left of politics. When, late in 1997, an electoral dispute forced a by-election in Winchester where the sitting Liberal Democrat MP had a majority of two, I was approached by an architect to use my good offices to persuade her party – the Labour Party – not to put up a candidate of its own against the Liberal Democrat. That is a measure of where most architects politically appeared to stand.

However, defeating John Major's Government, to the widespread applause of the profession, was probably seen as my major achievement at the RIBA. Since 1931, in order to practice as an architect, men and women with the necessary qualifications had been obliged to register with a statutory body. In the words then commonly used, 'the community was to be protected against the half-trained, the untrained and the absolute impostor'. Legislation had come to mean protection for the architect as well as the public, and other professions resented a privilege denied to them. The need to bring the law up to date was taken as an excuse by the Department of the Environment to launch an inquiry into the principle of registration, and ministers endorsed its main recommendation, that the protection of the title 'architect' should be abolished. This caused widespread dismay in the profession, downgrading years of professional education and opening the door to cowboys.

The first reaction of many architects was that the fight to retain registration was all over bar the shouting. The profession had lost. Others were reluctant to go into a head-on collision with the Government given the possibility of collateral damage to other negotiations in Whitehall over compulsory competitive tendering. Others again were concerned at the costs of a fight when the odds were against winning. But on my advice, and with the strong support of the RIBA President, Richard MacCormac, and the President-elect, Frank Duffy, and leadership from another well-regarded architect, Robin Nicholson, a campaign to persuade the Government to change its mind was launched.

The key to success as I saw it was for architects to approach their local MPs – using their own arguments and in their own words – who in turn would inundate ministers with letters. This needed a high degree of organisation and monitoring and would be supplemented by direct approaches to MPs by the President. We would concentrate on government backbenchers in marginal seats (seventy-two of them had majorities of less than 1,000) but make sure that ministers in all departments knew that any proposals in the Queen's Speech would be fiercely opposed, thus delaying their own legislation which would be competing for parliamentary time. Two members of the cabinet were important: Tony Newton, the Leader in the Commons, and John Wakeham, the Leader in the Lords. A constituent architect was seen by Newton in a long interview and I personally warned Wakeham of the dangers. In essence, the question put to them was: 'Is the game worth the candle?' when abolishing registration was hardly a Government priority.

To help us in the nuts and bolts of the campaign, we engaged the Advocacy Partnership, a lobbying firm run by my former PPS Ken Weetch and the former Conservative MP Fred Sylvester. They were most effective in looking for allies outside the profession and turning round some of the bodies, like the National Consumer Council, which previously had been indifferent to the ending of registration but who now told ministers that it would be a mistake. The Chairman of the Arts Council, Lord Palumbo, and the Chairman of the Royal Fine Art Commission, Lord St John of Fawsley (aka Norman St John Stevas) were strong in their support and some Commonwealth architects' associations wrote direct to the Prime Minister.

The campaign was launched at the beginning of June 1993, and by the middle of October my best estimate was that some 400 MPs had been in correspondence with or had been seen by architect constituents. Our various approaches – none of them round robins of the kind easy to discount – had probably generated as many as 2,000 letters to be prepared by officials and signed by ministers. There had been some selective briefing of national newspapers, and articles about the role of architects had been placed in regional newspapers, but we had chosen a soft approach to the media so as not to alert supporters of deregulation to our progress. In public we remained downbeat about our chances and I would shake my head in rather weary despair when asked how things were going 'Well …' I would say 'it isn't easy', and leave it at that.

I had always seen the last week in October as the decisive time and the climax of our campaign was timed to coincide with it, but I was taken by surprise when, in a Written Answer on 27 October 1993, the Government announced that they were backing down. Ministers had decided there would be no legislation. We had won.

The announcement came on the eve of my sixty-fifth birthday, and I had already told the RIBA that, subject to the completion of the registration campaign, I would like to leave the Institute in early 1994. I had enjoyed my executive responsibilities as Director-General, running things and being accountable. I had been supported by a loyal staff, learnt much about architecture and come to know and like many architects. I now had a real affection for the profession and hoped that my links would not be severed.

But my six years had been exacting and I was tired. The latter part of my time had involved a tight squeeze on my £5 million budget, which was declining in real terms, bringing redundancies and the sale of the RIBA journal to the Builder Group of publishers (although I was pleased to complete the deal, as it turned a deficit of £250,000 into a modest profit, with a bigger and much improved magazine).

There was also the unsolved problem of the future of the Institute's library, one of the finest architectural libraries in the world, but with quite inadequate space and resources. Shortly after my appointment I had backed a scheme for the reconstruction of 66 Portland Place, proposed by Sir Fred Dainton, Sir Denys Lasdun and Lord Rawlinson, 'the three wise men', as they were inevitably called, who had been asked for expert, independent advice. Subsequently, Peter Palumbo made £100,000 available to engage Stanton Williams, a rising architectural practice, to produce an exciting design. My deputy, Don Brooks, worked particularly hard to get planning permission and listed building consent and within a little over two years a full scheme was ready for council approval. But it then ran into the sand. With a contingent cost of up to £25 million, the Institute did not have the nerve or energy to push it forward in those pre-Lottery days, and the commitment was too great to carry without the wholehearted and active support of the profession. For me it was unfinished business, a failure of a kind. But my decision was made. In the spring of 1994 I said my farewells, cleared my desk and welcomed my successor. I was moving on, although where to I was not quite sure.

I enjoyed several relaxed months without obligations. There was nowhere I had to be at any particular time. In the autumn of the previous year we had left Kentish Town after thirty-two years living at 48 Patshull Road, a house to which I was devoted, where my children had grown up and many events in my public life had taken place. To give that period a historic perspective, it was as if we had moved to Patshull Road on the eve of World War One, when Asquith was Prime Minister, and left after World War Two, with Attlee at No. 10. We were now in a smaller house in Highgate, with the narrow hall and stairways almost blocked by the countless bound *Hansard* volumes of my Commons career. I set about finding a home for them (eventually with the Policy Studies Institute) and dealing with other domestic tasks, including the garden. I also began to speak more frequently in the House of Lords, if only to get a better feel for the place and make some contribution to the Liberal Democrat benches to remedy the neglect of the previous years. But by the end of 1994 I had accepted two new responsibilities: to become Chairman of the Advertising Standards Authority and as Liberal Democrat spokesman in the Lords on Home Office matters.

My time at the RIBA had led me to reflect on the role of the professions, which were neither the creatures of statute, although loosely overseen by the Privy Council, nor part of the profit-earning enterprise culture. They came within a complex network of self-regulating bodies integral to a plural society. The voluntary sector, including Citizens' Advice Bureaux and many other charities, provided important community services, raised money for medical research and sustained the arts. Beyond that there were cooperatives, mutual building societies, and housing associations. There was the Consumers' Association, for which I had briefly worked, the Howard League for Penal Reform, which I had joined when campaigning against capital punishment, and the

Town and Country Planning Association, another of my long-standing concerns. There were also the trade unions. Some of these bodies existed only to inform and protect the public; others primarily to advance the interests of their members. But they had in common that they were not dependent on the state nor beholden to shareholders.

Into this wide category, I decided, the Advertising Standards Authority fell, launched over thirty years earlier by an industry fearful of statutory regulation but evolving to establish its independence and provide safeguards that advertisements should be legal, decent, honest and truthful. Television, to which advertising had come in 1955, was the medium most sensitive to public attitudes and parliament had decided that it and commercial radio should be subject to statutory regulation. But the ASA dealt with advertisements in newspapers, magazines, brochures and other printed publications, as well as posters and cinema and video commercials. It was a wide field and produced well over 10,000 complaints a year, which it was the core work of the Authority to investigate and adjudicate upon. When asked to become Chairman of the Authority, it looked like a job I would enjoy, part-time without executive responsibilities, but with adequate resources and scope for visible achievement.

I started both well and badly. Well, by deciding to advertise vacancies for the eight lay members of my council of twelve, all of whom had previously been appointed on an informal, old-boy network; badly, by behaving like a minister in a new department, making decisions that he expected his Permanent Secretary to implement. I had inherited the lay members of my council from my predecessor, Sir Timothy Raison, who I had known first when he was a leading Bow Group member, and then as a Conservative MP, and he had chosen well. They included Elizabeth Filkin, who is now Parliamentary Commissioner for Standards, Professor Robert Pinker, who continues to serve as a member of the Press Complaints Commission, and a good mixture of able men and women of different ages and backgrounds. But I saw no reason why a body that was to take account of public attitudes to advertising should not recruit, through advertising, from the public itself. My first attempt at open competition found no shortage of candidates eager to serve and all lay members of council have since been recruited in this way. I also decided that council members should serve for no more than six years, where hitherto their contracts had been of indefinite duration, a change accepted without resentment by those passing into retirement. These innovations produced a good deal of anxiety in the industry, appearing dangerously radical, but they are now accepted and unlikely to be reversed by my successors.

I started badly by not recognising that a part-time chairman had a quite different relationship to a Chief Executive than a full-time minister to his civil servants. My role at the RIBA had been in a halfway house, as a Chief Executive appointing staff and in day-to-day control of business but serving a council elected by members that made policy decisions. The council of the Advertising Standards Authority was of a different kind, ultimately responsible as directors of the Authority for its success but mainly concerned with quasi-judicial adjudications on complaints. The Director-General, Matti Alderson, had a much freer hand than I had had with the architects and she and I had a number of tense encounters before we settled down to a professional partnership as harmonious and effective as any in my working life.

Some of the most complex investigations and difficult decisions arose from complaints by commercial competitors against each other – Virgin and British Airways, ASDA and Sainsburys, Unilever and Procter and Gamble, Miele and Dyson (fighting it out in the market for vacuum cleaners). One staple source of complaints was the holiday and travel industry, another, claims for health care and beauty treatment. Complaints against the offensive portrayal of women were relatively few but often high profile and, like complaints on the grounds of taste and decency, required largely subjective judgements. I was clear that it was not the task of the ASA to make social policy or to be politically correct or to be less strict with charities and campaigning organisations – now often highly professional and aggressive in their advertising – because of sympathy with their causes. Our duty was to make decisions that reflected public opinion as sensitively as possible, taking account of the advertising industry's own codes of conduct. Advertisements in laddish magazines like *Loaded* and *The Face,* whose readers would be shocked by very little, would be quite unacceptable as posters on street hoardings. A major cause of complaint were advertisements seen as unsuitable for or disturbing to children; and the use of bad language of the most routine kind. But public opinion could change and following the stabbing of the head teacher Philip Lawrence at the end of 1995, and the Dunblane tragedy in March 1996, there was an angry public response to violent advertising images. This in turn was reflected in the ASA's own judgements, which became more critical of advertisements showing knives and guns.

In 1996 the advertisement bringing the most complaints was of a woman wearing a translucent black bra and knickers lying in long grass. We did not hold it to be offensive, as it was relevant to the advertised product (lingerie by Gossard), although we might have been stricter in view of the innuendo: 'Who said a woman can't get pleasure from something soft'.

But the second largest number of complaints – over 150 – was about an advertisement even more controversial in the passions it aroused. This showed a sinister 'Demon Eyes' Tony Blair, then Leader of the Opposition, with the text: 'New Labour, New Danger'. It was placed by the Conservative Party as part of a larger campaign masterminded by M&C Saatchi and was said by complainants to be offensive both to readers and to Blair himself. There was great nervousness in the ASA about the damage that could be done to the Authority's reputation whichever way our decision went. As most political advertising was exempt from the strictures of the codes, it was suggested that we should find a way out of passing any verdict. I too was uncomfortable about the Authority's involvement in party politics, but believed that we had no choice in dealing with the case without delay. With one exception, I had no idea of the political opinions of my council members but knew they would be rigorous in applying objective criteria to their judgements. At my suggestion, the council member who had been a Labour MP (and was to become one again) willingly stood aside; and I followed my usual practice of not voting as chairman except in the case of a tie. Council then decided unanimously that the advertisement had not caused serious or widespread public offence, but by a majority, that it portrayed Tony Blair in an offensive way.

It was the latter adjudication that made the news and drew the fire. 'Drop "Demon Eyes" advert, watchdog tells the Tories', was the headline in the *Daily Telegraph*; and in the *Daily Mail*, columnist Andrew Alexander ridiculed 'the magnificent solemnity of it all'. But apart from claiming that the cost of the advertising had been far outweighed by the publicity that the ASA had helped to give it, Conservative Central Office was wisely silent. Although the complainants to the ASA had included Labour Party branches and a bishop, some were Conservatives who nevertheless objected to a personal attack of this kind. My guess is that John Major's postbag contained many letters with the same message from supporters who believed that this time the Saatchis had gone too far. One Tory backbencher made a half-hearted attack on me but the vice-chairman of the party was careful not to be drawn into any such criticism when we appeared together on television. Michael Portillo had said in advance that the party would respect the ASA's ruling whatever it might be, and the advertisement was not used again.

I am only one of many politicians, active or retired, involved in running voluntary bodies or serving as directors of public companies or deep into professional careers who find no difficulty in taking off one hat and putting on another. I mean by that the ability to leave aside political views, even when strongly held, as inappropriate to a quite different situation, which requires detachment and objectivity. I have never felt, in my time with the architects or my years as Chairman of the ASA, any difficulty in being politically neutral when this has been plainly required.

But where did my loyalties lie in the pre-election battle for the hearts and minds of voters as between the Conservative Party and Tony Blair? The Liberal Democrats were in opposition to a Tory government, but Paddy Ashdown had only just moved away from positioning his party equidistant from both Labour and the Conservatives. In the Lords, I was vehemently critical of Michael Howard's role as Home Secretary, but contemptuous of Jack Straw's willingness to go along with illiberal law-and-order policies. If my interest lay anywhere, it was in the Conservative and Labour Parties discrediting each other, leaving room for the Liberal Democrats to collect new support in between.

But it was not quite as simple as that. Since the 1992 election my views had shifted, much as the opinions of the voters had done. I had no faith in Neil Kinnock as a potential Prime Minister but John Smith and Tony Blair were a different matter. The realignment of the left had not taken place as the result of a breakthrough by the SDP and the Liberals, but an informal understanding between Labour and the Liberal Democrats might achieve as much.

In the early 1990s John Smith had suggested to me that, in view of Labour's recovery, I should think of rejoining the party. He had done so teasingly, without much hope but with a goodwill reflecting his days as a supporter of CDS and our brief time together in cabinet. In October 1992, not long after he had become Labour Leader, we had a similar exchange on coming out of Peter Jenkins' memorial service at St Margaret's, Westminster.

But six months later, as the Major Government declined into incompetence, I asked him to take an urgent but historic view of the need for some accommodation between the Labour Party and the Liberal Democrats. My approach was partly provoked by the forthcoming by-election at Newbury, where only the Liberal Democrats could take the seat from the Conservatives and Labour would inevitably spilt the anti-Tory vote (in the event David Rendel, the Liberal Democrat candidate, won by a landslide, and Labour's vote fell by two-thirds). But its purpose was to impress on John Smith that the Liberal Democrats were here to stay, and that Britain had a three-party system in which they would remain significant players. He had put two Liberal Democrats on his Commission on Social Justice, but had otherwise shown no imagination about an inclusive approach to the leadership of the centre-left. I wanted him to think beyond party and to recognise that just as Britain had changed permanently, the institutions and electoral assumptions of the centre-left must change too. 'You have no idea', I told him 'what energy, enthusiasm and hope you would release by ceasing to pretend that Labour can do it alone and that Labour's is the only way'.

But John Smith was not responsive. He was deep into getting his watered-down version of one member, one vote through his party conference – breaking down the trade union block vote but allowing them a bigger say than their party membership justified – and then turning away from further modernisation. He was, I concluded, still a 1960s' Gaitskellite with many of the right instincts about policy (which meant I shared them) but no vision about political change and the realignment of the left.

In June 1993 I wrote to David Marquand – who had become something of an intellectual bridge between the two parties – and mentioned my deepening gloom about John Smith. An increasing number of people, I said, talked sensibly about more relaxed relations between Labour and the Liberal Democrats, 'and all credit to Tony Blair in particular'. The fact remained that John Smith was not moving. I lobbied Bob Gavron and Sir Denis Foreman, trustees of the relatively new Institute of Public Policy Research, about transforming it from a Labour Party quango into a think-tank to serve the whole leftward-thinking body of opinion. Both were sympathetic but encountered reluctance to let it move away from its Labour roots. I had made clear to John Smith that mine were personal views and that many Liberal Democrats would be suspicious of closer relations with Labour, as Paddy Ashdown was finding. But there now seemed no chance of progress and, apart from advocating tactical voting in the next election, nothing further I could do.

Then suddenly in May 1994 John Smith died, and two months later Tony Blair was chosen as his successor. Blair had been elected in 1983 for Sedgefield, which abutted on to my own constituency of Stockton North, and I had campaigned against him in support of the SDP candidate, who won over 10,000 votes, a very good result in a former mining seat. Sharing a television show with him and Kenneth Clarke in the 1992 election I had found him tense and reserved, unable to gossip indiscreetly, unlike Ken Clarke who was quite open about his own party's shortcomings. But these were trivial considerations. I had been struck by the courage of his bid for his party's leadership, with no obvious compromises and no hostages given. There was a freshness and sense of vision about him which held the promise of a new kind of leadership, at last dragging the Labour Party into the 1990s. His success might threaten the Liberal Democrats and draw away some of our membership but a change of government after almost two decades of the Tories was now the first priority. In any case, he was ready for constitutional reform of the kind Liberal Democrats wanted, and on wider policy he had moved far into our own territory.

Roy Jenkins was quickly off the mark with an assessment of Tony Blair as 'the most exciting Labour choice since the election of Hugh Gaitskell', and Shirley Williams called for Labour and the Liberal Democrats to work towards a common programme. My own endorsement of Blair was seen to be the warmest because I said explicitly that I hoped he would win the next election, and that a new mutual tolerance between the two parties could lay the basis for a possible coalition. The headlines were predictable: 'Blair's Gang', said *The Times* and 'Gang Show for Blair', *The Observer*. *The Guardian* had a suitably vulgar cartoon with the three of us kneeling behind Blair's bottom, and Paddy Ashdown, trousers down, enjoying no such fawning. Paddy had every reason to be furious. This was not a concerted act of approval by Roy, Shirley and me, but that was how it was inevitably seen. As such, it undermined his policy of 'equidistance' and would be a signal to former Labour members that their way back to their old party was now clear. However, in my view there was every prospect that with the moderate-minded Blair as a potential Labour Prime Minister, and some tactical voting, if Labour won a majority there could well be a significant increase in the number of Liberal Democrat MPs. I had never believed in putting 'blue water' between political parties simply in order to emphasise differences and there would be no harm done if Liberal Democrats defined themselves as a party of the centre-left, close to Labour but with a mind of their own.

The arrival of Blair did provoke the early loss from the Liberal Democrats to Labour of some friends and allies. These included Andrew Adonis, an Oxford academic and *Financial Times* and *Observer* journalist who had become a Liberal Democrat parliamentary candidate and later joined the Blair team at No 10; and Roger Liddle, who had shared in all my political adventures since he joined me at the Department of Transport twenty years earlier. I was saddened by his leaving but I could hardly deny him the excitement of helping to make a new government when the Liberal Democrats could offer no comparable role. He too ended up in No 10, but lost none of the exuberance which makes him a one-man coalition of much that is best, regardless of party, on the centre-left.

It quickly became apparent to me that the Liberal Democrats could remain a voice to be heard when, with the new parliamentary session beginning in November 1994, I became the party's spokesman in the Lords on Home Affairs. Tony Blair's aphorism, 'tough on crime and tough on the causes of crime', had recognised that punishment alone would not diminish the number of criminal offences. But there seemed precious little of this in Jack Straw's approach to law and order, which Andrew McIntosh, his spokesman in the Lords, was required – often reluctantly – to follow. There was no love lost for Michael Howard – or his minister in the Lords, Baroness Blatch – on the Labour benches, but Jack Straw was terrified of being outflanked. As Howard moved Conservative policy rapidly away from the relatively liberal approach of his predecessors Douglas Hurd and Kenneth Baker, Jack Straw never seemed far behind. This left the Liberal Democrats taking the lead in deploring the rising prison population and exposing the attempt of the Home Secretary to make Derek Lewis, head of the Prison Service, the scapegoat for his own failings.

The opportunity for me to make a distinctive contribution to legislation in the face of resistance from both the Government and the Labour Party came with the Police Bill which reached the Lords in November 1996. This contained a provision to regulate the use of electronic surveillance by putting existing arrangements on a statutory footing, allowing senior police officers to authorise it. In the Second Reading debate, I expressed my reservations about these proposals for police bugging of private property, and my concern was greatly strengthened when Lord Browne-Wilkinson, a senior Law Lord, said this was an issue of constitutional importance affecting the freedom embodied in our belief that an Englishman's home was his castle. It was now clear to me that statutory surveillance must require judicial authorisation and on the first day of the committee stage I moved an amendment to make a circuit judge, rather than a senior police officer, responsible for the decision. The amendment was opposed by the Government on the grounds that it might compromise the impartiality of the judiciary by drawing them into police operations; and won no support from the Labour Party which was content that the Bill should relate only to serious crimes. There was no point in pressing the matter to a division at 10.30 at night – there seldom is in the Lords – so I decided to wait for the report stage that would come in January. This had the advantage of allowing a long period either side of Christmas in which to lobby for support.

This campaign was endorsed in *The Guardian* by Hugo Young, with all his steely anger, and I wrote an article for *The Observer* and spoke to as many other journalists as I could to lodge in their minds the importance of the issue. Freedom and privacy were concerns of both left and right and a helpful article by William Rees-Mogg in *The Times,* and editorial support from the *Daily Telegraph,* were amongst widespread comments that pushed the bandwagon along. My main objective was to get agreement to any form of judicial authorisation of police bugging, but there was no chance of winning except with 100 votes from elsewhere in the House to add to our own absolute maximum of about forty-five. Then, at the last moment, under the pressure that we had helped to generate, Jack Straw grudgingly changed course. He could not bring himself to endorse the Liberal Democrat amendment but he instructed Andrew McIntosh to put down one of his own to the same effect. Andrew McIntosh moved his amendment and I moved mine and a four-hour debate followed. I was able to welcome Andrew McIntosh as a sinner come to repentance but to demonstrate, so I thought, why my amendment was better. Then Jim Callaghan said that although he preferred his own party's amendment, he could cheerfully support mine, and Lord Browne-Wilkinson said he preferred my amendment but could also support Labour's. These speeches set the tone for much that followed. Andrew McIntosh's amendment was first to be called for a division and it was carried by 209 votes to 145. It was now a high risk to press my own amendment, as the two were incompatible and the Labour front bench would not support mine although Liberal Democrats had supported theirs. But as Nicolas Browne-Wilkinson had generously said in the course of his speech, I had fought the battle as a matter of principle and I wanted the record to give the Liberal Democrats credit. I took a chance, moved my amendment and won by 158 votes to 137. Here was sweet satisfaction, not least in the support of the Lord Chief Justice, of Jim Callaghan and others from the Conservative, Labour and Cross-Benches. The Government eventually tidied up the Bill in the Commons and my amendment did not survive as such. But judicial authorisation was in the Bill when it finally reached the Statute Book. It was proof that a third party using the opportunities provided by the House of Lords could occasionally determine the law of England.

There was a further opportunity only a few weeks later. The Crime (Sentences) Bill was another of Michael Howard's obnoxious measures that had wound its way through the House of Commons with only half-hearted opposition from the Labour Party. It reached the Lords for its Second Reading on 27 January 1997, when I condemned it as 'a bad bill with few redeeming features, foolishly conceived, wrong in principle and deceptive in its relevance to the real fight against crime'. More importantly, the Lord Chief Justice was scathing in his criticism, particularly in that it removed the discretion of judges to determine a case on its merits, and required the imposition of a mandatory sentence. There was strong cross-party support for this position and Andrew McIntosh, for Labour, eventually persuaded Jack Straw to allow him to table an amendment whereby in certain cases judges would be exempt from such a provision. This was carried against the Government by 180 votes to 172.

But a month later, before the Bill had completed all its stages, John Major announced the dissolution of parliament. Following the usual practice, consultations took place with a view to winding up all outstanding business in both Houses, in the course of which Jack Straw agreed that the Crime (Sentences) Bill should complete its passage with minimum further scrutiny and without the Lords amendment. In the Lords the Leader of the House, Lord Cranborne, with the support of the Labour front bench, presented this as a routine necessity but I was able to draw upon my personal experience as a minister on the eve of the elections of 1970 and 1979 in opposing the Government; and the Lord Chief Justice was again outspoken, as were Lord Carr of Hadley and Lord Carlisle of Bucklow, both former Tory cabinet ministers.

John Harris, the Liberal Democrat Chief Whip, had conducted a skilful delaying campaign against the Bill from the moment it had been announced in the Queen's Speech, and Michael Howard was fully aware that it was now the Liberal Democrats in the Lords who had its future in their hands. On the crucial day, 18 March, John ensured there were sufficient amendments on the order paper and encouraged colleagues to speak at length. I was sitting in the Bishops' Bar – the popular meeting place for gossip – having a lunchtime sandwich when I was approached by Lord Strathclyde, the Government Chief Whip, who asked me what we intended to do. 'Keep the House up all night', I replied and explained how John Harris had already arranged for relays of Liberal Democrat peers to be on duty. In the next few hours we showed our muscle while Black Rod and the authorities of the House became increasingly agitated about providing for an all-night sitting. Then, at 8.20 – it was time for a proper meal and I was in the dining room – I was asked to call on Lord Strathclyde in his room. 'You've won', were his first words and he offered the compromise we had been seeking of retaining the Lords amendment if we allowed the Bill to go through. John Harris was already with him and we agreed to accept the terms of the Government's climb-down. Once again, the Liberal Democrats had led when Labour had failed miserably to do so.

Like all new peers, my first port of call after my peerage had been gazetted at New Year 1992 was Garter King-of-Arms. The little I knew of his existence had been learnt from cigarette cards I had collected as a boy at the time of the coronation of King George VI in 1937. He was a ceremonial functionary with a splendid uniform whose status rested on nothing more than the traditional role of the College of Heralds, but whose assent was required to the title I might choose. Any connection with Stockton-on-Tees was ruled out – Harold Macmillan had become the Earl of Stockton – and there had been a Lord Liverpool since the eighteenth century. But I liked the idea of embodying in my title 'Quarry Bank', in recognition of the school to which I owed so much and the friends who had wished me well. 'Quarry Bank' said Garter, 'Where's Quarry Bank?' and I explained, having done my homework in the British Museum, that Quarry Bank was marked on the earliest Ordnance Survey maps. It was, I said, a district of Liverpool, although admittedly a rather small one (I did not confess that it was hardly more than the site of a substantial Victorian villa). 'Well, if I went to the local newsagents and said "Take me to Quarry Bank", would they know where to go?' The idea of Garter King-of-Arms catching a train to Liverpool, perhaps in his fancy dress, and calling on the local newsagent was more than faintly ridiculous so I confidently said 'Yes'. Without further discussion he settled for that, provided Lyon King-of-Arms (his opposite number north of the Border) confirmed that there was a Scottish peer whose name was sufficiently like mine to justify the addition of 'Quarry Bank' to identify me and to avoid confusion. I called again at the College of Heralds in Queen Victoria Street to discover the outcome, by which time I had learnt the language. 'And what has Lyon said to Garter, Garter?' I asked with a very straight face. And Garter confirmed that on Lyon's advice I should be 'Lord Rodgers of Quarry Bank'.

This was both a fitting introduction to my life in the Lords and a misleading one. Fitting because I found the Lords much more given to traditional styles and courtesies than the Commons; misleading, because the usual objects of ridicule distracted attention from the fact that for more than half the time, the Lords were involved in the expert and detailed scrutiny of legislation essential to the credibility of parliamentary government. It was easy to make fun of the Lords by dwelling on arthritic old backwoodsmen coming up from the country to vote against change and not even knowing their way into the Chamber; and that the House of Lords was an anomaly in a democratic society was not in dispute. Quite apart from the two-thirds of peers who sat in the Lords only because their forebears had given their wives as mistresses to the king (or, more likely, a great deal of money to a political party), most of the remainder of us had been appointed because the Prime Minister of the day exercised his discretion in our favour. But the indefensible composition of the House should not be confused with the way it did its job.

In the Commons it was long speeches and rhetoric; in the Lords, which was far better attended for routine daily business, much shorter ones and a lot more substance. This did not make for entertainment or drama. But the outcome of a division was more unpredictable than in the Commons and, with less attachment to party, votes could be won on the quality of the argument. It was better to say, 'We on these benches believe …' than, 'Liberal Democrat (or Labour or Conservative) policy is …' because it seemed to address the merits of the case, thus making it easier to win cross-party support. Circumlocution also had its place. 'I hope that the Noble Lord, whose robust contributions the House so much enjoys, will forgive me if I suggest that on this occasion he may possibly be a little wide of the mark …' meant 'You've got it wrong'. To use hard words, without emollience or humour, was to strike a discordant note. For those coming from the blunter worlds of the Commons or local government, this could all seem pompous and stifling, but once the language had been learnt the real business was much the same.

But it was important to retain a sense of proportion. Since the 1911 Parliament Act, the Lords had seldom been more than an irritant to governments. Harold Wilson had trouble with the Southern Rhodesia Order in 1969, and the nationalisation of ship-repairing in the 1970s, but the shocked reaction to the Lords' offence in opposing critical government business was a measure of how far its acquiescence was usually taken for granted. During my own time in cabinet a report on next week's business in the House of Lords normally followed a report on forthcoming business in the Commons. The Prime Minister would barely raise his head, as with 'Fred?', he invited Lord Peart to make the briefest comment. Only a delay in legislation in which they had a stake, or a rogue amendment tiresomely carried provoked other members of the cabinet into asking questions. As Secretary of State for Transport I had in Lady Stedman an excellent junior minister but I seldom invited her to departmental meetings, and never read her speeches in the Lords *Hansard*. The difficulty for a government with a secure Commons majority was in stomaching any defeat or delay in the Lords when tame back-bench MPs created no such problems. This was both a measure of the usefulness of the Lords, and its secondary place in the parliamentary system which the removal of hereditary peers would not change. Occasionally, when carried away by a good speech or the exposure of a government failing, I pulled myself up by asking, 'But who is listening?' It is a necessary corrective to going native in what can be a seductive place.

I had the most vivid sense of the weight of the Commons and the vulnerability of the Lords as I sat for the first time, dressed in a scarlet robe, on the crowded benches at the state opening of parliament. The red and gold Chamber was at its most glittering, with the Queen on the throne, the wives of peers in fine gowns and priceless tiaras (except for Silivia's, which came from a theatrical costumier), the Lord Great Chamberlain and the Earl Marshal in their ceremonial dress, and the diplomatic gallery packed with ambassadors loving this unfolding pageant. Black Rod had gone to summon the Commons to hear the formal reading of the Gracious Speech, and the Lords sat dutifully silent awaiting their arrival. Then there was a distant rumbling, voices raised, laughter, even, and it grew louder until, led by the Speaker with the Prime Minister at her elbow, noisy MPs burst into the Chamber in their everyday clothes. Was it my imagination, or did I feel for a moment the whole assembled company shrink in apprehension from the unruly mob, much as the victims of the French Revolution must have done with the arrival of the *sans-culottes* at the height of the Jacobin terror? It was the Commons, not the Lords, that mattered. No second chamber could challenge for long the primacy, strength and confidence of those who had been elected.

From May 1997, the citizenry had new representatives. I was delighted to see the back of the Tories after eighteen years and reasonably confident that Tony Blair had the potential to be the least ideological, the least adversarial of Prime Ministers. My bet with Ladbrokes had underestimated his majority – I expected it to be less than 100 – but had also given the Liberal Democrats no more than thirty MPs, whereas there were now forty-six. There was every reason to rejoice at the outcome of the election. But my feelings in the Lords were mixed. The Labour peers moved as a bloc from one side of the Chamber to the other but we Liberal Democrats remained in place, now squeezed on our benches by Conservative peers, including many hereditaries, with whom we had nothing in common. Liberal Democrats had been opposed to 70–80 per cent of the policies of John Major's Government but were now in favour of 70–80 per cent of what the Labour Government had on offer, particularly its constitutional proposals. The new Leader of the House, Ivor Richard, admitted to me that he would have joined the SDP in 1981 had it not been for David Owen, who as Foreign Secretary had reprimanded him for daring to come to London from his post at the United Nations to attend Tony Crosland's memorial service. As for Labour's front bench, many were old friends and, as a parliamentary team, they were much more impressive than their Tory predecessors. Yet, here we were, the Liberal Democrats, still in opposition and obliged in this respect to be the junior partners of the Tories. It was uncongenial.

I had hoped it might be otherwise. Despite the failures of Jack Straw as Shadow Home Secretary with which I was currently wrestling in the Lords, I had said at our Brighton conference in the autumn of 1996 that Liberal Democrats should be prepared to join a coalition with Labour if invited to do so. This message made many activists uneasy, although I had more correspondence complaining about my advocacy of tactical voting. They saw this as unfair to Liberal Democrat candidates who found it difficult enough to be taken seriously when in third place behind a Conservative MP. But we were not in coalition and the restraints that partnership would have placed upon Liberal Democrats in exchange for a share in decision-making could not apply when the Labour Government was going it alone. We were sitting across the Chamber from the Government in the Lords and our obligation was to provide constructive opposition, in Paddy Ashdown's carefully chosen phrase.

But when Paddy and Tony Blair announced a joint consultative committee I was unimpressed, because there was no point in such formal arrangements unless the Government was prepared to be significantly influenced by them. I was also certain that ministers would complain when Liberal Democrats were awkward on policy issues outside the committee's terms of reference because they would see the very act of setting up such a committee as a gesture of goodwill to Paddy Ashdown for which a price should be paid. In the Commons it would be painless; Liberal Democrat MPs could be faithful to their own views by voting against the Government; and the Government could be tolerant, knowing that, with their huge majority, they would always win. In the Lords it would be different. As we had demonstrated on the Police Bill and the Crime (Sentences) Bill, we could play a leading part in defeating the Government and although we would not seek confrontation with Labour ministers, they would be annoyed when we felt obliged to take a stand. I said to Paddy, reversing Stanley Baldwin's adage about the press barons of the 1920s, 'that the danger of the new consultative committee is responsibility without power', inhibiting the Liberal Democrats with nothing in exchange except the symbol of closeness. Blair would see the committee as a mark of his genuine liking for Ashdown and his desire to be inclusive; it would hint at the coalition he might have preferred. But without a proper agenda and Cabinet Office papers, there would be little, if anything, gained beyond what Blair and Ashdown might achieve one to one through mutual respect.

The experience of the next two years confirmed my view. The Government's constitutional agenda had been agreed in discussions between Labour's Robin Cook and Bob Maclennan, for the Liberal Democrats, before the election, and these had been wholly worthwhile. When legislation for proportional representation for elections to the European Parliament was omitted from the 1997 Queen's Speech we successfully lobbied for a bill. But this was done outside the committee, direct to the Prime Minister, and by other informal channels to No. 10. On the key question of open lists, where voters choose between individual candidates, and closed lists, where the choice is between parties, Liberal Democrats made strong representations for open lists, only to have them turned down by Jack Straw. The failure of the consultative committee to secure this reasonable concession did not prevent ministers being irritated when we continued to press our case in the Lords. I can think of only one measurable outcome from the committee: the reference to 'proportionate creations' (proportionate to the votes cast for other parties) of new Liberal Democrat life peers in the transitional House of Lords which was included in the Government White Paper at the eleventh hour, at the insistence of Bob Maclennan. I was involved in entirely friendly conversations with the Leader of the House, then Ivor Richard, and the Lord Chancellor, Derry Irvine, during the time the Government was deciding how to tackle Lords reform. But at no time did I see Cabinet Office papers or feel that consultation was anything more than a sensible picking of brains on the best way forward towards shared objectives. When, as a result of negotiations between the Lord Chancellor and Lord Cranborne, a major concession was made that breached the whole principle of the Bill and allowed ninety-two hereditary peers to stay on in the House – the Weatherill amendment – Paddy Ashdown was told only when the matter had been settled. The deal was done without reference to the Liberal Democrats and a thoroughly unsatisfactory, dog's breakfast of a deal it turned out to be, with Derry Irvine comprehensively outwitted by Cranborne, as wily a fox as many of his ancestors have been, back to Robert Cecil, first Earl of Salisbury, who served Queen Elizabeth I.

I was elected Leader of the Liberal Democrat peers, in succession to Roy Jenkins, who had led the party in the Lords for almost ten years with great authority and distinction, and took over in January 1998, with David Steel and later Shirley Williams as my deputy. I found that, as the Government got into its stride and brought forward legislation, much of my time seemed to be given to the consequences of the special relationship with Labour we were thought to enjoy. Liberal Democrat peers reacted positively to my wish for a higher level of activity in the Chamber, with at least one starred question to a minister (of four allowed) every day, more team work and a good vote in divisions, particularly on Liberal Democrat amendments. I also asked my spokesmen – in keeping with constructive opposition – to keep in close touch with ministers, make them aware of our intentions and look for compromises. John Harris said, and I agreed, that there should be no late-night ambushes when a vote might be won simply because the Government was off-guard and had too few Labour peers on duty. We were aware that the Government Chief Whip was finding difficulty in 'keeping a House' of back-bench peers to avoid unexpected defeats, when few of them grasped that staying late to ensure the passage of business was one of the prices to be paid for being in Government.

Nevertheless, there were soon complaints that Liberal Democrat peers were not acting in the spirit of the joint consultative committee when we helped to defeat ministers. On the majority of occasions we voted in the Government lobby, but eight times in the first six months of 1998 the Government was defeated on amendments moved by Liberal Democrat peers. That the Government Chief Whip Denis Carter should complain was par for the course, and did not affect good working relations between him and John Harris. But messages also came to me from Paddy Ashdown, to whom No. 10 had complained.

When the Government decided to charge tuition fees on English, Welsh and Northern Ireland students at Scottish universities, strong pressure was put on Paddy to persuade me to call off Liberal Democrat opposition in the Lords (where we were following the lead already given by Liberal Democrat MPs in the Commons); and on one occasion, he telephoned me from France, having just received an angry call from No. 10 complaining about our behaviour. The message I received from Margaret Jay shortly after she had become Leader of the Lords was that, apart from the Prime Minister and Peter Mandelson, there was no support in the cabinet for 'the project' (as close cooperation between our two parties was called). But given the extent to which we moderated our opposition in the Lords, the Government gained more than the Liberal Democrats from the first couple of years of the joint consultative committee. When it came to an increase in the financial assistance given to opposition parties ('Cranborne money' in the Lords matches 'Short money' in the Commons) Margaret Jay, now Labour Leader of the Lords, pushed through a mean-spirited settlement which reflected nothing of any special relationship.

Even more seriously, the idea was not reflected in the creation of new life peers. On the contrary, for both Ivor Richard and Margaret Jay as Leaders of the House complained about Liberal Democrat expectations as long as we continued to embarrass the Government by sometimes voting against it. New peers were to be, it seemed, a reward for good behaviour rather than an entitlement in keeping with Liberal Democrat standing in the country and votes won at a general election, despite the endorsement of this principle set out in the Government's White Paper. It is this power of the Prime Minister of the day to appoint – or not appoint – new peers from opposition parties in whatever numbers they choose, whenever they choose (and Margaret Thatcher and John Major starved both Labour and the Liberal Democrats of their share) that makes the prospect of a nominated House of Lords profoundly unattractive. Restricting Prime Ministerial patronage is an essential part of any further reform, and one more reason why a predominantly elected House has everything to recommend it (the exception being cross-bench peers).

As the Government moved inexorably, so it seemed, towards a second term I viewed it with mixed feelings. It was infinitely more acceptable either than the Thatcher–Major administrations that had preceded it or the Tory party in opposition, increasingly fractious, unpleasantly xenophobic and stumbling even further towards extremes. The middle England to which Tony Blair had appealed was very like the provincial suburbia in which I had grown up, frightened of strikes and trade unions, hostile to scroungers on the welfare state, unimpressed by the performance of nationalised industries, often prejudiced and sometimes smug but capable of imagination and generosity and offering a source of comfort and security that no-one should despise. The shortcomings and qualities of middle England have to be embraced by any political party hoping to win power. Clement Attlee had won middle England in 1945 and Margaret Thatcher in 1979. Tony Blair needs to hold it to win two terms in office and William Hague or his successor must win it back if Labour is not to enjoy a third.

In the balance sheet, I must also set today's ruthless management of the Labour Party, with the voice of dissent virtually silenced, against the history of the 1970s and 1980s when it was close to disintegration. I was on the inside then and witnessed the centripetal forces that tore it apart. Labour Party conferences were noisy, exciting and unpredictable but five minutes allowed for the Chancellor of the Exchequer at the rostrum – Denis Healey's ration of time, grudgingly given in 1976 – was hardly the mark of a government in control. The Labour conference turned its face away from the voters and made policy that satisfied only its militant delegates, with MPs marginalised and abused. Earlier I had played my part in trying to have chosen parliamentary candidates who were better disposed to the leadership at a time when local parties were often dominated by an organised caucus of the left. Many of the lessons to be drawn from Labour in decline were incorporated in the SDP, whether one member, one vote to avoid take-over by an activist minority, or the orderly progression of green and white papers to avoid policy-making on the hoof. I can hardly complain where Labour has learnt from the SDP or from its own troubled experience.

The Liberal Party's effective parliamentary life began with its emergence from a confusion of Whigs and radicals at the time of Palmerston's second administration of 1859. Barely sixty years later, as Asquith collapsed his government into a wartime coalition, it was almost over. The Liberals proved unable to respond adequately to profound economic, social and political change and the Labour Party came into its own. Why, almost a century later, should we suppose that the ideas and beliefs that then made the Labour Party should have any place in the philosophy of the centre-left if it is to win and hold the voters? New Labour is as different from the party of Clement Attlee as the Labour Party of Attlee was from the Liberal Party of Asquith.

For all that, for all my understanding of why the Labour Government is what it is, I am profoundly uneasy. Alone and unchallenged, Tony Blair could allow his missionary zeal to turn into a righteous intolerance close to Margaret Thatcher's terrifying certainties, and far from even a redefined centre-left.

Three main factors contribute to a government's success or failure: presentation, process and substance. Tony Blair's New Labour has handled presentation brilliantly. Never has a government had such a chorus of loyal and well-behaved MPs singing from the same hymn sheet; never such a professional team of spin doctors; and never such a cult of celebrity for its top ministers. Life round Westminster – with well-chosen sorties to hospitals, schools and housing estates – is a constant festival of events peppered with glossy policy statements that glow with smiling faces and tell of hard choices bravely faced. Cleverly using a willing media, New Labour has presented itself to the public over the heads of parliament. With overwhelming dominance in the House of Commons, and almost any revolt on its own submissive benches shrinking to a mild squeak of protest, no government has worried less about the views of elected representatives, least of all the new women MPs who were expected to change things but willingly settled for being 'Blair's babes'. The first parliamentary 'reform' of this Parliament was for the Prime Minister to reduce his commitment to answer questions from two days a week to one. If I were a back-bench MP, I would be very cautious of other parliamentary reforms, especially those claiming to make my life easier, with more time away in my constituency or with my family. 'Keep the lads busy', was Tony Blair's injunction to his Chief Whip, but his motive was to minimise mischief-making in idle hands, not to make his MPs more vigilant custodians of parliamentary democracy.

I am equally concerned about the diminution of cabinet government, both the creation of what is in effect a Department of the Prime Minister at No. 10, and the minimising of the decision-making role of the cabinet. Every Prime Minister is bound to have a small circle of friends and helpers with whom he feels at home. They will be a healthy influence if they talk frankly, but when the going gets tough and criticism of the Prime Minister inevitable, a kitchen cabinet becomes sycophantic. A Prime Minister must in the end rely on the creative talents of the ministers he appoints. Too much manipulation from No. 10 eventually causes resentment, undermines confidence and fractures the policy coherence it is meant to create. This government is run like a corporate business, with the Prime Minister as chairman and chief executive, a politically appointed former civil servant, Jonathan Powell, as managing director and cabinet ministers as heads of operating divisions marketing (and frequently re-packaging) their products. It owes little to parliamentary tradition.

As for the substance of New Labour's policy, leaving aside its welcome constitutional reforms, I cannot with confidence endorse its sense of direction. Its initial theme was a rigorous fiscal framework with a Chancellor often as unyielding as his predecessor, Philip Snowden, in the disastrous 1929 Labour Government of Ramsay MacDonald. In the 1970s it was Labour's social democrats who warned that public expenditure was getting out of hand; Tony Crosland's 'the party's over' contained that message. And in my own book, *The Politics of Change*, published in 1982, I devoted a chapter to arguing that it was wrong to assume that more public expenditure was the only or best way of meeting social needs. But it is foolish to embrace the other extreme of fiscal rectitude. If the choice is between lower levels of income tax and increased spending, in the circumstances of today the latter should prevail. Properly explained in terms of specific needs – health, education, transport – I believe that middle England would agree.

I would go further and address the central question of poverty. I am reminded here of R. H. Tawney in his *Religion and the Rise of Capitalism,* when he writes of the practical energy and technical skills that were transforming material civilisation from the latter part of the seventeenth century – times quite like our own:

> If, however, economic ambitions are good servants, they are bad masters. Harnessed to a social purpose, they will turn the mill and grind the corn. But the question, to what end the wheels revolve, still remains …

My question is this: to what end do the wheels of wealth creation revolve for New Labour as we enter the twenty-first century?

The idea of equality, embodying fairness (described as an 'obsession' by Blair's current guru, LSE Director Tony Giddens) has been watered down to 'equality of access', which seems to mean equal opportunity for the unequal. The able-bodied poor will be helped back to work, but the undeserving poor will remain an underclass as national wealth grows. Two hundred years ago a twelvefold increase in the cost of poor relief led to the invention of the workhouse. This Government's drive against poverty is inspired at least in part by the same wish to make savings in public expenditure. It shows a remarkable lack of understanding and compassion.

My concern is not simply that we are still two nations in Britain, but that the rich are getting richer and the gap between rich and poor (measured either by incomes or by the distribution of wealth) is widening. We take pride in being a more socially mobile society. But boys from managerial and professional families are still three times more likely to end up in such occupations as the sons of unskilled and semi-skilled manual workers. Similarly, children with an unemployed father are twice as likely to end up with a substantial history of unemployment themselves than those with no such background of unemployment. For the most part, in the next generation the rich still stay rich, while the poor remain trapped in their poverty.

Then there is the record of many inner-city comprehensive schools which offer nothing of the quality of learning of my grammar school sixty years ago. I supported the comprehensive principle and an end to selection at eleven to give subsequent generations of children the advantages I was lucky enough to enjoy. But good intentions – and too much rigidity in curricula and examinations – will get nowhere unless money is put into books and equipment and teachers are paid the proper rate for their exacting jobs. And despite genuine dilemmas about priorities, and without pretending that greater resources alone are required, the National Health Service will remain in decline – with those who can afford it opting out into private medicine – unless the proportion of GDP devoted to it rises at least to the levels of our principal partners in the European Union, as the government now promises that it will.

These are some of many examples of inequality capable of remedy. They are within the power of government to begin changing. There is no need to wait for another pamphlet from the Institute for Public Policy Research or a pronouncement from the Social Exclusion Unit at No. 10.

I will not labour these points further. My concern is that the Blair Government is not facing up to the question of inequality which, for me, is central to any party of the centre-left. Forty years ago, many of us were much influenced by J. K. Galbraith's *The Affluent Society*. Galbraith was writing again recently, saying that in those forty years the contrast between public services and affluent private consumption had become much greater. He then offered an explanation. The problem was not, he said, economics, but, as people became more fortunate in their personal well-being, there was 'a common tendency to ignore the poor or to develop some rationalisation for the good fortune of the fortunate. Responsibility is assigned to the poor themselves. Given their personal disposition and moral tone, they are meant to be poor. Poverty is both inevitable and, in some measure, deserved.' Tony Blair would certainly not give his name to that. And yet, underlying much of the discussion of 'welfare to work', and how to deal with benefits, there is a tendency to treat the poor not as victims but as perpetrators. The Blair Government has not created a political climate sympathetic to the poor. They are somehow an embarrassment, like the 'squeegee merchants' of Jack Straw fame.

So my support for New Labour remains qualified, and I am doubtful whether it will ever adequately address the concerns that in 1945 made a sixteen year-old Liverpool boy rejoice in the election of a Labour Government. I am a social democrat who now finds himself content in a party to which the flow of traditional Liberal ideas equally contributes. If the realignment of the centre-left is ever to take place, giving Britain a broadly social democratic government for much of the twenty-first century, it will not be within a 'big tent' presided over by Tony Blair or his New Labour successors, but as a result of proportional representation and a plurality of political parties. In the meantime, Liberal Democrats must pursue their own course, giving the Government the benefit of the doubt but having no obligations except on the basis of reciprocity.

I am writing this in the early evening, looking across olive groves to the monastery of Santa Anna where they made part of that marvellous film, *The English Patient*. Slightly to the right, but also in my line of vision, is Castelmuzzio, typical of the unspoilt hill towns of these parts; and slightly to the left in the hazy distance, the brooding, volcanic presence of Monte Amiata, that rises 5,700 feet above sea level. Over there, beyond Pienza, is the Val d'Orcia about which Iris Origo wrote in her memorable account of wartime and liberation. We are familiar now with this small corner of Italy, if familiarity can be claimed by anyone who makes only annual visits. My body and mind are quickly restored and I pinch myself into remembering that I have reached the age of seventy.

But my home is where I have spent most of those years, in and around London, England, and Liverpool, which I remember wistfully; and my life has been mainly through rough weather over the bumpy ground of politics. It has sometimes been a painful journey and I wince at the thought of what I have done and been, errors of judgement, moments of aberration. Perhaps I will do better in future; perhaps not.

Index

NOTTINGHAM UNIVERSITY LIBRARY